C20th

Pop Culture

Twentieth-Century Pop Culture

Dan Epstein is a freelance journalist whose work appears regularly in many publications including *L.A. Weekly, BAM, Book, Bikini, Raygun,* and *Guitar World.* He lives in Los Angeles.

Produced by Carlton Books Limited
20 St Anne's Court
Wardour Street
London W1V 3AW

Text and design copyright © Carlton Books Limited

This edition published in 1999 by CLB,
an imprint of Quadrillion Publishing Ltd.

Distributed in the USA by
Quadrillion Publishing Inc.,
230 Fifth Avenue,
New York, NY 10001

ISBN: 1-84100-304-2

EDITORIAL AND DESIGN: Andy Jones and Barry Sutcliffe
Executive Editor: Sarah Larter
PROJECT ART DIRECTION: Zoë Mercer
PICTURE RESEARCH: Emily Hedges/Sarah Moule
PRODUCTION: Sarah Schuman

Printed and bound in Dubai

C20th Pop Culture

Dan Epstein

CLB

Contents

1900
1945

An early Coca-cola bottle.

1900: A Century Begins

What a difference a century makes. The intrepid time-traveler from 1999 would barely recognize the America of 1900—a country where most people worked over sixty hours a week, the average summer wardrobe provided more body coverage than today's winter sportswear, and music lovers had to visit special "phonograph parlors" in order to hear the latest recordings. Expensive and generally unreliable, the few automobiles on the road (only four thousand were even manufactured in 1900) tended to belong to wealthy Americans; the rest relied upon ten million bicycles and eighteen million mules and horses to take them through the nation's unpaved streets. Not exactly the stuff of MTV programming, is it?

And yet, some things haven't changed much. In 1900, the US military was involved in a controversial conflict in a far-off land—though this one was taking place in the Philippines, as opposed to Kosovo. Then, as now, there were those who sought to impose their sense of morality upon their fellow citizens; prohibition crusader **Carry Nation** led her volunteers through the state of Kansas, using hatchets to destroy saloons and other businesses that sold liquor. And, while they weren't called "hate crimes" back then, anti-minority violence was still quite commonplace, with one hundred and five blacks reportedly lynched during that year.

On a lighter note, college football, boxing, and professional baseball were as popular as they are today (even more so, in the case of the latter two), and the lucky patron who frequented the Louis Lunch Counter in New Haven, Connecticut could partake of a new sandwich called the **hamburger**. The establishment's spartan beef-patty-on-toast presentation might well perplex the modern-day Big Mac aficionado, however; hamburger buns wouldn't be popularized until the St. Louis World's Fair of 1903, and it would take another three decades for someone to come up with the idea of dressing a burger with a slice of cheese.

1901–1914: A Brave New Era

In many ways, the new American century didn't really begin until September 14, 1901, when President William McKinley died of complications from a gunshot wound inflicted by anarchist Leon Czolgosz. A dour, conservative politician with ties to big business and decidedly "imperialist" leanings, McKinley was every inch a late-nineteenth-century president. **Theodore "Teddy" Roosevelt**, the man who succeeded him, was a different animal entirely; a charismatic renaissance man with "war hero," "state governor," "cowboy," and "historian" already on his resumé, his boundless energy and progressive politics were a perfect match for the optimistic young country.

Now that the US had finally extricated itself from the rebellion in the Philippines (itself a by-product of the recent Spanish-American War), Roosevelt was free to concentrate on strengthening the country by preserving its natural resources, busting big-business "trusts," and trying to improve race relations

Theodore "Teddy" Roosevelt—a new leader for a new age

(though many Americans protested when he invited black educator Booker T Washington to a White House dinner, Roosevelt stood firm). He also appointed a commission to investigate the country's meat industry, after Upton Sinclair's harrowing novel *The Jungle* (1906) exposed the terrible working conditions in meat-packing plants, as well as the fact that the beef sent to market often came from diseased cattle. The ensuing probe led to the government's passage of the Pure Food and Drug and Meat Inspection acts, which enforced new standards of cleanliness for the country's food manufacturers.

Beverage companies were also falling under a fair amount of scrutiny at this time; in 1903, the **Coca-Cola** Company was forced to remove unprocessed coca leaves from its recipe, after several newspapers and various concerned citizens began to rail against the (actually rather minuscule) quantity of cocaine contained in the soft drink. Coke had already been around for two decades, but many of the products we take for granted today were actually introduced or invented during this period. **Kellogg's Corn Flakes** hit the market in 1902; over a hundred thousand pounds of the cereal were sold during its first year on the shelves. New Jersey ice cream salesman Italio Marcioni patented the ice-cream cone in 1903; George Schmidt and Fred Osius of Racine, Wisconsin introduced the first electric milkshake mixer in 1904; Gennaro Lombardi opened the country's first pizzeria in New York's Little Italy in

1905; and in 1906, vendor Harry Mosley Stevens began wrapping sausages with buns at New York's Polo Grounds ballpark, thus establishing the still-intact connection between baseball and **hot dogs**.

Of course, the American spirit of invention spread far beyond the realm of foodstuffs. In 1907, the Ideal Novelty Company sold a million of their new "teddy bears," stuffed animals inspired by the then-popular (and probably apocryphal) tale of a friendly encounter between President Roosevelt and an orphaned bear cub.

The Model "T" Ford—the car that changed the world.

In 1913, Gideon Sundback, a Swedish engineer from Hoboken, New Jersey, patented the **zipper** fastener; a year later, New York debutante Mary Phelps Jacob patented the first elasticized, backless brassiere. And one certainly mustn't forget brothers Orville and Wilbur Wright, who made aviation history by flying their home-made, 750-lb aircraft along the beach at Kitty Hawk, North Carolina. The date was December 17, 1903, and it marked the first actual flight by a heavier-than-air vehicle.

Advances were also coming fast and furious in the automotive field. In 1900, Packard's Model C became the first car to be fitted with a steering wheel, a positively futuristic device compared to the tillers then in use for other models. The Olds Company of Detroit, Michigan established the first mass-production automobile factory the same year, but it was **Henry Ford** who really popularized the concept. Ford's Model T had sold well

from its 1908 debut, but the company's 1913 switch to mass production enabled Ford to crank out a thousand cars a day at remarkably affordable prices, resulting in the sales of nearly sixteen million Model T's between 1908 and 1927. Available "in any color you like, as long as it's black," the **Model T** proved such a success that most of the country's other manufacturers began producing their own front-engine, gas-powered (many earlier cars were powered by steam) models that looked remarkably like Ford's "Tin Lizzie." Oft-imitated but never quite duplicated, the reliable and wallet-friendly Model T almost single-handedly turned America into a nation of car drivers.

Thomas Edison applied similar mass-production techniques to his phonograph cylinders, but the cumbersome format was ultimately destined to fail. His chief competitor, the Victor Talking Machine Company, made phonographs (popularly known as "**Victrolas**") which played flat discs, a far more convenient format. As a result, Americans who used to gather around the family piano for

Kellogg's Corn Flakes

musical entertainment (wealthier homes often boasted automated "player" pianos) were starting to buy more records than sheet music. In 1905, Arthur Collins' "The Preacher And The Bear" (one of the many racist "coon" songs then in vogue) became the first record to sell a million copies. The ragtime music of Jelly Roll Morton became quite popular during this period, but it was four-part "**barbershop**" harmony singing that really defined the music of the era. One of the better-known barbershop quartets was the Haydn Quartet, whose renditions of "Sweet Adeline" (1904) and "By The Light Of The Silvery Moon" (1910) could be heard emanating from Victrolas everywhere.

The film industry grew by leaps and bounds during this period, though—like baseball, vaudeville, and burlesque shows—moving pictures were generally considered a vulgar and disreputable pastime. Of course, such snobbery didn't exactly hinder the proliferation of **nickelodeons** (which numbered between eight and ten thousand by 1908), or keep the hundreds of thousands of regular nickelodeon customers from paying five cents to view such three-minute shorts as *Gertie the Dinosaur* (a 1909 animated film featuring the drawings of newspaper cartoonist Winsor McCay), *In Old Kentucky* (a 1909 drama starring Mary Pickford, one of the industry's first stars, and directed by the tremendously prolific and influential DW Griffith), or the many slapstick "Keystone Cops" comedies of director Mack Sennett.

"Cultivated" persons tended to prefer the theater, flocking to see such stage productions as Florenz Zeigfield's *Ziegfield Follies* (featuring "the most beautiful girls in the world"), George M Cohan's *Forty-Five Minutes from Broadway*, and George Broadhurst's melodramatic *Bought and Paid For*. The influence of the period's theatergoers can best be gauged by the fact that, while thousands of American coal miners died in mine explosions and cave-ins during the first decade of the century, the demands for improved mine safety paled next to the outcry for new theater building codes that followed Chicago's Iroquois Theater fire, which killed 588 patrons in 1903.

Other significant disasters of the period included the 1912 sinking of the "unsinkable" British ocean liner *Titanic*, which killed nearly 1500 British and American passengers, and the massive **San Francisco earthquake** of 1906, which (along with the fire that followed) killed two and a half thousand San Franciscans, left three hundred thousand homeless, and destroyed over twenty-eight thousand of the city's buildings. Less massively cataclysmic, though far more preventable, was the 1911 fire at New York City's Triangle Shirtwaist Company, which killed one hundred and forty-six female garment workers—most of whom could have been saved had the building been equipped with fire escapes and emergency exits.

With the age of the "skyscraper" already in full swing, the substantial revisions of the city's building code that followed the Triangle Shirtwaist tragedy came not a moment too soon. On one evening in 1913, President Woodrow Wilson pressed a button that illuminated Manhattan's newly-completed **Woolworth Building** with eighty thousand light-bulbs.

At sixty stories and 792 feet, the gothic structure was now the world's tallest building, besting its closest competitor—1908's Metropolitan Life Tower, located several miles uptown—by almost a hundred feet. It would be nearly two decades before anybody built one higher.

1915–1929: A World War And "The Roaring Twenties"

As "The Great War" raged in Europe, debate raged at home about whether

■ Higher and higher—the Woolworth Building scrapes the sky in New York City.

or not the United States should enter the fray. The Peerless Quartet's "I Didn't Raise My Boy To Be A Soldier," a song with unabashedly pacifist sentiments, was one of the top sellers of 1915, despite the fact that one hundred and twenty-three Americans had been killed in May when the British steamship *Lusitania* was sunk by a German submarine.

Still, while President Wilson's 1916 re-election campaign used "**He Kept**

Us Out Of The War" as its slogan, both Wilson and the American people knew that it would only be a matter of time before US soldiers joined their British and French counterparts in the trenches along the Western Front. By June 26, 1917, when the first US troops landed in France, anti-German sentiment had built to the point where Tin Pan Alley songwriters were making piles of money cranking out ditties with titles like "We're All Going Calling On The Kaiser," "When I Send You A Picture Of Berlin," and "We Don't Want The Bacon (What We Want Is A Piece Of The Rhine)." Most popular of all was George M Cohan's "**Over There**," which spent most of the year at the top of the sales charts, thanks to an appropriately brash rendition by The American Quartet.

Though World War One was far less damaging to the United States than to its allies, the country hardly emerged unscathed; 116,708 American soldiers died in the war (more than half of them from disease), while another 204,002 returned wounded. The lingering memories of the war's horrors and privations (and of the influenza epidemic that killed over four hundred thousand Americans in the autumn of 1918) manifested themselves in both the harsh realism of authors like Ernest Hemingway, F Scott Fitzgerald, and John Dos Passos, and the general public's almost nihilistic desire to party as if there was no tomorrow.

It was in this environment that **jazz** music, once strictly the province of Kansas City and New Orleans brothels, began to flourish nationally, as the "hot" music of bandleaders like Paul Whiteman and Louis Armstrong—now coming into homes via a new invention called radio—tapped into the pent-up energies of the populace. In 1923, the Broadway musical *Runnin' Wild* helped turn the **Charleston** into the latest dance craze; as with the short hemlines of the new "flapper" fashions, the energetic dance was emblematic of the era's shift to a sexier, more carefree mood.

Of course, there was the slight matter of **Prohibition** to contend with. On January 29, 1919, the US Congress ratified the Eighteenth Amendment to the Constitution, outlawing the manufacture, sale, and transportation of alcohol throughout the entire country. Long considered a "noble experiment" by its many supporters, Prohibition had already taken hold in twenty-four states; but as of January 16, 1920, when the Amendment took effect, it was now impossible to purchase a drop of liquor anywhere in the country—legally, that is. While the rest of the economy was feeling the negative effects of the postwar manufacturing slowdown, business was absolutely booming for bootleggers. Every town had at least one "**speakeasy**," a clandestine saloon that served booze, and rare was the gentleman who travelled without his hip flask. Stories abounded about people who'd been blinded or sickened by drinking homemade "bathtub gin," but demand for the stuff continued to override any medical, moral, or legal concerns.

◼ Footloose and fancy free—flappers scale the heights

◼ Al Capone (1899–1947) with US Marshal Laubenheimer.

As Chicago gangster **Al Capone** put it, "When I sell liquor, it's bootlegging. When my patrons serve it on silver trays on Lake Shore Drive, it's hospitality."

In short, the "noble experiment" proved a tremendous failure. Over the course of the decade, federal and state officials arrested an estimated half-million people for manufacturing or importing alcohol, but the illegal booze continued to flow. If anything, Prohibition created a bigger problem than the one it sought to eradicate—namely, the rise of organized crime, which was primarily financed by bootlegging profits. The hub of gangland activity was Chicago, where gang warfare killed over six hundred people during the 1920s. The most famous gang-related incident of the era took place on February 14, 1929: "**The St Valentine's Day Massacre**," in which seven members of Bugs Moran's gang were gunned down in a Chicago warehouse. Though Al Capone was widely believed to have ordered the hit, police lacked enough evidence to bring him in. Capone's reign of terror was effectively ended three months later, when he was sentenced to a year in prison for carrying a concealed weapon. Tax evasion charges—and the ravages of syphillis—would keep "Scarface" out of action for the remainder of his life.

Charles Lindbergh became a national hero in 1927, when he piloted his "*Spirit of St Louis*" to Paris in the first solo flight across the Atlantic, but the era seemed to produce as many infamous figures as exemplary ones. Among the notable folks running afoul of the law were the Chicago White Sox, whose starting lineup was accused of taking bribes to intentionally lose the 1919 World Series. The players were eventually acquitted, but it took several years (and the ascendance of colorful slugger Babe Ruth, who hit a record 60 home runs in 1927) for professional baseball to completely lose the taint of "**The Black Sox Scandal**." Also beset by scandal was President Warren G. Harding, whose administration was positively riddled by corruption; his death on August 2, 1923 of a pulmonary embolism ˉsome have alleged that he was poisoned—was probably the only thing that saved him from being thrown out of office.

Perhaps the most notorious scandal of the era involved comedic actor **Roscoe "Fatty" Arbuckle**, whose star turns in films like *His Wedding Night* and *The Life of the Party* had, by 1921, earned him a million-dollar-a-year contract with Paramount Studios. The film industry had grown substantially since relocating from the East Coast in the years before the First World War, but many Americans perceived Hollywood as nothing less than a seething pit of godless iniquity. Therefore, when Arbuckle was accused of raping and mortally injuring aspiring actress Virginia Rappe, it only confirmed the

　Charlie Chaplin in "The Goldrush".

worst suspicions of the country's moral watchdogs. After two deadlocked trials, a third found Arbuckle not guilty, but it would be another decade before the rotund comic again found work in the industry.

DW Griffith, the most important director of the era, was another film great who found himself *persona non grata* in Hollywood, albeit for reasons far less tawdry. His 1915 epic *Birth of a Nation* was a box-office smash—even though it drew criticism for its sympathetic portrayal of the Ku Klux Klan, a late-nineteenth-century Southern hate group then experiencing a revival—but the multiple plot lines of his next film, 1916's *Intolerance*, left audiences scratching their heads. Griffith regained some of his commercial

momentum in 1919 with *Broken Blossoms*, a lovely film for United Artists, the new company he formed with popular stars Charlie Chaplin (already famous for his "Little Tramp" character), Mary Pickford, and Douglas Fairbanks; but for all his formidable artistry, the director's propensity for going over budget—and his inability to tailor his filmmaking style to the tastes of 1920s audiences— completely alienated him from his colleagues.

Along with Chaplin, Pickford, and Fairbanks, other leading lights of the "golden age of silent film" included Western stars William S Hart and Tom Mix, screen beauties Clara Bow and Norma Talmadge, acrobatic comedians Buster Keaton and Harold Lloyd, canine hero Rin Tin Tin, horror film star Lon Chaney (whose deft use of makeup earned him the nickname "Man of a Thousand Faces") and

romantic lead Rudolph Valentino, whose premature death in 1926 set off a wave of worldwide hysteria.

For the country, the period between 1922 and 1929 brought an unprecedented surge of prosperity; for the motion-picture industry, the attendant leap in box-office receipts resulted in lavish movie theaters—like the Roxy in New York City, and Grauman's Chinese in Hollywood—and tremendous advances in film technology. Though Charlie Chaplin was heard to opine that "moving pictures need sound as much as Beethoven symphonies need lyrics," the days of silent film were definitely numbered.

The Jazz Singer, which premiered in October of 1927, caused a sensation with its synchronized sound effects, talking sequences, and songs sung by recording star Al Jolson. The following year saw every major film studio hop on the sound bandwagon; some of the more notable early efforts included Warner Bros.' *Lights of New York* (helpfully billed as "100 percent all-talking") and Walt Disney's *Steamboat Willie*, the first animated sound film, which also starred an early version of Mickey Mouse. Unfortunately, the advent of "**talkies**" also spelled early retirement for many silent stars—including Norma Talmadge, John Gilbert, and Marie Prevost—whose speaking voices failed to live up to the personas they'd created for the silver screen.

Like the silent films themselves, the prosperity and *joie de vivre* that characterized the "Roaring Twenties" would not live to see the end of the decade. Stock prices had reached an all-time high on September 3, 1929, but it simply couldn't last; stocks soon began a drastic decline, with the biggest crash coming on October 29, better known as "**Black Tuesday**." Within weeks, holdings on the New York Stock Exchange had dropped twenty-six million dollars, and the country (indeed, much of the world) would spend the next decade trying to recover. The Great Depression was underway.

1930–1944: The Great Depression And Another Global Conflict

"Happy Days Are Here Again" went the most popular song of 1930, but for most Depression-era Americans, the sentiment strictly amounted to wishful thinking. "Brother Can You Spare A Dime," a 1932 hit for both Bing Crosby and Rudy Vallee, was probably more to the point: By October of 1930, four and a half million Americans were unemployed; two months later, New

America's silent film sweetheart, Mary Pickford.

York City's Bank of the United States suddenly went out of business, leaving four hundred thousand depositors empty-handed, and "bank panics"—wherein customers ran to withdraw their balances before their banks could close on them—soon became commonplace.

The Depression drove most of Detroit's auto makers out of business, and basically did the same for **Herbert Hoover**. Hoover, elected President in 1928 at the height of American prosperity, had responded to the country's economic plight by laying plans for government-funded public works programs, as well as voluntarily taking a twenty-percent cut in pay; but in the minds of voters—thirteen million of whom were unemployed by late 1932—Hoover was synonymous with the hard times that had recently come to pass. As a result, Franklin Delano Roosevelt, the former governor of New York, beat Hoover by a landslide in the 1932 elections. **FDR**'s runaway victory came as something of a surprise to the Hoover camp, who wrongly assumed that the American public would never elect a paraplegic to the country's highest office. In fact, Roosevelt's indomitable optimism, which had served him so well during his initial recovery from polio, was probably even more attractive to the voters of the day than his much-vaunted "New Deal" platform.

FDR's other major asset was his mellifluous speaking voice, which seemed tailor-made for the medium of radio. A few days after his initial inauguration, Roosevelt began delivering regular radio addresses to the nation. These genial "**fireside chats**," as he liked to call them, did a lot to improve the morale of the

country during the lean times; they also kept him in good standing with the voters—even when the country's newspapers called for his head, as they often did during the 1930s.

Of course, Roosevelt's "fireside chats" weren't the only thing Americans were listening to. Since 1922, when a system for parceling out wavelengths was first established, **the radio industry** had grown rapidly, with millions of Americans tuning in on a daily basis. Now, with unemployment at an all-time high, more Americans than ever were relying upon radio to provide them with their evening's entertainment. In 1930, NBC began airing live Sunday broadcasts of the New York Philharmonic Orchestra with Arturo Toscanini conducting, while CBS inaugurated the country's first regular broadcasting schedule in 1931, beginning with a telecast featuring performances by George Gershwin, the Boswell Sisters, and Kate Smith. The company also gave **Bing Crosby** a fifteen-minute spot each evening; Crosby's soft croon, like that of Rudy Vallee (who hosted NBC's *The Fleischmann Hour*, the first radio variety show), was perfectly suited to the intimacy of the medium, and listeners showed their undying appreciation by sending a seemingly endless string of hits to the top of the pop charts.

But if radio proved invaluable to the careers of crooners like Crosby and Vallee, its emphasis on classical music and mainstream pop could be frustratingly limited, especially for listeners who couldn't afford a phonograph. **Jukeboxes** had been around since 1906, when inventor John Gabel first introduced his "Automatic Entertainer," but by the late 1930s, the jukebox industry was

positively booming. Most restaurants and bars (yes, bars; by 1933, Congress had finally given in to public pressure and repealed Prohibition) had a Wurlitzer, Seeburg, Mills, AMI, or Rock-Ola jukebox in the corner, and a mere nickel would get you several plays of your choice: something by Duke Ellington, the Mills Brothers, Fats Waller, or Ethel Waters, perhaps? Or maybe The Glenn Miller Band's "*In The Mood*," which, sixty years after its release, remains the quintessential artifact of the Swing Era.

Other popular personalities on 1930s radio included gossip columnist Walter Winchell, "singing cowboy" Gene Autry, vocalist Eddie Cantor, and a variety of comedic refugees from the vaudeville circuit, including Jack Benny, Fred Allen, the husband-and-wife team of George Burns and Gracie Allen, and the ventriloquist-and-dummy team of Edgar Bergen and Charlie McCarthy. Popular programs included *Little Orphan Annie*, *The Lone Ranger*, *Jack Armstrong, The All-American Boy*, *Fibber McGee and Molly*, and Bob Hope's *Pepsodent Show*. There was also **Father Charles Coughlan**, whose anti-Semitic rants were so virulent that CBS actually kicked him off the air. Undaunted, Father Coughlan set up his own radio network and found a receptive audience; in a mid-1930s poll, he was named the second most popular man in America—behind FDR, of course.

Perhaps the most notorious example of radio's hold over the public imagination was the evening of October 30, 1938, when Orson Welles staged a radio play of HG Wells' **The War of the Worlds** as part of his *Mercury Theater on the Air* program. Though disclaimers were aired at the beginning of the broadcast, many who tuned in later on became convinced that New Jersey was actually being attacked by Martian invaders. Within minutes, the radio station's phone lines were jammed by panicked listeners, and hundreds of others ran screaming from their homes before order could be sufficiently restored.

Lakehurst, New Jersey had been the site of a real disaster a year earlier, when the German zeppelin *Hindenburg* (left) exploded while attempting to land. The tragedy was broadcast over radio station WLS, which had sent announcer Herbert Morrison to cover the aircraft's arrival. Fifteen passengers, twenty crewmen, and one line-handler were killed in the conflagration, the cause of which has never truly been determined; in an era where measured, unemotional announcements were the radio norm, Morrison's hysterical reportage—"Oh, the humanity!"—struck a deep chord with the American public. Not surprisingly, the *Hindenburg* disaster effectively ended the brief vogue for lighter-than-air travel.

Unemployment dropped substantially during FDR's first term in office, and his Works Progress Administration projects (**WPA** for short) created hundreds of thousands of jobs across the country; many of the buildings, bridges, highways and murals commissioned by the WPA are still in existence. But the country's economic recovery proved sluggish, and the droughts (and subsequent dust storms) that ravaged the Midwest didn't help any. Like the characters in John Steinbeck's *The Grapes of Wrath*, many Midwestern farmers packed up their families and meager belongings and headed for California,

only to be met by billboards imploring them to go back where they came from. Maps and guidebooks to 1930s Los Angeles included the friendly message: "WARNING! While the attractions for tourists are unlimited, please advise anyone seeking employment not to come to Southern California, as natural attractions have already drawn so many capable, experienced people that the present demand is more than satisfied."

In truth, the American economy didn't truly pick up again until 1939, when the growing possibility of war with Germany initiated a substantial increase in US manufacturing. Relations between the two countries had been tense since 1933, when the American Federation of Labor had protested the Nazis' rise to power by calling for a boycott of all German-made products, but most Americans continued to hope that war was not in the offing. Indeed, several prominent Americans (like Henry Ford, himself the proud publisher of a bilious pamphlet entitled *The International Jew*) pushed for improved relations with Germany; when New York mayor Fiorello

LaGuardia announced that he wished his city's 1939–40 World's Fair had included a "chamber of horrors" with a Hitler room, many government officials demanded that the mayor make an apology.

Just the same, on September 16, 1940 Congress passed the **Selective Service Act**, which stipulated that nine hundred thousand American men between the ages of twenty and twenty-six would be drafted each year. Seven weeks later, FDR was re-elected for an unprecedented third term. Though his decision to run was controversial, most Americans seemed to feel that it was better not to "change captains in the middle of a storm"—and the storm clouds from the war in Europe seemed to be drifting closer by the moment.

War finally came on December 7, 1941, when Japanese forces launched a sneak attack on the US naval base at **Pearl Harbor**, Hawaii. Congress declared war against Japan the next day, and against Germany and Italy on December 11. With most able-bodied men pressed into military service, women joined the American work

force in record numbers. After Roosevelt instituted a minimum forty-eight-hour working week for war industries in labor-scarce areas, many black Americans moved from the South to the northern cities to find factory work, and farmers from the Midwest finally found themselves welcome in California.

In addition to the average Joes, the war effort snapped up most of the country's young film, radio, music, and athletics stars; some, like Glenn Miller, never came back. With most of their male objects of desire overseas, millions of young American women became fixated on a scrawny young singer named **Frank Sinatra**, who had been excused from the armed services because of a punctured eardrum. Though not the masterful interpreter he would later become, Sinatra did project an appealing vulnerability in songs like "All Or Nothing At All" and "You'll Never Know." Appealing to the ladies, that is; most American men, especially those serving in the military, openly resented the shrieks and swoons the singer elicited from "their" girls.

With rents and goods prices frozen to halt wartime inflation, the sale of new cars and trucks banned by the US Office of Production Management, and rationing ordered for sugar, coffee, rubber tires, gasoline, shoes, canned goods, meat, fat, and cheese, Americans on the home front suddenly found themselves with a surplus of cash, and with little to spend it on. As a result, nightclub and movie theater profits suddenly went through the roof.

From the dark days of the Depression, through the uncertainty of World War Two, Americans counted on **Hollywood** to distract them from their troubles and worries. Talking pictures, a novelty in the late 1920s, had quickly moved through their awkward, microphone-in-the-flowerpot adolescence. By the early 1930s, Hollywood understood that it took more than talking and singing actors to excite paying customers; over the next fifteen years, the studios responded by making hundreds of films that are still considered classics.

The 1930s and 1940s were something of a **golden age of film comedy**, with the Marx Brothers (*Duck Soup, A Night at the Opera*), WC Fields (*The Bank Dick, Never Give a Sucker an Even Break*), Mae West (*She Done Him Wrong, My Little Chickadee*), and Abbott and Costello (*Buck Privates, Rio Rita*) holding court as the top comedic stars of the day. Charlie Chaplin, who would eschew spoken dialogue until 1940's *The Great Dictator*, also produced two of his finest films— *City Lights* (1931) and *Modern Times* (1936)—during this period.

The horror film experienced an impressive revival, with audiences flocking to see Boris Karloff in *Frankenstein* (1931), *The Mummy* (1932), and *The Bride of Frankenstein* (1935); **Bela Lugosi** in *Dracula* (1931), *White Zombie* (1932), and *Island of Lost Souls* (1932); Fredric March in *Dr. Jekyll and Mr. Hyde*; an animated ape climb up New York's newly-erected Empire State Building in *King Kong* (1933); and Lon Chaney, Jr. in *The Wolf Man* (1941). And with gangsters like Al Capone and John

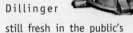
The Marx Brothers.

Dillinger still fresh in the public's memory, it was little wonder that films like *Little Caesar* (1931, with Edward G Robinson), *The Public Enemy* (1931, with James Cagney), and *Scarface: The Shame of the Nation* (1932, with Paul Muni) were so successful—or that a dapper actor named **Humphrey Bogart** would make a fortune playing tough guys in films like *The Petrified Forest* (1936), *The Maltese Falcon* (1941), and *Casablanca* (1943).

The period also produced a bumper crop of lavish musicals, including 1933's *42nd Street* and *Gold Diggers of 1933*, both of which were choreographed by the great Busby Berkeley. The same year saw **Fred Astaire and Ginger Rogers** paired for the first time in *Flying Down to Rio*; the coupling proved so popular that the

dancing duo appeared in nine subsequent films together, including *The Gay Divorcee* (1934), *Top Hat* (1935), *Swing Time* (1936), and *Shall We Dance?* (1937). Two other Rogers proved major draws: Will, the popular humorist who starred in several hits before his tragic death in a 1935 airplane crash; and Roy, who assumed the mantle of "top Western star" when Gene Autry joined the military.

Perhaps the two most successful (and enduring) musicals of the period were 1937's *Snow White and the Seven Dwarfs* and 1939's *The Wizard of Oz*. The former, the first feature-length

cartoon, was made by Walt Disney for a then-staggering 2.6 million dollars, while the latter featured several stunning color sequences, and made a star out of a young actress named Judy Garland. But the biggest stars of the era had to be **Shirley Temple** and **Clark Gable**. Not that they had much in common: Temple, a singing-and-dancing moppet with an excess of dimples and curls, was idolized by little girls for her roles in films like *Curly Top* (1935) and *Heidi* (1937); Gable, on the other hand, was idolized by men and lusted after by women. His role opposite Claudette Colbert in 1934's *It Happened One Night* made him a star, but it was his performance as Rhett Butler in 1939's epic *Gone With the Wind* that truly sealed his silver-screen immortality.

Curly top herself: Shirley Temple.

'45

"With the world at peace," cheered a holiday advertisement for Firestone tires, "this Christmas will be the merriest in years." The Second World War had been a long, arduous, bloody, and dispiriting affair. As 1945 drew to a close, most Americans were ready to relax and have a good time. Wartime rationing of shoes, oil, meat, butter, and tires had recently been discontinued and "the boys" were starting to come home.

TRANS-LUX PRESENTS A SPECIAL V-J DAY PROGRAM

Celebrating the end of the war, a sailor kisses his girl.

However, from bedsheets to building materials, many goods were still scarce, and radio and print ads regularly reminded the public to continue buying war and **victory bonds** "to insure your splendid postwar world."

Despite creeping anxiety about the ramifications of the newly deployed atomic bomb, the postwar world did seem to offer some splendid possibilities. "Precooked frozen foods have a brilliant future," proclaimed *Consumer Reports* and, indeed, improved refrigeration technology was enabling consumers to store more foodstuffs, including frozen dinners. Heating them up was quite another matter, however. 1945 saw Percy LeBaron Spencer invent the **microwave oven**, but at three thousand dollars a pop, the Raytheon Company's new "Raydarange" was priced far out of reach of most consumers.

45 Frozen foods were a boon for rationing-beset housewives.

US Signs Up For Austerity Drive

For the first time since 1941, Detroit's automobile factories began to roll out cars for civilian use; material shortages kept the assembly lines at a slow pace, however, and most folks looking to buy a new car had to sign up on a waiting list at their local dealer's showroom. General Motors hyped their "**Hydra-Matic Drive**—

the modern drive without a clutch pedal," while Ford boasted "more new developments than most prewar yearly models," but the truth was that most 1946 models did not differ appreciably from their 1942 counterparts; with the exception of minor alterations on the bumpers and radiator grille, Pontiac's 1946 **Silver Streak** sported virtually the same round-top design as the '42. The end of the year witnessed the introduction of Kaiser-Frazer's first cars. Though advertised as costing between twelve and fifteen hundred dollars (for the flashier Frazer) and a thousand dollars (for the more utilitarian Kaiser), the economical compacts hardly put a dent in the sales of Ford, General Motors or Chrysler-Plymouth, aka "The Big Three."

Radio Daze

After much discussion, the Federal Communications Commission decided to allocate thirteen channels for commercial television (Channel One was later reassigned for non-commercial

45 The Andrews Sisters, wartime favorites.

use). As only roughly five thousand American homes actually had TV sets, most people continued to depend on radio for their home entertainment. Popular radio programs included the humorous **Red Skelton Show**, the action-packed serials *Green Hornet* and *Superman*, and the unbelievably maudlin *Queen for a Day*, a game show that awarded prizes to the female contestant with the most heartrending tale of woe.

Music News

"Rum And Coca-Cola," The Andrews Sisters' whitewashed rendition of a bawdy Trinidadian calypso number, was on everyone's lips, followed closely by Johnny Mercer's "On The Atchison, Topeka And Santa Fe" and Perry Como's "Till The End Of Time." Based on the melody from Frederic Chopin's "Polonaise In A Flat," Como's

hit capitalized on the **Chopin craze** then sweeping the country; thanks to Cornel Wilde's star turn in the Chopin biopic *A Song To Remember*, listeners both young and old were snapping up any Chopin records they could find.

Les Brown and His Orchestra scored big with "Sentimental Journey" and "My Dreams Are Getting Better All the Time" (both featuring vocals by a young Doris Day), and Vaughn Monroe

and His Orchestra had a huge hit with "There! I've Said It Again," but the era of the big bands was quickly coming to an end. Listeners were transferring their attentions and affections to solo vocalists such as Bing Crosby, Perry Como, Frank Sinatra, and Dinah Shore, as well as to rhythm 'n' blues combos like Louis Jordan and his Tympany Five ("Caldonia") and novelty acts like Spike Jones and His City Slickers ("Cocktails For Two"). Frustrated by the restrictions of big-band arrangements, many musicians found themselves drawn to the frantic improvisations of bebop, then currently being explored by trumpeter **Dizzy Gillespie** and saxophonist **Charlie Parker**. Without steady commercial prospects, the big bands proved too expensive to maintain; within a year, bandleaders Tommy Dorsey, Harry James, Woody Herman and Les Brown would all disband their orchestras.

45 A boyish-looking Sinatra stood up for racial integration in 1945.

Movie News

1945 was a landmark year for **Bing Crosby**. Not only did the mellow-voiced crooner rack up three Number One pop hits ("I Can't Begin To Tell You," "It's Been A Long, Long Time," and the perennial holiday favorite "White Christmas"), but the success of *Duffy's Tavern* and *The Bells of St Mary's* proved him the most popular male box-office attraction. He had plenty of competition from **Gregory Peck**, whose status as a Hollywood heartthrob was heightened by leading roles in *The Valley of Decision* (opposite **Greer Garson**, the top-drawing leading lady of 1945) and Alfred Hitchcock's *Spellbound* (opposite Ingrid Bergman, who didn't do too badly for herself in *Saratoga Trunk* and *The Bells of St Mary's*). John Wayne kept the world safe for democracy in *Back to Bataan* and *They Were Expendable*; meanwhile, on the home front, Joan Crawford won a Best Actress Oscar for her portrayal of a housewife-turned-waitress in *Mildred Pierce*.

Humphrey Bogart and Lauren Bacall, who played lovers in 1944's **To Have and Have Not**, showed that their electric chemistry was not just an onscreen fluke; they married in 1945.

ACADEMY AWARDS

BEST PICTURE

The Lost Weekend

directed by Billy Wilder

BEST ACTOR

Ray Milland

The Lost Weekend

BEST ACTRESS

Joan Crawford

Mildred Pierce

45 Gregory Peck and Ingrid Bergman, spellbound by each other in Alfred Hitchcock's psychological mystery movie.

Life further imitated art in November, when Frank Sinatra, star of the recent Oscar-winning anti-racism short, *The House I Live In*, made a special appearance at a racial-tolerance rally in Gary, Indiana. White students at integrated Froebel High School had gone on strike against their new principal's "pro-Negro policies," which included letting black students join the orchestra and use the school pool. Between songs, "Ol' Blue Eyes" told the assembled students that racism was strictly for Nazis, and that if the Allied leaders could work out their differences, the kids of America could do the same.

Sounding a less optimistic note was **The Lost Weekend**, Billy Wilder's harrowing look at the life of a New York alcoholic, played by Ray Milland. Despite Paramount's uneasiness about releasing something so exceedingly bleak (much of the footage was actually shot in grimy New York City bars and the detox ward at Bellevue Hospital), the film took Best Picture honors, and Milland was awarded Best Actor. As Wilder told the *New York Times*, "If *To Have and Have Not* has established Lauren Bacall as The Look, then *The Lost Weekend* should certainly bring Mr Milland renown as The Kidney."

45 A stylish demonstration of Raytheon's electronic Raydarange.

As 1946 dawned, America woke up with a serious hangover. The jubilant victory celebrations of late 1945 were over, pre-empted by the **dark uncertainties** of the postwar world. The country was racked by spiraling inflation, labor disputes involving over four million workers, and a severe housing shortage.

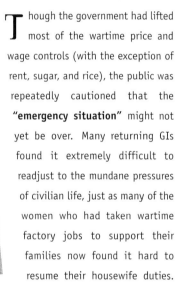

Though the government had lifted most of the wartime price and wage controls (with the exception of rent, sugar, and rice), the public was repeatedly cautioned that the **"emergency situation"** might not yet be over. Many returning GIs found it extremely difficult to readjust to the mundane pressures of civilian life, just as many of the women who had taken wartime factory jobs to support their families now found it hard to resume their housewife duties. From penthouse dinner parties to corner bars, Russian Communism and the atomic bomb were the main topics of conversation.

Movie News

No film better captured the uneasy mood of postwar America than William Wyler's **The Best Years of Our Lives**. The picture was an instant hit with American audiences, who saw their own hopes, fears, and travails reflected in the poignant story of three American vets returning home from World War Two. The film won seven Academy Awards, including Best Picture, Best Actor for Fredric March, and Best Supporting Actor for Harold Russell—an actual World War Two vet whose battle-mangled hands had been replaced with hooks. Best Actress went to Olivia de Havilland, for her performance in Mitchell Leisen's melodramatic *To Each His Own*. Failing to win anything at all was Frank Capra's **It's a Wonderful Life**, an uplifting, sentimental story of a depressed man who gets a second chance to straighten out his life. The Jimmy Stewart vehicle didn't even do much business at the box-office; in fact, it took several decades of televised screenings for the film to attain its present status as an American holiday classic.

Although Bing Crosby still reigned as the box-office king (thanks to *Road to Utopia* and *Blue Skies*), and Rita Hayworth's turn as the freewheeling *Gilda* established her as Hollywood's top sex symbol, Hollywood's 1946 output was decidedly less than frivolous. Ingrid Bergman, 1946's top female draw, spied on the Nazis with Cary Grant in Alfred Hitchcock's *Notorious*, and Tyrone Power and Gene Tierney pondered the meaning of life in Edmund Goulding's *The Razor's Edge*; but both films seemed like Walt Disney productions next to the cynical themes of such *films noir* as Howard Hawks' *The Big Sleep*, Tay Garnett's *The Postman Always Rings Twice*, Fritz Lang's *Scarlet Street,* and Otto Preminger's *Fallen Angel*. Such rampant pessimism did little to cloud **Norma Jeane Dougherty**'s skies, however; in August, 20th Century Fox signed the aspiring actress to a one hundred and twenty-five dollar a week contract, changing her name to **Marilyn Monroe** in the process.

July 1 – US atomic bomb tests held at Bikini Atoll in Pacific.

July 7 – Mother Francis Xavier Cabrini becomes the first American to be canonized by the Roman Catholic Church.

August 1 – Atomic Energy Commission created to promote peaceful application of atomic power.

Doin' What Comes Naturally

Show-business history was also being made in Atlantic City, New Jersey, where handsome crooner **Dean Martin** teamed up for the first time with pathologically goofy comedian **Jerry Lewis**, thus establishing a creative partnership that would make both of them rich and famous.

Across the state line, Irving Berlin's *Annie Get Your Gun*, starring Ethel Merman, was playing to sell-out crowds on Broadway. Perry Como's recording of the show's "They Say

It's Wonderful" and Dinah Shore's rendition of "Doin' What Comes Naturally" became huge chart hits, and Merman's showcase, "There's No Business Like Show Business," quickly entered the national consciousness.

Music News

Without question, the biggest song of the year was the Billy Reid composition "**The Gypsy**." Dinah Shore's recording of the song spent eight weeks at the top of the charts, whereupon it was promptly replaced by The Ink Spots' version—which, in turn, spent thirteen weeks at Number One. Other hits doing double duty at the top of the charts included Frankie Carle's "Oh! What It Seemed To Be," whose success was almost surpassed by Frank Sinatra's rendition, and the title song from *To Each His Own*, whose melody so captivated the American public that it hit Number One for no less than three artists (Eddy Howard and His Orchestra, Freddy Martin and

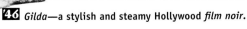
46 *Gilda*—a stylish and steamy Hollywood *film noir*.

His Orchestra, and The Ink Spots) and the Top Five for two others (Tony Martin, and The Modernaires with Paula Kelly).

Nat "King" Cole's Trio hit paydirt with the smooth "(I Love You) For Sentimental Reasons," and R&B superstar **Louis Jordan** continued to sell tons of records to black and white music lovers alike, hitting the pop charts four times ("Buzz Me," "Stone Cold Dead In The Market," "Choo Choo Ch'Boogie," and "Ain't That Just Like A Woman") over the course of the year. In the world of bebop, Dizzy Gillespie and Charlie Parker dissolved their partnership, after a two-month stand in Hollywood that puzzled audiences and critics as much as it excited their fellow musicians. Gillespie returned to New York City in February with the intention of organizing a bop orchestra, but Parker decided to stay in California. Unfortunately, Parker's precarious mental state (due, in part, to his raging heroin addiction) got the better of him; in July, he was committed to Camarillo State Hospital after accidentally starting a fire in his hotel.

Construction Goes On The Level

The postwar building boom going on across the nation was giving birth to a new kind of American dwelling: the **"ranch house."** The low-slung, single-story buildings were cheaper to build and to heat than the typical two-story-plus-attic house, and thus became immediately favored by a populace that was still experiencing the shortage of material goods. If it was still too costly to heat your ranch house, you could always spend your nights curled up under one of those new-fangled "electronic blankets," which the Simmons Company of Petersburg, Virginia, offered for $39.50 apiece.

Technology Starts To Count

American ingenuity, long directed towards the war effort, was now in full effect on the home front. The most interesting thing Detroit could come up with was a Nash 600 that could fit a double bed in its back seat, but things elsewhere were progressing rapidly. At the University of Pennsylvania, John P Eckert and John Mauchly developed the **ENIAC** (Electronic Numerical Integrator And Computer), the world's first electronic digital computer. The device required some eighteen thousand vacuum tubes, and so many components that they filled a 30- by 50-foot room; according to some witnesses, the ENIAC's initial power surge resulted in a brief brown-out throughout the city of Philadelphia.

...And Spring Arrives

The most momentous technological breakthrough, at least as far as American kids were concerned, was the invention of "**The Slinky**." Devised by marine engineer Richard James, the coiled spring that "walks up stairs,

46 Comedian Sammy Kaye tries out the brand new "Radio Chef," an electronic dime-in-the-slot frankfurter machine.

THE INK SPOTS
"The Gypsy"

FRANKIE CARLE AND HIS ORCHESTRA
"Oh! What It Seemed To Be"

FRANKIE CARLE AND HIS ORCHESTRA
"Rumors Are Flying"

EDDY HOWARD AND HIS ORCHESTRA
"To Each His Own"

DINAH SHORE
"The Gypsy"

alone or in pairs" became an immediate hit with the younger generation. Other offshoots, like "Slinky Dog" and "Cater-Puller," soon followed, but none of them ever matched the enormous success of the original item.

Time For A Fresh Look

Changes were afoot in the fashion world, as well; with the easing of wartime manufacturing restrictions, Americans now had a wider variety of clothes to choose from. The "slacks suits" popular with working women during the last years of the war were now out of favor, replaced by slim, belted dresses that rose to the knee. Also popular were dresses with shirtwaist tops, which buttoned all the way down the front. Colorful sports shirts were in for men, along with zipper-front casual jackets that could be worn with a shirt and tie.

46 The Inkspots—(*left to right*) Charles Fuqua, Bill Kenny, Herb Kenny, and Bill Bowen.

Car designers began to look across the Atlantic for new ideas.

The 1948 model Lincoln Continental, Studebaker Coupe, and Hudson were all influenced by the low, streamlined designs currently coming out of France and England. Davis, an independent manufacturer, anticipated consumer desire for smaller cars with its bubble-shaped, three-wheeled vehicle.

nineteen

47

47 Howard Hughes' *Spruce Goose* gets ready for takeoff in Los Angeles harbor.

The Davis could seat four persons on its single bench seat. Though it was priced at a reasonable $995, it was just too far ahead of its time to be successful. Also well ahead of its time was Cadillac; inspired by the Lockheed P-38 fighter plane, the company became the first to incorporate tailfins into its designs, putting them on all of their 1948 models. It would be several years, however, before the tailfin fad really caught on with American drivers.

Billed as "The first completely new car in fifty years," the Tucker, a six-passenger, four-door sedan, was the talk of the automobile world when it debuted in June of 1947. The car's rear-mounted, six-cylinder engine was made almost exclusively of aluminum, facilitating quick removal for repair purposes, and the front of the car sported three headlights, one of which would swivel to follow the curves of the road. "The car of the future" eschewed standard automobile parts like clutches, transmissions, differentials, and drive shafts, and the whole package was advertised at a little over a thousand dollars. There was only one catch: they weren't available yet. Despite selling millions of dollars worth of Tucker stock and franchises, Preston Tucker never seemed to have enough money to actually mass-produce his car. The Security Exchange Commission took a dim view of Tucker's dealings, and put him on trial for fraud. He was acquitted in 1949, but only fifty of his futuristic Tuckers were ever made. (The car and its inventor were eventually immortalized in Francis Ford Coppola's 1988 film, *Tucker: The Man and His Dream*.)

After a couple of years of treading water, the American automotive industry was finally starting to turn its eyes toward the future. In May, the BF Goodrich Tire Company introduced the tubeless tire, which was designed to seal itself when punctured. The **Harley-Davidson** company released its new **Panhead** motorcycle, featuring a redesigned Evolution engine. There were plenty of Harleys in attendance on July 4, when three thousand motorcycle enthusiasts rolled into Hollister, California, for a day of races. Fights with the local police quickly ensued, and the much-publicized incident, which indelibly molded the public's perception of the "outlaw" biker, later became the basis of the 1954 film *The Wild One*.

Set For Success

Commercial TV debuted in 1947; if it lacked much in the way of socially redeeming values—"It is a commercial reality but not yet an art," sniffed *Life* magazine—at least it was extremely entertaining. RCA marketed a small table television with a 6½- by 8½-inch screen, which sold for $325 plus a $55 "installation charge." Philco's 15- by 20-inch console model went for $795, plus

$85 installation, and Dumont's lavish Westminster emptied pocketbooks at $2,495, plus $75 installation. Most Americans, for the time being, did their TV watching in local taverns and bars, where the new invention was seen as a handy way to increase business.

Close Up And Dirty

Unsurprisingly, many of the year's more popular telecasts were of sporting events. Television exposure single-handedly resuscitated the popularity of **roller derby**, a brutal sport that essentially consisted of full-contact boxing on roller skates. Professional wrestling also reaped the benefits of the new medium; regular match broadcasts turned wrestler **"Gorgeous George" Wagner**—famous for wearing shocking pink shorts and his hair in a bleached-blond permanent wave—into one of the first television celebrities. At the peak of his popularity, he was earning seventy thousand dollars a year.

Major Breakthroughs

In September, the World Series of baseball was televised for the first time, although New York City, Washington, Philadelphia and Schenectady were the only cities to actually receive transmission. The seven-game contest between the New York Yankees and the Brooklyn Dodgers was notable for another reason: it featured the talents of Dodger **Jackie Robinson**, the first African-American player in the major leagues. Despite constant abuse from fans and opposing players, Robinson kept his cool and played well enough to win "Rookie of the Year" honors, becoming an overnight folk hero in the process. Other black players who made the majors in 1947 were the Dodgers' Dan Bankhead, the Cleveland Indians' Larry Doby, and Henry Thompson and Willard Brown of the St Louis Browns, but it would take until 1959 for the sport to be fully integrated.

Black Marx

Racial intolerance was also a hot issue in Hollywood, where Elia Kazan's *Gentleman's Agreement* (in which Gregory Peck pretends to be a Jew in order to understand how anti-Semitism feels) was released against the protests of many studio heads, who worried that the film would draw undue attention to their own Jewishness.

They needn't have worried. As October's **House Committee on Un-American Activities** hearings indicated, the American government was much more concerned about "the extent of **Communist infiltration** in the Hollywood motion picture industry"

'47 *Left:* **Jackie Robinson**
Below: Robinson signs autographs for young Dodgers fans.

than the influence of Jews. Called to testify before the committee, popular leading man Gary Cooper voiced the feelings of most of America, saying, "I never read Karl Marx, and therefore don't know so much about Communism except what I picked up from hearsay. But from what I heard I don't like it, because it's not on the level."

Starting To List

While many stars, writers, directors and studio heads testified before the committee that they were indeed fine, upstanding citizens, "**The Hollywood Ten**"—producer-director Herbert Biberman, director Edward Dmytryk, producer-writer Adrian Scott, and screenwriters Alvah Bessie, Lester Cole, Ring Lardner, Jr, John Howard Lawson, Albert Maltz,

Samuel Ornitz, and Dalton Trumbo—refused to divulge their political affiliations. Much to everyone's surprise, the ten men were convicted of contempt of Congress, and jailed for terms ranging up to a year. Wary of the specter of Communism, but even more frightened by the government probe, the film community effectively blacklisted the Hollywood Ten.

The Hollywood Committee for the First Amendment was formed in the fall by a group of Hollywood insiders (including Humphrey Bogart, Lauren Bacall, John Huston, Groucho Marx, Katharine Hepburn, Frank Sinatra, Fredric March, Gene Kelly, John Garfield, Ira Gershwin, and Danny Kaye) who claimed that, by forcing citizens to state their political views,

the government was violating their civil rights. Unfortunately, the group quickly splintered in the face of in-fighting and intense media pressure.

Movie News

While the paranoia of the time is certainly still palpable in the grimness of such *noir* offerings as Robert Rossen's *Body and Soul*, Henry Hathaway's *Kiss of Death* and Jacques Tourneur's *Out of the Past*, there was plenty of Hollywood sunshine to go around, as well. Bing Crosby, once again the leading male screen attraction, starred with Bob Hope and Dorothy Lamour in **Road to Rio**, one of the best of their six "Road" comedies, which featured musical numbers and comedic situations set in exotic locales. Betty

Grable, whose gorgeous gams adorned the wall of every self-respecting army barracks, livened up the screen (and the box office) with leads in *The Shocking Miss Pilgrim* and *Mother Wore Tights*. Natalie Wood warmed hearts as Kris Kringle's pal in *Miracle on 34th Street*, and cartoon characters Tweetie and Sylvester teamed up for the first time in Warner Brothers' Oscar-winning *Tweetie Pie*. Walt Disney mixed cartoon sequences with live action in **Song of the South**; while many have since derided the film as racist, it did provide the music industry with one of the year's most popular songs. Thanks to recorded versions by Johnny Mercer, Sammy Kaye, and The Modernaires with Paula Kelly, it was impossible to go anywhere without hearing "**Zip-a-Dee-Doo-Dah**."

Music News

In 1947, the most interesting musical developments were taking place off of the pop charts. In New York, **Dizzy Gillespie** introduced Afro-Cuban jazz to American listeners by incorporating Latin percussion and poly-rhythms into the music of his big band. Country star Merle Travis began making appearances with a solid-body electric guitar, constructed especially for him by luthier Paul Bigsby. Few others were ever made, but Bigsby's baby anticipated the solid-body electric boom by a good three years. On the country and western charts, a young Alabamian by the name of **Hank Williams** scored his first big hit with "Move It On Over." The sound of the song was pure country, but the attitude was pure rock 'n' roll.

Method In His Mumbling

On Broadway, musicals *Finian's Rainbow* and *Brigadoon* opened to immediate raves. The big news of the theater season, however, was Tennessee Williams' **A Streetcar Named Desire**, and its dynamic lead, **Marlon Brando**. Although often criticized for "mumbling" his lines, Brando drew praise for his performance, heralding the eventual rise of the empathetic "method" school of acting.

Nylon Clings

In 1947, American consumers were again hit hard by the rising costs of food, clothing, rent and other necessities. Still, many women managed to scrape up enough cash to outfit themselves in **"the Dior Look"** (also known as "the New Look")—padded-hip, full-skirted fashions that were becoming increasingly popular. Men's suits stayed conservative, although many men brightened up their wardrobes with madras shirts or wide, colorful ties. Synthetic blends of rayon and polyester also saw a rise in popularity, as postwar Americans found themselves with less time to actually do their ironing.

Tract House Dreams

Inspired by the postwar housing shortage, **Levittown**, the US's first mass-produced tract housing project, was built in Island Trees, Long Island, by developer William Levitt. Architectural critics and sociologists attacked its sterility and lack of individuality, but many returning GIs and their wives found the pre-fabricated community attractive, not to mention affordable—Levittown's Cape Cod-style homes could be had for $6,990 apiece. With its expansive front lawns, wide streets and look-alike houses, Levittown became the model for America's new suburbia. Sales of rotary lawn mowers soon increased dramatically, and the modern American cult of lawn care was on its way.

And Nevada Nightmares

After a disastrous grand opening in late 1946, the **Flamingo Hotel**, the first "sophisticated" hotel on "the strip," reopened in Las Vegas. Financed by mobster Bugsy Siegel (who, thanks to an assassin's bullets, would not live to see the end of 1947), the hotel helped shift the desert city's image from vice-ridden gambling town to glamorous vacation hot-spot.

47 Marlon Brando (far left) smolders in the Broadway production of *A Streetcar Named Desire*.

'48

"What time is it? Howdy Doody Time, of course!" Introduced during the last week of 1947, *The Howdy Doody Show* (originally titled Puppet Playhouse) quickly became required viewing for the youth of America. Hosted by "Buffalo Bob" Smith, and featuring occasional appearances from Clarabelle the Clown (aka Bob Keeshan, who later got his own children's TV gig as the titular host of Captain Kangaroo), the variety show's main draw was Howdy Doody, an inquisitive puppet with freckles and a plaid shirt.

The program took place in front of a live audience of children, known as "The Peanut Gallery." Savvy businessmen made millions from Howdy Doody dolls, records, toys, sleeping bags, wallpaper and wristwatches, convincing wary executives that television was indeed a profitable medium for advertising.

Popular from the get-go, TV was widely assailed as the eventual destroyer of American literacy, movies and theater. Although Ed Sullivan's *Toast of the Town* variety show (renamed **The Ed Sullivan Show** in 1955) lent the medium some class (well, just a touch of it—Sullivan's first broadcast did include singing fireman Fred Kohoman), the success of puppet shows like *Howdy Doody* and *Kukla, Fran and Ollie* didn't exactly reflect well upon its intellectual content.

What was most frightening, at least to the movie industry, was the obvious hold that television exerted over its viewers. Milton Berle's

48 The phenomenally successful Howdy Doody with Princess Summerfall Winterspring.

weekly comedy series, **The Texaco Star Theater**, was so popular that many restaurants would stay closed on Tuesday nights rather than compete; the show's October 19 broadcast earned a ninety-two-percent viewer share, still the highest rating ever. A former vaudevillian, Berle indulged in plenty of outrageous antics (including dressing up in women's clothing), but his real cultural contribution was the shot in the arm his show gave to the television industry—many Americans actually purchased their first TV sets just so they could watch "**Uncle Miltie**" in the privacy of their own homes.

System Breakdown

Television wasn't the only threat facing the major film studios in 1948. The US Supreme Court ruled that Columbia, Metro-Goldwyn-Mayer, Paramount, RKO, 20th Century Fox, Warner Bros., and Universal would all have to divest themselves of their

48 Right from the start, television had an irresistible attraction for the American people.

theater chains, effectively ending their monopoly over the exhibition of films. Thanks to competition from television, foreign filmmakers (Hollywood bigwigs were less than thrilled by *Hamlet*'s Academy Awards success), and smaller companies like Republic and Monogram, the late forties and early fifties saw the majors pumping more and more money into lavish productions. As a result, they found it increasingly difficult to afford to keep large numbers of actors and directors under contract. By the end of the fifties, Hollywood's "studio system" had virtually collapsed, giving actors and directors a greater degree of independence and control over their own careers.

Movie News

But the main reason to go to a movie theater in 1948 was the sheer quality of the stuff being screened. Bing Crosby (*The Emperor Waltz*) and Betty Grable (*That Lady in Ermine*, *When My Baby Smiles at Me*) retained their top box-office status despite the fluffiness of their vehicles, but folks were also buying plenty of tickets to see Bogart in **The Treasure of the Sierra Madre** and *Key Largo*, Ingrid Bergman in *Joan of Arc*, and John Wayne in *Red River* and *Fort Apache*. Orson Welles' *The Lady from Shanghai* led the pack of excellent *noir* thrillers, including Rudolph Maté's *The Dark Past*, John

Farrow's *The Big Clock*, and Anthony Mann's *Raw Deal*. Viewers who packed the theaters for *Rachel and the Stranger* didn't go for its pioneer-era love story, but rather for the chance to gawk at **Robert Mitchum**. In a bizarre twist of fate, Mitchum's recent arrest for **marijuana** possession lent an added dose of reality to his "outsider" characters, and actually made him more popular at the box office.

Still struggling to make it in Hollywood, **Marilyn Monroe** appeared in bit roles in *Scudda-Hoo! Scudda-Hay!* and *Dangerous Years* before being dropped by 20th Century Fox. She then signed with Columbia, but was released soon after playing the lead in *Ladies of the Chorus*. Out of

work and hungry, she posed nude for photos that would later see the light of day in the form of a million-selling calendar. Marilyn's modeling fee? Fifty dollars.

48 Aspiring young actress Marilyn Monroe.

Spike Jones and His City Slickers' crazed "All I Want For Christmas (Is My Two Front Teeth)". Rhythm 'n' blues continued to make its presence felt, most prominently in the form of Bull Moose Jackson and His Bearcats' "I Love You, Yes I Do" and The Orioles' "It's Too Soon to Know." Thanks to the tireless efforts of Dizzy Gillespie, bebop was rising in popularity; many swing bands tried to incorporate bop into their repertoires, often with awkward results. Meanwhile, trumpeter Miles Davis formed a nine-piece "**Birth of the Cool**" combo (including baritone saxophonist Gerry Mulligan and alto saxophonist Lee Konitz), which utilized softer tones, a smoother rhythm section and more concise arrangements than bebop, pioneering "cool" jazz in the process.

Revolution Loses Pace

In June, Columbia Records introduced their new 33⅓ rpm "**long-playing**" **record**. While the standard 78 rpm disc could only accommodate a maximum of four minutes of music, each side of Columbia's new album format could handle up to twenty-three, which made it ideal for classical selections. RCA also unveiled their new creation, the 7-inch 45 rpm disc. Originally intended for short classical pieces, the company quickly began using the format for pop singles.

Music News

1948's pop charts offered something for just about everyone, ranging from the comforting lilt of Bing Crosby's "Now Is The Hour (Maori Farewell Song)" and Nat "King" Cole's "Nature Boy," to the novelty charm of Art Mooney and His Orchestra's "I'm Looking Over a Four Leaf Clover," and

Full Metal

Over a million new homes were built in 1948, and Plymouth saluted America's burgeoning suburbia with its 1949 Suburban Wagon. The station wagon's

all-steel construction was cheaper to manufacture than the previously favored "woodies," and thus the car was more affordable to middle-class families.

Wedgewood USA

Another important suburban invention to surface in 1948 was Tupperware. "**Tupperware parties**," in which housewives gathered in someone's living room to examine and purchase various plastic Tupperware containers, became an important social ritual—you could meet your neighbors and outfit your kitchen at the same time.

Teenage The New Age

On December 20, *Life* magazine ran a cover story on **teenagers**, underscoring the fact that, for the first time in American history, teenagers were viewed as a demographic unto themselves. Thanks, in part, to the many extra jobs that were created by World War Two, teenagers had plenty of spending money, and it became Madison Avenue's avowed mission to get them to spend it on various clothing, dance and music fads.

Teenagers were also experiencing more independence than they typically had in the past, as the demands of the war meant that one or both parents were usually away from home; in some cases, this resulted in "**juvenile delinquency**," one of the biggest concerns of postwar white America. In general, teenage boys favored "collegiate" sweaters, pleated pants, and casual jackets, while teenage girls could be easily identified by their pleated skirts, baggy sweaters, bobby sox, and penny loafers.

48 A triumphant Harry S Truman holds up an early—and mistaken—report of his election defeat.

ACADEMY AWARDS

BEST FILM

Hamlet

directed by Laurence Olivier

BEST ACTOR

Laurence Olivier

Hamlet

BEST ACTRESS

Jane Wyman

Johnny Belinda

1949 held more than its share of bad news for the United States. For the first time, the American Cancer Society and National Cancer Institute warned adult Americans (over forty percent of whom enjoyed at least a pack a day) that **cigarette smoking might cause cancer.** To make matters worse, **the Soviet Union exploded its first atomic bomb.** Stalin's government claimed that the bomb was detonated as a means of stimulating agricultural growth in a barren region of the USSR, but **most Americans took it as a sign that a full-scale nuclear war was just around the corner.**

ACADEMY AWARDS

BEST PICTURE

All the King's Men

directed by Robert Rossen

BEST ACTOR

Broderick Crawford

All the King's Men

BEST ACTRESS

Olivia de Havilland

The Heiress

Beginning a pattern that would continue, more or less unabated, through to the present day, Americans responded to the ominous global developments by zoning out in front of the television. By 1949, Americans were buying one hundred thousand TV

sets a week. Critics noted a substantial increase in mystery and horror programming from the previous year, which was just fine with the viewers who tuned in regularly for gritty shows including *Lights Out*, *Man Against Crime* and *Hands of Murder*. **Captain Video**, featuring former radio actor Al Hodge, was American television's first science-fiction program; despite tremendously cheesy props and cardboard scenery, it gained a huge following. **The Lone Ranger**, based on the popular radio serial, also debuted in 1949, with Clayton Moore in the title role and Jay Silverheels as Tonto.

On a more wholesome note, **The Goldbergs**, based on a long-running radio sitcom, gave TV its first Jewish family. Though extremely popular with viewers, the hit show was dropped in 1951, when anti-Communist pamphlet *Red Channels* listed Phillip Loeb, who played Mr Goldberg, as "friendly to Communist causes." The show returned in 1952 with a different Mr Goldberg,

but only lasted a few more years. Unable to find further work, the blacklisted Loeb killed himself in 1955.

Show Of Hands Leads To Emmy

Los Angeles' Hollywood Athletic Club hosted the first annual Emmy Awards ceremony, an event which was all but ignored by the news media. As a result, America missed the once-in-a-lifetime opportunity to see Shirley Dinsdale and her puppet, Judy Splinters, win the Emmy for Outstanding Personality.

Movie News

Betty Grable was still America's most popular leading lady, but even her star power (and legs) couldn't save *The Beautiful Blonde from Bashful Bend* from laying an egg at the box office. Grable's main competition was from **Esther Williams**, a great swimmer and serviceable actress who turned heads in *Take Me Out to the Ball Game* and *Neptune's Daughter*. John Wayne was

undoubtedly the number one box-office draw in the country, putting in lead appearances in *Three Godfathers*, *The Fighting Kentuckian*, and *She Wore a Yellow Ribbon*. Errol Flynn, one of America's favorite male stars during World War Two, appeared in the title role of *The Adventures of Don Juan*, but the film did little to boost his sagging popularity.

Other popular films included Stanley Donen's musical **On the Town** (starring Gene Kelly and Frank Sinatra as swabbies on shore leave), the costume spectacle **Samson and Delilah** (with Victor Mature and Hedy Lamarr), and **Francis**, the first of several successful low-brow comedies starring Francis the Talking Mule. Just to show that it was on the right side of the anti-Communist cause, Hollywood produced three Red-bashing features, *The Red Menace*, *The Red Danube*, and *Guilty of Treason*. None of them did particularly well with filmgoers.

Two great entertainment duos made their film debuts in 1949: Dean Martin and Jerry Lewis in *My Friend Irma*, and the Roadrunner and Wile E Coyote in Chuck Jones' animated short, *Fast and Furryous*.

America's Driving Force

There were over thirty-four thousand miles of road improvements and construction carried out on American highways during 1949, and it was considered every citizen's patriotic duty to take advantage of them. In Detroit, the auto makers were gearing up for the coming decade with various improvements, both cosmetic and functional. Plymouth hailed its "Improved Air Pillow Ride" and "Safe-Guard Hydraulic Brakes," noting that its 1950 models were "Packed with value and ready to prove it!" 1950 Hudsons offered "the new step-down ride," with a lower center of gravity than any other American car, while ads for the 1950 Studebaker trumpeted its rocket-derived "Next Look." Flashiest of all were Oldsmobile's 88 and 98 models, both of which were part of Olds' new "Futuramic" line.

The postwar automobile culture also had a hand in shaping modern American architecture. In Los Angeles, John Lautner's design for **Googie's** coffee shop featured jaunty angles and

IN THE NEWS

Construction begins on UN Headquarters in New York City.

September 3 – Soviet Union explodes its first atom bomb.

October 21 – Judge Harold Medina sentences "eleven top US Communists" to prison terms of up to five years.

In The John Ford Tradition of Greatness

JOHN FORD and MERIAN C. COOPER present

SHE WORE A YELLOW RIBBON

JOHN WAYNE in his most heroic role as Captain Brittles of the U.S. Cavalry

Starring JOHN WAYNE · JOANNE DRU · JOHN AGAR
BEN JOHNSON · HARRY CAREY
with VICTOR McLAGLEN · MILDRED NATWICK · GEORGE O'BRIEN · ARTHUR SHIELDS
Story by JAMES WARNER BELLAH · Screen Play by FRANK NUGENT and LAURENCE STALLINGS
DIRECTED BY JOHN FORD

a dynamic exterior sign, both of which were created for the express purpose of attracting the attention of passing motorists. Once thought of as sleazy dives, coffee shops and diners were now considered respectable places for family dining, and Googie's comfortable spaces and bright color scheme virtually defined 1950s' coffeeshop architecture.

Music News

In 1949, music lovers could take advantage of the RCA's new 7-inch format with the Emerson 45 rpm record player, available at participating dealers for just $39.95. It's quite likely most folks who bought the Emerson player used it to listen to their new **Perry Como** singles. It was another stellar year for Como, who landed nine singles in the Top Twenty, including "Some Enchanted Evening", "Forever And Ever," and "Bali Ha'i"—the latter from the popular Rodgers and Hammerstein musical *South Pacific*, which was currently raking in the cash on Broadway. One of the year's biggest singles was Gene Autry's "**Rudolph The Red-Nosed Reindeer**." Autry's recording of Johnny Marks' Christmas song sold over two million copies in the month of December, and became a Yuletide standard. Louis Jordan and

Ella Fitzgerald's "Baby, It's Cold Outside" wasn't a Christmas hit (it came out in June), but it should have been.

Refugees from the country charts, Hank Williams' "Lovesick Blues" and Ernest Tubb's "Slipping Around" both snuck into the pop Top 25, although the latter song would eventually top the pop charts in a duet version by Jimmy Wakely and Margaret Whiting. "Drinkin' Wine Spo-Dee-O-Dee," a crossover R&B hit for "Stick" McGhee, was the first in a long line of R&B and rock hits for New York's Atlantic label.

In November, Charlie Parker recorded a groundbreaking jazz session with a string section. "Bird," Parker's nickname, was immortalized a month later when the **Birdland** jazz club opened on Broadway in New York City.

49 Charlie Parker (second from right) and friends at Birdland.

Pots Of Dough

Peter Hodgson, an unemployed ad copywriter, raised a few eyebrows when he placed a pink-looking compound of boric acid and silicone oil on the market. The compound had been invented during World War Two by General Electric engineer James Wright, but Wright could find no conceivable use for the stretchable, bounceable substance. Christened **Silly Putty**, Hodgson's product was an immediate hit with America's kids, who of course found innumerable uses for it. Priced at a dollar per one-ounce glob, Silly Putty eventually grossed Hodgson over a hundred and forty million dollars.

nineteen '50

As 1950 drew to a close, a pall of pessimism settled over the country like a black sheet. The situation in Korea seemed to confirm widely held fears that the Cold War was about to heat up. Soviet war production was said to far outstrip that of the United States, and Americans were getting rather jumpy; one evening in the New York City subway, one thousand riders stampeded when they mistook a short-circuited signal for an indication that World War Three had started.

50 US troops embark for Korea.

Movie News

In 1950, the surest way to mark yourself as a Communist sympathizer was to oppose the war in Korea. The *Los Angeles Times*, for instance, advised its readers to report **peace petitioners** to the FBI. "Don't punch him in the nose," the paper warned, "Reds are used to that. Get his name and address and phone the FBI." The *New York Times* also reported that Hollywood's Monogram Studio had shelved a film on the life and exploits of Indian brave Hiawatha, fearing that it might be regarded as Communist propaganda. The studio worried that Hiawatha's efforts as a peacemaker might cause the film to be interpreted as pro-peace, and therefore pro-Communist. However, there was no mistaking the political agenda of Robert Stevenson's ***I Married a Communist***, which starred Robert Ryan as a former Communist menaced by his old comrades.

When they weren't busy worrying about the Russians, Americans were loudly venting their disapproval over Ingrid Bergman's decision to have a baby with Italian director Roberto Rossellini—instead of her actual husband, Dr Peter Lindstrom. Never especially adept at distinguishing onscreen life from the real thing, the American public was positively appalled that the angelic star of *Joan of Arc* and *The Bells of St Mary's* could

ACADEMY AWARDS

BEST PICTURE

All About Eve
directed by Joseph L. Mankiewicz

BEST ACTOR

José Ferrer
Cyrano de Bergerac

BEST ACTRESS

Judy Holliday
Born Yesterday

50 Gloria Swanson turns on the charm for William Holden in *Sunset Boulevard*.

possibly behave in such a wanton manner. Sparing no amount of hyperbole, Senator Edwin C Johnson of Colorado assailed Bergman as a **"free-love cultist."** *Stromboli*, Bergman's first filmic collaboration with Rossellini, was widely boycotted during its theatrical release.

Far more popular with moviegoers were John Wayne (*Sands of Iwo Jima*, *Rio Grande*), Betty Grable (*Wabash Avenue, My Blue Heaven*), and Esther Williams (*Duchess of Idaho*, *Pagan Love Song*). Billy Wilder's humorously creepy *Sunset Boulevard* brought silent-screen beauty Gloria Swanson out of retirement; Walt Disney enchanted viewers with an animated adaptation of *Cinderella*; George Cukor's witty **Adam's Rib** was

perhaps the finest ever pairing of Spencer Tracy and Katherine Hepburn; and **Jimmy Stewart** was at his bumbling best as *Harvey*'s rabbit-befriending drunk.

Marilyn Monroe, once again under contract to Fox, scored small roles in *Love Happy, A Ticket to Tomahawk, The Asphalt Jungle, All About Eve, Right Cross,* and *The Fireball*. Judy

Holliday, perfectly essaying the sort of "dizzy blonde" role that Marilyn would later be typecast as, won an Oscar for *Born Yesterday*. Befitting his method-actor reputation, **Marlon Brando** prepared for his film debut in Stanley Kramer's *The Men*—in which he played an embittered paraplegic—by spending an entire month in a hospital's paraplegic ward.

January 21 – Alger Hiss found guilty of two counts of perjury, for having initially denied giving State Department papers to Communists in 1938.

January 31 – President Truman okays development of the hydrogen bomb, or "superbomb." Many take this as a sign that the US is losing the arms race.

February – Wisconsin Senator Joseph McCarthy begins his anti-Communist crusade, announcing that he is aware of Communist activity in the State Department.

A Lot To Take Comfort In

Despite all the turmoil overseas, America was doing just fine from a material standpoint. Before the Korean War reared its ugly head, the economy had finally just begun to stabilize; the average industry worker was making $60.53 a week, an all-time high. General Electric boasted that its new automatic dishwasher "will give you over 200 long hours of extra leisure time!" **Betty Crocker**'s *Picture Cook Book* topped the best-seller lists. Diners Club introduced the first plastic credit card, and the US Brewers Foundation wanted to let you know that beer, "America's beverage of moderation," was all right to drink "at mealtime, too!"

Wear To Be Seen

Younger girls were often seen wearing the bizarre combination of dungarees and ballet slippers; slim-figured, "man-tailored" suits and shirts were popular with young women, as were ornate

"**circle skirts**," which were usually combined with simple blouses or sweaters. For the first time since before the war, heavy eye-makeup was in. Increased leisure time also encouraged the purchase of "at home" clothes, which included comfortable skirts, lounging pants and flat-soled shoes.

The greased-back "da" (or "duck's ass") haircut, originally invented in 1940 by Philadelphia barber Joe Cirella, began to be favored by some young men, although most still preferred the slicked-back, side-parted look.

What It's All About

The "hokey pokey" dance, which involved putting your right foot in, putting your right foot out, putting your right foot in and then shaking it all about, experienced an inexplicable burst of popularity at US colleges across the country.

Driven To Distraction

Inflation rose again with the eruption of the Korean War, and material shortages were making things difficult

for auto manufacturers just around the time that they began introducing their 1951 models. For the first time since World War Two, whitewall tires were hard to come by, even on new cars.

Cars in the 1950s differed from their 1940s predecessors in that they often sported tailfins, excessive chrome ornamentation, and two- and three-tone exterior paints. **Color-coordinated** interiors and exteriors, with pastel shades that mirrored the postwar popularity of pastel fabrics in clothing and home furnishings, were a great leap forward from the relative drabness of the previous decade. Car bodies also tended to be longer and lower, as the "fastback" and rounded tops of the 1940s were replaced by flat, "hardtop" shapes. Extra **accessories**—everything from mudflaps to antenna foxtails—became a popular way for drivers to personalize their cars.

As vacationing became a popular pastime for Americans, and the automobile a primary means of vacation transport for the middle class, "motor lodges," reflecting the novel combination of driving and leisure, began to spring up all over

50 Nash cars offered "Hydra-Matic Drive" and "Nash Selecto-Lift Starting."

America in the 1950s, and cars got names from holiday spots, like **Riviera, Bel Air,** and **Newport.**

Bearing the new slogan, "True yesterday—true today," Chrysler debuted its dream-car program with the futuristic Plymouth XX500, built by Ghia in Italy. General Motors, meanwhile, introduced the Buick LeSabre dream-car, aka "the car of

the Sixties." The dream-cars never actually went into mass production, but their appearance at traveling "Motorama" shows definitely influenced the tastes of automobile buyers, as well as the designs of other car companies. For the first time ever, Fords were available with a fully **automatic transmission**, offered optionally as "Ford-O-Matic" or "Merc-O-Matic" (for Mercury). Nash previewed its one-thousand-dollar NXI model, a compact two-seater, to mixed reviews; *Life* magazine asked, "Does the US want a small car?" At the opposite end of the spectrum, Cadillac's thirty-five-thousand-dollar **Debutante** was displayed in the January auto show at New York's Waldorf-Astoria hotel. A tawny gold convertible with silver satin and Somaliland Leopardskin upholstery, it was truly an automotive work of art.

Picture This

Jackson Pollock caused a stir in the art world with *Lavender Mist*, widely considered to be the first "drip" or "action" painting. Charles Schulz's *Peanuts* comic strip, featuring Charlie Brown and his dog Snoopy, made its national debut. The first issues of EC's **comic books** *The Crypt of Terror* (later changed to *Tales from the Crypt*), *The Vault of Horror,* and *The Haunt of Fear* debuted on newsstands about this time. With their gruesome artwork, flowery language and fiendish (but ultimately moral) tales, EC's publications trounced those of the competition.

Old-Time Radio Waves Goodbye

Despite the unrelenting onslaught of television, radio was still trying to put up a fight. There were compromises, however; as time went on, local stations were relying more and more on music programming to keep the attention of their listeners. When **The Big Show**, a variety program hosted by Tallulah Bankhead, debuted in 1950, it garnered raves—but in retrospect, it was really the last gasp of old-time radio.

Television sets were coming down in price; the no-frills Philco model 1403, with a 12½-inch tube, was available for $199.95. Of course, the big spender could have Admiral's "complete home entertainment"

system, which included FM-AM Radio, two-speed phonograph, and "magic mirror" television, in "one luxurious console"—and all for the princely sum of $549.50. CBS began transmitting **color broadcasts** in November, much to the chagrin of RCA, which claimed to have the superior color system.

TV News

1950 saw the advent of many television programs which are now regarded as classics. Groucho Marx mixed comedy and quiz

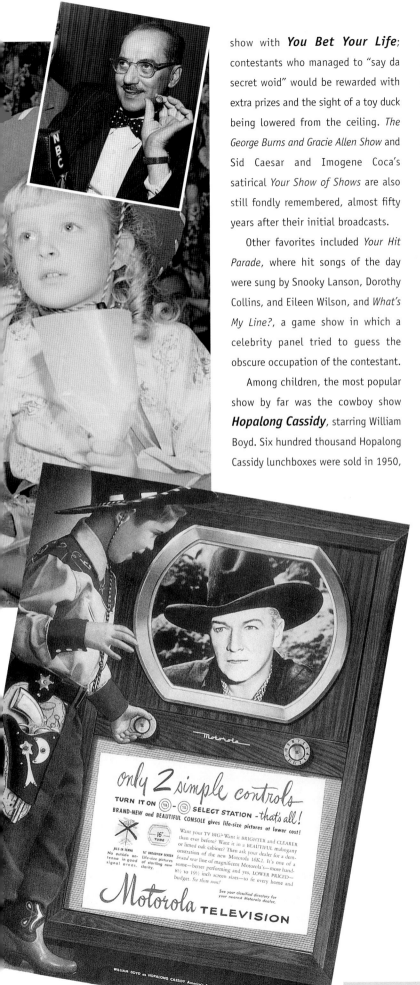

show with **You Bet Your Life**; contestants who managed to "say da secret woid" would be rewarded with extra prizes and the sight of a toy duck being lowered from the ceiling. *The George Burns and Gracie Allen Show* and Sid Caesar and Imogene Coca's satirical *Your Show of Shows* are also still fondly remembered, almost fifty years after their initial broadcasts.

Other favorites included *Your Hit Parade*, where hit songs of the day were sung by Snooky Lanson, Dorothy Collins, and Eileen Wilson, and *What's My Line?*, a game show in which a celebrity panel tried to guess the obscure occupation of the contestant.

Among children, the most popular show by far was the cowboy show **Hopalong Cassidy**, starring William Boyd. Six hundred thousand Hopalong Cassidy lunchboxes were sold in 1950,

and everything from Hopalong Cassidy bicycles to "bath roundup" kits were also available for purchase. And purchased they were.

Music News

1950 was a less than memorable year for music; about the only interesting aspect of the pop charts was that "The Thing," a trite novelty song, actually charted for three different artists (Phil Harris, Arthur Godfrey, and The Ames Brothers). More interesting were the technological advances: the Seeburg company produced the first **jukeboxes** to play 45 rpm singles, and they soon became regular fixtures in bars, bowling alleys and soda shops. Meanwhile, Columbia was advertising its 10- and 12-inch LPs as "The ultimate in uninterrupted listening pleasure." The 12-inch records, like the *Kiss Me Kate* Broadway cast recording, sold for $4.85, while the 10-inchers, like Doris Day's "You're My Thrill," were priced at $2.85.

Solid Body

Leo Fender's guitar company introduced their Broadcaster and Esquire models, the first mass-produced solid-body electric guitars on the market. As they could be turned up much louder than their hollow counterparts without causing unwanted noise or feedback, they soon became quite a common sight on bandstands across the nation. They also helped continue to elevate the electric guitar to the status of a lead instrument, rather than just part of the rhythm section.

50 *Above left:* **young Hopalong Cassidy fans.** *Inset:* **Groucho Marx.**

nineteen

51

As the Korean War dragged on, **America's Communist witch-hunt hysteria shifted into high gear.** The American Committee for Cultural Freedom was founded to "counteract the influence of mendacious Communist propaganda," and film director and "Hollywood Ten" member Edward Dmytryk, released from prison after confessing prior involvement in the Communist Party, became the star witness in the second round of HUAC's Hollywood hearings.

More than three hundred Hollywood personalities were implicated as Communists (usually by colleagues looking to save their own careers), and most of them were blacklisted. Many blacklisted actors and directors retired, looked for work in the theater, or left to find greener pastures in Europe. Some screenwriters, operating under aliases, managed still to find work in Hollywood.

Movie News

With the exception of Gordon Douglas' forgettable *I Was a Communist for the FBI*, Hollywood pretty much avoided the subject altogether, although **sci-fi** releases such as *The Thing from Another World* and *The Day the Earth Stood Still* certainly slipped plenty of pro-peace and anti-nuclear sentiments past the censors. Once again, the year's top stars were John Wayne (*Operation Pacific*, *The Bullfighter and The Lady*, *Flying Leathernecks*) and Betty Grable (*Call Me Mister*, *Meet Me after the Show*), but **Marlon Brando** made the biggest screen impression with his portrayal of Stanley Kowalski in Tennessee Williams' *A Streetcar Named Desire*. Older critics lambasted his method-oriented performance as being from "the torn T-shirt school of acting," but there was no doubt that a major new star had arrived. *Bedtime for Bonzo* pitted future US President **Ronald Reagan** against a precocious chimpanzee. Once a fairly successful B-movie actor, Reagan wasn't getting many parts any more. Despite the commercial success of films such as *A Place in The Sun* (an adaptation of Theodore Dreiser's *An American Tragedy*, starring Montgomery Clift and Elizabeth Taylor) theater owners complained that their audiences were down roughly forty percent. Television, of course, was considered the main culprit.

TV News

Seventeen million Americans now had their own TV sets, and there were plenty of reasons to stay home and watch them. *I Love Lucy*, a sitcom featuring the talents of comedienne Lucille Ball and her Cuban bandleader husband Desi Arnaz, became an immediate hit when it debuted in October. *The Cisco Kid*, starring Duncan Renaldo and Leo Carillo as a pair of wrong-righting desperadoes, was an appealing addition to the TV western genre. Edward R. Murrow's documentary series *See It Now* debuted on CBS, and families regularly gathered around the

'51 After a rollercoaster courtship, Frank Sinatra and Ava Gardner marry in November 1951.

set on Monday nights to see the array of amateur and professional performers on *Arthur Godfrey's Talent Scouts*.

The *Amos and Andy Show*, one of television's more controversial sitcoms, debuted in June; though often vilified for perpetuating racist stereotypes, the show was still the first television series with an all-black cast—and the last one until *Sanford and Son* debuted in 1971. Much whiter was **The Chevy Show**, a twice-a-day, fifteen-minute program starring Dinah Shore. "See the USA in your Chevrolet," she advised, ending each show by blowing a big kiss.

Cruising Stalls

In 1951, American automobiles were still in mid-evolution between the tank-like creations of the 1940s and the rocket-like stylings of the mid- and late 1950s. GM did produce the futuristic XP300 show car for Buick, but the year brought little in the way of innovation—although the 1952 Dodge Coronet Diplomat did feature an "Oriflow system" for smooth rides, and 1952 Chryslers came with "Hydraguide," later known as power steering. Willys-Overland's compact two-door Eagle was extremely practical, but also extremely unpopular—Americans just weren't ready for economy cars.

Pollocks Go On Show

Nor were Americans quite ready for **abstract expressionism**, although *Abstract Painting and Sculpture in America*, an exhibition at New York City's Museum of Modern Art, went a long way towards giving the New York-based movement some recognition and respect. Their approaches to painting varied, but Jackson Pollock, Willem de Kooning, Mark Rothko, Clyfford Still, Franz Kline, and Robert Motherwell were all lumped together by art critics of the time; their work did, at least, demonstrate a shared affection for open structures, pure color fields, and anonymous brushstrokes.

Lawn Jockeys Lose Out

In other art news, Don Featherstone designed the first plastic lawn flamingo for Union Products of Leominster, Massachusetts. The hollow, steel-legged bird soon replaced lawn jockeys as the lawn ornament of choice for taste-impaired American homeowners.

Write Stuff

Despite television's popularity, American's still had plenty of time for books. *Kon-Tiki*, Thor Heyerdahl's record of his South Seas expeditions, became a best-seller, as did James Jones' gripping Pearl Harbor tale, *From Here to Eternity*. Rachel Carson published *The Sea Around Us*, a dire warning that effectively kick-started the American ecology movement, and JD Salinger published **The Catcher in the Rye**, his acclaimed novel of alienated youth. Far more readers had eyes for Mickey Spillane's *One Lonely Night*, however; the gritty detective novel, in which Spillane hero Mike Hammer kills "Commies" and gloats about it, sold three million copies.

Music News

Balladeer Tony Bennett had his first big year, topping the charts with "Because Of You" and a smooth reading of Hank Williams' "Cold, Cold Heart." Thanks to "Be My Love," "Because," and "The Loveliest Night Of The Year," Mario Lanza became the most popular operatic tenor since Enrico Caruso. But the biggest buzz in the music (and film) world was about **Frank Sinatra**'s marriage to screen goddess **Ava Gardner**. The couple's tempestuous relationship had been going on for years, but Nancy, Sinatra's first wife, had been unwilling to grant him a divorce. The divorce finally came through on October 31, and Sinatra and Gardner were wed a few days later at a private home in Philadelphia. "Well, we finally made it," Sinatra beamed. Their marriage would last until 1957.

Lasting almost as long on the charts was "Cry," the melodramatic ballad that established Johnny Ray as the closest thing to a rock star in pre-Elvis America; given the hysteria that his concerts created, it's not unreasonable to see him as the missing link between Sinatra and Elvis. The Dominoes created some hysteria of their own with "Sixty Minute Man," an innuendo-laden R&B number that was way too raunchy for most white adult listeners, but which still managed to make the pop Top Twenty. "Rocket 88," considered by many to be the first actual **rock 'n' roll** song, topped the R&B charts in a version by Jackie Brenston and His Delta Cats that also featured a young Ike Turner on piano. Fender Instruments in Fullerton, California, pushed the world one step closer to rock 'n' roll with the introduction of their Precision electric bass.

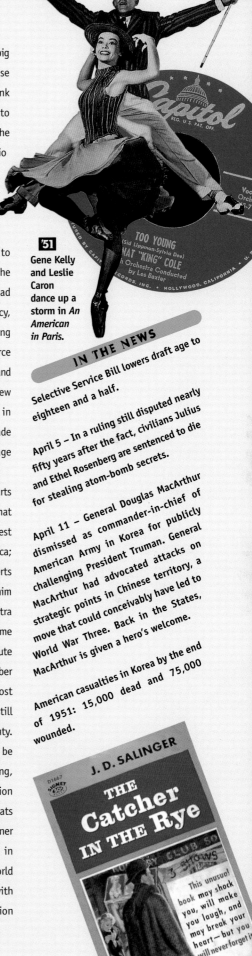

'51 Gene Kelly and Leslie Caron dance up a storm in *An American in Paris*.

IN THE NEWS

Selective Service Bill lowers draft age to eighteen and a half.

April 5 – In a ruling still disputed nearly fifty years after the fact, civilians Julius and Ethel Rosenberg are sentenced to die for stealing atom-bomb secrets.

April 11 – General Douglas MacArthur dismissed as commander-in-chief of American Army in Korea for publicly challenging President Truman. General MacArthur had advocated attacks on strategic points in Chinese territory, a move that could conceivably have led to World War Three. Back in the States, MacArthur is given a hero's welcome.

American casualties in Korea by the end of 1951: 15,000 dead and 75,000 wounded.

J.D. SALINGER

THE Catcher IN THE Rye

This unusual book may shock you, will make you laugh, and may break your heart—but you will never forget it

'52

Hollywood was in big trouble. **Between 1948 and 1952, television had caused film profits to drop by five hundred million dollars.** Hollywood tried to lure the public back to the theaters with big-budget musicals (*Singin' in the Rain, Hans Christian Andersen*), lavish costumers (*Moulin Rouge, Ivanhoe*), and slice-of-Tinseltown exposés (*The Bad and the Beautiful, The Star*), but folks were much more interested in staying home to watch *I Love Lucy*.

Stereoscopic cinema, or "3-D," was mooted as a possible cure to the box-office blahs, but **3-D films** like *Bwana Devil* tended to consist merely of shoddy scripts and lots of gimmicky action (such as spears, knives, and chairs being thrown towards the camera), and audiences quickly tired of the novelty. The 3-D glasses were also uncomfortable to wear, and 3-D's effectiveness depended on the location of your theater seat.

Movie News

Dean Martin and Jerry Lewis were the top marquee attractions of 1952, thanks to *Sailor Beware* and *Jumping Jacks*, and crowds did flock to see Doris Day do her stuff in *The Winning Team* and *April in Paris*. John Wayne played a romantic lead for a change in *The Quiet Man*, Marilyn Monroe played a mentally ill babysitter in *Don't Bother to Knock*, and Marlon Brando played a Mexican revolutionary in *Viva Zapata*. But it was Gary Cooper's turn as an embattled sheriff in **High Noon** that truly deserved the Best

52 Moviegoers wear 3-D glasses to get the full stereoscopic effect.

Actor Oscar. Screenwriter Carl Foreman later claimed that his film was an anti-HUAC allegory, but most viewers thought the film was just a really good western.

Hollywood's anti-Communist propaganda reached new levels of camp absurdity with *Seeds of Destruction* and *Red Planet Mars*. In the former, Kent Taylor plays a spy who assumes the identity of a missionary in order to spread Marxist filth in the US; in the latter, Peter Graves and Andrea King play scientists who discover that the planet Mars is actually ruled by God— knowledge that immediately results in the overthrow of the Russian Communist government by religious revolutionaries.

Final Flynn (And Other Exits)

Charlie Chaplin didn't find the "Red scare" so amusing, however. Criticized for never actually becoming an American citizen, the English-born actor was systematically harassed by the FBI and the IRS; having spoken out in defense of Russia during World War Two, he was now accused of being a Communist. While Chaplin traveled to London in 1952, the US Attorney General instructed immigration authorities to revoke Chaplin's re-entry visa until he agreed to allow his "Communist affiliations" to be examined. Refusing to testify before the House Committee on Un-American Activities, Chaplin simply decided to relocate to Switzerland.

In debt and with his popularity severely diminished, Errol Flynn also left the United States in 1952. Though the swashbuckling actor made several films in England, he was sadly unable to turn his career around.

TV News

Over two thousand new TV stations opened across the USA in 1952. Some sixty-five million viewers tuned into network coverage of the presidential conventions in Chicago, but the masses still preferred pure entertainment—it's said that Adlai Stevenson's popularity began to decline after he pre-empted an *I Love Lucy* episode with a campaign speech. Lucy was indeed "Queen of the Screen," but **Dragnet**, starring Jack

Webb as no-nonsense LAPD detective Sergeant Joe Friday, also did very well for itself in its first full season. Fridayisms like "Just the facts, ma'am" quickly became a part of the national vernacular, as did "And away we go," and "How sweet it is" from **The Jackie Gleason Show**. The second half-hour of the Gleason show was usually devoted to *The Honeymooners*, a semi-improvised sketch featuring Gleason as argumentative New York City bus driver Ralph Kramden, and Art Carney as Ed Norton, his dimwitted neighbor. The popular segment was given its own show in 1955.

Mash Hits

Hasbro's Mr Potato Head made television history in 1952 by

52 Mrs Potato Head (*right*) joined her husband in the sixties.

Desert Rats

The Sands Hotel, designed in an abstract modern style by Wayne McAllister, opened on the Las Vegas Strip. A favorite Vegas hangout of Frank Sinatra's, the hotel became synonymous with the "**Rat Pack**," a group of swinging drinking buddies that included Sinatra, Dean Martin, Sammy Davis, Jr, Joey Bishop, and Peter Lawford.

Greenhouse Effects

In New York City, the architectural firm of Skidmore, Owings and Merrill completed the mid-town Lever House; the building's spartan glass and steel

becoming the first children's toy ever to be advertised on TV. Unsurprisingly, the toy—basically just a boxed set of eyes, ears, noses, and mouths that you could stick into a potato—was an instant success. Mr Potato Head finally got his own plastic potato body in 1964, and there was much rejoicing.

Scoring Big-Time

Scrabble, a crossword spelling game invented in 1931, experienced a sudden popular resurgence, selling fifty-eight thousand sets in 1952. College students had other ideas about recreation—on March 21, the country's first official "**panty raid**" took place at the University of Michigan, as six hundred male students stormed a women's dormitory with the intention of stealing any undergarments they could find. The fad quickly caught on across the country, with women students occasionally raiding men's dorms in revenge.

Hat Designers Lose Headroom

As far as outer garments were concerned, the "casual look" was in for both sexes. Men were wearing pinstriped suits and solid-colored shirts without ties, while women preferred tailored suits, long skirts and no hats. The crowns of men's hats were actually growing lower, partially due to increasingly lowered automobile roofs.

Chain Male

Frustrated by the lack of quality lodgings along America's highways, Kemmon Wilson opened the first **Holiday Inn** in 1952. Easily identifiable from the road because of its bright yellow and green sign, the franchise eventually expanded to become the world's largest motel chain.

who had had numerous hits with his wife Mary Ford, and who contributed a great deal to the development of musical technology, the instrument would become one of the most popular rock guitars of all time.

Genius and MADness

Ralph Ellison published *The Invisible Man*, a scathing indictment of racism in America. Kurt Vonnegut published *Player Piano*, his first novel, while John Steinbeck published *East of Eden*.

EC's satirical **MAD** magazine was published for the first time; its avowed intention to make fun of anything and everything made it a must-read for smart-ass high school and college students everywhere. Alfred E Newman, the magazine's moronic-looking mascot, wouldn't be introduced until 1956.

construction set the standard for office building design in the next decade.

Lincoln Discovers Glass Ceiling

Lincoln slipped plenty of glass and steel into its 1953 XL-500 dream-car, which featured a roof that was made predominantly of glass. But it was Studebaker, a company not usually known for daring designs, who came up with the year's sleekest mass-produced 1953 car—interestingly, it was one of the few 1953 models to sport tailfins.

Music News

1952 was an especially strong year for female vocalists. Eddie Fisher hit the top of the charts with "Wish You Were Here," showbiz vets The Mills Brothers had great success with "The Glow-Worm," and Al Martino scored his first big hit with "Here In My Heart," but Dean Martin's version of "You Belong To Me" was beaten out by Jo Stafford, and none of Frank Sinatra's singles charted higher than number nineteen.

It was a year of ups and downs for **Hank Williams** as well; "Jambalaya

(On The Bayou)" gave him his first crossover hit in three years, but he soon found himself fired from Nashville's Grand Ole Opry for "erratic behavior." His divorce from his first wife, Audrey, was quickly followed by his wedding to Billie Jean Jones Eshlimar, a much-hyped event that Hank actually sold tickets to.

The Star's A Guitar

1952 was the year that Gibson introduced its **Les Paul** model electric guitar. Named for the guitarist

The US Government's Small Business Act of 1953 helped small firms and businesses obtain start-up monies; these came in handy, considering that, halfway through the year, a "mild depression" hit the country hard. One business that outlived this recession was **Playboy magazine,** founded in 1953 by Hugh Hefner. Hefner described his target audience as "that select group of urbane fellows who were less concerned with hunting, fishing, and climbing mountains than with good food, drink, proper dress, and the pleasure of female company."

The magazine's first centerfold was a nude photo of Marilyn Monroe, taken during the same 1948 session that yielded her million-selling calendar.

Burger Masters

Urbane fellows (and females) looking for good food and drink had plenty of options in 1953, but those who wanted a quick, cheap burger while on the run didn't have many places to choose from. This would soon change, as **McDonald's** franchises quickly began to spread across the country. The first franchise with golden arches (specifically designed to attract passing motorists) opened in Phoenix, Arizona, in 1953. "Speedee," the original McDonald's mascot, lasted until 1960, when "hamburger-loving clown" Ronald McDonald took over his coveted position.

Dreaming Tires

If you wanted to cruise your local McDonald's in a new car, there were a number of attractive models to choose from. Buicks sported tailfins for the very first time in their existence, the most eye-catching being the chrome fins

53 Gregory Peck romances Audrey Hepburn on their *Roman Holiday*.

on the 1954 Skylark. Buick's 1954 Skylark dream-car received such rave reviews that the company actually decided to make a limited production version for their customers. Mercury's 1954 XM-800 dream-car was for exhibit only, but there were plenty of auto enthusiasts who coveted its glass-roofed design. Chevrolet's super-sporty 1954 Corvette became the first mass-produced car to utilize a plastic body, and Hudson's small but attractive 1954 Italia was inspired by the increasing popularity of "continental" designs in clothing and automobiles. And, if you could afford to fork over six thousand dollars you could always get your hands on Cadillac's opulent 1954 El Dorado.

Movie News

An unintentional appearance in *Playboy* certainly didn't hurt Marilyn Monroe's popularity, but it was her luminous performances in *Niagara, Gentlemen Prefer Blondes,* and *How to Marry a Millionaire* that really established her as Hollywood's reigning **sex symbol**. The previous title-holder, Ava Gardner, wasn't doing too badly for herself, either, netting an Academy Award nomination for her role in John Ford's *Mogambo*. She also used her influence with Columbia Pictures boss Harry Cohn to help hubby Frank Sinatra land the part of Private Maggio in Columbia's film adaptation of James Jones' **From Here to Eternity**. Sinatra, who had blown his voice out the previous year, was widely considered to be washed up; the role, which he took for a measly eight-thousand-dollar salary, completely turned his career around. Gary Cooper, still riding high off the success of *High Noon*, helped *Blowing Wild* and *Return to Paradise* rack up better box-office notices than they probably deserved. **Audrey Hepburn**'s American screen debut in *Roman Holiday* made a big impression upon American women, many of whom immediately adopted her chic hairstyle.

IN THE NEWS

January – Following a Republican landslide in the November elections, Senator Joseph McCarthy is appointed chairman of the Senate Committee on Government Operations.

March 5 – Joseph Stalin dies of a stroke; Georgi M Malenkov named new Soviet Premier.

June 19 – Spies Julius and Ethel Rosenberg executed.

July 27 – Communist and United Nations delegates sign truce ending the Korean War. 54,246 Americans were killed, 103,284 were wounded and 7,955 reported missing in action.

Summer – Senator McCarthy begins investigating "rumors" of Communist infiltration of the US Army.

53 A suitably scary poster for *The War of the Worlds,* released in 1953.

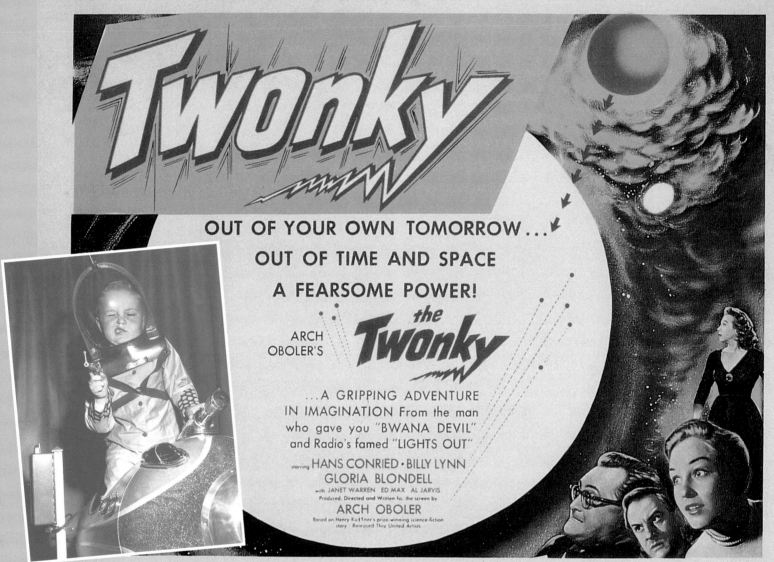

53 At the 1953 American Toy Fair, a young would-be astronaut tests the latest merchandise. The space theme—rocket styling and plenty of chrome—was definitely "in," especially with auto makers.

Overall, it was a pretty good year for films. Fans of lavish costume dramas had Richard Burton and Jean Simmons in *The Robe* (the first film shot using the widescreen **CinemaScope** process), and Marlon Brando and James Mason in *Julius Caesar*. *Calamity Jane*, featuring Doris Day, was one of the year's most popular musicals, and *The Band Wagon* proved that Fred Astaire could still cut a rug with the best of them. *Shane*, starring Alan Ladd, was easily the year's best western, even if it had taken two years to get it released.

House Of Wax, Vincent Price's first horror film since 1940's *The Invisible Man Returns*, was actually pretty decent for a 3-D feature, as was sci-fi thriller *It Came from Outer Space*. *The Beast from Twenty Thousand Fathoms* beat *Godzilla* to the nuclear-powered punch by a couple of years, and *The War of the Worlds* was a frightening filmic adaptation of HG Wells' Martian invasion tale. The year's oddest sci-fi entry had to be Arch Oboler's *The Twonky*, featuring a TV that came to life, hypnotized people and tried to take over their lives. Hmmm...

TV News

Goodyear Playhouse, which specialized in top-notch original teleplays, outdid itself on May 24 with a presentation of Paddy Chayefsky's **Marty**. A moving look at two people who find love despite their awkward social skills, the play starred Rod Steiger and Nancy Marchand. Chayefsky later expanded the play into a full-length film, which went on to win the 1956 Academy Award for Best Picture.

Person To Person, hosted by Edward R Murrow, took the viewing audience into the homes of famous personalities like Harry Truman, Marlon Brando, and Jackie Robinson.

Liberace, the man for whom the word "flamboyant" was practically invented, debuted with his own syndicated show. Enormously popular, the program featured the sequin-garbed pianist bouncing his way through lush arrangements of classical pieces, often assisted by George, his violinist brother.

I Love Lucy continued its reign as the most popular show in America, making television history when Lucy's writers decided to write her actual pregnancy into the scripts. In an age where you couldn't say "pregnant" on TV, and in which married characters had to sleep in separate beds, this was a fairly radical concept. Coincidentally, Lucille Ball's baby was born on January 19, the same day that the "having a baby" episode (filmed two months earlier) ran on national television. The episode was watched by seventy percent of the viewing audience, and the ensuing deluge of publicity completely eclipsed President Eisenhower's inauguration.

Music News

Superficially, it seemed like just another year in pop—perennial favorites like Perry Como, Tony Bennett, Eddie Fisher, Teresa Brewer, Nat "King" Cole, and Patti Page made regular chart-topping appearances, and Les Paul and Mary Ford's "Vaya Con Dios (May God Be With You)" sounded as if it

could have been sister to their 1951 smash, "How High The Moon."

But farther down the charts, things were beginning to stir. Eartha Kitt's "Santa Baby" was certainly the sexiest Christmas song anyone had ever heard. More importantly, the healthy sales of The Orioles' "Crying In The Chapel" and Bill Haley and His Comets' "**Crazy, Man, Crazy**" indicated that American listeners were hungering for a greater percentage of R&B in their aural diet.

Take These Chains

One man who would not live to hear these changes occur was Hank Williams. The twenty-nine-year-old Williams died on New Year's Day in the back of his limousine, his body worn down by a steady diet

53 "Long Gone Lonesome Blues"—Hank Williams bowed out in 1953.

of pills and booze. His songs "Your Cheatin' Heart," "Kaw-Liga," and "Take These Chains From My Heart" all topped the country charts after his death.

Ball Park Figures

The New York Yankees defeated the Brooklyn Dodgers in the fiftieth annual World Series, four games to two. The Yankee team, featuring such future Hall of Famers as Mickey Mantle, Yogi Berra, and Whitey Ford, were the first to win five consecutive World Series championships.

Turning Up The Heat

Arthur Miller drew a direct parallel between HUAC's investigations and the Salem witch trials in his new stage play, *The Crucible*.

A Breath of Fresh Air?

Bermuda shorts were the strangest male fashion fad to come along in the 1950s. Businessmen would actually wear the big, baggy shorts to work during the summer months, combining them with suit jackets, dress shirts, ties and knee-length socks for a look that could only be called indescribable.

**nineteen**

'54

For all its (not undeserved) reputation as an **"idiot box"** with no socially redeeming value, television did manage to do something no politician, reporter or movie star had been previously able to accomplish: **to demonstrate publicly what a paranoid, power-crazed and utterly unpleasant individual Senator Joseph McCarthy** actually was.

From April 22 to June 18, millions of Americans tuned in to watch the Army-McCarthy hearings, in which the US government charged that McCarthy and his chief counsel, Roy Cohn, had tried to get preferential treatment for a drafted member of McCarthy's staff. McCarthy, in turn, claimed that Secretary of the Army Robert T Stevens and Army lawyer John G Adams were conspiring to obstruct his attempts to uncover Communist infiltration in the military. For the first time, viewers got a good look at McCarthy, and most didn't like what they saw—a shrill, tyrannical bully given to statements heavily laden with innuendo and hyperbole; by contrast, Army lawyer Joseph Welch came across as eloquent, even-tempered, and clear-headed.

McCarthy was officially censured by the Senate in December, but by then he had already been publicly discredited. America's fear and

54 Appearing on television didn't win anti-Commie Senator Joseph McCarthy any friends.

distrust of Communism was now permanently ingrained, but at least the witch-hunt was over. McCarthy would spend the next three years drinking himself to death.

Comic Capers

There were plenty of other things to get hysterical about, however. Henry David Thoreau's *Walden* was banned from libraries across the country for being "downright socialistic," and Frederic Wertham's *Seduction of the Innocent*, a treatise charging that comic books were corrupting the youth of America, became something of a *cause célèbre*. Under pressure from distributors, law-enforcement officials and parental groups, twenty-six comic-book publishers adopted a voluntary code to eliminate obscene, vulgar and horror-oriented comics. Archie, Mickey Mouse, and superhero comics were still deemed acceptable by the new **Comics Code** (even though Wertham's book charged that Batman and Robin were homosexuals), but "all scenes of horror, excessive bloodshed, gory or gruesome crimes, depravity, lust, sadism, and masochism," as well as anything depicting the "walking dead, torture, vampires, ghouls, cannibalism, and werewolfism" were strictly out of the question.

As a result, EC was forced to discontinue its groundbreaking horror titles, as well as *Shock SuspenStories* and *Crime SuspenStories*, the company's two crime titles. EC replaced them with its "New Direction" line, but new titles like *Valor*, *Piracy*, and *Psychoanalysis* didn't exactly capture the imagination of the comic-buying public. Yet, despite the concerted efforts of Wertham and the Comics Code, the country's levels of crime and juvenile delinquency remained curiously unaffected.

Good Golly!

Music was not without its share of controversy, as well. Due to an uproar over "suggestive lyrics" in R&B songs (Hank Ballard and The Midnighters came under heavy criticism for their singles "Work With Me, Annie" and "Sexy Ways"), various radio stations, jukebox operators and trade papers launched a campaign to stamp out "off-color and offensive" records. Unfortunately for them, American record companies understood that many teenagers preferred the raw, sexually charged sounds of R&B to the sterile blandness of Eddie Fisher and Perry Como, and thus continued to release as many R&B records as possible.

Music News

Thanks in part to the efforts of Cleveland disc jockey and R&B enthusiast Alan Freed, The Crows and The Chords had the year's biggest crossover hits, with "Gee" and "Sh-Boom," respectively; employing a strategy that would become increasingly common over the next few years, white vocal group The Crew-Cuts took a smoothed-over version of "Sh-Boom" to the top of the charts.

Bill Haley and His Comets were the year's top rock 'n' roll combo, riding high with "Shake, Rattle, And Roll" and "Dim, Dim The Lights (I Want Some Atmosphere)." They would soon face some serious competition in the form of Elvis Presley, whose first single, "That's All Right, Mama," was released during the summer on Memphis, Tennessee's Sun Records.

Back in California, the Fender company introduced its new **Stratocaster** guitar, a streamlined electric that would become the preferred weapon of thousands of rock 'n' roll guitarists.

Latin Conjugations

While the young 'uns were busy getting their morals corrupted by that rock 'n' roll jungle beat, America's adults were getting their kicks by doing the **mambo**; the sexual repression of the times found a tailor-made outlet in the slinky Cuban dance. Rosemary Clooney's "Mambo Italiano," Perry Como's "Papa Loves

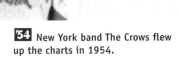

54 New York band The Crows flew up the charts in 1954.

TOP SINGLES

KITTY KALLEN

"Little Things Mean A Lot"

THE CREW-CUTS

"Sh-Boom"

PERRY COMO

"Wanted"

EDDIE CALVERT

"Oh, My Pa-Pa"

JO STAFFORD

"Make Love To Me"

Mambo," Vaughn Monroe's "They Were Doin' The Mambo," and umpteen Latinized versions of "Skokiaan" and "Hernando's Hideaway" all capitalized on the vogue for sexy Latin rhythms, with various degrees of authenticity.

Amore

Dean Martin, Doris Day and Sammy Davis, Jr all scored their biggest hits to date, Dino with "That's Amore," Doris with "Secret Love," and Sammy with "Hey, There." Unfortunately, Sammy's career almost ended in November, when a near-fatal car accident robbed him of his left eye and put him in the hospital for weeks. Frank Sinatra, his voice and confidence sufficiently recovered, had his biggest hit in years with "Young At Heart." He also recorded *Songs For Young Lovers*, the first of many collaborations with arranger/conductor Nelson Riddle, and his first extended-player for Capitol Records, thus beginning what many consider to be his finest period of work.

54 *The Wild One*—biker Brando stirs up trouble in a small town.

ACADEMY AWARDS

BEST PICTURE

On the Waterfront

directed by Elia Kazan

BEST ACTOR

Marlon Brando

On the Waterfront

BEST ACTRESS

Grace Kelly

The Country Girl

WARNER BROS. present 'A STAR IS BORN' starring Judy GARLAND and James MASON also starring JACK CARSON · CHARLES BICKFORD with Tom Noonan
Colour by TECHNICOLOR   Directed by GEORGE CUKOR   Produced by Sidney Luft   Musical Direction by Ray Heindorf
Screen Play by MOSS HART   They should be returned to Warner Bros. Pictures Ltd., after exhibition.
These Stills are Copyright. They must NOT be re-sold, traded, given away or sublessed
Cert 'A'

February 2 – Eisenhower announces that the US has detonated its first hydrogen bomb.

March 1 – Five congressmen shot on the floor of the House of Representatives by Puerto Rican nationalists.

April 22 – The nationally televised Army-McCarthy hearings begin.

May 7–8 – The French garrison at Dien Bien Phu falls to Ho Chi Minh and the Viet Minh. Vice-President Richard Nixon urges direct intervention.

May 17 – The Supreme Court's *Brown v The Board of Education* decision rules that segregated education is illegal.

Movie News

After only four years in Hollywood, Marlon Brando had taken the place by storm. 1954 saw him play the part of Napoleon in *Désirée*, but it was his roles in *On the Waterfront* and **The Wild One** that cemented his status as the country's new non-conformist icon. Though *On the Waterfront* won him an Oscar, his performance as *The Wild One*'s sullen, leather-jacketed biker leader is the one that remains indelibly stamped on the collective pop cultural memory; replying "Whaddaya got?" to the condescending question "What are you rebelling against?," Brando's character seemed to give the country a sneak preview of the look, attitude and charisma that would make Elvis Presley such a threat to the repressed adult establishment.

With her bleached-blonde locks and hourglass figure, Marilyn Monroe set the physical standard that all 1950s bombshells would be judged by. In January, she broke the hearts of millions of American males by marrying baseball great Joe DiMaggio. *River of No Return* and *There's No Business like Show Business* were hardly memorable films, but Marilyn's presence in them virtually assured them of commercial success.

Humphrey Bogart was also the envy of many men, appearing opposite Ava Gardner in *The Barefoot Contessa* and opposite Audrey Hepburn in *Sabrina*; his excellent performance in *The Caine Mutiny* rounded out an extremely successful year. John Wayne was still the country's most popular male star, however, as evidenced by the success of *The High And The Mighty*, an early air-disaster film.

A Star Is Born was Judy Garland's first film in four years; the actress,

'54 Monroe and DiMaggio tie the knot.

whose career had been plagued during the past decade, gave her finest performance as an up-and-coming singer married to slumping actor James Mason. Stanley Donen's *Seven Brides for Seven Brothers*, starring Howard Keel and Jane Powell, provided rather more wholesome and upbeat fare for musical fans.

There was good stuff out there for horror and science-fiction fans as well. **Twenty Thousand Leagues Under the Sea**, Walt Disney's CinemaScope adaptation of Jules Verne's submarine adventure, was glorious to look at (and the giant squid sequence was pretty cool), but *Them!*, in which nuclear radiation results in giant, angry ants, was truly terrifying. *Godzilla*, a nuclear- powered beast in his own right, made his first appearance in Japan; the version that was later shown in the United States was edited to include twenty minutes of footage featuring American actor Raymond Burr. And if it took way too long for *The Creature from the Black Lagoon* to emerge from his watery home, his bizarre half man/ half-fish appearance (and the film's 3-D effects) made it all worthwhile. Also filmed in 3-D was Alfred Hitchcock's *Dial M for Murder*,

54 A typical down-home breakfast for the all-American fifties family.

starring **Grace Kelly** in the first of her three Hitchcock productions. Kelly also won an Oscar for playing Bing Crosby's put-upon wife in *The Country Girl*, but she's now better remembered for her role as James Stewart's society girlfriend in Hitchcock's *Rear Window*, which also came out during the year.

Modern Mannas

A 1954 study found that the average American's ideal meal consisted of fruit cup, vegetable soup, steak and potatoes, peas, and pie for dessert.

Rocket Science

Chevrolet introduced its stylish new Nomad station wagon, which improved greatly on the clumsy shapes of previous station wagons. Ford introduced its sporty Thunderbird; the tiny two-seater came in an array of eye-catching pastel colors and with a base sticker-price of $2,944.

Packard introduced push-button transmissions in its 1955 models, while 1955 Lincolns offered an optional "Multi-Luber" button, which could be pressed to lube the chassis automatically for a "just-lubricated ride."

V-8 engines were also featured in most makers' 1955 models.

The big news in the auto world, however, was the **tailfin**; all of a sudden, fins were popping out all over the place. Buicks, Chevrolets, Lincolns and Hudsons all rolled off the lines wearing moderate fins, as did Cadillac's 1955 El Dorado, and the "flair-fashioned" '55 Dodge sported bold fins and twin-jet tail-lights. But it was Chrysler that stole everyone's thunder, with its new "**Forward Look**" line. The brainchild of design guru Virgil Exner, the Forward Look (also advertised as "the Hundred-Million-Dollar Look") featured prominent tailfins and a space-age sleekness that bore little resemblance to its predecessors of even a year ago. Chrysler was now the company the rest of the industry looked to for innovations in automotive design.

nineteen '55

It was the best of times, it was...well, the best of times. With the Korean War now but a memory, the United States was enjoying unprecedented prosperity and growth. The American steel, lumber and glass industries were thriving, with plastics taking its place beside them as the fourth largest American industry.

'55 Thousands of Americans bought one of the new "split-level" houses in 1955.

Thanks to a "**baby boom**," the US population increased by 15.6 million between 1950 and 1955. 1,320,000 new homes were built in 1955, many of them split-level dwellings with habitable basements; the age of the "rec room"—a furnished basement (often with carpeted or linoleum floors) where guests were entertained—had arrived. So had the age of the mall; America's first enclosed **shopping mall**, where shoppers could visit a variety of stores without ever having to go outside, opened in Appleton, Wisconsin. More and more Americans were installing central air conditioning in their houses, and it seemed as if a new age of convenience, leisure and luxury had come to pass—at least for the white middle and upper classes.

Poodle skirts—full skirts sewn with felt patches of animals, flowers, and other things—were *de rigeur* in 1955 for fashionable younger girls.

The Happiest Place On Earth

1955's ultimate expression of optimism and wholesomeness was Disneyland, an expansive amusement park built in Anaheim, California, under the auspices of Walt Disney. At a time when the words "amusement park" conjured up images of sleazy sideshows and rickety roller coasters, Disneyland was a revelation—an immaculate, well-organized "**Magic Kingdom**" staffed by friendly, clean-cut young people. Populated by walking Disney characters like Mickey Mouse and Donald Duck, the park was divided into four themed areas: Frontierland, Adventureland, Fantasyland, and Tomorrowland. Attractions like "Pirates of the Caribbean," "The Haunted Mansion,"

January 12 – US Secretary of State John Foster Dulles outlines the government's new "massive retaliation" nuclear policy, which calls for "a great capacity to retaliate instantly by means and at places of our choosing." The great US-Soviet Union arms race heats up even further.

April – Dr Jonas Salk introduces the polio vaccine.

September 24 – President Eisenhower suffers heart attack; recovers.

October 4 – The Brooklyn Dodgers, after years of World Series disappointments, finally beat the New York Yankees for baseball's World Championship.

November 25 – Racial segregation on interstate trains and buses banned by the Interstate Commerce Commission.

December 1 – 42-year-old black woman Rosa Parks arrested after refusing to give up her bus seat to a white man. Montgomery bus boycott begins within days, led by the Rev Dr Martin Luther King, Jr. Originally intended to be for one day only, the boycott continues for over a year, causing the bus company to go broke.

'55 Annette Funicello, Mouseketeer.

and "Mr Toad's Wild Ride" were designed specifically for the park, utilizing the finest in Disney "audio-animatronic" technology. Southern California's mild climate allowed the park to stay open all year, and "The Happiest Place on Earth" was an immediate hit; over one million visitors passed through Disneyland's entrance portal during its first two months of existence.

TV News

Disney wasn't doing too badly on the television front, either. **The Mickey Mouse Club** debuted in October, and became an immediate hit with the younger audience. The show was hosted by "The Mouseketeers," a group of twenty-four children (including future *Beach Party* babe Annette Funicello (*above*), future *Rifleman* star Johnny Crawford, and future Standells vocalist Dick Dodd) wearing T-shirts and mouse-ear hats. The shows, broadcast every weekday, were divided into five categories: Monday was "Fun with Music Day," Tuesday "Guest Star Day," Wednesday "Anything Can Happen Day," Thursday "Circus Day," and Friday "Talent Round-Up Day."

Disneyland, the company's Wednesday night showcase, struck gold with its **Davy Crockett** episodes, which starred Fess Parker

Sgt. BILKO and Doberman meet Aunt Mary!

as the legendary American pioneer. Almost overnight, the country was seized by Davy Crockett mania; over three hundred Disney-licensed Davy Crockett products (including bubble-gum cards, moccasin kits and "coonskin" caps) were snapped up by consumers, to the tune of three hundred million dollars in sales. "The Ballad Of Davy Crockett," with its indelible refrain of "Davy, Davy Crockett, King of the wild frontier," ruled the airways and jukeboxes in versions by Bill Hayes, Tennessee Ernie Ford, and Parker himself. Disney tried hard to repeat the phenomenon, writing dramas around such historical characters as Texas John Slaughter and General Francis Marion, but had little success; Parker would find further fame in 1964 as TV's *Daniel Boone*.

Honeymoon Season

The *Lawrence Welk Show* was another surprise hit. Debuting as a summer replacement series, the program—essentially a showcase for the "champagne music" of Welk's easy-listening orchestra—wound up hanging around for the next three decades. *The Honeymooners* was not so fortunate, however; given its own time-slot after years as a sketch on *The Jackie Gleason Show*, the sitcom failed to pull in the viewers, and was canceled after only one season. After five years of mildly successful ratings, **The Jack Benny Show** suddenly became one of the most popular shows in America; a mixture of variety show and sitcom, the program's sketches usually revolved around Benny's legendary stinginess and terrible violin playing.

Another popular comedy was *You'll Never Get Rich*, whose title was soon changed to **The Phil Silvers Show**. Silvers (*above*) played Ernie Bilko, a US Army sergeant whose get-rich-quick schemes were inevitably foiled by unforseen circumstances. You could strike an instant fortune on *The $64,000 Question*, just as long as you didn't give an incorrect answer. Hosted by Hal March, the program ushered in the era of big-money quiz shows.

Other new shows included CBS's *Mike Wallace Interviews*, a talk show that established journalist Wallace as a premier TV interrogator; *Gunsmoke*, a long-running TV western starring James Arness as Marshal Matt Dillon; Bob Keeshan's educational *Captain Kangaroo Show*; and *Alfred Hitchcock Presents*, a popular horror-anthology program.

Movie News

Alfred Hitchcock presented two films in 1955, *The Trouble with Harry* and *To Catch a Thief*; the former introduced Shirley MacLaine to the world, while the latter featured **Grace Kelly**, the most popular actress in America, who also received raves for her performance in Mark Robson's Korean War film, *The Bridges at Toko-Ri*. Marilyn Monroe, who divorced Joe DiMaggio during the year, stayed near the top of the popularity polls thanks to Billy Wilder's *The Seven Year Itch*, in which Marilyn very memorably straddled a subway grating while wearing a billowy white dress.

James Stewart was America's most popular actor, with appearances in *The Far Country*, *Strategic Air Command,* and *The Man from Laramie*. Marlon Brando and Frank Sinatra teamed up for the film

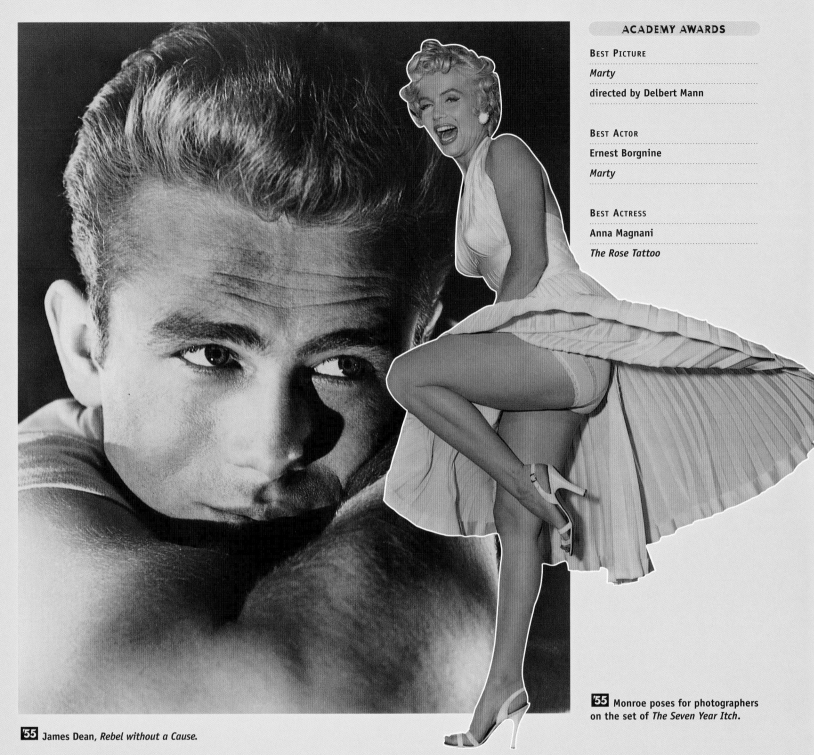

BEST PICTURE

Marty

directed by Delbert Mann

BEST ACTOR

Ernest Borgnine

Marty

BEST ACTRESS

Anna Magnani

The Rose Tattoo

'55 Monroe poses for photographers on the set of *The Seven Year Itch*.

'55 James Dean, *Rebel without a Cause.*

version of the Broadway musical *Guys and Dolls*, and Sinatra received an Oscar nomination for his turn as a junkie in the controversial *The Man with the Golden Arm*. Henry Fonda returned to the screen for the first time since 1949 in the title role of *Mr Roberts*, and Kirk Douglas donned sword and sandals for the title role of *Ulysses*.

Enter Ennui (Exit Jimmy Dean)

One of the brightest, and shortest, Hollywood careers of all time belonged to James Dean, who died in a car crash after starring in *East of Eden*, *Rebel without a Cause,* and *Giant*—the first two of which were released in 1955. Dean remains one of

Hollywood's most enduring icons; his onscreen appearances radiated the same alienation and restlessness that young people in the 1950s (and every subsequent decade) felt, but could not sufficiently articulate.

There was alienation and restlessness to spare in *The Blackboard Jungle*, Richard Brooks'

tough adaptation of Evan Hunter's juvenile delinquency novel. Glenn Ford delivered a top-notch performance as a frustrated high school teacher, and Vic Morrow made a fine debut as an angry student (who smashes his math teacher's jazz 78s!), but it was Bill Haley and His Comets' "(We're Gonna) Rock Around The

M·G·M's BLACKBOARD JUNGLE

IS THE MOST STARTLING PICTURE OF THE YEAR!

The sensational novel...now on the screen!

STARRING GLENN FORD

ANNE FRANCIS
LOUIS CALHERN
WITH MARGARET HAYES

SCREEN PLAY BY RICHARD BROOKS · BASED ON THE NOVEL BY EVAN HUNTER · DIRECTED BY RICHARD BROOKS · PRODUCED BY PANDRO S. BERMAN
AN M·G·M PICTURE

COUNTRY OF ORIGIN U. S. A.   Copyright 1955 Loew's Incorporated

Clock," which opened and closed the film, that made the biggest impression on the film's audience.

Out Of The Box

Everything about "(We're Gonna) Rock Around The Clock," from its opening chant of "One, two, three o'clock, four o' clock, ROCK!" to Danny Cedrone's wild guitar solo, seemed to indicate that a new era in music was beginning; the whole thing leaped out of the speakers with the excitement of a school bell announcing the arrival of summer vacation. Self-appointed guardians of public morality roundly denounced

this new music as "immoral" and contributing to juvenile delinquency (a perception that *Blackboard Jungle* did little to alleviate), but the kids were plainly aching for something loud and exciting to call their own. 45 rpm records were outselling 78s for the first time ever, and jukebox operators announced that plays of R&B records were up sixty percent from the previous year, so the timing was perfect for a former country and western artist like Haley to strike gold with a slightly cleaner (but still raucous) variation on the R&B sound. By the end of the year, Haley would earn over five hundred thousand dollars in bookings.

'Slumber party? Gee, that's dandy! Look your sharpest, everyone! Snappy PJ's come in handy— 'Fresh up' parties sure are fun!

"Fresh up" with Seven-Up!

THE ALL-FAMILY DRINK! Enjoy sparkling, crystal-clear 7-Up ... often. Seven-Up is so pure, so good, so wholesome that everybody—from tiny tots to grandmas and all ages in-between—may "fresh up" to his heart's content. And 7-Up makes food taste extra good. So have a Blackout with chilled 7-Up. Buy 7-Up wherever you see those bright 7-Up signs.

You like it...it likes you!

7up

Music News

For the rest of the year, rock 'n' roll records both real (Fats Domino's "Ain't That A Shame," Chuck Berry's "Maybellene") and watered-down (Pat Boone's cover of "Ain't That A Shame," Gale Storm's cover of Domino's "I Hear You Knockin'") jostled for elbow room on the charts with the likes of Perry Como's "Ko Ko Mo (I Love You So)" and Mitch Miller's "The Yellow Rose Of Texas." RCA, sensing which way the winds were turning, snapped up **Elvis Presley**'s Sun Records contract for forty thousand dollars. Elvis had continued to record regularly for Sun, but rockabilly singles like "Baby, Let's Play House" and "Mystery Train" were just too raw to dent the pop charts. In 1956, RCA would change all that...

Recently recovered from a debilitating heroin addiction, Miles Davis blew minds at the Newport Jazz Festival with his performance of "Round Midnight." Counted out by most jazz aficionados, Davis solidified his comeback by forming a mighty quintet with John Coltrane, Red Garland, Paul Chambers and Philly Joe Jones. Charlie Parker was not so lucky; unable to kick his heroin habit, the greatest saxophonist of the era died at age thirty-four.

Frank Sinatra recorded *In the Wee Small Hours*, his first 12-inch long-player for Capitol. Possibly his finest record, its emotional resonance seemed to many to be the result of his recent separation from Ava Gardner.

Falcon Flies

The Fred Gretsch Guitar Company of Brooklyn, New York, did its part for rock 'n' roll by introducing the Gretsch White Falcon, one of the flashiest and most expensive mass-produced electric guitars of all time, with a stunning white semi-hollow body and sparkling gold hardware. The White Falcon was advertised in *Guitars For Moderns*, the 1955 Gretsch catalog, with a list price of six hundred dollars.

Quiet, Sure Pride

The Gretsch White Falcon would have looked lovely perched in the back seat of the 1956 Lincoln Continental Mark II luxury coupe; priced at ten thousand dollars, it was the most expensive American-made car on the market. "Have you felt the quiet, sure pride of arriving in a Lincoln?" asked the company's ads. Lincoln also introduced its 1956 Futura dream-car which, with its bubble cockpit and sweeping tailfins, bore a suspicious resemblance to Batman's Batmobile. Pontiac's 1956 Firebird dream-car, on the other hand, looked more like a fighter plane than an actual automobile.

Indeed, since the advent of Chrysler's "Forward Look" line the year

55 "Don't just play—*do* something!" Bill Haley tells his Comets, rehearsing here at the Dominion Theatre in London.

before, auto makers were bending over backwards to give their products a **futuristic** slant. Ads for the 1956 Plymouth Belvedere praised the car's "youthful, dynamic" qualities, adding that "it has a generous touch of the future!" Chrysler was predicting that, by 1980, there would be electronically guided highway cars for long-distance travel, while the University of Michigan's College of Engineering predicted that electric cars would dominate the market by the year 2000. On a more down-to-earth note, bucket seats were offered for the first time in Chevy Corvettes and Ford Thunderbirds. Volkswagen of America was founded in 1955, but America was not quite ready for the tiny, no-frills VW Beetle.

"I have seen the best minds of my generation destroyed by madness," wrote Allen Ginsberg in *Howl*, the epic 1956 poem that served as the warning shot for the emergence of the beat movement. But most Americans weren't listening; they were more concerned that the minds (and morals) of their younger generation were being corrupted and destroyed by rock 'n' roll.

Elvis Presley, with his pompadour, sideburns, and perpetually swiveling hips, seemed like the most obvious threat to the American way of life, but in truth the music was coming from all corners; blues, country, pop, and gospel singers alike were jumping on **the rock 'n' roll bandwagon**, not just because the music was exciting, but because it sold. In 1956, the average American teenager had more pocket money than ever before (the minimum wage was now a dollar an hour), and the sexy, rebellious music held more than a little allure for those raised in the conservative climate of the Eisenhower era.

Rock Steady

Considered a fad the year before, rock 'n' roll had firmly established itself on the charts by 1956, making for a fairly schizophrenic hit parade. Rock 'n' roll singles like Little Richard's "Long Tall Sally," Gene Vincent's "Be-Bop-A-Lula," and Carl Perkins' "Blue Suede Shoes" rubbed shoulders with adult-oriented schmaltz like Andy Williams' "Canadian Sunset" or Kay Starr's considerably un-rock 'n' roll "Rock And Roll Waltz." A few acts, like The Platters and Pat Boone, managed to straddle both camps successfully—the former with soulful ballads like "The Great Pretender", and the latter with covers of Little Richard songs that were as white as his suede buck shoes.

'56 Beat poet Allen Ginsberg with Lee Forest.

'56 Little Richard was a big hit with teenage music lovers in 1956.

Despite its apparent staying power, there were those who insisted that rock 'n' roll would soon be supplanted by another form of music. **Calypso**, in fact, was widely touted as rock 'n' roll's successor, which made Harry Belafonte very happy; the calypso craze burned out quickly, but not before it turned Belafonte into an international singing sensation. The **cha-cha-cha** craze, a variation on the mambo, also swept the country during the year.

Pelvis Shakes America

Of course, the year's biggest music news was Elvis Presley. Newly signed to RCA, Presley hit Number One in March with "**Heartbreak Hotel**" and never looked back. By the end of 1956, Elvis had scored ten other Top Twenty hits, topping the charts with four of them ("I Want You, I Need You, I Love You," "Don't Be Cruel," "Hound Dog," and "Love Me Tender"). Not since Frank Sinatra's bobby-soxer days had a performer caused such **hysteria**, and not since Sinatra had a singer split American opinion down generational lines. If you were older, you probably thought Elvis was untalented and obscene. If you were younger, well, Elvis was probably the most exciting thing you'd ever seen or heard.

Most Americans' first glimpse of Elvis came through the magic of television. Manager Colonel Tom Parker astutely figured that his telegenic charge could only benefit from a judicious amount of TV exposure, and while Elvis's first-ever televised appearance—January 29 on

56 Elvis rocked to the tune of $50,000 on Ed Sullivan's show.

Stage Show—met with little response, the end of the year saw him commanding a then unheard-of sum of fifty thousand dollars for three appearances on **The Ed Sulllivan Show**. Elvis did have to make a few compromises, however; Sullivan's cameras blocked out his "scandalous" pelvic thrusts, and Steve Allen made him dress in tie and tails while singing "Hound Dog" to a nonplused canine.

TV News

In other televised rock 'n' roll news, a young disc jockey named Dick Clark was hired to host Philadelphia's local teen dance program, **Bandstand**. In a year's time, the show—renamed *American Bandstand*—would be broadcast nationally, becoming the country's most influential music program in the process; teenagers tuned into the show not just to hear the latest hits, but to learn the latest dances and pick up on the latest fashion trends.

The Adventures Of Gumby, Art Clokey's proto-psychedelic series of animated shorts about a flexible green humanoid and Pokey, his orange equine pal, debuted on as part of *The Howdy Doody Show*. **The Price Is Right**, a long-running game show in which contestants tried to guess the cost of various consumer goods, was also broadcast for the first time.

Ant Man Makes A Pile

Despite the evil lure of the rock 'n' roll beat, there were still plenty of wholesome hobbies available to American youngsters, and one of the most popular was ant farming. Invented by California entrepreneur Milton Levine, the transparent, sand-filled **Ant Farm** allowed you to observe the inscrutable doings of a colony of harvester ants. "Watch them dig tunnels! See them build rooms! Marvel as they erect bridges and move mountains before your very eyes!" read the ads. "The Ant Farm is a living TV screen that will keep you interested for hours!" It could be yours for only $1.98. During the next few decades, Levine would sell over twelve million of them.

Stranded At The Drive-In...

If you had a movie date in 1956, chances are it would be to a drive-in. Over four thousand drive-in theaters were in operation across the US, an all-time high. Convinced that lavish spectacles would pump up their box-office receipts, Hollywood was producing epics by the dozen (*Around The World in Eighty Days, The King*

and I, *The Ten Commandments*, *Giant*, and *Friendly Persuasion*, all at least two hours and twenty minutes long, were each nominated for Best Picture Oscars), but it also churned out low-budget trash like it was going out of style: if you timed it right, maybe you could catch a double bill of *The Creature Walks Among Us* and *The Mole People*. There were some real gems amid the junk, however; although it boasted both a sensational-sounding title and a star turn by Robby the Robot, Fred McLeod Wilcox's *Forbidden Planet* was actually a successfully ambitious sci-fi update of Shakespeare's *The Tempest*.

Movie News

Unsurprisingly, rock 'n' roll also got in on the box-office action. Influential DJ **Alan Freed** starred in both *Rock around the Clock* (featuring Bill Haley

and His Comets and The Platters), and *Rock Rock Rock* (featuring Chuck Berry and Frankie Lymon), which would be released the following year. **The Girl Can't Help It**— considered by many to be the best rock 'n' roll movie of all time—flirted with total sensory overload by showing Jayne Mansfield strutting her ample stuff to the sound of Little Richard, Fats Domino, and Gene Vincent and The Blue Caps.

Elvis also starred in his first film, a Civil War drama called *Love Me Tender*. While his notices were generally favorable, he hardly eclipsed the work of his filmic idols, Tony Curtis and James Dean.

Dean, in fact, was still the most popular actor in Hollywood. In January, James Dean got 4,038 fan letters, more mail than any other actor on the Warner Bros lot. The fact that he'd been dead for four months didn't seem to make a difference.

Still a popular draw, John Wayne managed to star in one of the year's best films (John Ford's *The Searchers*), as well as one of the its worst (*The Conqueror*, which featured "**The Duke**" in a role he definitely was not born to play: Genghis Khan!). William Holden was the year's most popular actor, thanks to leads in *Picnic*, *The*

'56 Yul Brynner, sternly majestic in *The King and I*.

'56 Jayne Mansfield, signed up by 20th Century Fox in 1956.

951-5-95

Proud and the Profane, and Toward the Unknown. Now that Grace Kelly had abandoned the US to marry Prince Ranier of Monaco, Marilyn Monroe was once again the country's most popular actress, and she surprised critics and

fans alike with a natural comic turn in Bus Stop. Even more surprising was her new marriage to playwright Arthur Miller.

Sufficiently recovered from his near-fatal auto accident, Sammy Davis, Jr made his Hollywood debut in The Benny Goodman Story. Dean Martin and Jerry Lewis's **Hollywood or Bust**

should've been titled Hollywood AND Bust—hardly able to stand the sight of each other despite their enormous success, Martin and Lewis went their separate ways after filming ended.

America Homes In On Suburbs

Over a million new houses were built in

1956. America's rural population was declining by about two percent per year, as more and more farms and ranches were turned into tract housing developments or shopping malls. Six million cars and one million trucks were produced by American assembly lines in 1956; responding to the needs of ever-expanding suburbs, one out of every

A Nation Entraced

The publication of Ginsberg's *Howl* was certainly an important milestone in modern American literature, but it was hardly the stuff that best-sellers, at least in 1956, were made of. **Peyton Place**, Grace Metalious' novel about sexual intrigue in a small town, was the talk of the country, as was Morey Bernstein's **The Search for Bridey Murphy**. In his best-seller, amateur hypnotist Bernstein wrote of his "age regression" experiments with Colorado housewife Virginia Tighe, which allegedly revealed evidence of Tighe's previous life. Over their several sessions, Bernstein claimed to have made repeated contact with Bridey Murphy, the nineteenth-century Irish farmwoman whom Tighe had apparently been in an earlier existence.

The book set off a nationwide fascination with reincarnation; *Life* magazine reported that people were holding "come as you were" parties, and that a bar in Houston was offering a "Reincarnation Cocktail." Various Bridey-inspired songs were released, and long-playing records of the Bernstein/Tighe trance sessions also sold well, at least until articles debunking Bernstein's book began to appear. It was revealed that many of Tighe's "historically accurate" details were not so accurate after all, and that, when she was a young girl, Tighe had lived near a Mrs. Bridie Murphy Corkell. Rather than "age regression," *The Search for Bridey Murphy* seemed to be just another case of hypnotic suggestion.

Ford's 1957 **Skyliner** came with a retractable hardtop; if you wanted to drive with the top down, a special mechanism automatically folded it back into the trunk. 1957 Fords also offered an optional safety package, the first ever offered by American auto makers. It included lap seat belts, a padded dash, sun visors, deep-dish steering wheel and safety door latches. American drivers just weren't interested in safety features, however, and the package was withdrawn a year later.

Another optional feature that proved unpopular was Chrysler's dash-mounted record player. Part of the problem was that you couldn't use it to play your favorite Gene Vincent singles; "The Highway Hi-Fi" only played unwieldy 16⅔ rpm discs.

eight cars built was a station wagon. Introduced on Labor Day, the 1957 Chevrolet sold seven hundred and fifty thousand units over the next year, with the two-door Bel-Air model proving especially popular. Popular with car customizers, the car, like most of its 1957 counterparts, featured bold tailfins and excessive chrome side-trim.

'57

By 1957, it seemed as if science and technology would soon solve all of our problems. Dr Jonas Salk's vaccine was proving extremely effective in **fighting polio**, cutting incidences of the dread disease by eighty percent. July 1 marked the beginning of International Geophysical Year, a coordinated study of the Earth's atmosphere, land, oceans, and the Sun by scientists from sixty-seven nations. IGY's first order of business was an experiment studying the effect of the Sun's radiation on communications.

'57 Raymond Burr stares out another witness in *Perry Mason*.

Petrochemical company Monsanto ('Without chemicals, life itself would be impossible!") opened its **House of the Future** attraction at Disneyland. Located in the park's Tomorrowland section (of course!), the pod-like house was constructed entirely from plastic, and was supposed to demonstrate how we all would live in "the future." The house was furnished with numerous "ultramodern" gadgets, including an "ultrasonic" dishwasher and an oven that could be folded away into a kitchen cabinet; forty years on, the only items from the house that have actually become common in American homes are microwave ovens and push-button phones.

Final Frontiers Opened Up

The average American production worker was now making $82.32 a week, and he could easily afford to avail himself of the estimated five thousand new grocery products introduced on supermarket shelves in 1957. These included the technological breakthrough that was Calentano Brothers' Frozen Pizza, the first-ever **frozen pizza** on the market. The Italian pie had been popular in East Coast cities since the early 1900s, but its popularity spread nationwide after World War Two, when GIs returned from the Italian campaign with a taste for the stuff; as a result, the pizza parlor became as integral a part of American life as the hot-dog stand. Thanks to Calentano Brothers, hungry Americans could now enjoy pizza at home with a minimum of inconvenience, and frozen pizza soon became the best-selling item in the frozens aisle.

There was one scientific development which completely rattled the US: the announcement that the Soviet Union had put a **satellite**, *Sputnik I*, into orbit. The USSR was off to a big head start in the space race, a fact made only more painfully obvious a month later, when the Soviets successfully launched *Sputnik II*. From its

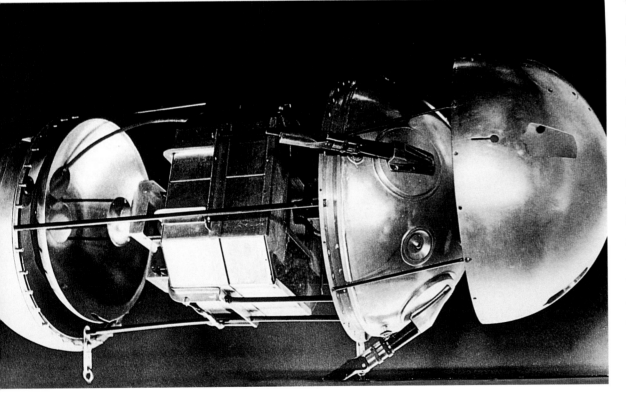

'57 The USSR's *Sputnik I* left the US way behind.

"Oh, Mamma Mia!... wait till you taste Pizza...home made with Hunt's Tomato Paste"

extremely well; available for seventy-nine cents, the aerodynamic plastic discs put a new spin on the game of catch.

Music News

Plastic discs of another kind were selling in dizzying numbers, although records by Bill Haley and His Comets were not among them. After a stratospheric 1955, Haley still managed some big hits in 1956 ("See You Later, Alligator," "R-O-C-K"), but by 1957 he had fallen off the charts completely. Some uptight observers cheered this development as evidence of rock 'n' roll's impending demise, but those who

churches to its saloons, America was abuzz with conjecture: Were the Commies spying on us from space? Would they launch a nuclear attack from the Moon? And why hadn't the US, the most technologically advanced nation in the world, been able to get into space before them? Embarrassed US scientists struggled to find answers to these questions, while frantically making plans to send up a satellite of their own.

Latest Disc-overy

Some other interesting items were spotted in American airspace. Originally marketed as "Pluto Platters," Wham-O's **Frisbees** were selling

HIS FIRST BIG DRAMATIC SINGING ROLE!

MGM PRESENTS

ELVIS PRESLEY AT HIS GREATEST

JAILHOUSE ROCK

JUDY TYLER with MICKEY SHAUGHNESSY · DEAN JONES · JENNIFER HOLDEN

heard (and bought) hits like Buddy Holly and The Crickets' "That'll Be The Day" and "Peggy Sue," Little Richard's "Jenny, Jenny" and "Keep A-Knockin', " or Jerry Lee Lewis's "Great Balls Of Fire" and "Whole Lotta Shakin' Going On" knew differently.

While Elvis and Pat Boone slugged it out for control of the singles charts (with the exception of Elvis, the more adult-oriented LP charts tended to be glutted with film soundtracks and original cast recordings of Broadway shows), numerous new faces appeared on the scene. The Everly Brothers crossed over from the country charts with "Bye Bye Love" and "Wake Up Little Susie," and former gospel star Sam Cooke hit Number One with "You Send Me." The gossamer-voiced Johnny Mathis appealed to more adult tastes with sophisticated ballads like "Chances Are" and "It's Not For Me To Say," but newcomers like Buddy Knox ("Party Doll"), The Del-Vikings ("Come Go With Me"), and The Diamonds ("Little Darlin' ") scored big by aiming their sound directly at teenage ears.

Movie News

Hollywood, correctly ascertaining that teenagers would go see anything

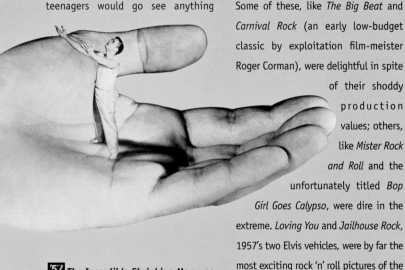

'57 *The Incredible Shrinking Man* was big at the box office.

having to do with rock 'n' roll, also made piles of money by releasing low-budget films spiced up with appearances by rock and R&B performers of the day. Some of these, like *The Big Beat* and *Carnival Rock* (an early low-budget classic by exploitation film-meister Roger Corman), were delightful in spite of their shoddy production values; others, like *Mister Rock and Roll* and the unfortunately titled *Bop Girl Goes Calypso*, were dire in the extreme. *Loving You* and *Jailhouse Rock*, 1957's two Elvis vehicles, were by far the most exciting rock 'n' roll pictures of the year, thanks to decent scripts and plenty

'57 "Great Balls of Fire"—Jerry Lee Lewis.

of musical numbers showcasing "**The King**" in his prime.

There was plenty of agreeably trashy horror and sci-fi to go around, too. What can one say about a year that followed *I Was a Teenage Werewolf* (starring a young Michael Landon) with *I Was a Teenage Frankenstein*, as well as both *The Amazing Colossal Man* and (the actually quite excellent) *The Incredible Shrinking Man*, other than, "Pass the popcorn"? William Asher's *The Twenty-Seventh Day*, in which an alien space capsule obliterates the USSR, also provided a timely bit of anti-Red wish-fulfillment.

Rock Hudson (*Written on the Wind, Battle Hymn, Something of Value, A Farewell to Arms*) and **Kim Novak**

(*Jeanne Eagels, Pal Joey*) were the year's hottest stars, while audiences turned out *en masse* for *Funny Face* (with Audrey Hepburn and Fred Astaire), *Twelve Angry Men* (with Henry Fonda), and, of course, *Peyton Place* (starring Lana Turner). Movie fans everywhere mourned the passing of Humphrey Bogart, who died of cancer of the esophagus at the age of fifty-seven.

Yee-ha!

Gunsmoke had already debuted a few years earlier, but it wasn't until 1957 that the western, a genre slowly dying at the box office, found new life on the small screen. *Have Gun Will Travel, Wagon Train, The Restless Gun, Tales of Wells Fargo,* and *Maverick* all debuted within months of each other, while ratings of older shows like *Cheyenne* and *Wyatt Earp* suddenly rocketed skyward. Though popular with the same younger demographic that fueled the Davy Crockett craze, subtler, more complex characters like *Maverick*'s cowardly title rogue (played by James Garner) were clearly written with an adult audience in mind.

Perry Mason, starring Raymond Burr as a methodical lawyer, was also a big hit with adult viewers.

US Senate subcommittee holds hearings on America's ability to withstand Soviet military attack.

US occupation forces leave Japan.

May 2 – Senator Joseph McCarthy dies of cirrhosis of the liver at age 48.

July 12 – US Surgeon General reports link between cigarette smoking and lung cancer.

September 19 – In the desert outside Las Vegas, the Atomic Energy Commission detonates first underground atomic blast.

September 24 – 1,000 army paratroopers called in by President Eisenhower to ensure the integration of Central High School in Little Rock, Arkansas.

October 4 – Soviet Union launches the first manmade satellite, *Sputnik I*.

November 3 – Soviet Union launches *Sputnik II*; canine passenger Laika becomes the first living Earth creature to travel (and die) in outer space.

TV News

In any case, there was plenty of stuff for the kids. *American Bandstand* debuted on ABC, and quickly ignited nationwide dance fads like the bunny hop, the bop, the slop, the pony, the chicken, the monkey, and the stroll. **Leave It to Beaver**, a sitcom revolving around the well-intentioned antics of young "Beaver" Cleaver (played by Jerry Mathers) and his friends, debuted on CBS; reruns of the show would continue to be popular for

decades afterward, partly because of its idyllic depiction of American suburban life in the late fifties and early sixties. And Robert Strom, a ten-year-old science buff, won $192,000 in three rounds of *The $64,000 Question*.

Kennedys Box Clever

No dummies themselves, brothers Robert and John F Kennedy received plenty of valuable exposure through the nationally televised hearings of the Senate Rackets Committee, in which the two Kennedys interrogated numerous known and alleged organized crime figures. JFK was also awarded a Pulitzer Prize for his book, *Profiles in Courage*, which saluted various US senators throughout history who had defied public opinion for the good of the country.

Dr Seuss (aka Theodore Seuss Geisel) published two classic children's books, *The Cat in the Hat* and *The Grinch that Stole Christmas*. **On the Road**, Jack Kerouac's compendium of cross-country musings and adventures, quickly became a must-read for any would-be hipster.

The Edsel Episode

Of course, for most Americans, "on the road" was merely where they drove, showing off their fabulously finned and chromed vehicles as they went to the supermarket, the drive-in or their jobs. Most auto makers were going overboard with their chrome trim-mings: heaps of chrome covered the doors, wheel-wells, and hoods, not to mention bumpers, radiator grilles and hood ornaments. Buick reintroduced and updated its "Limited" line from the 1940s, offering the extra-long,

ostentatiously trimmed Riviera coupe, Riviera sedan, and Riviera convertible for five thousand dollars apiece.

Also fabulously chromed, if rather awkwardly shaped, was Ford's 1958 Edsel. While hardly the worst car ever made, the car's over-the-top advance hype, questionable ornamentation (the new-fangled radiator grille was alternately compared to a cattle yoke, a toilet seat, and a vagina), excessive gadgetry (including a "teletouch" transmission and a speedometer that glowed red when the car exceeded a pre-set speed limit), and just plain bad luck (it was introduced in the middle of 1957's recession) ultimately set it up for failure; the fact that many of the early models seemed to experience endless technical difficulties didn't help improve its reputation and, in the minds of the American public, "Edsel" quickly became synonymous with "lemon." Ford tried again in 1958 with a slightly modified design and an understated ad campaign, but they still wound up losing two hundred and fifty million dollars on the car, which was finally discontinued in 1959.

There was a little bit of good news for Ford in 1957, however. The company's new four-door Thunderbird sedan proved far more popular than its previous two-seater incarnation.

'57 Michael Landon in *I Was a Teenage Werewolf*, billed as "The most amazing motion picture of our time!"

"The New-day woman won't sit still for the filling foods of yesteryear," noted a magazine ad for Pepsi-Cola. "She's thankful for the whole modern trend toward light food and drink. And don't you notice the slim-and-slender difference?" Actually, if your "New-day" woman was looking more "slim and slender" than usual, it might have been because she couldn't afford to eat on a regular basis.

The 1958 recession was the country's worst since World War Two, and almost five and a half million people were out of work. Not coincidentally, 1958 saw a rise in the sales of lower-priced "convenience foods"—according to one study, over four hundred million frozen pot pies were consumed during the year.

Time For Change

If you could afford new clothes, there were big changes afoot in the fashion world. Floral prints and knee-length skirts were now quite popular with women, as were short-sleeved dresses and "Empire waist" three-quarter coats. False eyelashes became a popular accessory, as did turbans. The bulky men's suits and wide neckties of the last few decades were out, replaced by sleek, narrow-lapelled suits and shiny, narrow ties. Brightly patterned sports shirts were also popular, and were often worn with solid-colored four-button cardigan sweaters.

58 Winning style: Catalina sweaters for him and her.

California magic in Sweaters

FOR HER: Cable-Knit Coat, 11.00
FOR HIM: Cable-Knit Pullover, 8.50

Catalina

LOOK FOR THE FLYING FISH

Hula-Hype

With hard times at hand, Americans were in need of distraction, and they got it in the circular form of the Hula-Hoop. The toy was brought back from Australia by Richard Knerr and Arthur "Spud" Melin of the Wham-O company, who had experienced great success the previous year with the Frisbee. Introduced in California in the Spring of 1958, the Hula-Hoop (now changed from the wood of the Australian "exercise rings" to light plastic) was a household item across the country by the end of the summer. Priced at $1.98, Wham-O's Hula-Hoop sold over seventy million units, and inspired a legion of imitators, including Spin-A-Hoop, Wiggle-A-Hoop, Hoop-Zing, Hooper Dooper, and Whoop-De-Do.

Spun from around the waist (or, in a popular variation, from around the neck), the Hula-Hoop required some dexterity to use successfully. It also required a fair amount of open space; consequently, when the winter of 1958 commenced, sales of the hoops immediately plummeted. Trying to cash in on the fad, Georgia Gibbs,

Teresa Brewer, and Betty Johnson all recorded Hula-Hoop-themed songs, but the Hula-Hoop craze died out before any of them could become hits.

Board Minds

In Dana Point, California, Bill and Mark Richards invented the first skateboard, attaching wheels from rollerskates to a square wooden board. The Richards sold the boards at their Val Surf Shop for eight dollars apiece.

Nation Tires Of Cruising

The needs of American drivers were changing, and cars were beginning to evolve along with them. Tailfins, now far more of a status symbol than an actual engineering necessity (despite the claims of various manufacturers), were larger and more popular than ever. 1959 Chevrolets and Buicks sported sideways "gull wing" fins, while the huge fins of the 1959 Cadillac were possibly the ultimate in automotive appendages. The "lion-hearted" '59 Chrysler New Yorker came with optional swivel seats (also available on all Plymouths, Dodges, DeSotos, Chryslers, and Imperials), and "Auto-Pilot" (an early version of cruise control), not to mention bold tailfins and expansive safety-glass windshields. Pontiac's "wide-track wheels" were moved five inches out from their previous position "for the widest, steadiest stance in America," while the '59 Oldsmobile's new "**Linear Look**" anticipated the full-sized cars of the next decade with its flat roof and tapered fins.

By 1958, however, many Americans no longer felt the need to impress others with the size of their tailfins, just as many could no longer afford to drive gas-guzzling luxury cars. The 1959 Ranchero was Ford's concession to the need for a more utilitarian vehicle, combining economy-car styling with the loadspace of a pickup truck. AMC's new economy-sized Rambler **compact** proved extremely popular, and Studebaker introduced the Lark, a compact smaller than the Rambler but larger than the VW Bug; "This is your new dimension," bragged Studebaker's ads. Foreign imports still weren't faring too well, though; Chrysler imported the compact Simca from France, but found few takers. Datsun, the first Japanese export available in the US, sold only eighty-three cars in its first year here.

To Rig Or Not To Rig...

Vladimir Nabokov's *Lolita*, the story of an older man's obsession with an underage girl, was 1958's most controversial best-seller, but the year's biggest scandal happened on television, when the game show **Twenty-One** was revealed to be rigged. As dramatized in the 1994 film *Quiz Show*, contestant Charles Van Doren had been given some correct answers in advance by the show's producers, enabling him to win one hundred and twenty-nine thousand dollars in prize money over fourteen appearances; a handsome, articulate English instructor at Columbia University, Van Doren was popular with the viewing audience, and the producers wanted to keep him on as many broadcasts as possible. When contestant Herbert Stempel (who had lost to Van Doren) went public with the truth, the ensuing brouhaha caused not only the cancelation of the program, but the cancelation of game shows *Dotto*, *The $64,000 Question*, and *The $64,000 Challenge*.

TV News

The "adult western" continued to flourish on television, with successful debuts by *The Rifleman*, *The Texan*, and *Wanted—Dead or Alive*. 1958 also witnessed the debut of two popular detective shows, *Peter Gunn,* and *77 Sunset Strip*. The latter starred Efrem Zimbalist, Jr as a Hollywood private eye, but the show's secret

ACADEMY AWARDS

BEST PICTURE
Gigi
directed by Vincente Minelli

BEST ACTOR
David Niven
Separate Tables

BEST ACTRESS
Susan Hayward
I Want to Live!

58 Efrem Zimbalist, Jr, Edd Byrnes, and Roger Smith of *77 Sunset Strip*.

School integration debate intensifies in South; many schools close or become privatized in order to avoid having to enroll black students.

January 31 – US launches *Explorer I* satellite into orbit.

March 17 – US launches *Vanguard 1* satellite into orbit; the 6.4-inch aluminum sphere goes into wider orbit than any previous manmade satellite.

July 7 – Alaska statehood bill signed by President Eisenhower.

October 11 – US launches *Pioneer* rocket in attempt to orbit the Moon. Project fails, but rocket does achieve a record altitude of 79,193 miles.

58 A mystery girl has eyes only for Rick Nelson on the *Ozzie and Harriet* show.

weapon was Kookie, the jive-talking parking lot attendant played by Edd Byrnes. Byrnes later parlayed his character into a briefly successful recording career, hitting biggest with "Kookie, Kookie (Lend Me Your Comb)."

Another TV actor with musical ambitions was **Rick Nelson**, the youngest member of the Nelson family, who played themselves on the long-running show *The Adventures of Ozzie and Harriet*. He performed regularly on the show, fronting a band that included future Elvis sideman James Burton, and had a series of chart hits, including "Be-Bop Baby" and "Poor Little Fool."

Music News

The musical events of 1958 were enough to try the patience of even the most die-hard rock 'n' roll fan. At the peak of his career, Elvis had been drafted into the army; Colonel Tom

58 Chart-topping teenager Laurie London.

Parker, his manager, thought that it would be better for Elvis's image to serve his allotted two years than to ask for a special dispensation from the draft board. **Jerry Lee Lewis** single-handedly derailed his own career by marrying his thirteen-year-old cousin, Myra Gale Brown; Lewis's concert and TV appearances were canceled as soon as the news slipped out, and "The Killer" became a pariah almost overnight. The country's new piano hero was the considerably more urbane Van Cliburn, the twenty-three-year-old pianist who had just won the international Tchaikovsky competition in Moscow.

Real rockers like Chuck Berry and Buddy Holly were also being crowded off the charts by an endless succession of novelty singles, such as David Seville's "Witch Doctor" and Sheb Wooley's "Purple People Eater," as well as treacly pap like Laurie

London's "He's Got The Whole World In His Hands." When The Kingston Trio had a successful hit with "Tom Dooley," many predicted that folk music would soon displace rock 'n'

TOP ALBUMS

South Pacific
soundtrack

The Music Man
original cast

Gigi
soundtrack

MITCH MILLER AND THE GANG
Sing Along With Mitch

VAN CLIBURN
Tchaikovsky: Piano Concerto No 1

roll. Perhaps that's why Gibson had a hard time interesting guitarists in its new, futuristically shaped Explorer and Flying V guitars, while the company's semi-hollow ES-335 was an immediate success.

"Rumble," a brooding guitar instrumental by **Link Wray**, was banned in many markets for "encouraging juvenile delinquency," and so enjoyed only moderate chart success. Wray's influence would be felt more heavily in the next decade, when guitarists on both sides of the Atlantic would draw upon his violent, feedback-laced sound to power their hard rock and heavy metal stylings.

Sounds More Like It

With the introduction of the stereophonic LP (RCA, Columbia and Atlantic also began releasing stereo 45s in 1958), "high fidelity" was the big buzzphrase in the music industry.

Consumers investing a bundle in expensive stereo components craved records that could really test (and show off) their stereo's sonic capabilities, and audiophile-oriented records like RCA's *Living Stereo* series were born. The king of "**hi-fi**" was Esquivel, a Mexican composer and conductor whose head-spinning arrangements were written to take utmost advantage of the stereo spectrum. His mastery could be heard on albums like *Other Worlds, Other Sounds*.

Miles Ahead

In New York, Miles Davis formed a sextet with John Coltrane, Cannonball Adderly, Bill Evans, Paul Chambers, and Philly Joe Jones, an aggregation that's still widely considered to be his finest band. Meanwhile, Duke Ellington was the hit of the Newport Jazz Festival, performing excerpts from his jazz suite, *Black, Brown And Beige*.

Movie News

There was still plenty of rock 'n' roll in the theaters, however; Jerry Lee Lewis raised hell on the back of a flatbed truck during the opening sequence of *High School Confidential* (which also starred popular B-movie bombshell Mamie Van Doren), Elvis delivered another respectable performance (this time as a boxer) in *King Creole*, and there was juvenile delinquency to spare in *The Cool and the Crazy, Dragstrip Riot, Hot Rod Gang,* and *Teenage Thunder*. *The Fly* and ***The Seventh Voyage of Sinbad*** were some of the year's better horror and adventure titles, respectively; the latter film's memorable "fighting skeletons" sequence still stands as a mighty testament to the mind-boggling abilities of animator Ray Harryhausen.

Look magazine named Rock Hudson its "Star of the Year" for his performances in *The Tarnished Angels* and *Twilight for the Gods*. However, it was Glenn Ford (*Cowboy, The Sheepman, Imitation General,* and *Torpedo Run*) who really cleaned up at the box office. **Elizabeth Taylor** had her finest role yet, as Maggie in Tennessee Williams' *Cat on a Hot Tin Roof*, but was severely traumatized by the airplane crash death of her third husband, producer Mike Todd.

Other highlights included *The Defiant Ones*, a gripping prison escape film starring Tony Curtis

and Sidney Poitier; *Touch of Evil*, Orson Welles' tale of corruption in a Mexican border town; and *The Young Lions*, Edward Dymytryk's World War Two film starring Marlon Brando, Dean Martin and Montgomery Clift. *Gigi*, starring Leslie Caron, and *Damn Yankees* (featuring the stage standard "Whatever Lola Wants") were the year's top musicals.

Off-Set Upset

Tragedy struck Hollywood on April 4, when Cheryl Crane, Lana Turner's fourteen-year-old daughter, was arrested for the stabbing to death of gangster Johnny Stompanato, Turner's boyfriend. Crane claimed that she heard Stompanato threatening her mother, and the jury ruled it a justifiable homicide. Later in the year, former matinee idol Tyrone Power died of heart attack on the set of *Solomon and Sheba*, a biblical costume epic starring Gina Lollobrigida. He was replaced by Yul Brynner.

'58 Hot property—Paul Newman and Elizabeth Taylor in *Cat on a Hot Tin Roof.*

"The new leisure is here," trumpeted *Life* magazine's year-end issue of 1959. "For the first time, a civilization has reached a point where most people are no longer preoccupied with providing food and shelter." The issue went on to note blithely that there were now over two hundred and fifty thousand swimming pools in US homes. Never before had the nation experienced such an overwhelming degree of opulence.

59 Hawaiian-style leisure wear for less formal times.

Put some romance in your "loof life"!

ARROW **Bali Cay**

Despite a 116-day steelworkers' strike—the longest in US history—the nation's economy was again in good shape, thanks in part to the government's "**Buy American**" campaign. America's aerospace industry was booming as the nation began to challenge Russia's lead in the space race. The average American worker earned $91.53 a week, and was looking for new ways in which to spend it.

Hawaiian Honeymoon

This abundance of disposable income, combined with Hawaii's recent entrance into the Union in 1959, manifested itself in a mania for all things Hawaiian. Polynesian restaurant-bars like Don The Beachcomber's and Trader Vic's had been serving mai-tais since before World War Two, but now "**tiki**" bars (usually furnished with excessive amounts of bamboo and blowfish lanterns) were springing up all over the place. Housewives were taking **hula** lessons, and suburbanites everywhere were holding weekend luaus in their back yards—which, in turn, were often transformed into miniature tropical paradises replete with palm trees, tiki torches, and statues of Polynesian gods. For many Americans (especially men who had served in the South Pacific during World War Two), the tropical South Sea Islands seemed the very embodiment of "the good life;" additionally, the wild "pagan" lifestyles associated with island cultures seemed to offer

59 Khrushchev doffs his hat as Eisenhower welcomes him to the US at Andrews Air Force Base, Maryland.

titillating relief, at least in theory, from the rampant sexual repression of the Eisenhower era.

Music News

One recording artist who reaped the benefits of the tiki craze was **Martin Denny**, the house pianist at Waikiki's Hawaiian Village hotel complex. Denny's combo incorporated birdcalls and exotic percussion into its easy-listening jazz and showtune repertoire, perfecting a sound and style that came to be known as "**exotica**." Recorded a year earlier, Denny's birdcall-saturated version of Les Baxter's "Quiet Village" became a huge hit in 1959, as did his albums *Quiet Village* and *Exotica*. Denny's records (and those of other exotica-oriented artists like Les Baxter, Arthur Lyman, Tak Shindo, Webley Edwards, and The Markko Polo Adventurers) were the perfect background music for backyard luaus, while their covers—usually featuring scantily clad beauties lolling about in tropical surroundings—perfectly summed up America's fascination with Polynesiana.

Despite being stationed in Germany, Elvis was still selling healthy quantities of records; he had recorded songs like "A Fool Such As I" and "Big Hunk O'

'59 Frankie Avalon.

Love" before his induction, in order to keep the charts warm until his return. Inferior Elvis substitutes Fabian ("Tiger"), Frankie Avalon ("Venus"), and Bobby Rydell ("We Got Love") all took advantage of Elvis's absence by ingratiating themselves into the hearts of his teenage fans—the female ones, at least.

But there were worse things than a missing Elvis to contend with. In February, Buddy Holly, Ritchie Valens, and The Big Bopper all ended their promising careers in a plane crash near Mason City, Iowa. In November, Alan Freed, one of rock 'n' roll's most influential proponents, was forced to resign his DJ post at New York City's

WABC. The US government was investigating reports that DJs were accepting monetary bribes in return for airplay, and was only too happy to make Freed the main scapegoat of the "**payola**" scandal. Freed received a four-hundred-dollar fine and a

Beatnik Branding

The Many Loves of Dobie Gillis debuted in the fall, starring Dwayne Hickman as the titular girl-crazy teenager. The character of Dobie's best buddy, Maynard G Krebs (*below*), was a good indication of how quickly the media had warped and commodified the image of the "beat generation." Instead of being hip, contemplative and creative (*à la* Kerouac and Ginsberg), Krebs was merely goateed, unwashed and extremely lazy. Coined in 1958 by San Francisco newspaper columnist Herb Caen, the term "beatnik" went into the American

suspended jail sentence, and was essentially drummed out of the music business; by 1965, "The Father of Rock 'n' Roll" was dead, the victim of alcoholism and a broken heart.

In what many consider to have been his finest year, Miles Davis completed *Kind Of Blue* and began

TOP ALBUMS

THE KINGSTON TRIO

The Kingston Trio At Large

HENRY MANCINI

The Music From Peter Gunn

THE KINGSTON TRIO

Here We Go Again!

JOHNNY MATHIS

Heavenly

MARTIN DENNY

Exotica

working on *Sketches Of Spain*. Both albums helped to popularize "**modal jazz**," in which the musicians improvised around scales rather than chord changes. Meanwhile, saxophonist Ornette Coleman recorded *The Shape Of Jazz*, a defining work of "free jazz," with trumpet player Don Cherry, bassist Charlie Haden, and drummer Billy Higgins. Billie Holiday, one of the finest jazz and blues vocalists ever, died broke and addicted at age forty-four.

TV News

Predictably, television also cashed in on the Polynesian craze: *Hawaiian Eye*, a detective show set in Honolulu, made its debut on ABC, as did *Adventure in Paradise*, about the captain (Gardner McKay) of a South Seas schooner. Other notable debuts included *Bonanza,* a long-running "ranch" western starring Lorne Greene as Pa Cartwright; *The Untouchables*, a crime show set in

1930s Chicago, starring Robert Stack as Eliot Ness; and *The Twilight Zone*, Rod Serling's impeccably written science-fiction anthology series. *Rocky and His Friends*, Jay Ward's cartoon featuring Rocky the Flying Squirrel, Bullwinkle Moose, and inept (and obviously Russian, though it was never explicitly stated) spies Boris and Natasha, debuted in November on ABC.

Superman Death Riddle

George Reeves, the former star of *Superman*, died during the summer in an apparent suicide. Forever typecast as "The Man of Steel," Reeves had not been able to find work since the show's cancelation in 1957, although some have since claimed that he was entertaining several offers at the time of his death, and that (as he left no note) his demise was either due to an accident or foul play. His death remains a mystery.

lexicon as a connotation for the likes of Krebs, rather than Kerouac's ideal of "a swinging group of new American men intent on joy." A decade later, the hippies would fall victim to a similar sort of media stereotype.

Movie News

Hollywood jumped on the beatnik bandwagon too, releasing Albert Zugsmith's *The Beat Generation* (in which detectives hunt a rapist against a backdrop of beatnik-populated

coffeehouses) and Roger Corman's *A Bucket of Blood*, a horror-comedy about a coffeehouse busboy whose grisly art projects bring him fame in the world of beats and hipsters.

ACADEMY AWARDS

BEST PICTURE
....
Ben-Hur
directed by William Wyler
....

BEST ACTOR
....
Charlton Heston
Ben-Hur
....

BEST ACTRESS
....
Simone Signoret
Room at the Top

Other cheap thrills were available in the form of *Teenagers from Outer Space*, *Attack of the Giant Leeches*, and *The Tingler*, a horror film by William Castle (whose status as an imaginative low-budget impresario was rivaled only by Corman) that utilized "**Percepto**"—the theater seats were wired with a mild electric current, so as to actually shock the audience! 1959 also produced Ed Wood's fabulously inept **Plan 9 from Outer Space**. The film was supposed to feature Bela Lugosi in a lead role, but the former *Dracula* star died just a little way into the shooting. Pressed for time, Wood mixed his minimal Lugosi footage with scenes of another (noticeably taller) man hiding his face with a cape.

Rock Hudson and Doris Day, who starred together in the popular romantic farce **Pillow Talk**, made for an extremely incongruous duo. Neither were exactly what they

'59 "Real gone" beatniks groove to Dick Contino in Corman's *The Beat Generation*.

seemed: the handsome Hudson, a closeted gay man, was lusted after by millions of American women, while Day, already well into her thirties, was usually depicted as the epitome of virginal innocence. The pair were easily the most popular stars of 1959.

Roles Apart

Speaking of virginal innocence, the most popular new face of the year was Sandra Dee, the seventeen-year-old actress who appeared in *Imitation of Life*, *Gidget* and *A Summer Place*. Four decades on, the contrast between the latter two films is especially interesting: *Gidget*, a light-hearted comedy-romance set on Southern California beaches, presented the stereotypical image of late-1950s life as carefree and uncomplicated. In comparison, **A Summer Place**, with its themes of adultery and teenage sex, seemed to come from another planet entirely. But melodramatic dialogue aside (not to mention a bizarrely stilted performance by Richard Egan, who appeared to have mistakenly wandered in from a science-fiction film), *A Summer Place* sharply depicted the frustrating social contradictions and confusing sexual mores of the era.

Off The Page

Suddenly Last Summer, Joseph L Mankiewicz's adaptation of Tennessee Williams' 1958 one-act play, starred Elizabeth Taylor as Katherine Hepburn's allegedly insane niece. In reality, Liz's own life continued to take soap-opera-worthy turns; her engagement (and subsequent wedding) to Eddie Fisher brought howls of outrage from fans who blamed Liz for breaking up Fisher's and Debbie Reynolds' "perfect" marriage.

William Wyler's epic **Ben-Hur**, starring Charlton Heston, swept the Academy Awards, thanks in part to Robert L Surtees' amazing cinematography; the film was back in the news in 1995, when writer Gore Vidal revealed that he had, unbeknownst to the notoriously conservative Heston, slipped a homoerotic subtext into the script. Heston was far from amused.

Zing In The Tail

In its 1960 sales catalog, the Plymouth company reported that—according to University of Detroit wind tunnel tests—"stabilizers" (aka tailfins) "bring the center of pressure back toward the rear" while driving, and that their fins actually reduced the need to make steering corrections in cross winds. Despite such lofty claims, the tailfin was now a shrinking, vanishing species. 1960 Chryslers still offered relatively sharp fins (along with push-button automatic transmission, air conditioning, power windows, and power seats), but many cars, including Oldsmobile's 1960 Super 88 Holiday SceniCoupe ("radiantly fashioned for the Rocketing Sixties"), sported flattened or angled fins. Others, like the 1960 Pontiac Ventura Sports Coupe, got rid of the fins entirely, relying instead on futuristically styled tail-lights for rear-end flashiness.

New Drift In Shifts

Car registrations were up forty-two percent from the beginning of the decade, and seventy-five percent of all new cars were now manufactured with automatic transmissions. Imports, including economy-sized Renaults and Volkswagens, had their first successful year, accounting for more than ten percent of the American market. Sensing America's increasing acceptance of smaller cars, Ford introduced the 1960 Falcon. Crossing its fingers, the company hoped that the car would help Ford recover from the Edsel fiasco.

Bell Company

"Phone-booth packing," the art of seeing just how many people you can fit into a phone booth, briefly became the rage on college campuses.

Just-over-the-knee "short" skirts and knitted sweaters were popular with women, with chokers as a common accessory. Panti-Legs, the first pantyhose, were marketed by North Carolina's Glen Raven Mills.

Barbie dolls, named after the daughter of Mattel Toy Company co-founder Ruth Handler, made their debut at the 1959 New York Toy Fair. Dealer interest was lukewarm at first—Barbie was thought to be a little too, er, "developed" for a young girl's doll—but picked up considerably when Mattel quickly sold out of its initial shipment of five hundred thousand dolls. Barbie, and her endless supply of outfits and accessories, have since become an integral part of life for pre-adolescent American girls.

'59 **Barbie-doll purse.**

As a new decade dawned and the Eisenhower era drew to a close, it became increasingly apparent that, beneath its well-chromed, luxury-laden facade, all was not well with the country. As of January 1, the US population stood at 179,245,000, including forty-seven million working women. Unemployment was high, however, and the average salary of $89.72 per week was actually down a few dollars from the previous year.

TOP TELEVISION SHOWS

Gunsmoke

Wagon Train

Have Gun, Will Travel

The Danny Thomas Show

The Real McCoys

On January 2, *The New York Times* further darkened the nation's spirits by announcing that America's space program was being consistently hampered by cost overruns, and was thus having trouble competing with the Soviets.

Powers Fall Out

Still, Americans could take comfort in the fact that US–USSR relations were at their warmest in years—at least until May, when the Soviets announced that they had downed Francis Gary Powers' U2 spy plane. Tensions quickly escalated between the two nations, and America's worldwide credibility was severely tarnished by the incident.

America Shuns Nixon

The US government was also having difficulty with its white constituents in the South, many of whom reacted violently to the government's attempts to integrate their public schools. Meanwhile, Southern blacks staged non-violent sit-ins, protesting the "Jim Crow" laws that prevented them from actually sitting down at dime-store lunch counters.

This tumultuous atmosphere was further exacerbated by the tight presidential race between Vice-President **Richard Nixon** and Massachusetts Senator John F Kennedy. The turning point in the presidential campaign came on September 26, when the two men met for the first of four nationally televised debates. Although the more experienced Nixon had been an odds-on favorite to win the debate, most of the viewing audience felt that the telegenic Kennedy seemed poised and confident, while Nixon (who was suffering from a broken knee-cap, and who had refused pancake makeup to cover his beard stubble) came off as haggard, ill-tempered, and downright seedy. The momentum from the televised confrontation, combined with running mate Lyndon Johnson's pull in the Southern states, carried Kennedy to victory in the November elections.

[60] JFK and Nixon poised for the 1960 TV debate.

IN THE NEWS

May 1 – An American U2 spy plane is downed inside the USSR. The Soviets announce that they will put the pilot, Francis Gary Powers, on trial as a spy.

May 7 – US admits that the downed U2 plane was on a spying mission.

May 16 – Nikita Khruschev cancels Paris summit meeting over U2. incident.

July 13 – Democratic party nominates John F Kennedy for presidency.

July 25 – Republican party nominates Vice-President Richard M Nixon for presidency.

August 19 – Francis Gary Powers sentenced to ten years in Soviet prison for espionage.

September – Fidel Castro visits Manhattan. Refused admission by New York's upscale hotels, Castro and his entourage eventually end up at the Hotel Theresa in Harlem.

September 12 – Kennedy assures the American public that, although he is a Catholic, his actions as President would not be dictated by the Roman Catholic Church.

September 26 – First of four nationally televised presidential debates held in Chicago.

October – Former President Harry Truman states publicly that Richard Nixon "never told the truth in his life" and that anyone who votes for Nixon "ought to go to Hell."

November.8 – Kennedy elected president by 0.3 percent of the popular vote, one of the slimmest margins of victory in US history.

TV News

While Kennedy and Nixon were slugging away at each other on the campaign trail, *The Andy Griffith Show* and *My Three Sons*, two of television's most enduring sitcoms, made their respective small-screen debuts. The former, which starred Andy Griffith as a small-town sheriff, was the first of many popular rural-themed comedies to spring up over the next decade. The latter, which featured Fred MacMurray as a widower raising three young boys, would run until 1972.

Yabba Dabba Doo!

Another popular show introduced in 1960 was **The Flintstones**, which was essentially an animated version of *The Honeymooners* set in prehistoric times. Although the show was originally created by William Hanna and Joe Barbera as a "cartoon for grownups," the Stone Age antics of Fred Flintstone (*right*), Barney Rubble, and Dino the Dinosaur quickly found favor with a younger audience.

Music News

The juvenile demographic was also making its presence felt in the music world—who else could be sending novelty songs such as Larry Verne's "Mr Custer," The Hollywood Argyles' "Alley-Oop," and Brian Hyland's "Itsy Bitsy Teenie Weenie Yellow Polka Dot Bikini" to the top of the charts?

Humor of a subtler nature was the specialty of stand-up comedian Bob Newhart, whose *Button-Down Mind*

album quickly became one of the biggest-selling comedy LPs to date.

Back on the teenage front, the fifteen-year-old **Brenda Lee** (whose remarkable powerhouse vocals sounded like those of a woman twice her age) established herself as a promising new talent, hitting Number

TOP SINGLES

PERCY FAITH

"The Theme From *A Summer Place*"

ELVIS PRESLEY

"It's Now Or Never"

ELVIS PRESLEY

"Are You Lonesome Tonight?"

THE EVERLY BROTHERS

"Cathy's Clown"

ELVIS PRESLEY

"Stuck On You"

One with "I'm Sorry" and "I Want To Be Wanted." Meanwhile, Mark Dinning's "Teen Angel" and Ray Peterson's "Tell Laura I Love Her" both successfully mined the "teen automotive death" genre.

No Cure For Cochran

One real-life rock 'n' roll traffic fatality was Eddie Cochran; the man behind "Summertime Blues," "C'mon Everybody," and "Somethin' Else" died in a car accident while touring England in April. The crash also injured tourmate Gene Vincent, who never fully recovered from the physical and psychological scars it left him with. Though he continued to record and tour, Vincent's addiction to drink and painkillers took a severe toll on his body and his once mighty musical abilities. In 1971, at the age of thirty-six, he died of a ruptured stomach ulcer.

The King And The Crooner

Rock 'n' roll fans did get a bit of good news on March 5, when Elvis was officially discharged from the army. If his 1960 hits were tamer than his pre-induction output, at least performances like "It's Now Or Never" proved that military life hadn't done the Presley voice any harm. Shortly after his return, Elvis made a guest appearance on Frank Sinatra's televised *Timex Special*; once one of Elvis's earliest and harshest critics, Sinatra—like the rest of the country— welcomed him back with open arms.

Movie News

In addition to filming his own TV special and recording the tremendously

successful *Nice 'n' Easy* LP, Sinatra also found time to star in **Ocean's Eleven**, a casino heist caper co-starring Dean Martin, Sammy Davis, Jr, and Peter Lawford. Though not an exceptionally strong film in its own right, *Ocean's Eleven* perfectly encapsulated the whole swinging "Rat Pack" aesthetic, providing a glimpse of that brief moment in time when Las Vegas was actually an elegant vacation destination for adults. In real life, Davis caused a bit of a stir by marrying Swedish actress May Britt; though he had campaigned ardently on behalf of the Kennedy election campaign, Kennedy's aides felt that Davis's interracial marriage was a political hot potato, and politely asked him not to attend the upcoming presidential inauguration.

Another Hollywood controversy revolved around the reappearance of formerly blacklisted writers and directors. Jules Dassin scored a huge hit with *Never on Sunday*, and Dalton Trumbo wrote the scripts for two of the year's biggest blockbusters, *Exodus* and **Spartacus**. (The latter, an epic costume drama starring Kirk Douglas, was widely praised for its ambitious battle sequences— although if you looked closely, you could spot Roman soldiers wearing wristwatches and tennis shoes!) Among those less than pleased with this Commie-lovin' turn of events was John Wayne, who took it upon himself to produce, direct, and star in **The Alamo**, an impressive spectacle which received luke-warm reviews; predictably, "The Duke" attributed these to a lack of patriotism among America's film critics.

A Many-Spendored Thing

Marilyn Monroe was experiencing some troubles of her own. Although *Let's Make Love,* her musical comedy with Yves Montand, opened to positive reviews, her marriage to Arthur Miller was falling apart. The couple announced their split shortly after the completion of John Huston's *The Misfits*, the filming of which also took a severe toll on co-star **Clark Gable**. Mere weeks after the cameras stopped rolling, Gable died of a heart attack at the age of fifty-nine.

Elizabeth Taylor won an Oscar for her portrayal of a high-class prostitute in

...the most desirable woman in town and the easiest to find...just call

BUTTERFIELD 8

IN CINEMASCOPE AND METROCOLOR

Butterfield 8, although most Hollywood observers felt that she was really being honored—two years after the fact—for her performance in *Cat on a Hot Tin Roof*. That was just fine with Liz; pressured by her studio to do *Butterfield 8*, she complained loudly that the film was trashy and that her character was nothing but a "nymphomaniac."

A maniac of a less appealing sort was on the loose in Alfred Hitchcock's **Psycho**, starring Anthony Perkins as a young motel owner controlled by his domineering "mother." One of the most influential (and truly terrifying) horror films of the postwar era, *Psycho* caused more than a few viewers to forgo showers for weeks afterwards.

Motown Sobers Up

"There's nothing like a new car for enchantment," promised an ad for the latest line of Oldsmobiles, but it was beginning to seem like Detroit was running out of new, enchanting ideas. Having produced miles of chrome and tailfins over the past five years, it now looked like auto makers were heading in the other direction. Buick's "clean look" emphasized sleekness over

ornamentation, while Dodge's 1961 Polara and 1961 Dart swapped fins for rounded, pod-like tail fixtures. Chrysler's "new direction in automotive styling" featured streamlined rears and low, flat roofs, although the 1961 Newport was allowed to keep its boldly angled fins. European cars were still selling slowly, but their competitive prices—$1,675 for a Volkswagen Beetle, $1,585 for a Renault Dauphine, and only $1,398 for a Fiat 600—indicated that Detroit would soon have a serious battle on its hands.

He Certainly Can Can-Can

In New York, Jasper Johns created *Painted Bronze*, a sculpture featuring painted replicas of Ballantine Ale cans. Drawing its inspiration from the packaging of an everyday commercial product, the work was an opening salvo in the pop art revolution.

Howdy Doodle

The closest most Americans got to pop art in 1960 was Ohio Art's Etch-A-Sketch, a popular device that enabled you to make disposable black-

and-white drawings on a television-like screen by twiddling two knobs. Drawing straight lines was easy, but curves were next to impossible; consequently, most people's Etch-A-Sketchings tended to veer towards the "abstract" side of things. Of course, if you messed up, you could just shake the screen and start over.

See Monkeys?

Another common household toy was "Mr Machine," a marching robot which could be taken apart and reassembled without tools. In theory, at least, the $11.95 toy was supposed to teach kids mechanical skills. Cheaper, if far less satisfying, were Transcience Corporation's Sea Monkeys. Colorfully advertised in countless comic books as aquatic, humanoid-type pets, Sea Monkeys were actually just ½- to ¾-inch brine shrimp, who swam randomly around in a tiny plastic tank.

60 Nancy Kwan as Hong Kong good-time girl, Suzie Wong

Lycra Chic

Oversized men's shirts and slim pants were popular with women, although Nancy Kwan's attractive turn in *The World of Suzie Wong* set off a brief vogue for *cheongsams*, patterned oriental sheaths with high collars and slit skirts. The fashion breakthrough of the year, however, belonged to the Warner Lingerie Company, which introduced the Little Godiva step-in girdle—the first mass-produced garment made of Lycra.

60 Etch-A-Sketch art—transient and tricky.

nineteen

61

America had never seen a presidential couple like **the Kennedys.** **Both were youthful, attractive and charismatic** (certain wags joked that John would have won the presidency by a wider margin had teenaged girls been allowed to vote), and **Jackie was without a doubt the chic-est First Lady** in memory. When Jackie wore a "pillbox" hat to the January 20 inauguration ceremony, she inadvertently set off a pillbox hat craze and became the nation's fashion barometer for the next half-decade.

TOP TELEVISION SHOWS

Wagon Train

Gunsmoke

The Andy Griffith Show

Candid Camera

Rawhide

From wrap-around sunglasses and bouffant hairdos to two-piece suits and slim A-line skirts that came to mid-knee—if Jackie wore them, millions of American women immediately had to wear them as well. Similarly, the couple's intellectual interests—which included classical music, Shakespeare, and collecting antiques—were reflected in the increasingly cultured tastes of the American public.

Chilled But Not Always Cool

Not surprisingly, this newfound emphasis on youth and sophistication quickly found its way into the product advertisements of the day. Pepsi's slogan "For those who think young" proved enormously successful, much more so than Coke's outdated "Zing! What a refreshing new feeling!" Conscious of the steadily rising sales of imported beer, the Anheuser-Busch brewing company introduced Michelob; intended as an up-scale

61 Jackie Kennedy, fashion icon and role model.

IN THE NEWS

January 3 – US breaks off diplomatic relations with Cuba.

January 28 – US announces establishment of the Peace Corps.

April 12 – Russia's Yuri Gagarin becomes the first man in space, orbiting the Earth for 108 minutes.

April 17 – In the CIA-backed "Bay of Pigs" invasion of Cuba, 1,500 anti-Castro Cuban exiles are soundly defeated by Castro's forces.

April 24 – Kennedy accepts full responsibility for "Bay of Pigs" incident.

May 5 – Navy Commander Alan Shepard, Jr makes a successful suborbital flight aboard Project Mercury capsule Freedom Seven, thus becoming the first American in space.

May 14 – Freedom riders traveling to New Orleans to protest Southern racial segregation are physically attacked by whites in the Alabama cities of Anniston and Birmingham.

61 Armed officers of the Communist People's Police help fasten barbed wire along the Berlin Wall.

IN THE NEWS

July 21 – Virgil "Gus" Grissom becomes the second American in space, making a suborbital flight aboard Project Mercury's *Liberty Bell Seven*.

August 13 – East German and Soviet guards seal off East Berlin, preventing refugees from fleeing to the West; the barrier of concrete and barbed wire becomes known as the Berlin Wall.

December 5 – Noting that five out of every seven men drafted by the US Army are turned down for reasons of physical inadequacy, President Kennedy calls for Americans to get more physical exercise. The US, Kennedy says, is becoming a nation of spectators rather than a nation of athletes.

December 11 – The first two US military companies arrive in South Vietnam, in order to help fend off the North Vietnamese Communist threat. The 4,000 men are ordered to fire only if fired upon.

alternative to the company's own Budweiser product, the beer's "sophisticated" image was reinforced by its futuristically styled bottle.

Backyard Bunkers

There were dark, mushroom-shaped clouds on the horizon, however. As relations with Cuba and the Soviet Union further deteriorated in the wake of the ill-conceived "Bay of Pigs" invasion, Kennedy urged Americans to build their own **fallout shelters**; as a result, the fallout shelter construction industry experienced an unprecedented boom. In back yards across the country, Americans stocked their shelters with all the canned goods, eating utensils, sanitation supplies, first-aid kits, reading material and drinking water needed to wait out the two weeks of fallout from a nuclear explosion. Until the bombs actually started dropping, many families used their new shelters as family rec rooms, or as clubhouses for the kids.

Strung Up And Married

Certainly, no self-respecting rec room was complete without a Duncan **Yo-Yo**; Donald F Duncan's company sold fifteen million of their tricky stringed double-discs in 1961, as American kids everywhere busied themselves learning how to "walk the dog." Also popular was **The Game of Life**, a nineteenth-century boardgame updated by Milton Bradley in honor of the company's one-hundredth anniversary. As in life itself, the object of the game was to get rich, get married and have as many children as possible.

Home Run Gets Footnote

In the game of baseball, all eyes were on the New York Yankees' **Roger Maris** as he closed in on Babe Ruth's single-season record of sixty home

61 Some fallout shelters had all the comforts of home, including fake windows to combat claustrophobia.

ACADEMY AWARDS

BEST FILM

West Side Story

directed by Robert Wise and Jerome Robbins

BEST ACTOR

Maximilian Schell

Judgment At Nuremberg

BEST ACTRESS

Sophia Loren

Two Women

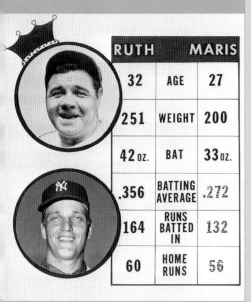

RUTH		MARIS
32	AGE	27
251	WEIGHT	200
42 oz.	BAT	33 oz.
.356	BATTING AVERAGE	.272
164	RUNS BATTED IN	132
60	HOME RUNS	56

'61 Roger Maris (*below*) challenges Babe Ruth's record.

runs. As the baseball season had recently been extended to 162 games from the previous 154, critics argued that Maris (reviled by some for even having the temerity to approach such a legendary benchmark) had an unfair eight-game advantage over the late Ruth. The controversy didn't affect Maris's play, but it did wreak plenty of havoc on his hair; by September, the constant stress was causing it to fall out in clumps. Maris didn't hit his sixty-first home run until the 162nd game of the season; consequently, his impressive feat has been forever tagged with an asterisk.

'61 Chubby Checker in *Twist around the Clock*.

Twisting Kids And Parents In Limbo

If you were young in 1961 (or one of those young-thinking Pepsi drinkers), you doubtless spent a fair amount of time dancing the twist. Initially popular in the autumn of 1960, thanks to **Chubby Checker**'s chart-topping version of "The Twist" (originally recorded by Hank Ballard), the dance craze continued to build momentum as 1961 progressed. Checker (real name: Ernest Evans) kept the twist fires burning with the summer single "Let's Twist Again," and when he performed the dance on *The Ed Sullivan Show* in October, "The Twist" again headed for the upper reaches of the charts.

Adults seemed to prefer **the limbo**, an island dance that was, in its own way, as sexually suggestive as the twist. "How low can you go?" was the cry at limbo parties across the land; all you needed was some festive friends, a long pole (a broomstick would do in a pinch) and a calypso record, and the fun could begin. Chubby Checker, never one to miss out on a dance fad, would have a huge 1962 hit with "Limbo Rock."

Medics Bag Audiences

The two biggest teen heartthrobs of 1961 were produced not by the pop charts, but by the world of television. ABC's *Ben Casey* and NBC's *Dr Kildare* were the first of a new wave of medical shows, but their appeal was hardly limited to their story lines; young women around the country regularly tuned in to moon over the surly, brooding Casey (Vince Edwards) or the charming and witty Kildare (Richard Chamberlain); whom you preferred presumably said much about your own personality.

Dumbing Down Meets Mr Ed

The little girls may have understood, but Newton Minow, chairman of the Federal Communications Committee, was less than pleased with network programming. In a speech to the National Association of Broadcasting, Minow called TV "a vast wasteland," remarking that "I do not think the public taste is as low as some of you appear to believe." Minow's pronouncement was proved wrong when *Mr Ed*, a situation comedy about an architect who discovered a talking horse in the barn of his new house, became an immediate hit.

Untouchables Fingered

More controversial was the popular crime drama, *The Untouchables*. Objecting to the show's stereotypical representation of Italian-American characters, the Federation of Italian-American Democratic Organizations announced a boycott of all products made by Ligget & Meyers, the main sponsor of *The Untouchables*. In order to make peace, producer Quinn Martin agreed to stop giving Italian surnames to fictionalized criminals, to give a greater role to Rico Rossi, Eliot Ness's right-hand man (played by Nicholas Georgiade), and generally to stress the positive effect of Italian-American officials on the reduction of crime in the United States.

New Show Goes Bear

Yogi Bear, previously a recurring character on *Huckleberry Hound*, got his own cartoon in 1961. Self-proclaimed as "smarter than the average bear," Yogi lived with his pal

'61 Richard Chamberlain set pulses racing as Dr Kildare.

shouts and sings with life... explodes with love!

Seven Arts Productions presents

CLARK **Gable** MARILYN **Monroe** MONTGOMERY **Clift**

in the **the Misfits.** Co-starring **Thelma Ritter Eli Wallach**

John Huston production

A UNITED ARTISTS

Screenplay by **Arthur Miller** Produced by **Frank E. Taylor** Directed by **John Huston** Music by **Alex North**

TOP SINGLES

BOBBY LEWIS

"Tossin' And Turnin' "

JIMMY DEAN

"Big Bad John"

DEL SHANNON

"Runaway"

THE TOKENS

"The Lion Sleeps Tonight"

THE MARCELS

"Blue Moon"

Boo Boo in Jellystone Park, where they spent most of their time trying to steal food from picnicking families. Extremely popular with kids, Yogi eventually graduated to the silver screen in 1964, with *Hey There, It's Yogi Bear*.

Movie News

Warren Beatty and Natalie Wood gave Hollywood its first onscreen French kiss in *Splendor in the Grass*, but the year in films was otherwise remarkably short on controversy. Rock Hudson remained the top male box-office attraction, thanks to *The Last Sunset* and *Come September*; Elizabeth Taylor, off filming *Cleopatra* in Italy, had no new films to speak of, but people continued to line up around the block to see *Butterfield 8*. Paul Newman and Jackie Gleason played pool sharks in Robert Rossen's *The Hustler*, while Clark Gable and Marilyn Monroe's world-weary performances in *The Misfits* were almost too painful to watch. Stanley Kramer relived the

Nuremberg Trials with *Judgment at Nuremberg*, and Gregory Peck led a band of Allied commandos to victory in J Lee Thompson's gripping *The Guns of Navarone*. Meanwhile, everyone was singing Leonard Bernstein and Stephen Sondheim's songs from **West Side Story**, a Romeo and Juliet musical set in the world of New York street gangs.

On a lighter note, Audrey Hepburn was charming as Holly Golightly in *Breakfast at Tiffany's*, while children everywhere flocked to see Disney's *101 Dalmatians*. Elvis Presley tried his hand at a serious role in *Wild in the Country*, but fared much better as a hormonally overloaded tour guide in *Blue Hawaii*. Predictably, the twist made it into the theaters before the year's end; Chubby Checker twisted yet again in *Twist Around the Clock*, while Joey Dee and The Starliters tore up New York's Peppermint Lounge in *Hey, Let's Twist*.

Americans Flock to T-Birds

Major auto makers seemed hellbent on making their new cars as unattractive as possible. The 1962 Chevrolets ("with Jet-Smooth ride") were flatter and boxier than in previous years. Chevy's 1962 Corvair, advertised as "built for budget-minded people who go for sports car driving," featured a rear-mounted engine, but precious little else of note. Chrysler's 1962 models were similar to their 1961 counterparts, only without fins; Virgil Exner, who resigned from the company late in the year, referred to them as "plucked chickens." Plymouth's 1962 models were all downsized by up to eight inches in length, which proved a big mistake at a time when ads for

the Oldsmobile 98 were urging buyers to "relax in luxury-lounge interiors fashioned in the tones and textures of modern living."

By far the year's most attractive car was still Ford's **Thunderbird**. Buyers found the car so attractive, in fact, that when JFK requested twenty-five T-birds for his inaugural parade, Ford had to turn him down. They were already completely sold out.

TOP ALBUMS

ELVIS PRESLEY

Blue Hawaii

soundtrack

Exodus

soundtrack

JUDY GARLAND

Judy At Carnegie Hall

LAWRENCE WELK

Calcutta!

VARIOUS ARTISTS

Stars For A Summer Night

61 Natalie Wood in *West Side Story*.

As 1962 drew to a close, the United States (and the rest of the world) drew a collective sigh of relief. Nuclear war, the predicted outcome of October's Cuban missile crisis, had been narrowly averted. President Kennedy, having been burned by the advice of hawkish military aides during the "Bay of Pigs" fiasco, ignored them this time around, opting instead for a methodical, diplomatic solution. For the time being, at least, Americans everywhere would live to twist another day.

A nd twist they did. Chubby Checker's version of "**The Twist**" became the first record since Bing Crosby's "White Christmas" to return to the charts and hit the Number One spot for a second time. Banned by concerned citizens in Tampa, Florida, and Buffalo, New York, the dance was now big business, spawning hit sequels (Joey Dee and The Starliters' "Peppermint Twist," Sam Cooke's "Twistin' The Night Away," The Isley Brothers' "Twist And Shout," and Gary "US" Bonds' "Dear Lady Twist" and "Twist Twist Señora"), clothing (Thom McAn's "Chubby Checker Twister Shoe" proved rather popular), and all manner of twist merchandise.

Bobby "Boris" Pickett and The Crypt Kicker Five's "The Monster Mash," released in October, managed to spoof both the twist and another hit dance, the mashed potato. Other dances, including the frug, the jerk, the swim, the monkey, and the Watusi, would follow, but none would capture America's imagination in quite the same way.

IN THE NEWS

January 12 – American communists barred from traveling abroad as the US State Department denies passports to all Communist Party members.

February 7 – US ban on trade with Cuba goes into effect.

February 8 – US government announces the deployment of Military Assistance Command (MAC) in South Vietnam.

February 10 – USSR releases U2 pilot Francis Gary Powers to the US in exchange for Soviet spy Rudolf Abel.

February 20 – Lt Col John Glenn becomes the first American to orbit the Earth. Glenn's voyage is televised by all three networks, and watched by 135 million viewers.

February 26 – US Supreme Court rules that segregation in interstate and intrastate transportation facilities is illegal.

April 8 – Cuba convicts 1,179 "Bay of Pigs" prisoners of treason, and sentences them to 30 years in prison. Cuban officials offer to free all of them to the US for a $62 million ransom.

July 10 – *Telstar*, an experimental communications satellite developed and owned by AT&T and Bell telecommunications companies, successfully placed in orbit. It later relays television pictures from Maine to Great Britain and France.

September 20 – James Meredith, a black student, is denied admission to the University of Mississippi by Mississippi governor Ross R Barnett.

62 Ray Charles topped the singles charts in 1962.

New Wave Cresting

Out on the West Coast, surf music was poised to make a national breakout; Dick Dale, a guitarist who had gained a fanatical following playing "surfer's stomp" dances at the Rendezvous Ballroom in Newport Beach, California, was its first major figure. Though they failed to break nationally, Dale's 1962 instrumentals "Misirlou" and "Surf Beat" were incredibly influential, sending staccato guitar picking through the newly invented **Fender Reverb** unit for a sound that captured perfectly the power and the majesty of the Pacific surf. Soon, every surf band worth its salt was shelling out for a Fender Reverb unit and emulating Dale's cascading lead runs.

Ironically, the most successful proponents of surf music were, with one exception, not really surfers at all. **The Beach Boys**, a vocal group from the Los Angeles suburb of Hawthorne, hit the national charts with "Surfin' Safari," a sprightly rocker crammed with surfing lingo. Leader Brian Wilson, inspired by the surfing stories related to him by his drummer brother Dennis, painted evocative three-minute pictures of sunshine, bikinis, and blue waves. Suddenly, every kid in America wanted to catch a wave and head for California.

62 "Key clubs," gentlemen's clubs featuring scantily clad hostesses and waitresses, experienced a sudden surge of popularity, with Hugh Hefner's Playboy Clubs leading the way.

At Home With JFK

The First Family, Vaughn Meader's good-natured spoof of the Kennedy White House, became one of the fastest-selling records of all time upon its release in December. A talented comedian and JFK mimic, Meader was so closely identified with the president that, when Kennedy was assassinated in 1963, Meader's career unfortunately died along with him. Consequently, *The First Family* ranks as one of the all-time easiest albums to find in American thrift shops.

Blame It On...

In jazz, tenor saxophonist Stan Getz and guitarist Charlie Byrd headed for even warmer climes, recording the Brazilian-influenced *Jazz Samba*. The best-selling record introduced the seductive music of Antonio Carlos Jobim to American listeners, paving the way for the bossa nova craze that would sweep the country over the next two years.

Movie News

The box-office popularity of Doris Day's *Lover Come Back* (with Rock Hudson) and *That Touch of Mink* (with Cary Grant) notwithstanding, the film highlights of 1962 were far removed from the sphere of comedy. *Days of Wine and Roses* starred Jack Lemmon and Lee Remick as downward-spiraling alcoholics; *The Manchurian Candidate* set Frank Sinatra in a paranoid tale of political intrigue; Gregory Peck played a scrupulous Southern lawyer in the film adaptation of Harper Lee's *To Kill a Mockingbird*, and *The Longest Day* placed an all-star cast at the Normandy Beach invasion. Robert Aldrich's bizarre *Whatever Happened to Baby Jane?* was

62 Bette Davis and Joan Crawford in *Whatever Happened to Baby Jane?*

SPACELY SPROCKETS

The first movie from the family that's truly ahead of its time!

A UNIVERSAL RELEASE
©1990 UNIVERSAL CITY STUDIOS, INC.

JETSONS
The Movie ⓤ

Distributed by
UNITED INTERNATIONAL PICTURES

TOP ALBUMS

West Side Story
soundtrack

RAY CHARLES
Modern Sounds In Country And
Western Music

HENRY MANCINI
Breakfast at Tiffany's
soundtrack

VAUGHN MEADER
The First Family

PETER, PAUL AND MARY
Peter, Paul And Mary

at least good for some dark laughs, with screen divas Joan Crawford and Bette Davis chewing the scenery as faded movie stars.

Brits A Hit

David Lean's *Lawrence of Arabia* made an international star of Peter O'Toole, but *Dr No* was the English film that really made the biggest impression on these shores. American audiences flipped for Sean Connery's suave portrayal of Ian Fleming's special agent "007," and would continue to support both Connery and the James Bond film series loyally during the ensuing decades.

Dick, Liz and Oscar

In the year's biggest scandal, the still-married Elizabeth Taylor carried on a very public romance with Richard Burton on the set of *Cleopatra*, which was being filmed in Rome. Upon hearing of the affair, the disapproving Academy of Motion Picture Arts and Sciences asked Liz to return her Best Actress Oscar. She refused.

Goodbye, Norma Jeane

Tongues were also wagging about Marilyn Monroe's apparent suicide in

August. The coroner's report ruled that the thirty-six-year-old actress had died from an overdose of barbiturates, but rumors of foul play (and a politically motivated cover-up, based on Monroe's alleged affairs with both John and Robert Kennedy) have only gotten louder in the decades since her death.

TV News

September 1962 saw the debut of two of television's most popular shows, *The Jetsons* and *The Beverly Hillbillies*. The former, an animated comedy set in the twenty-first century, was ABC's first

TOP TELEVISION SHOWS

Bonanza

The Red Skelton Show

Candid Camera

The Andy Griffith Show

Hazel

regular series to be broadcast in color, which the Hanna-Barbera artists used to their advantage in creating the show's "ultramodern" feel. The latter, a sitcom that revolved around a backwoods clan suddenly transplanted to Beverly Hills, made *The Andy Griffith Show* seem positively profound by comparison. Widely reviled by critics upon its introduction, the show proved wildly popular with viewers, as did *The Lucy Show*, Lucille Ball's post-Desi sitcom, which also debuted in the fall.

Televisionary

Up at the Century 21 Exposition World's Fair in Seattle, attractions such as the 600-foot Space Needle (*right*), a monorail, and a 25,000-pound cake baked by Van de Kamp's Holland Dutch Baker were joined by General Electric's "Television of the Future"—a TV that projected a color picture on to a four-by-six-foot panel.

Fame For Clay As Mets Eat Dirt

In basketball, Wilt Chamberlain, the towering center for the Philadelphia

Warriors, set an NBA record by scoring one hundred points in a game against the New York Knicks. In baseball, the newly created New York Mets logged a pathetic record of forty wins and one hundred and twenty losses, the worst ever posted in the major leagues.

Boxing, a sport declining in popularity, received a shot in the arm with the success of newcomer **Cassius Clay**. In November, the twenty-year-old fighter knocked out Archie Moore, enabling him to move closer to a title match-up with heavyweight champion Sonny Liston.

Tops Pop

Helen Gurley Brown's *Sex and the Single Girl*, a groundbreaking work

which encouraged "nice" girls to have (and enjoy) pre-marital sex, became a best-seller, as did **Silent Spring**, Rachel Carson's indictment of the use of toxic chemicals in agriculture and industry. The extremely influential book inspired mainstream media coverage of chemical-related environmental damage, thus helping to spread ecological awareness in Americans. Unfortunately, 1962 was also the year that the brewing industry introduced "pop-tops" on beer cans. While this was certainly good news for beer drinkers (now you didn't need to bring a "church key" can opener along on picnics or fishing trips), the sharp-edged pull rings would soon pose their own problems to the environment.

Avanti Moves In Right Direction

A glorious last gasp for the Studebaker company, the Avanti lived up to its name with a fiberglass body, cockpit-style overhead dashboard controls, and an angular modern exterior that eschewed fins and radiator grilles. Almost as exciting was Chevrolet's new Corvette Sting Ray. The car featured hidden headlights, sleek fastback styling, and a split rear window; the latter feature was removed after only a year, making the 1963 models extremely collectable.

62 The Sting Ray Sports Coupe.

nineteen '63

It would be an understatement of the severest sort to say that the assassination of **President John F Kennedy** cast a pall over the year that came before it. For while JFK barely sneaked into office in 1960, by 1963 he **was widely admired**, and adored by the American public. Certainly, much of this adoration had more to do **with the popular image** of the Kennedy White House as a modern-day Camelot than with his actual abilities and accomplishments as a leader, but the country he presided over did seem, at least superficially, to be changing rapidly for the better.

63 "I have a dream." Martin Luther King, Jr at the Lincoln Memorial.

TOP TELEVISION SHOWS

The Beverly Hillbillies

Bonanza

The Dick Van Dyke Show

The Lucy Show

The Andy Griffith Show

The Cuban missile crisis over, America started 1963 on a note of unbridled optimism; by the end of the year, it was all most Americans could do to shake themselves out of their depression and get on with the daily business of living.

Music News

1963 still stands as a pretty incredible year for pop music. The received wisdom has it that rock 'n' roll died between Elvis's army induction and The Beatles' arrival, but nothing could be further from the truth. Admittedly, American record buyers sent the unbelievably insipid "Sugar Shack" and "Dominique" to the top of the charts for weeks at a time, but they also bought fistfuls of great records by The Beach Boys ("Surfin' USA," "Surfer Girl"), Jan and Dean ("Surf City," "Drag City"), Ray Charles ("Busted," "Take These Chains From My Heart"), and Roy Orbison ("In Dreams," "Mean Woman Blues").

Dubbed "The Tycoon of Teen" by writer Tom Wolfe, the prolific Phil

Spector was also at the top of his game, writing and producing thunderous "**Wall of Sound**" hits for the likes of the Ronettes ("Be My Baby"), the Chiffons ("He's So Fine," "One Fine Day"), and the Crystals ("Da Doo Ron Ron," "Then He Kissed Me").

America Gets The Message (Mostly)

The folk scene that had been bubbling under for years in New York City's Greenwich Village was now exploding, thanks to the recent national success of Joan Baez and Peter, Paul and Mary. "Blowin' In The Wind" and "Don't Think Twice, It's All Right," two of the latter's Top Ten hits, were written by an unkempt young man from Minnesota who called himself **Bob Dylan**. "Blowin' In The Wind," sung at civil rights marches around the country, summed up perfectly the hopeful tenor of the times; by the end of the year, Dylan (*left*) was being touted as the pre-eminent poet of his generation.

TOP SINGLES

JIMMY GILMER AND THE FIREBALLS

"Sugar Shack"

THE SINGING NUN

"Dominique"

THE CHIFFONS

"He's So Fine"

THE FOUR SEASONS

"Walk Like A Man"

THE ANGELS

"My Boyfriend's Back"

If Dylan's lyrics were often controversial for their politics, the lyrics to The Kingsmen's "**Louie Louie**" caused a huge uproar, chiefly because no one could actually understand them. Everyone seemed to think that they were probably obscene, however, and the single was subsequently banned from airplay in many markets. After many spins, government experts finally judged that "Louie Louie" was utterly indecipherable, and thus totally harmless. But there are people who still claim, to this day, that you can clearly hear the words "At quarter to ten, I lay her again" and love the song all the more for it.

Really Got A Hold

Over in Detroit, a former assembly line worker named Berry Gordy, Jr was presiding over his own poetry press, known to the rest of the world as Motown Records. Formed in 1959 with a loan of eight hundred dollars, the label was now a force to be reckoned with, releasing hits by "Little" Stevie Wonder ("Fingertips – Pt. 2"), Martha and The Vandellas ("Heat Wave," "Quicksand"), The Miracles ("You've Really Got A Hold On Me," "Mickey's Monkey"), and Marvin Gaye ("Pride And Joy," "Can I Get A Witness") in 1963. Unlike other black music labels of the time, **Motown** was finely tuned to appeal to both white and black audiences, a strategy that paid massive dividends.

Guggenheim Goes Pop

The first large-scale exhibition of pop art was held at the Guggenheim Museum in New York City, featuring works by Andy Warhol, Robert Rauschenberg and Jasper Johns. Collectors and the public alike were rapidly becoming fascinated with pop art's representation of everyday objects of American life, including advertisements, commercial packaging, canned foods, electrical appliances, and comic strips. Artists like Warhol (himself a former commercial illustrator), Johns, Tom Wesselmann, and Roy Lichtenstein all simultaneously celebrated and sent up America's

all-pervasive culture of consumerism, blurring the distinctions between commercial art and "high" art.

Though not displayed in any museum or gallery at the time, Jay Ward's successful cartoon advertising campaign for Quaker Oats' **Cap'n Crunch** cereal can now be seen as a perfect example of pop art. Correctly surmising that children would be more apt to ask their parents for a cereal they'd seen in a cartoon, Quaker Oats hired Ward, the acclaimed creator of Rocky the Flying Squirrel and Bullwinkle Moose, to create a series of cartoon characters to help advertise the company's new cereal. Only after Ward developed such characters as Cap'n Crunch, Seadog, and pirate Jean LaFoote did the company actually get around to creating the product—which, of course, turned out to be enormously successful.

Fruit Cup Hooks Kids

The TV spot for Hawaiian Punch fruit drink was another popular animated advertisement. "How'd you like a nice Hawaiian punch?" asked a character known as "Punchy;" when his hapless companion replied in the affirmative, Punchy hauled off and socked him. Life imitated art as the scene was repeatedly replayed in schoolyards across America.

Beverage Brands Slug It Out

Packing a serious alcoholic punch was malt liquor, a newly introduced beverage with fifty percent more alcohol than regular beer. Colt .45 and Schlitz were among the most popular brands. Meanwhile, Coke and Pepsi tried to emulate the recent success of Royal Crown's sugar-free Diet Rite Cola, introducing Tab and Patio Diet Cola, respectively. Still, nothing matched Seven-Up's slogan of "You Like It—It Likes You" for sheer Orwellian creepiness.

Now Everyone Gives A Dam

Troll dolls—ugly, brightly colored, naked gnomes with wild hair—inexplicably experienced a sudden wave of popularity among children and college students. Originally called Dammit Dolls, after their creator, Danish woodcarver Thomas Dam, the **Trolls** found favor in America as good-luck charms. Selling at $5.95 apiece ($1.98 for the tiny ones), they certainly brought plenty of good luck to their inventor.

Argument And Sentiment

Betty Freidan's *The Feminine Mystique*, a book which took serious issue with the notion that a woman can only truly fulfill herself as a wife and mother, was one of 1963's biggest best-sellers, as was Charles Schultz's *Happiness Is a Warm Puppy*. The collection of Peanuts drawings and pithy maxims spawned the best-selling sequel *Security Is a Thumb and a Blanket*, as well as Johnny Carson's best-selling spoofs, *Happiness Is a Dry Martini* (1965) and *Misery Is a Blind Date* (1967).

Movie News

John Wayne (*Donovan's Reef, McLintock*) and Doris Day (*The Thrill of It All, Move Over Darling*) may have been the year's most consistent box-office performers, but all anyone could seem to talk about were the romantic exploits of **Elizabeth Taylor and Richard Burton** (*below*). Though *Cleopatra* was, at thirty-seven million dollars, the most

63 *Nutty Professor* Jerry Lewis with Stella Stevens.

expensive Hollywood film to date, the perpetual gossip surrounding its stars went a long way towards helping the film make a handsome profit.

Also recouping its (admittedly less impressive) investment was **Beach Party**, starring Frankie Avalon and former Mousketeer Annette Funicello. The first of many films featuring the wholesome pair, *Beach Party*'s simple formula (a beach, some musical numbers, lots of bikinis) inspired a legion of imitations over the next few years—the most amusing of which was certainly 1963's *The Horror of Party Beach*, which featured a radioactive sea monster terrorizing teens at a beach in sunny Connecticut.

1963 was, in fact, a great year for low-brow movie fun. Not only did it witness the release of *From Russia with Love*, the second film in the Bond series, but it also brought us *The Raven* (a great low-budget horror-comedy with Boris Karloff, Peter Lorre and Vincent Price), Jerry Lewis's immortal *The Nutty Professor*, and *Fun in Acapulco,* and *Viva Las*

Vegas, two of Elvis's more enjoyable films of the decade. (Ann-Margret, the King's co-star in *Viva Las Vegas*, also received rave revues for her performance in *Bye Bye Birdie*.)

More Than The Sum Of Its Parts

Nobody realized it at the time, of course, but *Blood Feast*, an ultra-low-budget horror film by Herschell Gordon Lewis, would turn out to be an extremely influential work in its own right. Filmed in "**Blood Color**," this sordid tale—concerning an Egyptian caterer who murders women in order to use their body parts in ancient rituals—would be hailed decades later as the first true "gore" flick. Lewis's disgusting special effects have been imitated time and time again, but no film has ever truly matched *Blood Feast*'s winning combination of realistic gore and thoroughly inept acting.

IN THE NEWS

April 10 – Nuclear-powered US submarine *Thresher* floods and sinks in Atlantic Ocean during a test dive.

June 10 – Federal legislation requires that women receive equal pay for equal work.

June 11 – University of Alabama is desegregated, over the protests of Governor George C Wallace, who only steps aside to let black students in the University doors when confronted by the National Guard.

August 28 – 200,000 marchers converge on Washington DC to listen to speeches by ten civil rights leaders, including the Rev Dr Martin Luther King, who delivers his "I have a dream" speech.

September 15 – A church bombing in Birmingham, Alabama, leaves four young black girls dead.

November 1 – The South Vietnamese government of Ngo Dinh Diem is overthrown by South Vietnamese forces. The US recognizes provisional government of Nguyen Ngoc Tho, Diem's vice-president.

November 22 – President Kennedy assassinated while riding in Dallas motorcade. Lee Harvey Oswald captured as suspect. Lyndon Baines Johnson sworn in as president. Nation goes into state of shock and mourning.

November 24 – Lee Harvey Oswald shot and killed by Jack Ruby while in police custody. Televised murder further shocks country.

63 *Opposite, top:* **Ann-Margret and Elvis have fun in Vegas.**

ACADEMY AWARDS

BEST PICTURE

Tom Jones

directed by Tony Richardson

BEST ACTOR

Sidney Poitier

Lilies of the Field

BEST ACTRESS

Patricia Neal

Hud

TV News

Some of the most popular new shows of 1963 included *My Favorite Martian* (starring Ray Walston as an alien who moves in with newspaper reporter Bill Bixby), *Petticoat Junction* (a rural-themed offshoot of *The Beverly Hillbillies*, but with the added attraction of three pretty girls), and *The Fugitive*, a gripping adventure series starring David Janssen as a man wrongly accused of his wife's murder. Also doing well in the ratings, despite a slow start, was **The Dick Van Dyke Show**, a witty sitcom starring Dick Van Dyke and Mary Tyler Moore (*right*). American women picked up on Moore's preference for wearing slim-fitting trousers, which in turn

became known as "Laura Petries," after Moore's character on the show.

TV Helps America Mourn

From November 22 to November 25, the regular network schedules were canceled in order to broadcast news coverage of President Kennedy's assassination and its aftermath. Polls taken in December showed that, by and large, the American public felt that the round-the-clock coverage helped them come to terms with their feelings of loss. On November 26, the networks returned to their regularly scheduled programming, indicating that the official period of mourning was now at an end.

63 The twist hits The *Dick Van Dyke Show*

"Come Alive!

You're in the Pepsi Generation!" crowed the ads for the country's second leading soft drink, one of many products aiming squarely at the "people who think young" market. Indeed, plenty of people were thinking young in 1964—Ford sold a hundred thousand of its sporty new Mustangs, initially advertised as "a young people's car," in their first three months of production; buyers included such notable youngsters as Frank Sinatra and Debbie Reynolds. Those too young to actually drive could ask Mom and Dad for their own "Midget Mustang" kiddie car, available at local Ford dealers for only $12.95.

64 Skateboarding finally took off in 1964.

64 The Beatles at Kennedy Airport.

64 Pepsi: the drink for a new generation.

Only the very young could get away with wearing Rudi Gernreich's new topless swimsuit in public; New York and Los Angeles police warned that women wearing them on local beaches would be arrested for indecent exposure. Predictably, Gernreich's creation was not included in *Sports Illustrated*'s first "swimsuit edition," but the issue, an editorial attempt to compensate for an otherwise-dreary sports week, did just fine without it; loaded with lovely models, the yearly photo spread has since become one of the magazine's most popular features.

Ali Takes Title

On February 25, Muhammad Ali (formerly known as Cassius Clay) won the world heavyweight boxing title from defending champ Sonny Liston. Ali's brash attitude (and his very public conversion to Islam) annoyed many observers, but he was without a doubt the most charismatic boxing figure to come along in years.

Surfers Seize Sidewalks

Six years after its invention, skateboarding was experiencing its first big burst of popularity; the sport gained its own anthem in September, when Jan and Dean released "Sidewalk Surfin'." When you got hungry, you could skate over to McDonald's, where an order of a hamburger, French fries, and a shake would get you three cents change on your newly minted John F Kennedy half-dollar coin.

Beatlemania

Musically, 1964 can best be summed up with one word: Beatlemania. In January, "I Want To Hold Your Hand" became the first of thirty-one Beatles songs to hit the *Billboard* singles charts over the next twelve months. **The Fab Four** made their first live appearance on US TV on February 9, singing "All My Loving," "She Loves You," and "This Boy" on *The Ed Sullivan Show*. By the first week of April, "Can't Buy Me Love," "Twist And Shout," "She Loves You," "I Want To Hold Your Hand," and "Please Please Me" occupied the top five slots of the singles chart, and American teens

were snapping up every piece of Beatles-related merchandise they could lay their hands on; in New York, the Lowell Toy Group was said to be manufacturing fifteen thousand **Beatle wigs** a day. Dozens of British acts hit the US charts in the wake of The Beatles' success, with Peter and Gordon, Manfred Mann, and The Animals each scoring Number One singles by the year's end.

American musicians tried to pretend like the "British Invasion" was no big deal; after all, homegrown groups like The Beach Boys, The Four Seasons, The Dixie Cups, and The Shangri-La's still managed to top the singles charts, and Berry Gordy's Motown label had its best year to date, with Number One showings by The Supremes and Mary Wells. Still,

The Beatles dominated the American consciousness to a staggering degree. Later in the year, when New York World's Fair buried a time capsule to be opened by denizens of the seventieth century, officials included such 1964 artifacts as a bikini, filtered cigarettes, birth control pills—and a copy of The Beatles' *A Hard Day's Night* LP.

TV News

Network television also reaped plenty of rewards by targeting younger (or at least less discerning) audiences, as evidenced by the runaway ratings of utterly inane shows like *The Beverly Hillbillies* and *Gomer Pyle, USMC*. In response to the popularity of such dim but lovable TV characters as Pyle, *Bonanza*'s Hoss, and *The Beverly Hillbillies*' Clampett family, many products incorporated mush-mouthed yokel-speak into their advertisements, best exemplified by Mountain Dew's successful "**Yahoo! It's Mountain Dew!**" campaign.

1964 saw the introduction of several offbeat situation comedies, including *Bewitched* (which featured Elizabeth Montgomery as a witch trying to keep a lid on her supernatural talents), *Gilligan's Island* (in which seven people are stranded together on a Pacific island, yet never wind up having sex with each other or resorting to cannibalism), and the ghoulishly similar *The Addams Family* and *The Munsters*. *The Man From UNCLE*, a spy series inspired by the success of the James Bond films, made a teen idol out of David McCallum, who played secret agent Ilya Kuryakin.

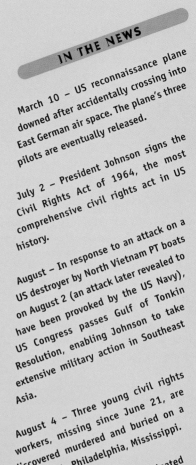

IN THE NEWS

March 10 – US reconnaissance plane downed after accidentally crossing into East German air space. The plane's three pilots are eventually released.

July 2 – President Johnson signs the Civil Rights Act of 1964, the most comprehensive civil rights act in US history.

August – In response to an attack on a US destroyer by North Vietnam PT boats on August 2 (an attack later revealed to have been provoked by the US Navy), US Congress passes Gulf of Tonkin Resolution, enabling Johnson to take extensive military action in Southeast Asia.

August 4 – Three young civil rights workers, missing since June 21, are discovered murdered and buried on a farm outside Philadelphia, Mississippi.

August 26 – Lyndon Johnson nominated for re-election by the Democratic party.

ballito Beatles
TEXTURED MESH
Seamfree nylons

George Harrison   Paul McCartney
Ringo Starr   John Lennon

Made in England by ballito for Scott-Centenaire Ltd. and solely

'64 The Munster family.

Popular soap opera *Peyton Place* became the first daytime serial to move to prime time, debuting on ABC two nights a week, but television's biggest advance in 1964 was strictly technological. On Sunday, December 20, between 9 pm and 10 pm, ABC, NBC, and CBS simultaneously broadcast in color for the very first time.

Movie News

Hollywood, continuing to feel the heat from its televised competitors, relied mostly on musicals (*My Fair Lady*, *Mary Poppins*), lavish costume spectacles (*Becket*, *The Unsinkable Molly Brown*) and all-star comedies (*It's a Mad Mad Mad Mad World*, *What a Way to Go*) to bring customers back to the theaters. Interestingly, two of the most popular films that deviated from the above

Left, centre: **Elizabeth Montgomery of *Bewitched* with the boys from *Bonanza* (*left*), and the castaways of *Gilligan's Island* (*right*).**

formulas came from England—Richard Lester's *A Hard Day's Night*, and Stanley Kubrick's *Dr Strangelove; or, How I Learned to Stop Worrying and Love the Bomb*. Like its stars, the former proved as popular in the United States as it had in the United Kingdom, while the latter was hailed by many as the year's best film (even if some conservative critics felt that its war-mongering portrayal of the US military was downright libelous).

Sean Connery once again packed theaters with his third Bond film, *Goldfinger*, although he was even better as Tippi Hedren's blackmailing employer in Alfred Hitchcock's *Marnie*; unfortunately, American audiences found Hitchcock's film confusing, and stayed away in droves. **Julie Andrews**, who had lost out to Audrey Hepburn for the lead in *My Fair Lady* (studio boss Jack Warner didn't think anyone in "the sticks" had ever heard of Andrews), won the Best Actress Oscar for her heartwarming turn as Mary Poppins.

Frankie and Annette were back in *Muscle Beach Party* and *Bikini Beach*, while Elvis settled comfortably into his post-army rut with a trio of abject mediocrities that combined musical numbers with even lamer comedic scripts—*Girl Happy*, *Kissin' Cousins*, and *Roustabout*. At least **Get Yourself a College Girl** featured some stellar musical performances by British invaders The Animals, jazz organist Jimmy Smith, and Astrud Gilberto and Stan Getz, whose gently swinging cover of Antonio Carlos Jobim's "The Girl From Ipanema" was one of the year's biggest hits.

Fair Flops But Art Goes Pop

Though it featured such attractions as Pepsi-Cola's "It's A Small World" ride, animatronic figures of Abe Lincoln and various dinosaurs (all of which eventually ended up at Disneyland), plus "picturephones" that allowed callers to see each other on four- by five-inch video screens, the New York World's Fair was actually a total financial disaster. Much more successful was Upper East Side gallery owner Paul Bianchini, who attracted plenty of media attention by turning his gallery into a faux-supermarket for an exhibition of pop art. **Andy Warhol**'s *Campbell's Soup Can* painting was on display, priced at fifteen hundred dollars, although you could get autographed cans of the actual stuff for only six dollars. You could also bring home a Warhol Brillo box for a measly three hundred and fifty dollars, while Billy Apple's *Slice of Watermelon* sculpture went for five hundred dollars.

Role Models

Though books like *The Feminine Mystique* were doing their best to thaw America's frozen gender roles, Kenner's new Easy Bake Oven and Hasbro's new **GI Joe** doll (*above*) indicated that society still had a long way to go. The Easy Bake Oven was a working miniature oven that taught young girls to "bake like Mom," while Hasbro's "action soldier" was specifically invented to keep young

boys from playing with Barbie dolls. Armed with various weapons of death and a nasty facial scar (for added masculinity value), GI Joe could be outfitted as a World War Two infantryman, marine, sailor or pilot. Immensely popular during the mid-sixties (Hasbro sold two million dolls in 1964), GI Joe fell out of favor towards the end of the decade, mostly due to increasing anti-war sentiment. In 1969, Hasbro recast him as an adventurer; instead of slaughtering the enemy, the new GI Joe was into manly pastimes like scuba diving, treasure hunting and space travel. Sales improved immediately.

IN THE NEWS

September 27 – The Warren Commission releases its report on the Kennedy assassination. The report concludes that there was no conspiracy, either domestic or international, to assassinate the president, and that Lee Harvey Oswald acted alone. Over 50 books on JFK are published by the end of the year, many of which dispute the Commission's findings.

October 14 – The Rev Dr Martin Luther King, Jr receives the Nobel Peace Prize.

November 3 – Lyndon Johnson re-elected President in landslide over Barry Goldwater, whose hard-line conservative views were widely viewed as racist, not to mention dangerously capable of leading the country into World War Three.

November 27 – *Life* magazine's cover story on Vietnam reports that the crisis is worsening.

ACADEMY AWARDS

BEST PICTURE

My Fair Lady

directed by George Cukor

BEST ACTOR

Rex Harrison

My Fair Lady

BEST ACTRESS

Julie Andrews

Mary Poppins

TOP ALBUMS

THE BEATLES

A Hard Day's Night
soundtrack

THE BEATLES

Meet The Beatles!

LOUIS ARMSTRONG

Hello Dolly

BARBRA STREISAND

People

THE BEATLES

The Beatles' Second Album

'65

The British invasion continued to roll over America, as groups like The Rolling Stones, The Kinks, Herman's Hermits, Freddie and The Dreamers, and Wayne Fontana and The Mindbenders capitalized on the country's appetite for all things "fab" and "gear." While many American musicians resented the attention paid to their English counterparts, The Beatles' success actually had a very positive effect on the country's music scene.

Before the advent of The Beatles, few American groups (outside of The Beach Boys and The Four Seasons) actually wrote their own material, relying instead on outside songwriters to keep them on the charts. Now, hundreds of American bands were following Lennon and McCartney's lead and bashing out songs of their own.

Shutting The Folk Up

The Byrds, an LA combo motivated and inspired by countless screenings of *A Hard Day's Night*, were one of the best of this new crop of Anglophilic American bands. But although the band included such talented songwriters as Roger McGuinn, Gene Clark, and David Crosby, it was a rocked-up cover of Bob Dylan's "Mr Tambourine Man" that sent them to the top of the charts in the summer of '65. Before you could say "**folk rock**," artists like The Turtles (who initially scored with a cover of Dylan's "It Ain't Me, Babe"), Barry McGuire ("Eve Of Destruction"), The Lovin'

65 **The Byrds, with Roger McGuinn wearing his trademark sunglasses.**

Spoonful ("Do You Believe In Magic"), and Sonny and Cher ("I Got You Babe") were arming themselves with twelve-string guitars and marching to the top of the charts. Much to the displeasure of hardcore folk fans, even Dylan himself "went electric,"

hitting the Top Ten with "Like A Rolling Stone" and "Positively 4th Street."

Movie News

The hills were indeed alive with the sound of music, but the endless

65 **Way-out sixties fashion from Pierre Cardin.**

parade of *Beach Party* knock-offs indicated that the surf and sand were really where the action was. Frankie and Annette popped up in *Beach Blanket Bingo*, *How to Stuff a Wild Bikini*, and *Dr Goldfoot and the Bikini Machine* (a *Goldfinger* spoof), but beach-movie addicts could also catch *Beach Ball*, *The Girls on the Beach*, *Wild on the Beach*, and *A Swingin' Summer*, not to mention *Endless Summer*, Bruce Brown's acclaimed surfing documentary. There was also *Ski Party* and *Winter A Go-Go*, which moved the beachfront shenanigans to the ski slopes.

But, for cheap thrills, you just couldn't beat *Faster, Pussycat! Kill! Kill!* Car

65 **Pop duo Sonny and Cher first climbed the charts in 1965.**

65 Russ Meyer's outrageous *Faster, Pussycat!* won an enthusiastic cult following.

crashes, judo chops and curvaceous women filled the screen in Russ Meyer's bizarre tale of three go-go dancers raising holy hell in the California desert. Although some Meyer cultists prefer his later, more sexually explicit films, *Faster, Pussycat!* still stands as the director's most inspired work.

Sean Connery continued to break hearts and box-office records with *Thunderball*, the latest installment in the Bond series, while Elvis continued his apparent quest to lose every vestige of credibility with *Frankie and Johnny, Harum Scarum,* and *Tickle Me*. Ten years after his starring role in *Sincerely Yours*, **Liberace** returned to the screen for two appearances: a musical spot in *When the Boys Meet the Girls*, and a hilarious turn as a funeral director in Tony Richardson's film adaptation of Evelyn Waugh's *The Loved One*. Rod Steiger, who played a Liberace-like embalmer in *The Loved One*, also received an Academy Award nomination for his portrayal of a concentration camp survivor in *The Pawnbroker*.

Camp Comedy

Ironically, the same year that produced *The Pawnbroker* also saw the debut of *Hogan's Heroes*, a television comedy set in that wackiest of all places, a Nazi prison camp. Bob Crane starred as Col. Robert Hogan, an American soldier who, along with his multi-cultural band of fellow POWs, made life miserable for Stalag Thirteen's foolish Colonel Klink (Werner Klemperer) and his bumbling aide, Sergeant Schultz (John Banner). Somewhere, the gods of bad taste were smiling ecstatically.

Jeannie Finds A Magic Formula

Green Acres, which starred Eddie Albert and Eva Gabor as a pair of Park Avenue swells roughing it in the country, was basically a reverse version of *The Beverly Hillbillies*. It seemed almost complex compared to *I Dream of Jeannie*, starring Barbara Eden (*below*) as a gorgeous genie indentured to astronaut Major Tony Nelson (Larry Hagman), whom she constantly referred to as "Master." Though screamingly sexist, the show did exude a great deal of good-natured (if vacuous) charm, and remained extremely popular with viewers during its five-year run. Less fortunate was *My Mother the Car*, in which an antique automobile was possessed by the spirit of its owner's deceased mother.

IN THE NEWS

February 21 – Civil rights leader Malcolm X assassinated by rival Black Muslims during a speech at Harlem's Audubon Ballroom. A vocal opponent of Dr King's non-violent measures, Malcolm X (born Malcolm Little) had pressed for blacks to seize equality "by any means necessary."

March 8–9 – 3,500 marines land in South Vietnam.

March 26 – 25,000 civil rights marchers converge on Montgomery, Alabama.

June 3 – Major Edward White completes the first US space walk, floating in space for 20 minutes while attached to Gemini 4.

June 28 – President Johnson announces that, in order to increase troop levels in South Vietnam, the military draft will soon be doubled from 17,000 to 35,000 a month.

November 20 – A week-long battle in Vietnam's Iadrang Valley leaves 240 US soldiers dead and 470 wounded.

November 27 – 25,000 anti-war demonstrators march on Washington DC.

December – US losses in Vietnam since 1961 now exceed 1,300 dead and 6,100 wounded.

December 24 – US temporarily suspends bombing runs in North Vietnam.

The sitcom set a new television benchmark for jaw-dropping stupidity, and was canceled after only a year.

Undercover And Outer Space

The success of the Bond films spawned two popular spy shows, *I Spy* and *Get Smart*. The former featured Robert Culp and Bill Cosby as globe-trotting undercover agents, while the latter, a comedy starring Don Adams and Barbara Feldon as agents 86 and 99, sent up the whole spy genre with ridiculous plots and fantastic gadgetry that never seemed to work.

Lost in Space, essentially *The Swiss Family Robinson* with a sci-fi twist, also debuted in the fall of 1965. It's best remembered for Jonathan Harris's bulging-eyed performance as the evil Dr Smith, and for the familiar "Danger, Will Robinson!" warning cry of the Robinson family's trusty robot.

Small-Screen Dean

Having already carved tremendously successful film and recording careers for himself, Dean Martin moved on to the realm of the small screen in 1965 with *The Dean Martin Show*. Though the show's comedy-variety format offered little in the way of innovation, Martin's affable, unpretentious, and seemingly inebriated manner made him an enormous favorite with the viewers.

More All Round

America's auto makers got some good news at the end of 1965: 9.3 million Detroit cars had been sold since January, the highest total in ten years. Not coincidentally, after shrinking steadily for the past five years, the average size of American cars was beginning to increase again. Most makers were also offering tons of "extras," essentially enabling customers to custom-build their own cars. The Toronado, the most innovative Oldsmobile in years, was introduced towards the end of 1965. The immensely popular fastback featured a 385 horsepower engine, a "split" automatic transmission (for a more even distribution of weight), a curved and contoured body, and flared wheel arches.

Bad news for General Motors—and the automobile industry in general— came in the form of *Unsafe at Any Speed*, **Ralph Nader**'s searing indictment of the industry's lax safety standards. Singled out for special criticism was Chevrolet's Corvair; Nader claimed that the car's rear-mounted engine made it especially susceptible to spin-outs. Although many through the years have insisted that the Corvair got a bum rap, Nader's book went a long way towards convinging the US government to impose heightened safety restrictions on American cars.

Hi-Balls At The White House

No safety restrictions were placed on slot cars; then again, at only a few inches in length, they didn't really require any. By mid-decade, slot car racing had become a popular pastime spanning elementary schools to college campuses; many towns even boasted special slot car centers, which allowed you to rent track time and race your car. Predictably, Aurora's Mustang model quickly became the biggest-selling slot car of all time.

Also popular with kids from eight to eighty was Wham-O's **Super Ball**, an impossibly high-bouncing ball made from high-density synthetics. Priced at ninety-eight cents a pop, the company sold close to seven million of them in only six months; McGeorge Bundy, special assistant to President Johnson, bought sixty of them for White House staffers as a means of stress relief.

Lava Light Fantastic

Another way of letting off steam (one that would become increasingly popular as the decade progressed) was to get stoned and stare at the waxy bubbles in your "Lava Lite." Chicago businessman Adolf Wertheimer first saw the English-made "Astrolight" in 1965 at a German home furnishings show; Wertheimer paid for the rights to market the eye-catching product in the States, changing its name to the "Lava Lite." By the end of the decade, he'd sold two million of them.

65 "Lava Lite"—the turned-on lamp.

Granny's Stuff Gets Strutted

Also good for long bouts of staring were Bridget Riley's "Op" art canvases. The artist's visually arresting black-and-white designs were immediately picked up on by fashion designers, who incorporated them into the **mod** styles that were becoming increasingly popular. Inspired by The Beatles, men were beginning to grow their hair longer, while fashionable young women were wearing Vidal Sassoon's "bangs and shingles" look; ironing one's hair to make it straight and shiny became an increasingly popular pastime. Must-have items for the feminine wardrobe included ruffled blouses, "helmet" hats, A-line dresses, skirts two inches above the knee, and high white boots. Granny dresses were "in" on the West Coast, as were granny glasses—Roger McGuinn of The Byrds, who wore granny-style sunglasses to shield his eyes from the glare of the stage lights, started the latter craze.

Dome Sweet Dome

The Astrodome, a stadium whose plastic dome protected players and spectators from the elements, opened April 9 in Houston, Texas. The first of the many "enormo-dome" sports stadiums that have since popped up across the country, the Astrodome—with its exploding scoreboard and "futuristic" orange color-scheme—looked something like an escaped Disneyland attraction.

Nation Favors Fun Flavors (But Bans Bad Taste)

In attempt to cut into Cool-Aid's dominance of the powdered drink market, Pillsbury introduced Funny Face, a new line of fruit-flavored drink mixes. Flavors included Goofy Grape, Freckle Face Strawberry, Rootin' Tootin' Raspberry, Lefty Lemonade, Loud-Mouth Lime, Injun Orange and Chinese Cherry, although complaints of racism got the latter two nixed. Taking a page from Cap'n Crunch's book, the flavors were given corresponding cartoon characters, all of which were seen in TV ads for the product. Needless to say, lots of kids asked Mom to put Funny Face on the shopping list.

In other beverage news, Pepsi changed Patio Diet Cola's name to Diet Pepsi. Dr Robert Cade, a sports physician studying the effects of heat exhaustion on the Florida Gators college football team, invented Gatorade, a drink that quickly replenished body fluids lost through perspiration. In 1967, Dr Cade sold the product to the Stokely-Van Camp corporation, who turned it into a billion-dollar product.

nineteen

As 1966 began, most Americans thought that **turning on** was what you **did** to your television, and that **taking a trip** was something that happened in the family car. By the year's end, however, both phrases had assumed entirely different meanings. Thanks to Dr Timothy Leary's exhortation to **"turn on, tune in, drop out,"** 1966 was the year that the concept of psychedelia first entered the public lexicon.

Mercury Cougar Dan Gurney Special

Hipsters and intellectuals had been experimenting with hallucinogenics for years (as had the CIA, as part of experimental mind-control programs known as Project Bluebird, Project Artichoke, and MK-ULTRA), but times were changing. Whether they were searching for spiritual enlightenment, looking for a distraction from their mind-numbing existences, or just trying to be "cool," young people everywhere were beginning to dabble with marijuana, **LSD** and (when they could find them) psilocybin mushrooms. Authorities around the country moved quickly to outlaw the hallucinogens (marijuana had already been illegal for decades), but the acid vibrations were already spreading from the hippie enclaves of New York's East Village and San Francisco's Haight-Ashbury district, on out to the endless tracts of suburbia.

Heroin, a drug still not readily available outside of urban areas, killed comedian **Lenny Bruce** on August 3. Harassed for years by various guardians of public morality over the "obscene"

nature of his act, Bruce was, in reality, one of the era's brightest and most irreverent humorists; while many stand-up comics have namechecked Bruce as an important influence, few have actually been able to match his combination of foul-mouthed outrage and wickedly perceptive social commentary.

High Moral Stand

As stories of illicit drug usage increased in the American media, musicians exponentially found their lyrics under scrutiny for drug references. "Eight Miles High," The Byrds' breathtaking new single, immediately ran afoul of radio

66 Acid-trip guru Dr Timothy Leary and his son Jackie in 1966.

censors who believed the song was about a drug trip; a quick scan of the lyrics revealed that the song was actually (as The Byrds insisted) about a plane flight to England, but the single was still banned in many regional markets.

Music News

The pop charts of 1966 were a strange mix of the turned on and the terminally unhip; The Beach Boys' groundbreaking "Good Vibrations" rubbed shoulders with The New Vaudville Band's corny "Winchester Cathedral," while Sgt. Barry Sadler's reactionary "The Ballad Of The Green Berets"—a bad-trip record if ever there was one—spent five weeks at the top of the charts. Frank Sinatra and daughter Nancy both had Number One singles in 1966; Ol' Blue Eyes with "Strangers In The Night", and Nancy with "These Boots Are Made For Walkin'." Nancy's long white "go-go" boots became an immediate fashion sensation, especially when worn with a mini-skirt for maximum eye-catching effect.

Free Wheelin'?

Bob Dylan, riding high on the charts with "Rainy Day Women #12 and 35" and "I Want You" (both from his acclaimed *Blonde On Blonde* LP), was the subject of much conjecture after a summer motorcycle accident took him out of action for the rest of the year. Some claimed he was dead; others that he was paralyzed, never able to perform again. While both rumors have obviously proved untrue, the accident, and the circumstances surrounding it, have never been fully explained; the prevailing opinion seems to be that the accident was less serious than originally reported, and that it provided a road-weary Dylan with a much-needed excuse to get away from it all for a while.

66 "Are you ready, boots?" Nancy Sinatra wears the archetypal sixties look she popularized.

The Monkees—pre-fab, but fab.

TOP SINGLES

THE MONKEES
"I'm A Believer"

SGT BARRY SADLER
"The Ballad Of The Green Berets"

THE NEW VAUDVILLE BAND
"Winchester Cathedral"

THE ASSOCIATION
"Cherish"

THE BEATLES
"We Can Work It Out"

Here We Come...

The Beatles' summer tour of America was a tense and relatively sour affair, as an out-of-context John Lennon quote about The Beatles being

playing on their first two albums (the band rebelled against producer Don Kirshner and took the artistic reins in time for 1967's *Headquarters*), "I'm A Believer" and "Last Train To Clarksville" were still some of the year's most enjoyable pop singles.

Batman and Enterprise Take Off

The other big television sensation of 1966 was *Batman*, a campy live-action interpretation of the popular comic book. Adam West and Burt Ward starred as "caped crusaders" Batman and Robin, whose seemingly endless supply of villainous opponents included The Joker (Cesar Romero), The Penguin (Burgess Meredith), The Riddler (Frank Gorshin), and Catwoman (variously played by Julie Newmar, Eartha Kitt and Lee Meriwether). Also making its de but was *Star Trek*, which followed the adventures of twenty-third century space voyagers boldly going **"where no man has gone before,"**. It was quite literally ahead of its time; though the show fared only moderately well in the ratings during

"**bigger than Jesus Christ**" inspired countless Bible Belt burnings of Beatles records and memorabilia, as well as boycotts of their concerts. Though the band was still massively popular in the US, many fans put off by the druggy, experimental sounds of *Rubber Soul* and *Revolver* (or the mildly tasteless "butcher cover" of their *Yesterday...And Today* collection) pined for the simpler "mop-tops" of yore. The Knickerbockers, a bar band from New Jersey, capitalized on this nostalgia for the early Beatles with "Lies," a Top Twenty single that wouldn't have sounded out of place on *A Hard Day's Night*. Even more successful were **The Monkees**, a prefabricated group whose weekly TV show of the same name blatantly replicated the groovy high jinks of The Beatles' films. Though the band was widely derided for not actually

its three years of existence, the crew of the starship *Enterprise* grew enormously in stature during the 1970s, thanks to a symbiotic combination of televised reruns and fan conventions. Still, the show had enough of a cult following during its original run that three of its cast members—William Shatner (Captain James T Kirk), Leonard Nimoy (Science Officer Spock) and Nichelle Nichols (Lieutenant Uhura)—all enjoyed brief recording careers. Although Nimoy and Nichols could actually sing, Shatner's album, *The Transformed Man* (which featured unintentionally

IN THE NEWS

February 21 – US resumes bombing raids on North Vietnam.

April 12 – B-52 bombers used for the first time on North Vietnamese targets.

May 1 – US forces fire on Cambodian targets for the first time.

May 15 – 10,000 anti-war demonstrators picket the White House, while the pledges of 63,000 voters to vote only for anti-war candidates are displayed at the Washington Monument.

June 2 – Surveyor 1, launched May 30, makes the first US soft landing on the Moon's surface. The spacecraft sends back more than 11,000 televised pictures before its batteries go dead.

August 4 – US announces a draft call of 46,200—the highest ever—for October.

Holy capes—it's Batman and Robin!

hilarious recitations of songs like "Lucy In The Sky With Diamonds" and "Mr. Tambourine Man"), was easily the most memorable release of the bunch.

Mission: Impossible, a popular TV espionage show, also debuted in the fall, although it would be another year before Peter Graves, the actor most closely associated with the series, would take the role of IMF head Jim Phelps. As good as the show was, it never truly lived up to the excitement of its kinetic opening sequence, which featured a lit fuse combusting in time to Lalo Schifren's memorable theme.

Movie News

America's appetite for all things James Bond-related continued to flourish— the Colgate-Palmolive company made plenty of cash marketing "007" grooming products for men. But with no new Bond film for 1966, Hollywood had to make do with *The Silencers* (starring Dean Martin as Matt Helm) and *Our Man Flint*, a stylish spy spoof starring James Coburn. If *The Ghost in the Invisible Bikini* represented the last gasp of the *Beach Party* series, *The Wild Angels* was the first of many low-budget films to exploit the **"sex, drugs, and motorcycles"** formula successfully. In the film's most memorable sequence, Peter Fonda's bike gang holds a raucous wake for deceased compadre Bruce Dern, whose last words were, "I just want to get high, man!"

The Wild Angels also helped solidify Nancy Sinatra's standing as the year's pre-eminent tough-cookie sex symbol, but even Nancy's boots were no match for the fur bikini sported by Raquel Welch in **One Million Years BC**; though dull in the extreme, the prehistoric cave opera did plenty of box-office business thanks to Raquel's considerable, er, charms. The underground film sex symbol of the year had to be Edie Sedgwick, the doe-eyed blonde whose performance enlivened Andy Warhol's otherwise interminable *Chelsea Girls*.

Cut Above

Following the lead of English designer Mary Quant, fashionable young women across America were going mad for the miniskirt. Featuring hemlines ranging from four to seven inches above the

knee, the skirts were often worn with decorative pantyhose. Another must-have 1966 item was the paper dress, whose disposable nature led *Life* to dub it "The Wastebasket Dress." Originally conceived by the Scott Paper Company, the sleeveless dresses came in a variety of wild patterns, and could be altered with a pair of scissors.

Twister Gains

"Left foot to red, right hand to yellow..." These familiar words echoed through rec rooms across the country, as children of all ages got down with Twister, Milton Bradley's "game that ties you up in knots." The game got a big boost when Johnny Carson and Eva Gabor played it on *The Tonight Show*; viewers picked up on the game's rather obvious sexual subtext, and three million sets were quickly sold.

Wild Things

The reverberations of the Ford Mustang continued to be felt throughout the auto industry. Mercury introduced the Cougar, essentially an upscale version of the Mustang, while Dodge weighed in with the Charger fastback. Even Cadillac got into the act; although not technically a sports car, the new four-wheel drive El Dorado was definitely aimed at a younger, hipper demographic. Most successful of all the Mustang clones was Chevy's new Camaro, a sporty four-seater with a base price of $2,466.

66 Raquel Welch's "cavewoman" charms boosted *One Million Years BC* at the box office.

"If you're going to San Francisco," sang Scott McKenzie, "be sure to wear some flowers in your hair." If you were young and hip in 1967, San Francisco seemed like the very center of the universe, the capital of the psychedelic sub-culture. It was home to KMPX, the country's first underground FM radio station, as well as *Rolling Stone*, whose first issue would hit the streets towards the end of the year.

Thousands of would-be flower children flocked to the city's Haight-Ashbury neighborhood, hoping to immerse themselves in the newly declared "**Summer of Love**"—or at least wear some tie-dye, score a bag of grass and find a place to crash. Tourists came to the Haight as well, looking to catch a glimpse of this mystifying new society; for only a few dollars, you could hitch a ride on Gray Line's "Hippie Hop" bus tour ("a safari through psychedelia") of the Haight. Annoyed Haight residents held a "Death of a Hippie" ceremony in October, hoping to convince the media, the would-be hippies and everyone else to get lost. It didn't work.

Monterey Blows Minds

The most memorable musical event of the year was the Monterey International Pop Festival, held June 16–18 in Monterey, California. If "The Summer of Love" was largely a media construct, the good vibes at Monterey Pop were definitely for real. The Monterey city fathers, who had braced themselves for an onslaught of debauched hooligans, were pleasantly surprised to see thousands of well-

'67 Hippies at a love-in.

mannered, neatly-groomed (most of the men weren't even sporting shoulder-length hair) flower children milling peacefully around the festival grounds.

Organized by record mogul Lou Adler and John Phillips of The Mamas and The Papas, the festival showcased the cream of the San Francisco music scene, including The Grateful Dead, Country Joe and The Fish, Big Brother and The Holding Company, Moby Grape, Quicksilver Messenger Service, The Steve Miller Band, and Jefferson Airplane, who were currently bringing some San Francisco magic to the charts with "Somebody To Love" and "White Rabbit," from the *Surrealistic Pillow* LP. The festival also fielded a diverse array of acts from around the globe, including The Who, Ravi Shankar, and **Jimi Hendrix**. The latter, a former sideman with Little Richard and The Isley Brothers, had transformed himself into a psychedelic guitar god during his recent stay in England. Monterey marked the first time Jimi had performed for an American audience since 1966, and he made it count; by the time the set was finished, his Stratocaster was in ashes and the audience shaking their heads in disbelief.

Otis Redding also experienced a major breakthrough at Monterey. A recording artist for Memphis's legendary Stax label (whose roster included Rufus Thomas, Booker T and The MGs, Eddie Floyd, and Sam and Dave), Otis specialized in down-home soul; given the fair to moderate pop success of singles like "Try A Little Tenderness" and "I've Been Loving You Too Long (To Stop Now)," he was completely unprepared for the ecstatic response he received from the Monterey festival-goers. Back home in Georgia after the festival, Otis penned "(Sittin' On) The Dock Of The Bay," a heartfelt tribute to the San Francisco "love crowd" that had made him feel so welcome. Sadly, he died in a plane crash on December 10, just three days after recording the song. Released in early 1968, it would become his first and only Number One single.

Imaginations Get A Goosing

Psychedelic poster art was everywhere, as talented folks like Wes Wilson and Carl Lundgren transformed handbills for upcoming shows at San Francisco's Fillmore Auditorium and Detroit's Grande Ballroom into truly eye-popping masterpieces; viewed under a fluorescent "black light," the effect could be positively mind-blowing. Working a more commercial (and legible) side of the street was Peter Max, an artist whose colorful, art nouveau-derived designs could be seen on clothes, inflatable pillows, General Electric wall clocks, dinner plates, and television commercials. *Rolling Stone* called Max "**The Walt Disney of Psychedelia**," adding that, "He blew our minds and goosed our imaginations with his stoned designs and colors, and then he Sold Out."

Walking a similar line between Haight Street and Wall Street were the lapel-less "Nehru jackets" that experienced a brief vogue around this time. Usually worn with turtleneck sweaters and love beads, the Nehru was especially popular with showbiz types like Johnny Carson and Sammy Davis, Jr. Maxis—ankle-length coats worn over miniskirts—were in with women, many of whom tried desperately to emulate the boyish look of **Twiggy**, the English model popping up on the cover of every fashion magazine.

Hollywood's Mood Swings

For the first time, the anti-establishment feelings swelling throughout the country were starting to be reflected in big-budget Hollywood productions, and not just in exploitation flicks like *The Trip*, *The Love-Ins* and *Riot on Sunset Strip*. In *The Dirty Dozen*, **Lee Marvin** (currently America's most popular box-office draw) led a group of murderers, rapists and other anti-social psychopaths in a successful mission against the Nazis. *Bonnie And Clyde* (starring Warren Beatty and Faye Dunaway) made heroes out of a pair of 1930s bank robbers, while *Cool Hand Luke* featured Paul Newman as an uncooperative inmate at a prison labor

67 Lee Marvin—leader of *The Dirty Dozen*.

detective (Poitier) and a redneck sheriff (Rod Steiger) investigating the same crime. But the film that touched the biggest nerve with audiences was **The Graduate**, which starred Dustin Hoffman as a directionless college grad involved in an affair with a middle-aged woman, played by Anne Bancroft. The poignant comedy made a star out of Hoffman, and the film's soundtrack (featuring "Mrs. Robinson") turned Paul Simon and Art Garfunkel into household names.

Just-So Stories

Of course, if you weren't into heavy messages, there was always *Doctor Dolittle* (starring Rex Harrison as the gent who "talks to the animals"), *Barefoot in the Park* (a light Neil Simon comedy about a young New York City couple, played by Jane Fonda and Robert Redford), or

The Jungle Book, Disney's enjoyable animated adaptation of Rudyard Kipling's jungle tales. Then, too, there was *The Valley of the Dolls*, an unintentionally campy adaptation of Jacqueline Susann's best-selling novel about the pitfalls of show business.

Hair Gets Everywhere

Offscreen, everybody was talking about the new hippie musical that had just opened off-Broadway in New York. Billed as "an American tribal

love-rock musical," *Hair* took the nation by storm, inspiring like-minded productions at college campuses around the country and spawning a best-selling original cast recording.

camp; the film's running line, "What we have here is a failure to communicate," would be shouted at anti-war demonstrations for years afterwards.

Sidney Poitier starred in *Guess Who's Coming to Dinner* and *In the Heat of the Night*; the former poked fun at the controversy surrounding mixed marriages, while the latter explored the tense relationship between black

JOSEPH E. LEVINE presents

A MIKE NICHOLS-LAWRENCE TURMAN PRODUCTION

"THE GRADUATE" x

starring ANNE BANCROFT

and DUSTIN HOFFMAN · KATHERINE ROSS

Produced by
LAWRENCE TURMAN

Directed by
MIKE NICHOLS

Technicolor® · Panavision® · United Artists

Macho Plymouth Now Even Hornier

America's appetite for sports cars seemed to grow greater with each passing year, and the folks in Detroit were only happy to oblige. In 1967, Pontiac introduced its Camaro-like Firebird, while AMC unveiled the Javelin; visually similar to the Ford Mustang and Plymouth Barracuda, the roomier car was a smashing success. Chevrolet responded to the sports car trend by restyling its Corvette, giving the car a curvier design that made the cockpit seem lower than usual. Though the new look was criticized by purists, the 1968 model set a Corvette sales record. Plymouth drew raves for its new muscle car, the 1968 **Road Runner**. Named after the popular Warner Brothers cartoon character, the tremendously powerful car came complete with Road Runner decals and a horn that actually went "Beep-Beep!" Priced at only three thousand dollars, it was a real steal.

Defiant Over Draft

As the anti-war movement continued to swell, heavyweight boxing champ Muhammad Ali made headlines for refusing to comply with the draft. Ali claimed exemption on religious grounds, adding that "No Viet Cong ever called me nigger." Failing to see his point, the World Boxing Association stripped Ali of his boxing title. Ali was also fined ten thousand dollars by the government and sentenced to five years in prison. The conviction was later overturned by the US Supreme Court.

TV Waist Deep In The Big Muddy

Almost as skinny as Twiggy, but considerably more animated, was Goldie Hawn, one of the many talented cast members of **Laugh-In**, a rapid-fire hour of comedy that debuted in a special NBC broadcast on September 9. Hosted by Dan Rowan and Dick Martin, the show's blink-and-you'll-miss-it humor (often based around cameo appearances by various celebrities) was a breath of fresh air compared to the predictable pacing of programs like *The Red Skelton Show*; given its own regular slot in January 1968, *Laugh-In* became an immediate favorite with viewers.

Other variety shows introduced in 1967 were *The Carol Burnett Show* and **The Smothers Brothers Comedy Hour**; the latter immediately got in trouble with CBS censors for openly criticizing the Vietnam War and the Johnson administration. A segment of Pete Seeger singing the anti-war "Waist Deep In The Big Muddy" was deleted from the show's debut episode, setting the tone for future battles between Dick and Tommy Smothers and the network. Though immensely popular with viewers under the age of thirty, the brothers received plenty of hate-mail over their liberal opinions and their regular inclusion of black performers on the show.

Far less controversial was *The Flying Nun*, starring a young Sally Field as the wing-taking Sister Bertrille, and *Gentle Ben*, about the adventures of a young boy (Clint Howard) and his pet bear. But for sheer televised offensiveness, you couldn't beat **The Frito Bandito**, Frito-Lay's Mexican mascot for their new Fritos Corn Chips commercials. A devious, perpetually grinning cross between Pancho Villa and Alfonso Bedoya in *The Treasure of the Sierra Madre*, with an extra dollop of racism thrown in for good measure, Señor Bandito was always thinking of new ways to steal bags of "cronchy Fritos corn cheeps." Not surprisingly, the Mexican-American Anti-Defamation Committee raised an objection to the animated spots. Although Frito-Lay denied any racist intentions, The Frito Bandito was eventually replaced by WC Fritos, whose WC Fields-like shtick was as inoffensive as it was unfunny.

IN THE NEWS

January 10 – Anti-segregationist Lester Maddox sworn in as Governor of Georgia.

January 27 – A space demilitarization treaty, forbidding the orbiting of nuclear weapons and territorial claims on celestial bodies, is signed by the US and USSR. On the same day, a launching pad fire kills US astronauts Virgil "Gus" Grissom, Edward White and Roger Chaffee.

April 15 – Massive anti-war protests take place in San Francisco and New York City.

May 13 – 70,000 people attend a pro-Vietnam War parade in New York City.

July 23 – The worst race riot in US history occurs in Detroit, killing 43 people and causing $200 million in damages. During the summer, race riots occur in 127 different cities.

October 21–22 – Anti-war protestors clash with police outside the Pentagon; 647 are arrested.

December – US casualty reports show that over 17,000 soldiers have died in Vietnam since 1961.

67 A young Sally Field plays *Flying Nun* Sister Bertrille.

'68
nineteen

1968 often seemed like one continuous riot. **Martin Luther King's assassination** set off a week of violence and destruction in ghettos across America. **James Brown, "The Godfather of Soul,"** single-handedly calmed the riots in Boston by staging a televised concert; faced with the options of **burning and looting or staying home to watch the Godfather**, most folks opted for the latter.

TOP TELEVISION SHOWS

Gomer Pyle, USMC

Bonanza

Gunsmoke

Family Affair

Laugh-In

With Dr King gone, there was talk that the civil rights movement would take a considerably more militant turn, a prospect that made a lot of folks in the government extremely nervous. The FBI stepped up its harassment of Eldridge Cleaver's **Black Panther** party; at the Summer Olympics in Mexico City, US track stars Tommy Smith and John Carlos were suspended from further competition merely for giving the clenched-fist "black power" salute during the 200-yard dash medals ceremony.

The anger and frustration in the air completely boiled over during August's Democratic Convention. According to most eyewitness accounts, Chicago's notoriously brutal police force actually started the trouble, wading into a peaceful anti-war demonstration with billy clubs raised. As pitched battles raged between protesters and police,

'68 America elects Nixon, and Streisand (*top*) wins an Oscar.

television cameras filled America's living rooms with disturbing images of cops beating anyone within reach. Vice-President **Hubert Humphrey** received the Democratic nomination over popular pro-peace candidate

Eugene McCarthy, but the Democratic Party's image was marred considerably by the violence at the convention; third-party candidate George Wallace also hurt Humphrey's cause by siphoning off important votes in Midwestern and Southern states. Claiming to have a "secret plan" to end the war in Vietnam, Republican candidate Richard Nixon squeaked to victory by a mere 0.7 percent of the popular vote.

Old Enough To Die

In 1968, American International Pictures released *Wild in the Streets*, a teen-exploitation film in which a rock star (Christopher Jones) is elected president of the United States after getting the minimum voting age reduced to fourteen. One of the new leader's first decisions is to pack up everyone over thirty and put them in concentration camps, where they're fed a steady diet of LSD. Though meant as a satire, the film had some obvious parallels with real life—the **Yippies**, a far-left political organization led by Jerry Rubin and Abbie Hoffmann, were fond of the slogan "Never trust anybody over thirty;" and many Americans were indeed questioning a system which stipulated that eighteen-year-olds were old enough to die for their country, but not old enough to vote.

Monochrome Fare For Color TV

For the first time in TV history, color television sets outsold black-and-whites, six million to five and a half million. But whether or not you watched them in color, the televised reports from the Democratic Convention riots seemed worlds removed from the whitebread fluff that dominated network programming. *Family Affair*, a sickeningly sweet sitcom about a swinging bachelor (Brian Keith) and his faithful butler (Sebastian Cabot, as the worryingly named Mr French) who are suddenly entrusted with the care of three children (Johnny Whitaker, Cathy Garver, and Anissa Jones), was more popular than ever in its third year on the small screen, while *Mayberry, RFD* and *The Doris Day Show* were two more entries in the seemingly endless string of wholesome sitcoms about small-town life.

Painful Hip

Laugh-In and *The Smothers Brothers Comedy Hour* aside, network TV could be even more embarrassing when it tried to be hip. *Julia*, the first series to star a black woman since 1950's *Beulah*, injected a bit of realism into the sitcom format, featuring Diahann Carroll as a young nurse whose husband was killed in Vietnam. *The Mod Squad*, however, was completely absurd; the plot followed three ultra-groovy youngsters (Michael Cole, Clarence Williams III, and Peggy Lipton), all of whom had abandoned their anti-establishment ways in order to work for "The Man" as undercover police officers. Much more plausible were *Adam-12* and *Hawaii Five-O*, two cop shows that were short on gimmicks, and long on intelligent scripts. The latter show, starring Jack Lord as the fabulously coifed Steve McGarrett, wound up running until 1980, a record for a crime-oriented TV show.

Calling The Shots

Bullitt, starring Steve McQueen as a cop who must play by his own rules in order to survive, was easily the most exciting cop film to come along in several years. Worth seeing for the amazing **car-chase** sequence alone, the innovative picture was a huge influence on 1970s cop films such as *Dirty Harry* and *The French Connection*. For pure creaking anachronism, you couldn't beat *The Green Berets*, an ultra-patriotic vehicle in which John Wayne convinces a cynical reporter (David Janssen) of the righteousness of America's involvement in Vietnam. Almost as frightening was *Rosemary's Baby*, Roman Polanski's adaptation of Ira Levin's best-selling novel; **Mia Farrow**'s neurotic screen presence was never better utilized than in her role as a pregnant woman who may be carrying the spawn of Satan himself. Stanley Kubrick's

68 Mia Farrow in *Rosemary's Baby* and (*inset*) Jack Lord in *Hawaii Five-O*.

January 30 – The Viet Cong's "Tet Offensive" begins, surprising US forces in South Vietnam.

March 28 – Violence mars a Dr Martin Luther King-led march in support of striking Memphis sanitation workers. Dr King promises to return for another march in April.

March 31 – In the face of increased anti-war sentiment and a strong primary showing by anti-war candidate Eugene McCarthy, President Lyndon Johnson announces that he will not seek another term.

April 4 – The Rev Dr Martin Luther King assassinated in Memphis.

April 15 – Chicago Mayor Richard J Daley issues a "shoot to kill" order to the city's police force for anyone involved in cases of arson, looting or rioting.

June 3 – Andy Warhol shot and seriously wounded by radical feminist Valerie Solanis.

June 5 – Senator Robert F Kennedy assassinated in Los Angeles, shortly after acknowledging his victory in the California Democratic primary. Sirhan B Sirhan, a Jordanian, is arrested in connection with the shooting.

2001: A Space Odyssey was the ultimate "head" film of 1968, a dazzlingly visual sci-fi epic which took on mystical meanings when viewed through a marijuana haze. Also ambitious, but not nearly as successful, was *Head*, The Monkees' markedly psychedelic attempt to rid themselves of their teeny-bopper reputation. Unfortunately, it served only to alienate their core following, while the unconverted stayed well away. They were probably all at **Planet of the Apes**, anyway; the sci-fi film, about a group of astronauts who encounter a strangely familiar world ruled by talking apes, was one of the year's biggest hits.

Singles Slip From Cutting Edge...

A year after the release of *The Graduate*, Simon and Garfunkel continued to sell records like crazy, hitting the singles charts with "Scarborough Fair/Canticle" and "Mrs Robinson", and the album charts with *Bookends* and *The Graduate*. In fact, the album charts were becoming noticeably hipper than the singles charts. Thanks to *Sergeant Pepper's Lonely Hearts Club Band*, singles were now increasingly seen as **a disposable medium**, a prejudice that was only intensified by the singles chart success of bubblegum acts like John Fred and His Playboy Band ("Judy In Disguise [With Glasses]") and The Lemon Pipers ("Green Tambourine"). There were a few exceptions, of course; James Brown's "Say It Loud—I'm Black And I'm Proud" was one of the best and boldest Top Ten singles of 1968, while The Temptations tackled the subject of drug abuse with "Cloud Nine," which made it to number six on the charts by the year's end.

...As Albums Make Their Mark

Albums, on the other hand, were where musicians could extend their songs, experiment with sounds and really make an artistic statement, *man*. Copies of Big Brother And The Holding Company's *Cheap Thrills*, Jimi Hendrix's *Electric Ladyland*, or The Doors' *Waiting For The Sun* were as ubiquitous in hippie pads as beanbag chairs, while albums like Love's *Forever Changes* and The Velvet Underground's *White Light/White Heat* proved incredibly influential despite their relative lack of sales. Of course, albums were also an open invitation to **unbridled self-indulgence**, best exemplified by Iron Butterfly's phenomenally successful *In-A-Gadda-Da-Vida*; most people bought it for side two, which consisted entirely of a seventeen-minute version of the title track, complete with seemingly endless drum solo.

Up And Way Or Over The Top?

When The Fifth Dimension scored a huge 1967 hit with "Up Up And Away," suddenly everybody wanted a piece of young Oklahoma-born songwriter **Jimmy Webb**. Webb's complex, impressionistic pop compositions made their mark again in 1968, as Glen Campbell took "Wichita Lineman" to the top of the country and adult contemporary charts (as well as number three in the pop charts), and Richard Harris made it into the number two spot on the pop charts with a fabulously overwrought "MacArthur Park."

68 Glen Campbell with Bobbie Gentry.

Raiders Praise Judge

Paul Revere and The Raiders, an excellent singles band whose Revolutionary War uniforms and fratboy humor were the very antithesis of the psychedelic age, stemmed the decline in their fortunes by doing commercials for The Judge, Pontiac's new, improved GTO. "The Judge will rule," sang The Raiders; with its

June 6 – James Earl Ray arrested in London for the assassination of Dr King.

June 23 – Vietnam War officially becomes the longest war in US history. Death toll passes 30,000 by the end of the year.

August 8 – Richard M Nixon nominated for presidency by Republican National Convention.

August 26–29 – Hubert H Humphrey nominated for presidency by Democratic National Convention.

October 3 – George Wallace announces third-party candidacy.

October 19 – Jackie Kennedy marries Greek shipping magnate Aristotle Onassis.

November 5 – Richard Nixon narrowly elected president.

November 14 – "National Turn In Your Draft Card Day" inspires draft-card burning at college campuses across the country.

powerful engine, loudly striped paint job and flared wheel arches, it most certainly did.

If You're Lookin' For Elvis

Just when it seemed like Elvis would never come back from his self-imposed purgatory of forgettable records and worse films, NBC's Elvis special, broadcast December 3, showed that The King still had life left in him yet. Fondly remembered as "The '68 Comeback," the show featured a newly slim Elvis garbed in black leather and singing, for a change, as if he actually meant it. "If you're lookin' for trouble," he sneered in the opening number, "you're in the right place." Elvis fans everywhere breathed a sigh of joy and relief.

Emissions Now A Big Issue

In 1968, Detroit auto makers were feeling heat from two sides: not only were Volkswagens and Japanese imports selling steadily, but now the federal government was imposing strict emissions and safety standards on all US models. Detroit attempted to fend off the foreigners by continuing to produce and refine their sports car lines. Ford introduced its sporty Torino Cobra, a mid-sized car that could go from zero to sixty in 7.2 seconds. Mercury lengthened and widened its Cougar models, while Pontiac had massive success with its new Firebird Trans Am, a sexily striped sports car in the Camaro vein.

Crumb Leads Break Away

R Crumb's Zap Comics debuted in 1968. Sold by hand on the streets of Haight-Ashbury, the tremendously influential comic single-handedly started the underground comics boom. Artists like Gilbert Shelton, S Clay Wilson, Spain Rodriguez, Rick Griffin, Dan O'Neill, Justin Green, Kim Deitch, and Crumb himself delved deeply into subjects that the likes of Marvel Comics would never touch—namely, sex, drugs, and the warped realities of daily life.

Like The Circles That You Find...

Aspiring psychedelic artists received an unexpected hand when the Kenner toy company introduced Spirograph, a drawing aid that allowed you to make

68 The outrageous "Springtime For Hitler" number from Mel Brooks' *The Producers*, a 1968 movie release.

colorful mandalas with the push of a pen (push too hard, though, and you ripped the paper). Soon, schoolkids everywhere were making their own tripped-out masterpieces, as parents and teachers looked on in approval.

TOP SINGLES

THE BEATLES
"Hey Jude"

MARVIN GAYE
"I Heard It Through The Grapevine"

PAUL MAURIAT
"Love Is Blue"

BOBBY GOLDSBORO
"Honey"

THE RASCALS
"People Got To Be Free"

"That's one small step for a man, one giant leap for mankind," announced astronaut Neil Armstrong on July 20, as he touched the surface of the Moon for the first time. A month later, many were making the same claim for Woodstock. A three-day music festival held near Bethel, New York, the Woodstock Music and Art Fair began life as benefit to raise money for the construction of a recording studio in the artists' enclave of Woodstock, New York. But once the town got wind of the anticipated size of the event, the festival organizers had to find somewhere else to hold it.

'69

Finally, a local farmer named Max Yasgur donated the use of one of his cow pastures, and the festival was able to go on as planned on August 15. Expecting an attendance figure of about a hundred thousand people, the promoters were shocked to see roughly three to four times that many converging on the festival grounds; realizing that it would be futile to attempt to keep people from sneaking in, the promoters threw up their hands and declared it a free festival.

Woodstock: Mellow In The Mud Bath

The concert itself featured performances by such luminaries as Jimi Hendrix, The Who, Sly and The Family Stone, Janis Joplin, The Jefferson Airplane, Crosby, Stills and Nash, Santana, Arlo Guthrie, Richie Havens, Ten Years After, Joe Cocker, Joan Baez, Canned Heat, Mountain, and Country Joe and The Fish, all of whom further bolstered their careers and/or legends about them by making the scene. Captured for posterity on film and

tape, the festival went a long way towards establishing the hierarchy of rock performers throughout the next decade; if talented bands like The Rascals and Tommy James and The Shondells hadn't turned down invitations to play, their present standing among rock fans and pop historians would probably be much higher.

In the end, though, the festival wasn't so much about the performers (many of whom left by helicopter as soon as their sets were finished) as about the attendees themselves. The sanitation facilities provided would have proved woefully inadequate for a gathering one quarter of its size, and steady rains turned the festival grounds into a mini-disaster area. And yet, in spite of the appalling conditions, the food shortages and the massive amounts of questionable drugs being consumed—"The brown acid now circulating among us is not specifically too good," was one of the more memorable stage

'69 Getting on down at Woodstock.

'69 The *Sesame Street* puppets made learning fun.

announcements—everybody just smiled, rolled in the mud and grooved on the good music and **happy vibes**. The festival had swelled to the size of a small city but, with the possible exception of Pete Townshend booting Abbie Hoffman off the stage during The Who's set, no incidents of violence were reported. (Of the two fatalities recorded, one was due to drug overdose, the other to a tractor accident.)

Altamont: Angels Rush In

For many, this was proof that the "Age of Aquarius" was indeed at hand. Unfortunately, the violence that permeated The Rolling Stones' disastrous Altamont Raceway concert proved, just months later, that such optimism was somewhat premature. Hired (for five hundred dollars' worth of beer) to serve as security guards for the free show, a group of Hell's Angels beat hundreds of concertgoers within inches of their lives, and stabbed a young black man named Meredith Hunter to death. If this was the dawning of a new age, it obviously had the potential to get extremely ugly.

In The Moog

Johann Sebastian Bach made the Top Ten in 1969, courtesy of *Switched-On Bach*, Walter Carlos' LP of Bach compositions played on the Moog synthesizer. The album's success inspired a deluge of records like Martin Denny's *Exotic Moog*, Marty Gold's *Moog Plays The Beatles*, and The Moog Machine's *Switched-On Rock*, all of which featured familiar pop and rock melodies tapped out on the

Moog. While none of these records matched *Switched-On Bach*'s success, they did plant the seeds for the coming integration of synthesizers into the rock format.

Joining Forces

Miles Davis paved the way for the jazz fusion movement of the 1970s with the release of *In A Silent Way* and *Bitches Brew*, two albums that mixed jazz rhythms and changes with an amplified rock sound. Over in Ann Arbor, Michigan, The MC5 and The Stooges were experimenting with their own fusions of high-energy rock and free jazz; though their records would ultimately prove extremely influential, both bands were continually beset by label hassles, bad press (*Rolling Stone* was particularly dismissive) and drug problems—a recipe for disaster that became all too familiar during the next decade.

Big Country

Musical programming of the country variety was especially popular in 1969, which many observers took as a sign of

increasing Middle-America backlash against the counter-culture. In any case, The *Glen Campbell Goodtime Hour*, *The Johnny Cash Show*, and *Hee Haw* all brought some of country music's finest talents into America's living rooms. First broadcast as a summer replacement for the *Smothers Brothers Comedy Hour* (canceled by CBS after Tommy Smothers had gone to Washington to petition support from liberal Congressmen), *Hee Haw*'s combination of musical segments and corny "farmer's daughter" skits proved so popular that the show remained in syndication for over twenty years.

Another of the year's televised musical highlights was the wedding of **Tiny Tim** and Miss Vicki. Tim, whose real name was Herbert Khaury, was a ukulele-playing eccentric who'd had a huge hit with 1968's "Tip-Toe Thru' The Tulips With Me." Now, with his novelty starting to wear thin, Tim correctly surmised that marrying Miss Vicki (Victoria Budinger) on *Johnny Carson's Tonight Show* would give his career another boost.

Sesame Opens

Two new medical dramas were added to the fall lineup, with immediate success—ABC's *Marcus Welby, MD*, starring Robert Young as the kindly physician of the title, and *Medical Center*, starring James Daly and Chad Everett. Also debuting in the fall was *Sesame Street*, an educational children's program broadcast on the

TOP SINGLES

THE 5TH DIMENSION
"Aquarius/Let The Sunshine In"

ZAGER AND EVANS
"In The Year 2525 (Exordium And Terminus)"

THE BEATLES
"Get Back"

THE ARCHIES
"Sugar, Sugar"

SLY AND THE FAMILY STONE
"Everyday People"

new, federally-created PBS network. In no time at all, American pre-schoolers were treating *Sesame Street* characters Big Bird, Ernie and Bert, and Oscar the Grouch like members of the family.

X For Xcess?

American pre-schoolers (or anyone under eighteen, for that matter), were strictly forbidden from seeing *Midnight Cowboy*, the first major studio film to be given an "X" rating under the Motion Picture Association of America's new rating system. Actually, whether it was the wife-swapping of *Bob & Carol & Ted & Alice* or the bloody violence of Samuel Peckinpah's *The Wild Bunch*, there was much in the theaters that was unsuitable for younger viewers. But despite (or perhaps because of) the prohibitive rating, *Midnight Cowboy*'s tale of two New York City hustlers (Jon Voight and Dustin Hoffman) proved immensely lucrative at the box office.

Buck In The Trends

Easy Rider, a low-budget film about two hippie bikers (Peter Fonda and Dennis Hopper) who set off to find "the real

ACADEMY AWARDS

BEST PICTURE

Midnight Cowboy
directed by John Schlesinger

BEST ACTOR

John Wayne
True Grit

BEST ACTRESS

Maggie Smith
The Prime of Miss Jean Brodie

quarterback who led AFL upstarts the New York Jets to a 16–7 victory over the NFL's Baltimore Colts in Super Bowl III. Once a shy boy from a small town in Alabama, "Broadway Joe" was now the epitome of the swinging, late-1960s bachelor, and was often spotted hitting the hot Big Apple nightspots decked out in bell-bottoms, medallions and questionable facial hair. Hollywood beckoned (1971's *CC and Company*, with Ann-Margret), as did the restaurant business (the "Broadway Joe's" chain failed to outlive the next decade),

but Namath remains best remembered for his football accomplishments—and for a bizarre series of pantyhose ads in which he remarked, "If they make my legs look this good, just think what they'll do for yours!"

Sweet Sorrow

As the 1960s ended, the grand American tradition of "nickel candy" ended with it; when Hershey raised the prices of its chocolate bars from five to ten cents apiece, the nation's other candy manufacturers quickly followed suit. In other not-so-sweet news, cyclamates—chemicals used to sweeten sugar-free sodas—were determined to cause cancer, and soft drink companies scrambled to find a suitable sugar substitute. There weren't any cyclamates in Hop 'N' Gator, the new beverage from Gatorade inventor Dr Robert Cade, but consumers apparently found the idea of a specially-brewed mixture of beer and Gatorade to be extremely off-putting. After a few months, the product vanished from the market, never to be seen again.

IN THE NEWS

August 9 – Sharon Tate and four others murdered in Los Angeles by followers of cult leader Charles Manson. Manson and several others are indicted for the murders in December.

October 15 – Vietnam Moratorium Day observed by millions across the country with prayer vigils, candlelight processions, and black armbands. Vice-President Spiro Agnew calls protest leaders "an effete corps of impudent snobs."

November 3 – Nixon announces that North Vietnamese have rejected his secret US peace proposals; asks nation to support "Vietnamization" of the war.

November 11 – Pro-war demonstrators, called "the great silent majority" by Nixon, march on Veterans' Day.

November 14 – Single-file "march against death" brings 250,000 to Washington DC; 100,000 march against the war in San Francisco.

November 16 – News reports accuse a US infantry unit, led by Lt William Calley, of committing a massacre at My Lai 4, a South Vietnam village. More than 450 villagers were killed in the attack, which took place in March 1968.

America" and wind up riddled with bullets from a redneck's shotgun, was another of the year's big box-office successes; soon, every Hollywood studio wanted its own low-budget, counter-culture project. They also all wanted **Robert Redford**; *Butch Cassidy and The Sundance Kid*, another anti-hero film in the vein of *Bonnie And Clyde*, elevated Redford to the same heartthrob status his co-star, Paul Newman, had occupied for the past decade.

Broadway Joe

Another new male sex symbol for 1969 was Joe Namath, the brash

69 Jack Nicholson hangs out with "Captain America" (Peter Fonda) in *Easy Rider*.

nineteen

'70

With the **killings at Kent State on May 4**, the divisions between the political left and right, between the **anti- and pro-war factions**, between the young and the old all seemed to grow ever wider. In the spring of 1970, anti-war demonstrations were part of virtually every college commencement ceremony in the country. Vassar grads wore **peace signs** on their gowns and mortarboards, while Tufts students boycotted their official ceremony to stage their own program.

'70 The Carpenters.

'70 The President meets The King.

The Tufts ceremony featured Simon and Garfunkel songs and a tribute to Tufts alumni killed in Southeast Asia. Even small-town schools got into the act; at Wilson college in Chambersburg, Pennsylvania, students greeted guest of honor Mamie Eisenhower with placards depicting black-shrouded skulls.

Troubled Water

Not surprisingly, the tension in the air made its way into the music. In July, Crosby, Stills, Nash, and Young followed their version of Joni Mitchell's hopeful "Woodstock" with the release of Neil Young's scathing "Ohio;" the song, which placed blame for the deaths of the four Kent State students directly on the doorstep of the White House, made it to number fourteen in the pop charts. The Temptations scored a number three pop hit the same month with "Ball of Confusion (That's What The World Is Today)," a single that seemed like a polite understatement next to Edwin Starr's angry "War," which spent three weeks at the top of the charts in September.

Sound Surround

But record buyers were looking for solace as well as catharsis, and many of them found it in the disparate worlds of soft rock and heavy metal. James Taylor's *Sweet Baby James* and Joni Mitchell's *Ladies Of The Canyon* were the dual cornerstones of the burgeoning "sensitive singer-songwriter" movement, while Bread's "Make It With You" and The Carpenters' "(They Long To Be) Close To You" filled the AM airwaves with melodic softness. On the flip side of the coin, Blue Cheer, Vanilla Fudge, and Iron Butterfly had all struck individual blows for **heavy rock** during the late sixties; but now Mountain, The Amboy Dukes, Frijid Pink, Cold Blood, The Frost, Rare Earth, Moloch, and dozens of other like-minded bands were coming out of the woodwork, cranking their amps past the threshold of physical pain, and playing simplified blues licks like there was no tomorrow. Biggest of all these bands was Michigan's indefatigable **Grand Funk Railroad**, who landed no less than three albums in the charts in a period

70 Janis Joplin

of ten months: *Grand Funk* came in at number eleven, *Closer To Home* at number six, and *Live Album* made it all the way to number five. If their music lacked a certain subtlety, at least it was really loud and you could boogie to it.

Tragic Chemistry

All of which made the death of rock's leading innovator even more tragic. Jimi Hendrix, whose approach to the electric guitar had completely revolutionized the instrument, choked to death on his own vomit on September 18th. He was twenty-seven. **Janis Joplin**, America's most popular white blues singer, was the same age when she died of a heroin overdose on October 4. Elvis Presley, no stranger to pharmaceuticals himself, was nonetheless concerned about the spread of illicit drugs in America. Or so he said in his letter to

President Nixon. In the year's most bizarre summit meeting, the President invited Elvis to the White House to award him a Drug Enforcement Agency badge, something that the badge-collecting Elvis had been coveting for some time. Nixon's aides mistakenly thought that Elvis might have some pull with young voters; for his part, Elvis advised Nixon that the best way to calm student unrest was to kick John Lennon out of the country.

TV News

One of Nixon's few popular moves in 1970 was signing a bill banning cigarette advertising on radio and television. Other good news for TV viewers was the introduction of three new high-quality comedy programs: the sitcoms *The Odd Couple* (starring Jack Klugman and Tony Randall) and *The Mary Tyler Moore Show*, and the variety-format *Flip Wilson Show*. The three most popular new shows among children were all about people (or animals) in rock bands: *Josie and the*

Pussycats, animated forerunners of bands like The Go-Gos and The Bangles; *Lancelot Link, Secret Chimp*, a live-action spy spoof starring a cast of chimpanzees, who also played together as The Evolution Revolution; and **The Partridge Family**, a sitcom about a family that decided to form a rock band. In the grand tradition of The Monkees, The Partridge Family (based on real-life family pop group The Cowsills) actually had several chart hits, including "I Think I Love You" and "I'll Meet You Halfway." David Cassidy, who played the family's eldest son and lead singer, was featured regularly in teeny-bopper magazines like *16* and *Tiger Beat*.

Import Fighting Grows Ugly

As America experienced its worst recession in several years, Detroit became increasingly concerned with the growing popularity of import cars. AMC responded to the situation with the Gremlin, a tiny two-door hatchback with a base price starting below two thousand dollars. Available in various unpleasant earth tones, the Gremlin was one of the quintessentially ugly cars of the 1970s. Much better looking was Chevy's new, sportier-styled Camaro; an immediate hit with consumers, the car would later be seen every week on TV's *The Rockford Files*. Less popular was the company's import-fighting Vega; along with an unattractive exterior, the compact was notorious for oil leaks and rapid body rust.

Rearguard Action Damages Ford

Ford's Pinto was, without question, the most notorious car of the decade. The popular compact's fuel tank was

mounted in such a way that left it extremely vulnerable in rear-end collisions, and the 1971–76 models were plagued by often-fatal fires and explosions. Numerous lawsuits ensued; instead of settling with the victims, Ford's lawyers fought the litigation all the way to the Supreme Court, thus severely hurting the company's reputation.

June 15 – US Supreme Court rules that "conscientious objector" status can also apply to those opposing the Vietnam War on moral grounds.

July 4 – "Honor America Day" observed in Washington DC by thousands of people marching in support of the Nixon administration's war policies.

September 13 – Timothy Leary escapes from a minimum-security prison near San Luis Obispo, California. Leary flees to Algiers, where he joins exiled Black Panther leader Eldridge Cleaver.

October 7 – President Nixon presents five-point peace plan to North Vietnamese, who reject it.

December – US troop deaths in Vietnam War rise to 44,000.

December 21 – Reduction of minimum voting age to eighteen approved by US Supreme Court.

ACADEMY AWARDS

BEST PICTURE

Patton

directed by Franklin Schaffner

BEST ACTOR

George C Scott

Patton

BEST ACTRESS

Glenda Jackson

Women in Love

70 "Love means never having to say you're sorry." O'Neal and MacGraw star in *Love Story*.

Movie News

Paul Newman (*WUSA*) and Barbra Streisand (*On a Clear Day You Can See Forever*, *The Owl and the Pussycat*) were the year's most popular movie stars, but audiences also flocked to see George C Scott command a tank battalion in *Patton*, Dustin Hoffman age a century in *Little Big Man*, and Jack Nicholson order a chicken salad sandwich in *Five Easy Pieces*.

The decidedly anti-war *M*A*S*H* starred Donald Sutherland and Elliott Gould as a pair of irreverent US Army surgeons serving in the Korean War. **Airport**, based on Arthur Hailey's best-selling novel about a plane in peril, started the vogue for all-star cast disaster movies that would last through the end of the decade. Written by future film critic Roger Ebert, *Beyond the Valley of the Dolls* was Russ Meyer's raunchy morality tale about an all-girl rock band trying to make it to the top—and with everyone in sight.

But the year's biggest smash was **Love Story**, based on Erich Segal's best-selling novel. Ryan O'Neal and Ali MacGraw were perfectly cast as the film's tragic lovers; O'Neal was nominated for an Academy Award for his performance, and MacGraw instantly became one of the most sought-after actresses in America.

Some Positions Examined

America's struggle to come to terms with the thorny issues of sexual revolution and women's liberation was reflected by the best-selling books lists. Dr David Reuben's *Everything You Always Wanted to Know About Sex*, J's *The Sensuous Woman*, Kate Millet's *Sexual Politics*, and Dr William H

Masters and Virginia Johnson's *Human Sexual Inadequacy* were some of the books taking up residency on the country's nightstands. Also popular, on a more underground level, were Jerry Rubin's *Do It!* (billed as "The most important political statement made by a white revolutionary in America today"), and *Soledad Brother*, a collection of George Jackson's prison writings. Jackson, serving a sentence for murdering a prison guard, was killed while trying to escape San Quentin in August 1971.

Tie-Dyed And Earth Bound

Fashion in 1970 seemed to have little rhyme or reason; while both sexes were wearing tie-dyed shirts, "unisex" bell-bottoms and second-hand military attire (for an ironic-yet-stylish comment on the Vietnam War), women were also wearing mid-calf hemlines, granny dresses, and "hot pants." The latter, an even shorter update of the previous decade's "short-shorts," were often made from suede or velvet and sewn with colorful patches.

"Earth shoes," designed so that one's heel sits lower than one's toe ("the way your feet were born to walk," according to the ads) became all the rage, despite being horribly unattractive. On the other hand, platform shoes were starting to make serious inroads with the "glam" set.

Search And Rescue

As the decade began, the search for self-awareness—a subject of much fascination in underground and collegiate circles since The Beatles' 1967 visit to India—became an increasingly mainstream concept. After the rampant consumerism of the fifties and early sixties, and the tremendous social upheavals of the last few years, many Americans believed that the solutions to their problems lay in "finding themselves;" as a result, many **self-help movements**, from Werner Erhard's EST to Transcendental Meditation (or "TM"), became extremely trendy.

70 Hot pants. Hmmm...

'71

As seekers of spiritual enlightenment began to explore various forms of Native American mysticism, the early seventies gave rise to increasing public awareness of Native American history and culture. In 1971, Dee Brown published *Bury My Heart at Wounded Knee,* a meticulously researched and deeply depressing account of the US government's genocidal ninetenth-century campaign against the American Indians.

Now also on the wrong end of the government's rifles, many young people began to realize that the "Cowboys good, Indians bad" attitude drummed into them by countless westerns might actually have been a gross over-simplification. One famous pro-ecology commercial even featured Indian actor Iron Eyes Cody shedding a tear over America's trash-strewn landscape.

Ejected From Alcatraz

On June 11, a group of American Indians ended their nineteen-month occupation of Alcatraz Island in San Francisco. The fifteen protesters, who were forcibly removed by US marshals, had claimed the island under a provision in a treaty between the US and the Indian nations which gave American Indians free run of unused federal lands.

Chart Topical

Native American consciousness made it into the pop charts as well, courtesy of The Raiders' "Indian Reservation."

Originally recorded by English vocalist Don Fardon, the song presented the plight of modern Native Americans in an empathetic, straightforward manner. Social commentary continued to be a viable way to have a hit record, as proved by The Undisputed Truth's "Smiling Faces Sometimes," The Chi-Lites' "(For God's Sake) Give More Power To The People," and Freda Payne's anti-war anthem, "Bring The Boys Home." Even Cher's melodramatic "Gypsies, Tramps And Thieves," her first major hit since 1967, dealt with the still-topical issue of racial prejudice.

Family Fortunes

There was still plenty of room on the charts for good clean fun, however. The Jackson Five, a group of brothers from Gary, Indiana, continued their chart dominance (they'd already scored four Number One singles between 1969 and 1970) with "Mama's Pearl," "Never Can Say Goodbye," and "Sugar Daddy", while thirteen-year-old lead vocalist Michael even stepped out for a solo smash, "Got To Be There." The Osmonds, another of the year's top acts, were like a white, Mormon version of The Jackson Five; while the band had hits with "One Bad Apple," "Double Lovin'," and "Yo-Yo," teen heartthrob Donny had hits of his own with "Go Away Little Girl," "Sweet And Innocent," and "Hey Girl."

Outrageous, Paranoic, Shafted

Alice Cooper (real name Vincent Furnier) stepped to the forefront of the rock scene; notorious for outrageous onstage antics (he was even rumored to have slaughtered chickens during a concert), Alice and his band actually produced two of the best hard-rock records of the year, *Love It To Death* and *Killer*. Frightening on a much deeper level was Sly and The Family Stone's *There's A Riot Goin' On*, which

'71 The Jackson Five.

viewed the current American malaise through a cocaine-laced veil of paranoia. *Shaft*, Isaac Hayes' wah-wah-fueled soundtrack to the popular film about a bad mutha ("Shut yo' mouth"), set the musical tone for the "blaxploitation" scores of the next half-decade.

Tapestry Puts The Pieces Together

James Taylor and Joni Mitchell were back, with *Mudslide Slim and The Blue Horizon* and *Blue*, respectively, but the light-a-candle-and-have-a-good-cry album of the year honors truly belonged to Carole King's **Tapestry**. At a time when everyone was still trying to come to terms with the radical changes of the last five years, songs like "It's Too Late" and "So Far Away" hit the zeitgeist square on the forehead, and kept *Tapestry* at the top of the album charts for nearly five months.

You've Been A Wonderful Audience...

Doors vocalist Jim Morrison, aged twenty-seven, died of a heart attack in Paris on July 3; he was followed three days later by Louis "Satchmo" Armstrong, whose gravelly voice made him even more famous than his superb trumpet playing. Duane Allman, the promising guitarist for The Allman Brothers Band, died October 29 in a motorcycle accident, aged twenty-four. Many also shed tears when Bill Graham announced the closing of his Fillmore East and West ballrooms; the venues, which were the hip places to play in New York City and San Francisco during the late sixties, had been hemorrhaging money for years.

Creative Accounts

Though the continuing recession caused many of the major film studios to tighten their budgets, the belt-tightening didn't really seem to hurt the quality of their projects. William Friedkin's *The French Connection*, Robert Altman's *McCabe And Mrs. Miller*, Alan J Pakula's *Klute*, Peter

'71 Gene Hackman as Popeye Doyle in *The French Connection*.

relied on excellent direction, good stories and en-gagingly complex characters rather than big budgets, and yet all except *Two Lane Blacktop* still made money at the box office.

Bad Ass Cinema

1971 was also the year that "blaxploitation" films—action pictures geared towards black audiences—began to appear regularly, led by Gordon Parks' *Shaft* and Melvin Van Peebles' *Sweet Sweetback's Baad Asssss Song*. *Billy Jack*, starring writer-director Tom Laughlin as a half-breed karate expert who faces off against "The Man," was another massive low-budget hit.

Bogdanovich's *The Last Picture Show*, Samuel Peckinpah's *Straw Dogs,* and Monte Hellman's *Two Lane Blacktop* all

jane fonda · donald sutherland in an alan j. pakula production

klute

Pricier, but just as silly, was Boris Sagal's *The Omega Man*; as the last living man in Los Angeles, Charlton Heston fought off an army of zombies, grimaced meaningfully and watched endless screenings of *Woodstock*. Watch out for the brown acid, Chuck!

TV News

In the grand tradition of Milton Berle, American viewers tuned in every week to see **Flip Wilson** dress up in drag. His female character, Geraldine, was *The Flip Wilson Show*'s most popular feature; her signature lines, "What you see is what you get!" and "The Devil made me do it!" became two of

IN THE NEWS

January 25 – Charles Manson, Susan Atkins, Leslie Van Houten, and Patricia Krenwinkel are convicted of the Tate-LaBianca murders.

January 31 – Apollo 14 mission launched; returns to Earth on February 9 with 100 lb of Moon rocks for study.

February 9 – The Sylmar earthquake kills 65 and causes $500 million in damage in Southern California.

March 1 – A bomb planted by the Weather Underground damages the Senate wing of the Capitol building; no one is injured.

March 29 – Lt William Calley convicted of premeditated murder in the deaths of 22 South Vietnamese civilians at My Lai. Calley's superiors are all acquitted, leading many to speculate that Calley is being used as a scapegoat.

71 *Shaft*—Richard Roundtree.

April 23 – Numerous Vietnam veterans return their medals and decorations as part of an anti-war protest in Washington DC.

May 3 – Anti-war demonstrators attempt to stop government activities by blocking traffic into Washington DC during the morning rush hour.

May 30 – US spacecraft *Mariner 9* achieves a successful orbit of Mars.

June 13 – The first installment of "The Pentagon Papers"—excerpts taken from the Pentagon's classified study, *History of the US Decision-Making Process on Vietnam Policy*—is published in *The New York Times*. Former Defense Department analyst Daniel Ellsberg admits to leaking the material to the *Times*, and is indicted for theft and possession of secret documents.

September 9–13 – 43 people die in riots at Attica State correctional Facility in Attica, NY.

November 24 – Somewhere between Seattle, Washington and Reno, Nevada, hijacker DB Cooper parachutes from a Northwest Orient jet with $200,000 in ransom money. Cooper, who is never apprehended, becomes an instant folk hero.

December 26 – The heaviest bombing of North Vietnam since November 1968 commences.

the year's most oft-uttered catch-phrases. People tuned in to **All in the Family** for very different reasons; as the bigoted, lower-middle-class dock worker Archie Bunker, Carroll O'Connor played a character that appealed as

'71 Peter Falk as Columbo.

BEST PICTURE

The French Connection

directed by William Friedkin

BEST ACTRESS

Jane Fonda

Klute

BEST ACTOR

Gene Hackman

The French Connection

ROD STEWART

Every Picture Tells A Story

much to those who laughed at his ignorance, as it did to those who shared his discomfort with the rapidly changing world around them.

Sanford and Son, an all-black adaptation of the popular British show *Steptoe and Son*, was almost as popular as *All in the Family*, and received almost as much criticism; many viewers felt that Redd Foxx's portrayal of a lazy, scheming junkman Fred Sanford (and Whitman Mayo's portrayal of Grady, Fred's wine-headed pal) only perpetuated **stereotypes** about black people. No complaints were made about the stereotypes of fat people perpetuated by *Cannon*, even though William Conrad's portly private eye was often seen helping himself to the delicacies of whatever locale he happened to be investigating.

Featured as a regular installment of *The NBC Mystery Movie*, **Columbo** (with Peter Falk in the title role) was one of television's more popular detectives. Decked out in a ratty raincoat and wrinkled suit, Columbo's mind was as sharp as his appearance was disheveled;

half the fun of the show was seeing him toy with criminals who almost never took him seriously. Clothes, or the lack thereof, were a big part of *The Sonny and Cher Comedy Hour*'s appeal, as viewers regularly tuned in to see what **Cher** would (or wouldn't) be wearing. Originally introduced as a summer-replacement variety show, the highly rated series gave the duo's career a new lease of life.

Smiley All The Way To The Bank

Manhattan button manufacturer NG Slater brought out his new line of yellow "smiley-face" buttons in 1969, but nobody seemed to want them. Perhaps it was increasing unemployment rates, or maybe people were just looking for an alternative to the ubiquitous peace sign, but in 1971, the buttons suddenly started to sell like crazy. Twenty million of the "Have a nice day" pin (as they became known) were sold in six months, ensuring that Slater would indeed have numerous nice days to come.

Wet Dreams

Also selling well was the Boogie Board, a new, smaller-sized surf board that anyone—even non-surfers—could ride. Real surfers, bemoaning the sudden influx of Boogie Boarders on their hallowed turf, cursed the name of inventor Tom Morey loudly and often.

In other aquatic news, furniture designer Charles Prior Hall patented a new invention of his own: the **waterbed**. Though it was the butt of many jokes (don't leave the windows open in the winter—it might freeze, ha ha ha), the waterbed soon became a necessary home furnishing for any self-respecting swinging single.

Disney Reveals Massive Plot

Walt Disney World opened in Orlando, Florida, on a 27,500-acre site, several times larger than that of Disneyland. The Disney company had spent years buying up lots in and around Orlando, hoping to avoid the buildup of sleazy motels like the ones that ringed their Anaheim park. The two parks themselves were similar in terms of rides and attractions, although Disney World's ample plot would eventually enable the park to accommodate larger attractions, such as the Epcot Center.

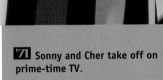 Sonny and Cher take off on prime-time TV.

CAROLE KING

Tapestry

JANIS JOPLIN

Pearl

GEORGE HARRISON

All Things Must Pass

SANTANA

Santana III

ROD STEWART

Every Picture Tells A Story

nineteen '72

In the wake of the Kent State shootings, and **with the Vietnam War still raging,** it was a matter of some debate as to whether **Richard Nixon** (and Spiro Agnew, his loose cannon of a vice-president) **would actually be re-elected in November.** But **"Tricky Dickie,"** as his detractors called him, **proved to be extremely resourceful** when the chips (and his approval ratings) were down.

Foreign policy was always Nixon's strong suit, and his historic visits to China and Russia not only improved relations between the US and those countries, but substantially boosted his popularity back home.

Though rumors of his administration's involvement in the Watergate affair continued to surface, Nixon received some unwitting help in the election from his Democratic opponent, Senator **George McGovern**. McGovern's original running mate, Senator Thomas Eagleton, was forced to withdraw from the race on July 31, when evidence surfaced that he had received psychiatric treatment for nervous exhaustion during the early sixties. McGovern's indecision over whether or not to stand by his man (R Sargent Shriver, the former head of the Peace Corps, took Eagleton's place in August) severely hampered his campaign's momentum; in addition, many moderate and conservative voters were put off by his proposal of amnesty for draft-

dodgers. On November 5, Secretary of State Henry Kissinger's casual hint of an impending Vietnam peace settlement sealed McGovern's fate; two days later, Nixon was re-elected with 60.7 percent of the popular vote.

Ms-Information

The burgeoning strength of the Women's Liberation movement was reflected in the US Senate's passing of the Equal Rights Amendment, which prohibited discrimination on the basis of sex. The amendment was then sent to the individual states for ratification; by the end of the year, twenty-two of the required thirty-eight states had ratified it.

Ms magazine, a monthly periodical edited by noted feminist Gloria Steinem, first appeared in 1972. Radically different from publications such as *Redbook* and *Good Housekeeping*, *Ms*, according to Steinem, wouldn't tell you "how to make jelly, but how to seize control of your life."

(platform shoes, flare-collared shirts, wide-lapelled suits) into the American mainstream. *Dirty Harry*, Don Seigel's fast-moving drama about a rule-breaking cop, turned journeyman actor **Clint Eastwood** into a film icon, and his "Feel lucky, punk?" line into a popular catchphrase. Burt Reynolds also saw his career take off in 1972; he received critical raves for his adrenalized performance in John Boorman's *Deliverance*, but it was a nude spread in the April issue of *Cosmopolitan* that really increased his popularity.

Women In The Spotlight

Marlon Brando, whose career had taken an erratic turn during the past decade, gave a memorable performance as Don Vito Corleone in Francis Ford Coppola's *The Godfather*. Even more memorable, for Academy Award viewers, was the sight of Sacheen Littlefeather, dressed in traditional Apache garb, stepping to the podium to accept Brando's *Godfather* Oscar. Ms Littlefeather, President of the National Native American Affirmative Image Committee, was allowed to read only a short excerpt from Brando's fifteen-page acceptance speech.

Barbra Streisand (*What's Up, Doc?* and *Up the Sandbox*) was the year's most popular female

Detective Harry Callahan. He doesn't break murder cases. He smashes them.

Clint Eastwood Dirty Harry x

CLINT EASTWOOD in "DIRTY HARRY" A Malpaso Company Production Co-Starring HARRY GUARDINO · RENI S LARCH and JOHN VERNON as "The Mayor" · Executive Producer Robert Daley · Screenplay by Harry Julian F Story by Harry Julian Fink & R. M. Fink · Produced and Directed by Don Siegel · PANAVISION® · TECHNICOLOR® Released by COLUMBIA-WARNER DISTRIBUTORS LTD.

Movie News

Superfly, directed Gordon Parks, Jr (the son of the man who directed *Shaft*), starred Ron O' Neal as a nattily attired coke dealer looking to make one last big score before getting out of the business. In addition to further fanning the flames of the "blaxploitation" fad (1972 also produced Barry Shear's *Across 110th Street* and William Crain's *Blacula*), the film presaged the infiltration of **cocaine** and flashy "pimp" clothes

ROBERTA FLACK

"The First Time Ever I Saw Your Face"

GILBERT O' SULLIVAN

"Alone Again (Naturally)"

DON MCLEAN

"American Pie"

NILSSON

"Without You"

JOHNNY NASH

"I Can See Clearly Now"

star, and Liza Minnelli and Diana Ross received raves for their turns in *Cabaret* and *Lady Sings the Blues*, but **Jane Fonda** received far more press—good and bad—than all of them put together. In protest at the Vietnam War, Fonda visited Hanoi and posed for pictures with a North Vietnamese anti-aircraft gun, a move which alienated her from many citizens and GIs. Even in the 1990s, long after she had settled into ruling-class respectability as the wife of broadcasting mogul Ted Turner, bumper stickers reading "Boycott Jane Fonda, America's Traitor Bitch" could still be seen on the occasional passing car.

Deep Blue

Linda Lovelace also received plenty of notoriety for her performance in *Deep Throat*, the first hardcore porn film to be released in commercial movie houses. Lovelace cheerfully made the rounds on the talk-show circuit (and even showed up at the Academy Awards) to promote the film, which ushered in a brief period where porn flicks were treated with the same curiousity and respect afforded to French art films. Years later, she published a book claiming she was forced into the porn business by her abusive husband/manager.

TV News

Maude, an offshoot of *All in the Family*, featured Bea Arthur as a voluble feminist, and *M*A*S*H* (starring Alan Alda as Army surgeon Hawkeye Pierce) continued in the anti-war vein of its filmic namesake; the popularity of both shows proved that programs with pronounced liberal themes could still be successful. Nothing beat good old-fashioned family values, something **The Waltons**, a heartwarming series about a rural family living in the Depression era, had by the wagonload. **The Bob Newhart Show**, another popular new show, was a well-crafted comedy whose basic premise—a psychiatrist and his group of eccentric patients—was tailor-made for Newhart's deadpan brand of humor. One of the year's surprise hits was *Emergency!*, an hour-long, multi-vignette drama that followed events at a Los Angeles hospital as well as a neighboring fire department. *The Rookies*, an early Aaron Spelling production about three new police recruits, also did well with viewers, although the show was one of many criticized for **excessive violence**. When the US Surgeon General released a study claiming that TV violence had little effect on children, it was widely slammed as slanted in favor of the TV industry.

IN THE NEWS

February 5 – Due to increased airplane hijackings, the screening of passengers and luggage becomes mandatory on all domestic and foreign flights by US airlines.

February 21–28 – President Nixon makes a historic visit to China, in which the two nations agree to work to lessen risk of war, to normalize relations, and to increase scientific and cultural ties.

April 16 – Apollo 16 launched; astronauts Charles Duke and Thomas K Mattingly walk on Moon's surface on April 20, conducting tests and collecting rocks.

May 15 – Alabama Governor George Wallace shot while campaigning for the presidency in Laurel, Maryland. The assassination attempt leaves Wallace paralyzed from the waist down.

May 22–30 – Nixon travels to Moscow, the first visit by a US president in history.

June 4 – Black activist Angela Davis is found innocent of abetting a 1970 courtroom escape that left four dead.

June 17 – Police arrest five men for breaking into the Democratic Party headquarters in the Watergate apartment complex in Washington DC. One of them is James McCord, a former CIA agent currently working for the Republican National Committee and the Committee to Re-elect the president. Democratic Party chief Larry O'Brien charges Nixon's campaign staff with "political espionage."

July 10–14 – Democratic National Convention nominates Senator George McGovern for president. McGovern vows to end the Vietnam War within 90 days of taking office.

Music News

AM radio was still king of the airwaves in 1972, embracing a wide cross-section of material that included soul (The Chi-Lites' "Oh Girl," Billy Paul's "Me and Mrs Jones"), soft rock (America, Don McLean), full-on schmaltz (Sammy Davis, Jr's "The Candy Man," Neil Diamond's "Song Sung Blue"), and novelty discs (Hot Butter's Moog opus "Popcorn," The Jimmy Castor Bunch's "Troglodyte"). Helen Reddy hit Number One with her feminist anthem "I Am Woman," while Michael Jackson topped the charts with "Ben," the lovely title song from a gory film about a killer rat.

Soul and funk music was growing in leaps and bounds, with the innovative arrangements of The Temptations' "Papa Was A Rollin' Stone," The O'Jays' "Backstabbers," and The Dramatics' "In The Rain" leading the way. **James Brown**, the hardest-working man in show business, paused between his successful "Talking Loud And Saying Nothing" and "Get On The Good Foot" singles to deliver the earnest anti-smack recitation, "King

TOP ALBUMS

CHICAGO
Chicago V

DON MCLEAN
American Pie

ELTON JOHN
Honkey Chateau

ROBERTA FLACK
First Take

AMERICA
America

Heroin," which also made the Top Forty. Stevie Wonder's *Talking Book* and Curtis Mayfield's *Superfly* were two of 1972's finest albums; the former featured "Superstition" and "You Are The Sunshine of My Life," while the latter provided the funky soundtrack to one of the year's most popular movies.

VD Catches On

With the economy at its healthiest since 1967, unemployment and inflation were way down from the previous year. The same could not be said for sexually transmitted diseases, however; according to Federal health officials, some 2,300,000 new cases of gonorrhea were reported in 1972, as well as a hundred thousand new cases of infectious syphillis, the biggest increase for either disease since the introduction of antibiotics. As many Americans participating in the "**sexual revolution**" were woefully uninformed about venereal disease, a series of "VD is for Everybody" public-service television ads were put into regular rotation on televison. Across the nation, confused children looked up from the family TV set and asked, "Mom, what's VD?"

The Denim Decade

Just when you thought that AMC's Gremlin couldn't get any uglier, the company attempted to capitalize on America's current infatuation with denim by introducing the "Levi's Edition" Gremlin, which came complete with copper rivets and denim-like blue nylon on the seats and door panels. Much easier on the eyes were the 1973 Lincoln Continentals, the first Continentals to be manufactured with padded vinyl roofs and oval "opera" windows. Lincoln stayed true to the popular look through the end of the decade.

Going For Gold

1972 produced American heroes in two unlikely sports. In Munich, swimmer Mark Spitz set an Olympic

72 Olympic champion Mark Spitz.

record by winning seven gold medals at the 1972 Summer Olympics, and was immediately deluged by offers of endorsements and movie roles. In Reykjavik, Iceland, **Bobby Fischer** became the first American to win the World Chess Championship, beating the USSR's Boris Spassky for the title. In the wake of his victory, retailers reported record sales of chess sets.

nineteen

'73

The draft had been ended, and the war in Vietnam was finally drawing to a close, but America was in no mood to celebrate. Everywhere you turned, there was unsettling news. In California, for example, Juan Corona was sentenced to twenty-five consecutive life terms for the 1971 murders of twenty-five migrant workers.

In Wounded Knee, South Dakota, armed members of the militant American Indian Movement held Federal forces at bay while calling for the free election of tribal officials, the investigation of the Bureau of Indian Affairs, and a review of all US–Indian treaties. There were endless lines at gas stations, thanks to the OPEC oil embargo, and nationwide meat boycotts resulting from inflated hamburger prices.

More troubling were the continued rumblings about the **Watergate** break-in, and the growing suspicion that the Nixon administration was unbelievably corrupt. Under sworn testimony, John Dean stunned the country with revelations of the White House "enemies list," a running tally of people targeted for IRS and FBI harassment because of their opposition (real or imagined) to the Nixon administration. On November 17, Nixon remarked to the Associated Press Managing Editors Convention: "People have the right to know whether or not their president is a crook. Well, I am not a crook." But as the House of Representatives busied itself preparing eight impeachment resolutions, it was looking increasingly as if nobody believed him.

Movie News
Given the downcast state of the nation, the success of period films like Paper Moon and The Sting made perfect sense; people were looking to escape to another time and place, and the simpler, the better. George Lucas' American Graffiti, with its big cars, teenage traumas, and soundtrack of rock 'n' roll classics from the late fifties and early sixties, provided a bittersweet snaphot of a time only ten years past, yet seemingly centuries away. Martin Scorsese made a name for himself with Mean Streets, a memorably intense film about two-bit hoods in New York's Little Italy, starring little-known actors Harvey Keitel and **Robert De Niro**; De Niro also starred in Bang The Drum Slowly, John Hancock's moving portrait of a baseball player dying of leukemia. Almost as gritty and exciting as Scorsese's film was Serpico, starring Al Pacino as a cop battling corruption in his own department, and The Harder They Come, a Jamaican film about a criminal who becomes a reggae idol. The latter film made an international singing star out of Jimmy Cliff, and went a long way towards popularizing reggae music in America.

Science And Religion On Film
Westworld (about robotic rebellion at a fantasy resort) and Soylent Green (in which the US government solves the overpopulation problem by turning corpses into food) were the year's two most popular science fiction flicks, while the filmic adaptations of popular God-rock musicals Godspell and Jesus Christ Superstar provoked endless arguments about who was the better Jesus, Victor Garber or Ted Neeley.

'73 American Graffiti captured the spirit of 1962—and grossed $55 million.

But, for the most part, if moviegoers weren't lining up to see Marlon Brando butter up Maria Schneider in Bernardo Bertolucci's *Last Tango in Paris*, they were plunking down money to see Linda Blair vomit pea soup in William Friedkin's **The Exorcist**. Blair became famous overnight as the twelve-year-old girl possessed by the devil, even though Mercedes McCambridge (voice) and Eileen Smith (body) deputized for her during the possession scenes (both actresses had to sue to get screen credit). In any case, the truly frightening film made more money than any horror movie before it.

Dragon Exits

After many years as a star in Hong Kong martial-arts films, Bruce Lee had finally broken through to the US mainstream (thanks to films like *Fists of Fury* and *The Chinese Connection*) when he died mysteriously of a brain edema at the age of thirty-two. *Enter The Dragon*, his final complete film, was a box-office smash.

Rock On The Box

Americans watched a lot of Watergate coverage in 1973; from May 17 to November 17, the three networks split live broadcasts of the hearings during the day, while PBS aired taped highlights in the evenings. Education of a cheerier note was provided by *Schoolhouse Rock*, three-minute educational cartoons broadcast during ABS's Saturday morning programming. The musical segments included "Multiplication Rock," "Grammar Rock", "America Rock," and "Science Rock," all of which proved remarkably effective as learning tools; today, you'd be hard-pressed to find an American adult between the ages of twenty-five and thirty-five who doesn't remember songs like "Three is a Magic Number," "A Noun Is A Person, Place Or Thing," or "Sufferin' Until Sufferage."

Equally instructive, in its own depressing way, was Elvis Presley's *Elvis:* **Aloha From Hawaii**; broadcast to over one and a half billion viewers in forty different countries on April 4, the concert showed what happens when a man believes his own press and eats too many double cheeseburgers. Just four and a half years after his remarkable "Comeback Special," The King looked haggard and overweight as he sleepwalked through classics like "Hound Dog" and "Blue Suede Shoes," but his notoriously forgiving fans still sent the soundtrack from the broadcast to the top of the album charts.

After *Kojak* made him a superstar, **Telly Savalas** also tried his hand at recording, but albums like *Who Loves Ya, Baby?* and *Telly Like It Is* weren't nearly as memorable as the wise-cracking, lollipop-sucking (a substitute for cigarettes, you see) New York cop he played on TV. Buddy Ebsen, an old song-and-dance man himself, came back from *Beverly Hillbillies* purgatory as the titular mild-mannered, milk-drinking detective on *Barnaby Jones*.

An American Family, Craig Gilbert's twelve-week PBS documentary about the Loud family of Santa Barbara, California, anticipated MTV's *Real World* by a good twenty years. Edited

73 Telly Savalas.

IN THE NEWS

June 25–29 – White House counsel John Dean testifies before the Senate Watergate Committee, implicating himself, White House Chief of Staff HR Haldeman, Assistant of Domestic Affairs John Erlichman, former Attorney General John Mitchell, and President Richard Nixon in the Watergate cover-up.

July 16 – Former White House aide Alexander Butterfield reveals the existence of secret recordings Nixon made of White House conversations. Though subpoenaed for them by special prosecutor Archibald Cox, Nixon refuses to release them.

July 28 – *Skylab 3* makes a rendezvous with the orbiting *Skylab* station; astronauts Alan Bean, Owen Garriott, and Jack Lousma perform further repairs and experiments.

September 4 – John Erlichman and G Gordon Liddy indicted in connection with the burglary of the office of Daniel Ellsberg's psychiatrist; following Ellsberg's leak of the "Pentagon Papers," the two were allegedly looking for evidence that would link Ellsburg to the KGB.

TOP SINGLES

ROBERTA FLACK

"Killing Me Softly With His Song"

DAWN, FEATURING TONY ORLANDO

"Tie A Yellow Ribbon Round The Ole Oak Tree"

PAUL MCCARTNEY AND WINGS

"My Love"

CARLY SIMON

"You're So Vain"

ELTON JOHN

"Crocodile Rock"

down from three hundred hours of footage, the controversial program is best remembered for the episode in which teenaged son Lance comes out.

Pop At A Low Ebb

1973 was, quite frankly, a rather dire year for American music. The New York Dolls recorded their legendary first album, and Iggy Pop and The Stooges released *Raw Power*. However, most Americans ignored them in favor of novelties like Tony Orlando and Dawn's "Tie a Yellow Ribbon Round The Ole Oak Tree" or sappy pop songs like Maureen McGovern's "The Morning After," the theme from the previous year's flipped-ship disaster flick *The Poseidon Adventure*. The Watkins Glen Music Festival, the last big Woodstock-style festival for several years, drew five hundred thousand people to see The Allman Brothers Band, The Grateful Dead, and The Band, but none of the performers played particularly memorable sets.

Sole Saviors

Soul music was once again radio's saving grace, with Gladys Knight and The Pips and former Temptation Eddie Kendricks scoring back-to-back Number Ones with "Midnight Train to Georgia" and "Keep On Truckin'," respectively, and The Isley Brothers offering up a sweet summer hit in "That Lady." Marvin Gaye's "Let's Get It On," The O'Jays' "Love Train," and Billy Preston's "Will It Go Round In Circles" all also topped the charts during the year, while War came close with the Latin funk of "The Cisco Kid" and "Gypsy Man." **Soul Train**, a black version of *American Bandstand* hosted by the impossibly smooth Don Cornelius, became *the* TV show to watch for black (and white) kids interested in the latest steps, sounds and threads.

Bach Bores, But Sex Scores

Richard Bach's *Jonathan Livingston Seagull*, an existential fable about an individualistic seagull, continued to top the book best-seller lists for the second year running, although it was tough to decide which was more boring—the

book, Hall Bartlett's film of it, or Neil Diamond's meandering score for the film. Alex Comfort's **The Joy of Sex** was much more exciting and enlightening, and became *the* sex

manual of choice for liberated seventies couples. The book's runaway success inspired a 1974 the imaginatively titled *More Joy of Sex*. Oh, and in case you were still wondering, the American Psychiatric Association boldly reversed its one-hundred year stance and announced that homosexuality was not in fact a mental illness.

Game, Set, And Match

In sports, George Foreman beat Joe Frazier for the World Heavyweight boxing title, while the nationally televised "Battle of the Sexes" saw tennis champ Billie Jean King beat Bobby Riggs in three straight sets at the Houston astrodome.

In football, **OJ Simpson** set a seasonal record for rushing yardage (2,003 yards); movie roles and product endorsements (including the ad for Dingo boots, *below*) followed in quick succession.

Glassy Smooth

A skateboard boom again swept the nation's sidewalks and parking lots, as newly introduced urethane wheels and fiberglass boards enabled skaters to enjoy a faster, safer ride.

Loungin' Around

The "leisure suit," a loose-tailored suit with flat jacket pockets, experienced a brief popularity as an after-work outfit. Often made from textured polyester blends and offered in distinctly non-professional colors like lemon yellow and robin's egg blue, leisure suits quickly became recognized as the mark of a lounge lizard, especially when worn with the winning combination of a half-unbuttoned shirt and a gold medallion. Hey, baby, want to swing?

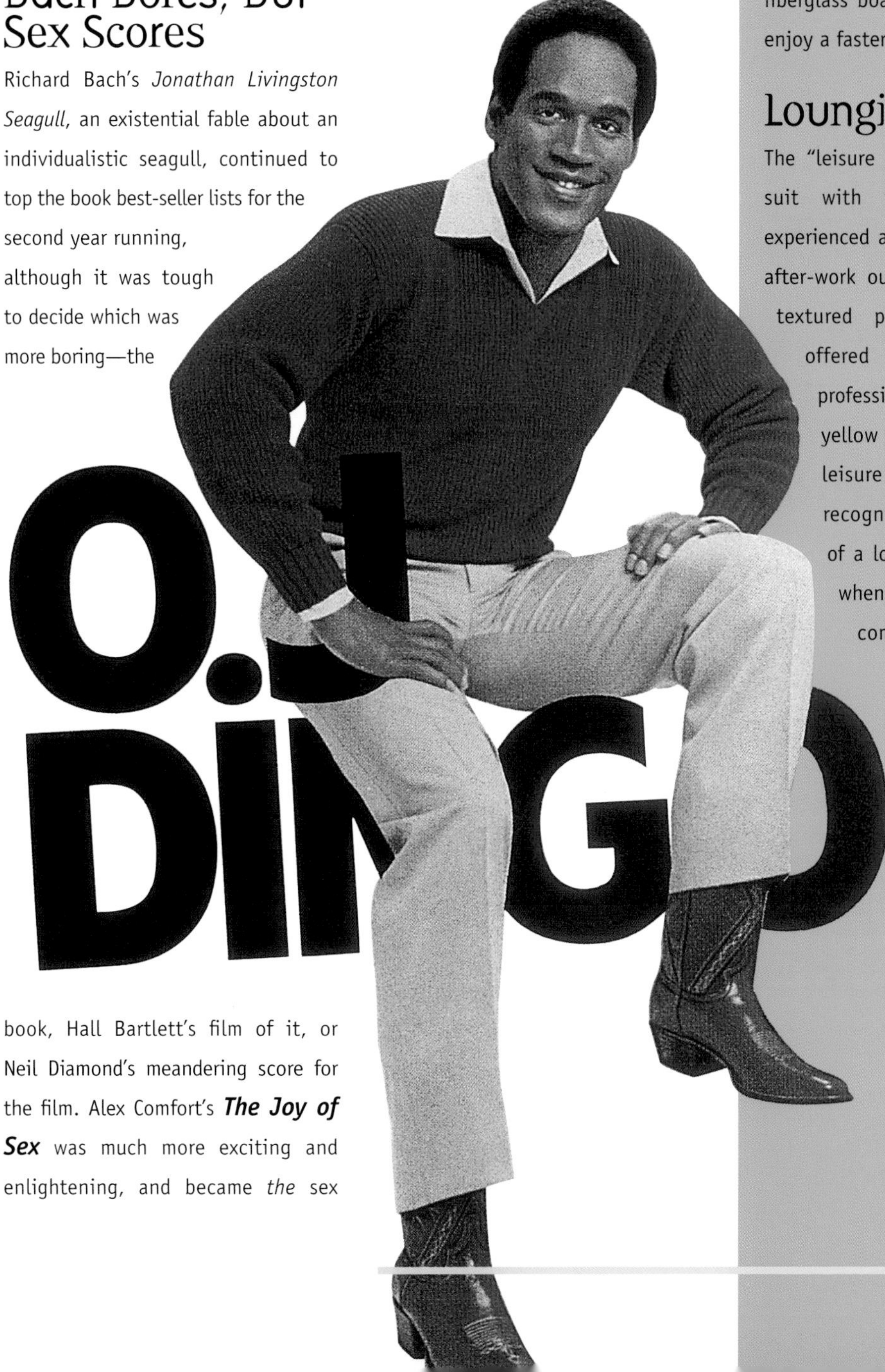

O. DINGO

TOP ALBUMS

Elton John

Goodbye Yellow Brick Road

The Allman Brothers Band

Brothers and Sisters

Carly Simon

No Secrets

Chicago

Chicago VI

George Harrison

Living In The Material World

'74

Unless you were actually there, it's hard to imagine just how utterly loathed and reviled Richard Nixon was in the America of 1974. "Impeach Nixon" bumper stickers and placards were everywhere you turned. On playgrounds across the country, schoolchildren sang obscene songs about him. Accompanied by the appropriate combination of clenched eyebrows and jowly frown, the declaration of "I am not a crook!" was an unfailing laugh-getter at fondue parties, regardless of political persuasion.

TOP TELEVISION SHOWS

All in the Family

Sanford and Son

M*A*S*H*

The Waltons

The Sonny and Cher Comedy Hour

ACADEMY AWARDS

BEST PICTURE
The Godfather Part II
directed by Francis Ford Coppola

BEST ACTOR
Art Carney
Harry and Tonto

BEST ACTRESS
Ellen Burstyn
Alice Doesn't Live Here Anymore

Nixon's "stonewalling" strategy— a carefully plotted series of public denials (given the sublimely Orwellian name of "Operation Candor" by White House strategists) and continued refusals to comply with requests for the Watergate tapes— only made things worse for him, although it's unlikely that anything could have improved his public image, short of stripping naked and **streaking** across the White House lawn. Hell, everyone else seemed to be doing it; from college campuses to downtown financial districts, Americans everywhere were shedding their clothes and going for a quick run. "The Streak," Ray Stevens' top-selling novelty single, served as a rallying cry, and the sudden appearance of various streakers lent a touch of

'74 Following his resignation, Richard Nixon says goodbye to his White House staff.

absurdity to live performances by pianist Van Cliburn and dancer Rudolf Nureyev, *The Tonight Show*, and even the Academy Awards telecast.

Stripped To Essentials

Nudism was growing increasingly popular, spreading—much to the displeasure of local authorities—from the time-honored "nudist camps" to public beaches. Not that sunbathers within the legal limit of the law were wearing much, either; the **string bikini**, originally introduced in Rio, was now a fairly common sight on US beaches, as were men's French-cut bikini trunks. All you needed was a puka shell necklace, and your stylish beachgoing outfit was complete.

Monster Gas Guzzlers

American automobile sales were down twenty percent in 1974, due in part to the OPEC oil embargo and the accompanying "energy crisis." Chrysler was hit especially hard, suffering a sales drop of thirty-four percent; the company attempted to rectify the situation with the 1975 Cordoba, the shortest Chrysler since World War Two. Billed as "the new small Chrysler," the car remains most memorable for its

TV spots, in which actor Ricardo Montalban seductively extolled such extras as "rich, Corinthian leather."

The quintessential 1970s automobile was probably The Pacer, introduced by AMC as "the first wide small car." The car's bubble-like styling made it look like some "car of the future" from a 1950s showroom, but its heavy six-cylinder engine made handling awkward, and caused the car to gobble far more fuel than the average domestic subcompact. For all its hype, sales were disappointing, and the Pacer barely made it to the end of the decade.

Experiencing far more longevity was the "monster truck" craze, inspired by Robert Chandler's **Bigfoot**—a souped-up Ford with four-foot high tires, named after the hairy, ape-like creature currently popping up all over the Pacific Northwest. At county fairs across the country, people flocked to see Chandler demonstrate Bigfoot's prowess, which usually involved rolling over heaps of junked cars.

Evel Genius

Folks also came from all over to see daredevil Robert Craig "Evel"

Knievel jump Idaho's Snake River Canyon on September 8. The staunchly right-wing Knievel became one of the most unlikely heroes of the 1970s, idolized both by the denizens of America's myriad trailer parks, and by hyperactive young boys who tried to jump trash cans and other obstacles with their bikes, in emulation of the man who'd allegedly broken every bone in his body two or three times. The latter demographic was undoubtedly a factor in the US government's ban on European mopeds, although officials finally relaxed anti-moped regulations in 1974. As a result, more than two hundred and fifty thousand of the half-bike-half-motorcycles were sold by 1977.

New Handles

Of course, the one drawback to a moped was that there was no room on it for your Citizen's Band radio. CB radio, primarily the domain of truckers who used it as a way to warn each other in code of speed traps and other manifestations of the highway patrol (aka "Smokey the Bear"), suddenly took off in 1974. Two million new CB radio licenses were issued in 1974,

74 Bigfoot, the world's first monster truck, steps out in style at its press launch.

IN THE NEWS

January – A Gallup poll shows that 79 percent of American voters are in favor of impeaching President Nixon.

February 5 – Patricia Hearst, daughter of publisher Randolph Hearst, is kidnapped in Berkeley, California by members of the Symbionese Liberation Army. The radicals demand ransom of $70 in food for every poor person in California; the Hearst family begins $2,000,000 food giveaway on February 22.

February 6 – An House Judiciary Committee impeachment inquiry against Nixon is approved by the House of Representatives.

March 18 – Arabs lift oil embargo against US following Henry Kissinger's diplomatic missions to Egypt and Israel.

April 3 – Patricia Hearst announces that she has changed her name to Tania and is joining the Symbionese Liberation Army of her own free will. On April 15, a bank camera takes a picture of her participating in a bank robbery.

April 8 – Nixon signs bill to raise the minimum wage to $2.30 an hour.

May 17 – Police open fire on Symbionese Liberation Army headquarters in LA, leaving six of eight known members dead. Patty Hearst was not in the building at the time.

July 24 – The Supreme Court orders the White House to honor Leon Jaworski's subpoena of tapes and documents, ruling that executive privilege does not apply to Watergate-related evidence.

August 5 – Nixon releases tapes and transcripts which reveal his approval the Watergate cover-up.

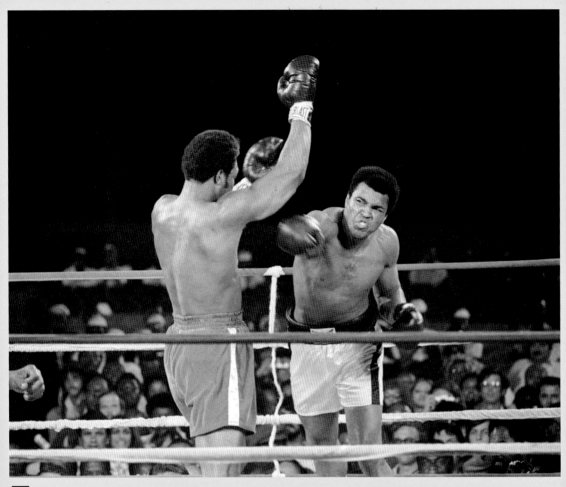

74 KO'd in Kinshasa—Foreman takes a punishing right from Ali.

twice the number of licenses issued between 1958 and 1973. Dictionaries of CB lingo became hot sellers, and expressions like "Ten-four, good buddy" (ie, "Yes, sir") quickly entered the mainstream lexicon.

Rumble In The Jungle

In baseball, Henry "Hank" Aaron entered the record books by breaking Babe Ruth's career record of 714 home runs. Although the media was generally more supportive of Aaron than they had been of Roger Maris, many fans behaved much worse, sending him piles of racist hate mail. Despite these distractions, Aaron remained true to his mission, hitting

home run number 715 on April 8th, and finishing the season with 733.

In a comeback that had taken the better part of a decade, Muhammad Ali regained the World Heavyweight title, defeating George Foreman in a brutal match held in Kinshasa, Zaire.

Music News

Hand-to-hand combat was all over the radio, in the form of Carl Douglas' "Kung Fu Fighting." Inspired by the current mania for all things martial-arts-related (even the GI Joe action figure now featured "Kung Fu Grip"), the deliciously absurd song topped the December charts—helped, no doubt, by promotional TV appearances in which Douglas traded Kung Fu moves with *ghi*-attired dancers.

There were thirty-five different Number One pop singles in 1974, the

most ever for a single year, and the diversity of AM radio playlists now bordered on the schizophrenic. Singles buyers were snapping up everything, including novelty hits, teeny-bop pop (Bo Donaldson and The Heywoods' "Billy, Don't Be A Hero," Andy Kim's "Rock Me Gently"), disco soul (The Hues Corporation's "Rock the Boat," George McRae's "Rock Your Baby"), polished hard rock (Bachman-Turner Overdrive's "You Ain't Seen Nothin' Yet," Grand Funk's cover of "The Loco-Motion"), and folky ballads by Gordon Lightfoot ("Sundown"), Harry Chapin ("Cat's In The Cradle"), and John Denver ("Sunshine On My Shoulders," "Annie's Song").

Stevie Wonder topped the charts with "You Haven't Done Nothin'," a vicious attack on President Nixon, but **Barry White** was all

about love (pronounced "*Luuuuuvv*"), scoring with "Can't Get Enough of Your Love, Babe" and "You're The First, The Last, My Everything," as well as writing, producing, and conducting "Love's Theme" for The Love Unlimited Orchestra.

Cool And Collected

Intent on getting some value for their money, Americans took home a number of "Best of" albums. John Denver's *Greatest Hits* and Crosby, Stills, Nash and Young's *So Far* were huge sellers, as was *Photographs and Memories*, a collection of hits by Chicago singer-songwriter Jim Croce ("Bad Bad Leroy Brown"), who had died the previous year in a plane crash. *Endless Summer*, a compilation of Beach Boys hits from the early 1960s, totally turned the group's career around; as a new generation of kids discovered the joys of "Fun, Fun, Fun" and "California Girls," The Beach Boys were once again in high demand as a concert draw.

TV News

The theatrical success of last year's *American Graffiti* paved the way for *Happy Days*, a popular comedy nostalgically set in a blurry late-fifties/early sixties time period. The show featured *American Graffiti*'s Ron Howard (who, a decade earlier, had played Opie on *The Andy Griffith Show*), and made a surprise star out of Henry Winkler, who played the leather-jacketed, preternaturally cool Arthur "**The Fonz**" Fonzarelli. Recurring Fonz expressions like "Sit on it!" and "Aaaaay!" (accompanied by an affirmative thumbs-up gesture) were some of the most oft-repeated phrases of 1974-75, rivalled only by "Dy-No-Mite!," which was shouted *ad nauseam* by Jimmy ("JJ") Walker on *Good Times*.

Other popular new comedies included *Chico and the Man* (starring comedian Freddie Prinze) and *Rhoda*, a *Mary Tyler Moore* spin-off starring Valerie Harper.

The Rockford Files and **Police Woman** were two of the year's most popular crime shows; the former featured James Garner as a down-on-his-luck private eye, while the latter starred Angie

'74 Jack Nicholson in *Chinatown*

Dickinson as Sgt Pepper Anderson, an undercover LAPD officer who always seemed to have to impersonate a prostitute when solving a case. Other new shows, *Little House on the Prairie* (based on Laura Ingalls Wilder's books about life as a pioneer family in the 1870s) and **The Six Million Dollar Man** (starring Lee Majors as "Steve Austin, a man barely alive..."), were big favorites with the kids.

Movie Audiences Quake In Their Seats

While 1974 produced some truly great films (Francis Ford Coppola's *The Godfather Part II*, Roman Polanski's *Chinatown*), it also gave us some really memorable trash. *Airport 1975* continued in the air-disaster vein of the original (but was set this time

on—ooh!—a 747), while *The Towering Inferno* menaced Steve McQueen and an all-star cast of thousands with a flaming skyscraper. *Earthquake*, an almost unwatchably bad disaster film starring the ubiquitous Charlton Heston, was slightly redeemed by its use of "**Sensurround**," which added rumbling realism to the quake sequences; doctors claimed this new effect damaged your eardrums, but it sure was fun. And who could ever forget Gunnar Hansen wearing a mask of human skin and brandishing Black and Decker's finest hardware in **The Texas Chainsaw Massacre**? Tobe Hooper's bloody (and extremely frightening) film, loosely based on the ghoulish career Wisconsin farmer Ed Gein, set a new standard for "splatter flicks" and proved enduringly popular with college film clubs.

Mel Brooks' *Young Frankenstein* just slips into the list of great 1974 films. All of his later efforts were pretty terrible; if we're gonna give the man his due, this is probably the best place to do it (though let's not forget 1968's *The Producers*).

'74 *Happy Days'* **Howard and Winkler, and (*right*) The Texas Chainsaw Massacre.**

IN THE NEWS

August 8 – Nixon makes a televised resignation speech; as 100,000,000 people watch on three networks, Nixon admits to having made some wrong decisions, but insists that the real reason he's leaving is because Congress no longer supports him.

August 9 – Nixon resigns. Gerald R Ford sworn in as president.

September 8 – Nixon pardoned by President Ford for any crimes he may have committed or participated in while in office. Ford claims that his actions are motivated by a desire to end the national divisions caused by the Watergate scandal, but the move will effectively doom his re-election campaign in 1976.

September 16 – Ford offers limited amnesty to Vietnam War draft resisters and deserters, on the condition that they swear allegiance to the US and perform up to two years of public service.

December 19 – Nelson A Rockefeller, former Governor of New York, is sworn in as vice-president.

December 21 – *The New York Times* reports that the CIA, during the Nixon administration, had maintained files on some 10,000 US citizens, as well as engaged in illegal domestic operations against opponents of the Vietnam War.

75

The Vietnam War ended in 1975, but nobody in the States seemed to feel much like celebrating. Among most Americans, the pervasive attitude towards the war's ignominious conclusion seemed to be a mixture of relief and embarrassment; unsurprisingly, **there was a conspicuous absence of ticker-tape parades for returning vets.** With food prices at an all-time high, electricity rates up thirty percent from 1974, and unemployment hitting levels not seen since 1941, Americans were more concerned about the prospect of another depression than with healing the scars left by the war.

Indeed, there were plenty of new wounds being wrought by forced busing, the government's attempt to desegregate public schools by sending white kids to schools in black neighborhoods, and vice-versa.

First-Family Misfortunes

Gerald Ford's first full year in office was as difficult for him as it was for the rest of the country. His wife Betty caused a stir when, during a televised interview, she lauded the US Supreme Court's controversial 1973 *Roe v Wade* ruling legalizing abortion as a "great, great decision." Shortly thereafter, his son Jack, twenty-three, publicly admitted using marijuana.

75 As the US pulls out of Vietnam, the Saigon embassy is evacuated.

In September, the president nearly fell victim to not one but *two* assassination attempts—first in Sacramento, California by Manson

Monster hits: *One Flew over the Cuckoo's Nest* and (below) *Jaws*.

Pepper, *Three Days of the Condor*) and Barbra Streisand (*Funny Lady*) were the year's biggest stars, or rather, the year's biggest *human* stars—"Bruce," the twenty-foot mechanical Great White shark who handily upstaged **Jaws** co-stars Roy Scheider, Robert Shaw and Richard Dreyfuss, was easily the year's top box-office attraction. In the wake of the film's runaway success, sharkmania gripped the nation; a puzzle book called *Shark Mazes* was a big seller among schoolkids, shark's-tooth pendants hung from men's necks, and "Mr Jaws," Dickie Goodman's novelty "answer" record, even made it into the Top Five.

follower Lynette A "Squeaky" Fromme, and two weeks later in San Francisco by estranged FBI informant Sara Jane Moore.

Movie News

If the president was getting off to a rather shaky start, Hollywood was running at full steam, raking in a record two billion dollars in profits. Milos Forman's **One Flew over the Cuckoo's Nest** (starring Jack Nicholson as the likeable trouble-maker who stirs things up in an insane asylum, and Louise Fletcher as the hard-as-nails Nurse Ratchet) and Robert Altman's *Nashville* garnered heaps of critical plaudits, but it was ultra-violent pictures like *Rollerball* and *Death Race 2000* that really had 'em lining up at the box office.

Warren Beatty slept his way through Beverly Hills in *Shampoo*, and Al Pacino tried to rob a bank to pay for his lover's sex-change operation in *Dog Day Afternoon*. Robert Redford (*The Great Waldo*

IN THE NEWS

February 21 – For their roles in the Watergate cover-up, HR Haldeman, John D Ehrlichman, and John Mitchell are each sentenced to 30 months in prison.

April 30 – The Vietnam War ends, as the last remaining US citizens are air-lifted out of Saigon. Cambodia and South Vietnam fall to Communist forces.

May 12 – The US merchant ship Mayaguez is seized in Cambodian waters, and the crew are charged with espionage. On May 14, the 39 crew members are freed by a US military raid which leaves fifteen US soldiers dead and 50 wounded.

July 15 – The US and USSR's joint Apollo-Soyuz space mission begins. The Russian and American spacecrafts dock with each other on July 17; the crews perform a number of scientific experiments together during the 44-hour linkup.

July 30 – Former Teamsters Union President Jimmy Hoffa disappears after making a phone call from the Manchus Red Fox Restaurant in suburban Detroit. Though he is presumed murdered by underworld figures, Hoffa's fate has never been officially solved.

Good, Clean Fun?

Perhaps most damaging of all the new president's troubles were Chevy Chase's Ford impersonations on NBC's new *Saturday Night Live*, which mercilessly lampooned his lumbering, slow-on-the-draw demeanor and his propensity for accidental pratfalls. President Ford may not have been a fan of *Saturday Night Live*, but the late-night comedy program was

V75 Love keeps The Captain and Tennille together.

unquestionably one of the year's bright spots. Most of the show's cast (which included Chase, Dan Aykroyd, John Belushi, Jane Curtin, Garrett Morris, Laraine Newman, and Gilda Radner) and writers had been previously involved with various *National Lampoon* projects, a connection evidenced by the show's irreverent (and usually somewhat tasteless) brand of humor, which suited perfectly the cynical tenor of the times.

Across the dial, ABC weighed in with the similarly titled—and far less successful—*Saturday Night Live with Howard Cosell*. Though the verbose Cosell seemed far more comfortable in his regular gig as an ABC sportscaster than as the host of a variety show, the program did feature regular appearances by talented comedian Bill Murray, who coincidentally would go on to replace Chevy Chase as a member of NBC's *SNL* cast in the fall of 1976.

Thanks to the National Association of Broadcasters' new emphasis on "family viewing time," network affiliated stations were encouraged to set aside two hours in the early evening as a sex- and violence-free zone; the stations generally made the best of the situation by programming syndicated game shows and sitcoms. *Welcome Back, Kotter*, starring Gabe Kaplan as a high-school teacher saddled with a group of under-achieving students known as "The Sweathogs," was one of the year's most popular new sitcoms; **John Travolta** got his first big break in show business as Vinnie Barbarino, an exceptionally dim-witted member of the class.

Up-Beat Cops

All in the Family and *The Mary Tyler Moore Show* continued to produce popular new spin-offs (*The Jeffersons* and *Phyllis*, respectively). *Barney Miller* was one of the few violence-free cop shows on the air, while newcomers

SWAT, *Baretta*, and *Starsky and Hutch* had gunplay and grittiness to spare. The latter two shows at least offered occasional comic relief; *Baretta*'s Robert Blake spent a portion of each episode communing with his pet cockatoo, Fred, while **Starsky and Hutch**'s Antonio Fargas played Huggy Bear, the jive-talking informer to end all jive-talking informers.

West Meets East

The Night Stalker and *Kung Fu*, two of the decade's most intriguing shows, were canceled by ABC halfway through the year. One of the few horror shows to actually boast some good scares, *The Night Stalker* starred Darren McGavin as Carl Kolchak, a rumpled Chicago reporter constantly doing battle with the forces of evil. Forever insisting that "I come in peace," **Kung Fu**'s Kwai Chang Caine (David Carradine) had ample opportunity to showcase his slow-motion martial arts skills, usually against cowboys who reacted to his exotic presence with greetings of, "I'm gon' *kill* you, Chinaman!" The show was also famous for its atmospheric flashback sequences, during which the young "Grasshopper" Caine pondered pearls of inscrutable wisdom at the knee of blind Master Po.

Winning Game Plans

Possessing a similar Zen-like intensity was Pong, the video table tennis game that hooked up to your television set. Invented by Atari founder Nolan Bushnell, the home version of Pong sold one hundred and fifty thousand units in its first year on the market, kick-starting the whole home videogame craze in the process.

Meanwhile, over at the local arcade, Bally's new Wizard (a pinball game based on Ken Russell's film of The Who's *Tommy*) was working overtime coaxing hard-earned quarters from the pockets of pinball fanatics.

Car Industry Cutbacks

"It's about time for a new kind of American car," sang the ads for Chevrolet's new Chevette, an economical (if plain-looking) sub-compact that could get up to thirty-five miles per gallon on the highway. In truth, it was time for any kind of American car that could bring consumers into the showrooms. On February 3, auto industry layoffs cut Detroit's automotive workforce by over thirty-three percent, with poor sales taking most of the blame.

Still, some makes and models were selling well. Ford's new Granada, a slightly smaller and more fuel-conscious version of the Ford Maverick, quickly became the company's top-selling car, while Cadillac's new Seville, an "intermediate" luxury vehicle *à la* Mercedes-Benz, racked up sales of forty-three thousand.

Van-Tastic!

If the fifties and early sixties produced a rash of car-oriented songs, it's only appropriate that it took one of 1975's biggest singles to finally give vans their due. Whether you were traveling in the "Mystery Machine" with *Scooby-Doo* and the gang, or just pulling bongs in the back of a Dodge Econoline

airbrushed with a scene out of Norse mythology, the customized van was like a clubhouse on wheels for the groovy youngsters of the early and mid-seventies. A Top Five hit, Sammy Johns' "Chevy Van" perfectly encapsulated the van fantasy: Man in van picks up nubile hitchhiker; man has sex with hitchhiker in back of van (whose interior is doubtless covered in thick shag carpeting); man deposits hitchhiker in out-of-the-way town and drives on. This archetypal scenario was later the basis for *The Van*, a 1976 film starring a pre-*Taxi* Danny DeVito.

Meet The New Boss...

Similarly vehicular-minded (although a good deal more romantic), Bruce Springsteen's new *Born To Run* LP sold like hot cakes and landed the scraggly New Jersey singer on the covers of *Time* and *Newsweek* in the same week. Springsteen's three-hour concerts were the stuff of legend, causing many rock critics to swoon like schoolgirls. Also legendary were the incendiary live performances of **Kiss**, the fire-breathing, blood-spitting, makeup-wearing rock band that all the critics seemed to hate. Although it received almost no support from radio or the

media, word of mouth and nonstop touring helped their live *Kiss Alive* album slither into the Top Ten.

The Magic of Manilow

Flamboyant soft-rocker Barry Manilow had a fabulous year, scoring huge hits with "Mandy," "Could it Be Magic," "It's a Miracle," and "I Write The Songs." A former jingle writer and erstwhile Bette Midler accompanist, Manilow became an instant heart-throb of America's housewife set.

Blown Away

All-in-one stereos (which, like Zenith's "The Wedge," usually included AM/FM receiver, an eight-track tape recorder and a turntable) were especially popular among seventies music buyers. Also popular were portable eight-track players, the most memorable being the Panasonic Dynamite 8, which came in a variety of bright colors and looked like a detonator; just pop in your favorite rock eight-track, and push down on the handle for an explosion of sound.

Emotional Appeal

Of course, as anyone in 1975 could've told you, nothing rocked like the Pet Rock. The brainchild of California businessman Gary Dahl, the Pet Rock was the year's hottest-selling novelty gift. Costing a mere four dollars, the rocks came in miniature pet carrying-cases filed with straw, accompanied by an owner's manual that told you how to teach your pet to roll over, play dead, and generally be on its best behavior.

Almost as popular (and just as memorable) were **Mood Rings**,

whose heat-sensitive liquid crystal stones supposedly changed color according to your mood. Black meant you were anxious or excitable, amber meant nervous or tense, green meant sensitive, red meant passionate, blue meant happy, and it only cost $19.95 to figure out what you were feeling.

Cosmic Cash for Football Star

In the world of sports, Brazilian soccer star **Pelé** (born Edson Arantes do Nascimento) came out of retirement to play for the New York Cosmos of the North American Soccer League, thanks to a three-year, seven-million-dollar contract that made him the world's highest-paid team athlete. Cosmos executives hoped that his presence would help boost the sport's popularity in America.

75 Barry Manilow.

'76

America celebrated its two-hundredth birthday in 1976, and the entire country seemed to be swathed in stars and stripes. Eveywhere you looked, people were painting fire hydrants in shades of red, white, and blue, donning tri-colored clown wigs, and plunking down newly minted Bicentennial twenty-five-cent and dollar coins for clothes, dishes, coffee mugs and anything else with a flag pattern on it.

TOP TELEVISION SHOWS

Happy Days

Laverne and Shirley

The Six Million Dollar Man

*M*A*S*H**

The Bionic Woman

The Bicentennial celebrations culminated on July 4 with the nationwide ringing of bells, the convergence of fifty warships and sixteen tall ships from around the world in New York harbor, and the largest display of fireworks anyone had ever seen. In retrospect, the timing couldn't have been better. For all its gaudiness and self-congratulation, the Bicentennial did a lot to bring the country back together after the divisive traumas of the Vietnam era. Not coincidentally, most Bicentennial celebrations seemed to downplay America's military might, highlighting instead the country's domestic accomplishments and the resilience of its people.

America Reborn With Carter

It's hard to imagine another year in the late twentieth century in which Jimmy Carter could have been elected president. A peanut farmer and former one-term Governor of Georgia, Carter was the perfect candidate for a country grown increasingly cynical

about lawyers and career politicians. Both Miss Lillian, Carter's mother, and Billy, his down-home younger brother, became national celebrities thanks to their outspoken ways (Jimmy himself proved almost too outspoken, nearly capsizing his campaign by admitting to *Playboy* that he had "committed adultery in my heart many times"), and Carter generally exuded a warmth and sincerity that contrasted strongly with Gerald Ford's almost Frankensteinian stiffness. Of course, Ford's inability to stem the rising inflation and unempoyment rates was certainly a decisive factor in the election, but when Carter pledged "**I will never lie to you**," many Americans took him at his word. It's interesting to note that Carter was the first (and, to date, the only) "born again" Christian to be elected to the White House. Although his own politics were moderately liberal, Carter's election presaged the rise in profile and power of the religious right during the next decade.

'76 Rocky *(left)* suffers but Laverne and Shirley *(above)* bloom.

'76 Keitel and De Niro in *Taxi Driver*, and Sissy Spacek (right) in *Carrie*.

TAXI
DRIVER
A COLUMBIA PICTURES RELEASE

Movie News

Despite its humiliation in Vietnam, America maintained its status as the wealthiest and most powerful nation in the world, yet most Americans still instinctively identified with rebels and underdogs. *Rocky*, starring **Sylvester Stallone** as a boxer who gets a "million to one" shot at the world heavyweight boxing title, was the ultimate underdog tale; the previously unknown Stallone had risked his entire savings to bring his script to the screen, a fact with gave the already uplifting film an added bit of resonance. The film was a runaway smash, and Stallone became a matinee idol literally overnight.

Less uplifting, but equally resonant, was Sidney Lumet's **Network**, an amazingly prescient satire of network television; Peter Finch's crazed admission that "I'm mad as hell, and I'm not gonna take it anymore!" became one of the seventies' most familiar battle cries, along with Robert De Niro's "You lookin' at me?" from Martin Scorsese's unbelievably seamy **Taxi Driver**.

Robert Redford (who starred with Dustin Hoffman as Bob Woodward and Carl Bernstein in *All The President's Men*) and thirteen-year-old Tatum O'Neal (*The Bad News Bears*, *Nickelodeon*) were the year's biggest male and female draws. John Wayne made his last film appearance as a dying gunfighter in *The Shootist*, while Barbra Streisand and Kris Kristofferson tried unsuccessfully to breathe new life into *A Star is Born*. Another remake, Dino DeLaurentis' *King Kong* sent the titular ape to the top of New York's World Trade Center, but had little other than ace special effects to recommend it. Much better were horror films **Carrie** and **The Omen**; the former starred Sissy Spacek as a telekinetic teenager who lays waste to her teasing classmates, while the latter featured Gregory Peck and Lee Remick as a couple who come to the unsettling realization that their son is the anti-Christ.

BEST FILM

Rocky

directed by John G Avildsen

BEST ACTOR

Peter Finch

Network

BEST ACTRESS

Faye Dunaway

Network

Stay Hungry gave Austrian body-builder Arnold Schwarzenegger his first major film role, while *Logan's Run*, a futuristic look at a world of compulsory pleasure, got much of its box-office juice from a supporting appearance by one of television's hottest new stars: Farrah Fawcett-Majors.

Superwomen Take Over TV

Debuting in the fall of 1976, *Charlie's Angels* immediately took the television world by storm. As three gorgeous detectives capable of tackling any case, Kate Jackson, Jaclyn Smith and **Farrah Fawcett-Majors** became the idols of millions of young girls, and the lust objects of millions of American males; all feathered blonde hair and shiny teeth, Farrah (who was married at the time to *Six Million Dollar Man* Lee Majors) was the most popular pin-up to come along in years. Other female superheroes popping up on television in 1976 included *The Bionic Woman*, a *Six Million Dollar Man* spin-off starring Lindsay Wagner, and ***Wonder Woman***, starring Lynda Carter as the Nazi-fighting Amazon princess, while Electra-Woman (Deidre Hall) and Dynagirl (Judy Strangis) were regulars on Saturday morning's *Krofft Supershow*. Living slightly more mundane existences were *Alice*, a widowed mother and waitress played by Linda Lavin, and Louise Lasser's titular Ohio

'76 Arnie—hungry for stardom.

housewife in the soap-opera parody ***Mary Hartman, Mary Hartman***.

Of the year's new sitcoms, *Laverne and Shirley* (a *Happy Days* spin-off starring Penny Marshall and Cindy Williams) and *What's Happening!!* (an updated version of the 1975 film *Cooley High*, itself something of a black *American Graffiti*) were easily the most popular. Also doing quite well were musical variety shows starring The Captain and Tennille ("Love Will Keep Us Together"), Donny and Marie Osmond, and Jim Henson's Muppets.

For *real* bottom-of-the-barrel entertainment, you couldn't beat **The Gong Show**, a talent show wherein the celebrity judges regularly negated contestants by rapping a large gong. Host/co-producer Chuck Barris was a true renaissance man; not only was he responsible for those twin pillars of popular culture, *The Dating Game* and *The Newlywed Game*, but he also wrote "Palisades Park" for Freddy Cannon in 1962.

John Travolta further cemented his teen-heartthrob status as the lead in *The Boy in the Plastic Bubble*, an ABC Friday Night Movie. Travolta also managed to score two Top Forty hits—"Let Her In" and "Whenever I'm Away From You"—though he would have to wait another year for his disco apotheosis.

Music News

In 1976, there were an estimated ten thousand discos open in the United States, as opposed to only fifteen hundred in 1974. The hustle, a combination of mambo and jitterbug steps, was the favored dance of the day, although the bump was almost as popular. Cheaper than going to a rock concert and less hassle than a singles

February 18 – President Ford issues an executive order curtailing domestic surveillance of US citizens by the FBI and CIA.

May 28 – The US and USSR sign a nuclear test pact limiting underground tests to a maximum of 150 kilotons; the pact also allows the US to inspect Soviet test sites.

July 14 – Former Georgia governor James Earl "Jimmy" Carter, Jr is nominated for president at the Democratic convention. Senator Walter Mondale is nominated for vice-president the next day.

July 20 – *Viking 1*, launched eleven months earlier, lands on Mars. *Viking 2* lands on Mars on September 3. Both spacecraft collect data showing the planet to be barren, rocky—and generally devoid of Martians.

August 19 – The Republican National Convention narrowly nominates Gerald Ford for re-election over Ronald Reagan. Senator Robert Dole is nominated for the vice-presidency.

September 1 – Ohio Representative Wayne Hays resigns from the US House of Representatives in the wake of a sex scandal involving him and former secretary Elizabeth Ray.

September 17 – In light of recent revelations of malfeasance and abuse of power by the country's intelligence agencies, a special committee to review the assassinations of John F Kennedy and Martin Luther King, Jr is created by the House of Representatives.

September 24 – Patricia Hearst sentenced to seven years in jail for her participation in a 1974 bank robbery.

'76 The Ramones

bar, the disco was a combination of both, one which also allowed gays, straights, blacks, and whites to party together as one underneath the mirror ball.

Arena Yields To The Ramones

There was still an audience for rock records, as evidenced by the phenomenal success of Boston's first album, The Steve Miller Band's *Fly Like An Eagle*, Heart's *Dreamboat Annie,* and Kiss's *Destroyer*. New York's Ramones didn't exactly storm the Top Forty with their self-titled debut, but their loud-and-fast aesthetic made a positive impression on many music fans and critics sick of the bloated excesses of arena rock. The P-Funk Earth Tour, led by funk pied piper George Clinton, landed the Parliament-Funkadelic mothership in sold-out arenas across the country, but most older black acts had a tough time in the disco era. Johnnie Taylor, who had a number five hit in 1968 with "Who's Making Love," was one of the few to successfully

make the adjustment, topping the charts for four weeks with "**Disco Lady**," a cash-in almost as blatant as CW McCall's "**Convoy**," which capitalized on the Citizen's Band radio craze by using CB lingo to recount a tale of renegade truckers.

Volare Takes Off

Due to declining sales, US auto companies ceased production of convertibles in 1976; Cadillac's El Dorado was the last convertible model released. One of the few bright spots for Detroit was the success of Plymouth's Volare; thanks to a memorable ad campaign featuring crooner Sergio Franchi, the upscale compact sold four hundred thousand units in its first year on the market.

Videogame News

Encouraged by the success of Atari, other companies tried dipping their joysticks into the home videogame market. Coleco introduced Telstar Pong, while the Fairchild Camera and Instrument Company weighed in with the Fairchild Channel F; the first programmable home game console, it came with large cartridges that could be inserted in order to play different games.

Cutting-Edge Style

After winning a gold medal at the Winter Olympics in Innsbruck, Austria, US figure skater Dorothy Hamill quickly became an icon for young girls, who adopted Dorothy's "Wedge" haircut as their own—at least until Farrah showed up. Bruce Jenner also become a national hero for winning the Decathalon at the Summer Olympics in Montreal, but exerted little sartorial influence on the country's youth. Nor did many folks adopt the grown-out Harpo Marx hairdo of Mark "The Bird" Fidrych, the rookie pitcher who won nineteen games for the lowly Detroit Tigers. So named for his resemblance to *Sesame Street*'s Big Bird, "The Bird" was famous for talking to the ball between pitches; the technique's effectiveness only lasted for one season, however, and Fidrych was out of baseball completely after only a couple of years.

Having narrowly defeating Ken Norton in a Heavyweight title bout, **Muhammad Ali** announced his retirement from boxing, a pledge that proved about as realistic as the then-circulating rumor that Bubble Yum bubblegum contained spider eggs. Within a year, Ali would be back in the ring.

1977 was yet **another banner year for the movie industry,** with box-office registers ringing to the tune of $2.3 billion in revenues thanks to the holy trinity of *Star Wars*, *Close Encounters of the Third Kind*, and *Saturday Night Fever*. **Kids of all ages flocked repeatedly to see Luke Skywalker** (Mark Hamill) and Han Solo (Harrison Ford) take on Darth Vader's Death Star with the help of a couple of robots and a Wookie.

ACADEMY AWARDS

BEST PICTURE

Annie Hall

directed by Woody Allen

BEST ACTOR

Richard Dreyfuss

The Goodbye Girl

BEST ACTRESS

Diane Keaton

Annie Hall

S tar Wars bubblegum cards, toys, watches, masks, towels, T-shirts and records sold in unimaginable numbers, and the phrase "May the Force be with you" became a part of everyday conversation. Unlike *Star Wars*, Steven Spielberg's **Close Encounters** was less *Flash Gordon* and more *War of the Worlds*, only with suitably updated special effects and an uplifting ending.

Saturday Night Fever, which came out later in the year, featured John Travolta (in his first leading film role) playing Brooklyn disco king Tony Manero. The film's success pushed the already thriving disco scene to new heights of popularity; male disco denizens everywhere copied Travolta's white-suit-and-dark-shirt look, usually set off with gold chains and Italian snaggle-tooth pendants. Flared slacks and platform shoes also became an integral part of the disco look, along with form-fitting, vividly patterned polyester shirts.

Many women picked up on Diane Keaton's unorthodox **Annie Hall** wardrobe; ensembles consisting of

'77 Diane Keaton and Woody Allen in *Annie Hall*, aptly subtitled *A Nervous Romance*.

floppy hats, oversized men's shirts, tise, vests, and baggy chinos were soon spotted on the streets of most major metropolitan areas. Though already highly regarded for a string of hilarious films that included 1969's *Take the Money and Run*, 1971's *Bananas* and 1973's *Sleeper*, Woody Allen had his greatest commercial and critical success to date with *Annie Hall*.

Completely reviled by critics, *Smokey and the Bandit* was a box-office smash. Starring **Burt Reynolds** as a daredevil bootlegger endlessly pursued by small-town sheriff Jackie Gleason, the film proved (as did *Semi-Tough*, his other 1977 project) that audiences would pay to see Reynolds in just about anything. Arnold Schwarzenegger would have to wait until the next decade for similar treatment, although *Pumping Iron*, George Butler's documentary about the Mr Olympia bodybuilding championships, went a long way towards establishing "Ah-nold" as an appealing screen personality.

Where do you go when the record is over ...

SATURDAY NIGHT FEVER

January 17 – Gary Gilmore, convicted for murdering a Utah gas-station attendant, is executed by firing squad. Gilmore is the first person executed in the US since 1967.

January 20 – Jimmy Carter is inaugurated president.

January 21 – Carter issues a presidential pardon for the majority of Vietnam draft-resisters.

January 28–29 – A blizzard paralyzes most of the East and Midwest, resulting in a severe shortage of natural gas.

April 18 – Calling it "the moral equivalent of war," President Carter calls for an all-out campaign for energy conservation.

May – Richard Nixon appears in a series of televised interviews with David Frost. Although he admits that he "let the American people down" with his actions surrounding the Watergate cover-up, Nixon argues that illegal activities against dissidents aren't illegal "when the president does it." America remains unconvinced.

May 4 – At normalization talks in Paris, the US agrees to stop blocking Vietnam's application for admission to the United Nations.

May 9 – Patricia Hearst is released from jail on probation.

June 6 – *The Washington Post* reports that the US is developing a neutron bomb, a weapon designed to kill people but cause minimal destruction of property.

'77 "We are not alone..." Spielberg's *Close Encounters of the Third Kind*.

TV News

The big news in TV land was Farrah Fawcett-Majors' decision to leave *Charlie's Angels* after only a year, ostensibly to pursue film projects. Her replacement, Cheryl Ladd, became almost as popular a pin-up as Farrah, as did Suzanne Somers, star of the hot new sitcom *Three's Company*. *Chico and the Man*'s Freddie Prinze chose to leave his show in a much more dramatic manner—with a bullet in his head. Overwhelmed by sudden fame and a nagging drug problem, the twenty-two-year-old comic shot himself to death in January.

Other popular new shows included *The Love Boat*, *Lou Grant* (featuring Ed Asner in a serious take on his *Mary Tyler Moore Show*

character), and *CHiPs*, an action series starring Erik Estrada and Larry Wilcox as California Highway Patrolmen. **The Life and Times of Grizzly Adams** and **The Man from Atlantis** were big favorites with younger viewers; the former starred Dan Haggerty as a fugitive from justice (over a crime he didn't commit, of course) who lived in the woods of the Pacific Northwest with a large grizzly bear, while the latter starred Patrick Duffy as a web-footed, acquatic native of a lost continent. Also popular with the kiddies (especially pre-pubescent girls) were *The Hardy Boys*, played by Parker Stevenson and Shaun Cassidy (younger brother of former teen idol David).

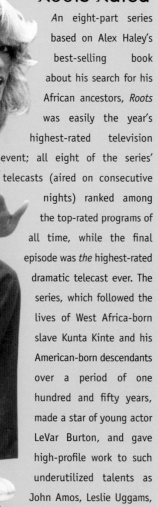

77 Runaway success—Farrah Fawcett-Majors.

Roots Rated

An eight-part series based on Alex Haley's best-selling book about his search for his African ancestors, *Roots* was easily the year's highest-rated television event; all eight of the series' telecasts (aired on consecutive nights) ranked among the top-rated programs of all time, while the final episode was *the* highest-rated dramatic telecast ever. The series, which followed the lives of West Africa-born slave Kunta Kinte and his American-born descendants over a period of one hundred and fifty years, made a star of young actor LeVar Burton, and gave high-profile work to such underutilized talents as John Amos, Leslie Uggams, and Ben Vereen.

Tut-Mania

Next to *Roots*, King Tut was the biggest American obsession of 1977. For the first time since their excavation in the 1920s, the contents of the ancient Egyptian King Tutankhamen's tomb made the rounds of American museums; the traveling exhibition set off a mania for all things Egyptian, and gave rise to the brief **"pyramid power"** fad, which claimed that you could harness certain spiritual energies through the judicious placement of pyramids around your household.

The King Is Dead

On August 16, while Americans stood in line for hours at a time in order to gawk at the lavish treasures of King Tut's tomb, the King of Rock and Roll died on the throne of his Graceland Mansion bathroom, aged forty-two. Heart failure aggravated by "straining at stool" was ruled as the official cause of death, although Elvis's prodigious pill-gobbling certainly helped to hasten his end—"Dr Nick," aka Dr George Nichopoulos, had prescribed over eleven thousand depressants, stimulants, and painkillers to Elvis during the last fifteen months of his life. Countless tribute records—including Ronnie McDowell's "The King is Gone," Ral Donner's "The Day the Beat Stopped," and JD Sumner's "Elvis Has Left the Building"—were immediately waxed, and rock 'n' roll fans everywhere went into deep mourning.

Perhaps the saddest thing of all about The King's death was that, at the time he checked out, there was precious little evidence of his influence left on the charts. Of all of 1977's chart-toppers, only Shaun Cassidy's watered-down cover of The

Crystals' "Da Doo Ron Ron" actually qualified as rock 'n' roll—and just barely, at that. The punk revolution may have been raging in England, but underground American bands like Television, Talking Heads, and The Dead Boys couldn't even get on the radio, much less compete with the likes of Bill Conti's "Gonna Fly Now (Theme from Rocky)," Alan O'Day's "Undercover Angel," or Mary MacGregor's "Torn Between Two Lovers." **David Soul**, who had spent the earlier part of the decade trying to make it as a masked folksinger known as "The Covered Man," cashed in on his popularity as one-half of *Starsky and Hutch*, and scored a Number One hit with "Don't Give Up On Us." Debby Boone, daughter of whitebread pop scourge Pat, had the biggest hit of the decade with "You Light Up My Life."

As the continued success of Aerosmith, Ted Nugent, and Kiss proved, there was still an audience for loud guitars and bad attitudes, although it seemed to be dwindling under the onslaught of disco and soft

TOP SINGLES

DEBBY BOONE
"You Light Up My Life"

THE EMOTIONS
"Best of My Love"

ANDY GIBB
"I Just Want To Be Your Everything"

STEVIE WONDER
"Sir Duke"

BARBRA STREISAND
"Love Theme From *A Star Is Born* (Evergreen)"

'77 The King nears the end of his reign.

rock. **Lynyrd Skynyrd**, a hard-drinkin' band that virtually defined the whole "Southern Rock" movement with songs like "Sweet Home Alabama" and "Free Bird," called it a day after October 20, when the crash of their ancient touring plane killed three members, including leader Ronnie Van Zant.

Throwbacks Battle Industrial Blues

In Detroit, the $337 million Renaissance Center complex, which included a seventy-three-story hotel and four thirty-nine-story office blocks, opened its doors. The city hoped that the complex would spur an economic revitalization of the riot-torn downtown area, but nothing of the sort occured. Nor did the city's auto makers have much luck stemming the tide of Japanese and European imports with new subcompacts like Dodge's Omni and Ford's Fiesta. In many ways, the

most interesting new models were throwbacks to an earlier era. Chevrolet's 1978 Silver Anniversary Corvette came with a Stingray-like fastback, while Ford's Mustang King Cobra was a throwback to the muscle-car days, sporting tape stripes, a cool snake decal and a 122-horsepower engine. Lincoln's limited-edition Continental Mark V Diamond Jubilee coupe was typically excessive, coming with a gold grille, special midnight-blue metallic paint, and a leather-bound owner's manual and tool kit.

Cheering News

To the surprise of few, Muhammad Ali came out of retirement in 1977, and defeated Ernie Shavers. Baseball attendance was up twenty-four percent from the previous year, but even that sport's popularity was no match for that of football's Dallas Cowboy Cheerleaders. Practically more famous than the Dallas Cowboys themselves, the scantily clad pom-

pom girls even served as the basis for a TV movie starring Jane Seymour.

Apple Blossoms

The Atari Video Computer System (later renamed Atari 2600), which included such games as Tank, Pong, Centipede, Galaxian, Breakout and Pole Position, totally dominated the home videogame market upon its release in 1977. Atari also opened the first Chuck E Cheese restaurant, a nightmarish "fun-for-the-whole family" eatery featuring robotic animals and electronic games. In other technological news, twenty-six-year-old Steve Wozniak and twenty-one-year-old Steve Jobs marketed their new invention, the Apple II **personal computer**.

Bottoms Up, Y'All!

Beer-can collecting was a popular hobby in the late 1970s, and few new brands were more sought after than Billy Beer, a heady concoction brewed to the exact specifications of President Carter's beer-swilling brother.

TOP ALBUMS

FLEETWOOD MAC
Rumours
....

THE EAGLES
Hotel California
....

BARBRA STREISAND
A Star Is Born
soundtrack
....

LINDA RONSTADT
Simple Dreams
....

BARRY MANILOW
Barry Manilow Live

nineteen

'78

Three years **after the end of the Vietnam War,** Hollywood finally felt comfortable enough to tackle the subject. Although Michael Cimino's *The Deer Hunter* had some **unbelievably gripping Vietnam sequences,** it and Hal Ashby's **Coming Home** both dealt primarily with the after-effects of the war on everyday existence in America. Like *The Best Years of Our Lives* thirty-two years earlier, both films **touched a nerve with American audiences,** who made them two of the year's bigger hits.

American audiences seemed to have a higher tolerance than usual for serious films, if the success of *An Unmarried Woman*, *Interiors*, and *Midnight Express* was anything to go by. *An Unmarried Woman* featured a memorable performance by Jill Clayburgh as a woman trying to deal with the breakup of her marriage, while *Interiors* was Woody Allen's respectable stab at Ingmar Bergman-style family drama. Of the many who sat through Alan Parker's brutal *Midnight Express*, most would probably think twice before trying to smuggle

 Frathouse fun for Belushi *(above)* and teen romance for Newton-John and Travolta in *Grease.*

drugs out of Turkey in the future. *Foul Play* (a surprisingly effective supense-murder-comedy starring Chevy Chase and Goldie Hawn) and *Up in Smoke* (a completely gratuitous yet absurdly funny drug comedy starring Cheech Marin and Tommy Chong) were two of 1978's most popular comedies, but the surprise comedy hit of the year was

National Lampoon's Animal House. Set somewhere in the early 1960s, the film followed the anarchic antics of a fraternity house at fictional Faber College, and provided a perfect showcase for John Belushi's manic brand of physical comedy. As cries of **"Toga! Toga! Toga!"** rang through the air, college kids everywhere re-enacted the film's toga party sequence, and a whole new generation discovered the unintelligible joys of The Kingsmen's "Louie, Louie."

1978 also saw Christopher Reeve save the world in *Superman*, and offered a surplus of music-related films, both good and truly awful. The better ones included *The Last Waltz*, Martin Scorsese's documentary of The Band's final concert, and Steve Rash's *The Buddy Holly Story*, whose stunning performance by Gary Busey (in the title role) more than made up for the liberties the script took with Holly's life. **Grease**, a film version of the popular Broadway musical, starred John Travolta and Olivia Newton-John as the two halves of a greaser-debutante romance. Much worse were

TOP SINGLES

THE BEE GEES
"Night Fever"

ANDY GIBB
"Shadow Dancing"

CHIC
"Le Freak"

THE BEE GEES
"Stayin' Alive"

EXILE
"Kiss You All Over"

the vapid disco comedy *Thank God It's Friday*, and *FM*, in which a radio station defies its stiff parent company by spinning the rebellious sounds of Linda Ronstadt and Jimmy Buffett. Lamest of all was *Sergeant Pepper's Lonely Hearts Club Band*, record mogul Robert Stigwood's woefully misguided attempt to make movie stars out of The Bee Gees and Peter Frampton.

Dead Scary

Horror films proved immensely successful in 1978, with *Damien—The Omen II*, *Magic* and *Invasion of the Body Snatchers* (a remake of the 1956 "pod people" classic) all doing well in the theaters. George Romero's *Dawn of the Dead* was an update of his earlier *Night of the Living Dead*, given a late-seventies twist; instead of attacking a farmhouse (as they did in the 1968 film), Romero's army of zombies invaded a suburban shopping mall. **Halloween**, a low-budget film by John Carpenter, kicked off a slasher-flick craze that would make millions over the next decade, and effectively introduced the crazed-killer-in-a-hockey-mask archetype to the horror genre.

TV News

"Boss! Boss! Ze plane! Ze plane!" Uttered by the diminutive Herve Vellechaize, these magic words heralded the beginning of each week's **Fantasy Island** episode. Villechaize (who played the white-suited assistant to Ricardo Montalban's omniscient Mr

Roarke) was just part of 1978's odd parade of new TV stars—*The Incredible Hulk* featured hearing-imparied bodybuilder Lou Ferrigno; *Diff'rent Strokes* made a star out of Gary Coleman, whose congenital kidney condition made him look much younger than his real age; *Mork and Mindy* starred comedian **Robin Williams** (*left*) as an alien (from planet Ork) given to exclamations of "Shazbat!" and "Na-Nu, Na-Nu," while *Taxi* introduced the bizarre genius of Andy Kaufman to the world. And speaking of bizarre genius, both adjectives (but mostly just the former) were used to describe *The $1.98 Beauty Contest*, a *Gong Show*-like game show (produced by Chuck Barris, of course) hosted by flamboyant comedian Rip Taylor.

Other new shows included *WKRP in Cincinnati*, a radio station sitcom based loosely on *FM*, and *Battlestar Galactica*, a science fiction series

IN THE NEWS

February 8 – Egyptian President Anwar Sadat visits the US, urging the country to exert pressure on Israel to negotiate a Middle East peace settlement.

April 7 – President Carter postpones production of the neutron bomb, pending further research.

May 26 – The first legal casino in the US outside of Nevada opens in Atlantic City, New Jersey.

June 6 – Proposition 13, a controversial California constitutional amendment to cut state property taxes by 57 percent wins over California voters. Amendment reduces the state's revenues from $12 billion to $5 billion.

'78 "Hey, man—what's happenin'?" *Up in Smoke*'s Cheech and Chong (*above*), and (*left*) Dr Bannister changes into *The Incredible Hulk.*

whose three-hour, three-million-dollar premiere was said to be the most expensive premiere telecast to date.

Soap Strikes Oil

Far less costly, but much more popular, was *Dallas*, the highest-rated nighttime soap opera since *Peyton Place*. Revolving around the various philanderings and business dealings of two Texas oil families, the show boasted an attractive cast (including Victoria Principal, Charlene Tilton, Linda Gray, and Patrick Duffy) and starred Larry Hagman as the fantastically amoral JR Ewing.

Fighting Fit

Inflation continued to rise in 1978, but it didn't seem to affect the sales of jogging suits and other sportswear, which went through the roof as the result of a renewed American interest in physical fitness. Major league baseball's popularity was at an all-time high, with a record forty million fans attending games in 1978. In an attempt to rack up similar attendance numbers, the NFL extended the regular football season from fourteen to sixteen games. In boxing, gap-toothed **Leon Spinks** made headlines on February 15 by winning the World Heavyweight title from Muhammad Ali. Ali defeated Spinks in a September 15 rematch, becoming the first heavyweight boxer to regain the title three different times.

Electronic Invasion

Atari continued its domination of the home videogame market with the release of Atari Football. Meanwhile, the Midway company imported Space Invaders from Japan; the game quickly became the hottest arcade attraction in the country. Mattel's hand-held Electronic Quarterback sold particularly well at Christmas time, as did other electronic games like Simon, Merlin, and the 2XL talking robot.

Killer Candy?

Also popular with the kids were Pop Rocks, a candy that fizzed noisily when placed in one's mouth. The big rumor going around school playgrounds at the time was that "Mikey," a small child who appeared in commercials for Life Cereal, had died after ingesting a combination of Pop Rocks and Coca-Cola.

Music News

One of the year's most important television events, at least as far as **Kiss** fans were concerned, was the broadcast of *Kiss Meets the Phantom of the Park*. Filmed at Southern California's Magic Mountain amusement park, the gloriously cheesy made-for-TV movie (which actually received a theatrical release in Europe) featured Kiss as extra-terrestrial superheroes who defeat a mad scientist (Anthony Zerbe) and his Kiss look-alike robots. Though the broadcast scored reasonably well with viewers, the Kiss phenomenon was beginning to peak. After eight Kiss albums in three years (including 1978's *Double Platinum* compilation), and Kiss merchandise ranging from dolls to makeup to comic books, the band further inundated the market with solo albums by members Paul Stanley, Gene Simmons, Ace Frehley, and Peter Criss; Casablanca, the band's label, insisted that retailers order the same amount of each solo record,

thereby burdening record stores with thousands of unwanted LPs.

Record Return

Similar over-saturation of the market occurred in the case of *Don't Look Back*, Boston's follow-up to their tremendously successful 1976

debut. Retailers ordered millions of copies of the record, thereby insuring its "multi-platinum" status; however, once fans realized that the album was a rush job devoid of decent songs, thousands of unopened boxes of *Don't Look Back* wound up being returned to Epic, the band's record

company. As a result, US record companies began to impose harsher restrictions on album returns from retailers—who, in turn, began to order smaller amounts of new releases from the record companies, setting the stage for the record industry panic of 1979.

Disco Fever Epidemic

The *Saturday Night Fever* soundtrack stayed at the top of the album charts for half the year, spawning massive hits for The Bee Gees and Yvonne Elliman. Once limited to black and gay subcultures, disco had completely infiltrated the mainstream; "roller disco," a combination of disco dancing and roller skating, was a popular new variation. The *Grease* soundtrack, packed full of disco-fied 1950s pastiches like "Summer Nights" and "You're the One That I Want," also sold extremely well. Chic's "Le Freak" and Donna Summer's thumping remake of Jimmy Webb's "MacArthur Park" kept the dance floors packed, and even teen idol Leif Garrett boogied onto the disco bandwagon with "I Was Made For Dancin'."

The Village People, the creation of French disco producer Jacques Morali, gave Kiss a run for their outrageousness dollar. Although the group's six members dressed as obvious gay archetypes (a policeman, a construction worker, a cowboy, an indian, a soldier, and a leatherman), straight America didn't catch the thinly veiled gay references in hits like "Macho Man," "YMCA," and "In The Navy." Steve Martin, whose albums *Let's Get Small* and *A Wild And Crazy Guy* made him the premier comedian of the late seventies, dressed up in Egyptian garb for his novelty hit, "King Tut." Akron, Ohio natives Devo were about twenty years ahead of their time with their futuristic outfits, herky-jerky music and complex theories of "Devolution;" dismissed by many as a novelty record, Devo's *Are We Not Men?* LP would exert a great deal of influence on American indie bands in the 1990s.

'78 Uninhibited performance artists **The Village People**, and *(above)* Kiss.

IN THE NEWS

June 28 – In the case of *Bakke v the University of California*, the US Supreme Court rules that the college has to admit white applicant Allan Bakke to its medical school. Bakke claimed his civil rights had been violated by the school's minority-student admission quotas.

August 4 – Having recently discovered that their land was used as a toxic waste dump between 1947 and 1952, the residents of Niagara Falls, New York's Love Canal community begin to evacuate their homes.

September 17 – Anwar Sadat and Israeli Prime Minister Menachem Begin sign an agreement at the White House to conclude a peace treaty between their two nations within three months.

October 6 – Congress extends the deadline for the ratification of the Equal Rights Amendment to June 30, 1982. So far, 35 of the required 38 states have ratified it.

November 18 – 911 people, most of them Americans, commit mass suicide at the People's Temple commune in Guyana. After ordering the murder of California Representative Leo J Ryan, who had come to the commune on a fact-finding mission, Reverend Jim Jones orders the commune's members to drink poisoned Flavoraid.

November 27 – San Francisco Mayor George Moscone and city supervisor Harvey Milk are shot to death at City Hall by disgruntled former supervisor Dan White. White later pleads "Twinkie insanity" (ie, he had been eating too much junk food in the weeks leading up to the attack) and actually receives a reduced sentence.

1979 was a troubled and **troubling year** for the United States.

Inflation hit 13.3 percent, the highest rate in thirty-three years;

thanks to strained relations with the OPEC nations, oil prices were rising as well.

Odd-even gas sale days were instituted for motorists in California and many other states;

in the East and Midwest,

truckers rioted over fuel rationing.

'79 New Wave band The Knack.

Right-wing Christians responded to what they saw as a direct correlation between the country's troubles and the "decline of American morals" (ie, increased tolerance of drug use, gay rights, and abortion rights) by becoming increasingly politicized. With more than seventy million Americans claiming to be "born again," the Christian Right (or "**Moral Majority**," as they ostentatiously called themselves) were now a political faction to be reckoned with—a fact that would not escape the notice of the Republican Party during the next presidential election.

Fallout Flops

In July, people began to stare nervously at the sky; *Skylab*, the orbiting US space laboratory, was due to re-enter the Earth's atmosphere, but no one knew where the seventy-seven tons of equipment would actually land. On the evening of July 11, revelers across the country painted target symbols on their roofs and held "The Sky is Falling" parties, but eventually went to bed disappointed; the spacecraft, disintegrating upon re-entry, scattered debris over the Indian Ocean and Australia. No injuries were reported, although many Australians were miffed about having their country used as a dumping ground for American space junk.

July also witnessed the introduction of the US Mint's new Susan B. Anthony dollar coin. The first US coin to feature a historical personage of female persuasion, the eleven-sided Anthony dollar was a resounding flop, mostly because of its similarity in size to a twenty-five cent piece—a similarity which caused numerous folks to accidentally spend them in payphones and videogames like Space Invaders and Asteroids.

Discs Slip...

1979's increased oil prices didn't just inconvenience motorists; as petroleum was needed to press records, the shortages hit American record companies squarely in the pocketbook. This development was further compounded by the news that,

for the first time in twenty-five years, record sales were slipping. Many industry analysts blamed disco for this turn of events, arguing that most disco fans bought singles, not albums.

While this was a huge over-simplification, disco was indeed an easy scapegoat; with disco music having thoroughly saturated nearly every aspect of the market (*Mickey Mouse Disco*, featuring Donald Duck quacking his way through "Macho Duck," was a three-million seller), a backlash was inevitable. The opening shot was fired July 12 at Chicago's Comiskey Park where, between the first and second games of a Chicago White Sox-Detroit Tigers double-header, radio disc jockey Steve Dahl blew up a mountain of disco records as part of a "Disco Demolition Night" promotion. The ensuing riot caused the second game to be canceled, and the "**disco sucks**" movement was off and running.

...And New Wave Breaks

Ironically, one of the year's biggest disco singles was released by veterans of New York City's punk scene. After their first two albums went nowhere, **Blondie** broke through to the mainstream with the blatantly discofied "Heart of Glass;" yet the band—along with such disparate acts as The Knack, The B-52s, and Cheap Trick—was widely considered to be "New Wave," the industry's shorthand term for more accessible (and apolitical) variations on punk rock. Though New Wave was hotly tipped to

be "the next big thing," it turned out to have a relatively short shelf life. (The oft-repeated story that the Carter administration pressured American record companies to steer clear of the punk movement is probably apocryphal; more likely, the industry merely understood that most American rock fans were even more leery of punk than they were of disco.)

In other music news, **Bob Dylan** freaked out his longtime followers by converting to Christianity and releasing the dour *Slow Train Coming*; The Charlie Daniels Band unwittingly primed the world for the advent rap music with "The Devil Went Down to Georgia;" eleven Who fans died during a stampede for seats at a Who concert in Cincinnati, Ohio; and moustachioed singer-songwriter Rupert Holmes scored the last Number One of the "Me Decade" with the sleazy "Escape (The Pina Colada Song)." *Off The Wall*, **Michael Jackson**'s first solo album since the early seventies, was a huge hit, though it was in reality just a warm-up for his forthcoming blockbuster.

Movie News

It was almost too spooky to be a coincidence. *The China Syndrome*, a drama about an accident at a California nuclear facility (and its subsequent cover-up), had barely opened when the **Three Mile Island** leak occurred; the accident silenced the energy companies who had derided *The China Syndrome*'s premise as far-fetched, and lent an extra measure of terror to the Jane Fonda-Michael Douglas vehicle. Even more frightening was ***Apocalypse Now***, Francis Ford

79 *Above:* **Debbie Harry, lead singer of Blondie.**

September 23 – 200,000 demonstrators attend the "No Nukes" anti-nuclear rally and concert in New York City.

October 8–12 – The Dow Jones Industrial plunges 58 points in panic trading triggered by the Federal Reserve Board's raising of interest rates. Though the market eventually rights itself, the new high interest rates spell bad news for the automobile and construction industries.

November 4 – The US embassy in Teheran, Iran is seized by Iranian student revolutionaries. All foreign, black and female hostages are quickly released, but 52 white American males remain in custody. The revolutionaries demand the return of the deposed Shah to Iran in order to stand trial; the US refuses, and the "hostage crisis" begins.

December 4 – President Carter announces candidacy for re-election, despite polls showing his approval rating at its lowest levels yet.

TOP ALBUMS

THE EAGLES

The Long Run

LED ZEPPELIN

In Through The Out Door

SUPERTRAMP

Breakfast In America

THE BEE GEES

Spirits Having Flown

DONNA SUMMER

Bad Girls

Coppola's hallucinatory adaptation of Joseph Conrad's *Heart of Darkness*, which starred Marlon Brando as an out-of-control US officer in Vietnam, and Martin Sheen as the special agent assigned to kill him. And for sheer visceral thrills, you couldn't beat the worm-like creature busting out of a man's stomach in *Alien*, the sci-fi thriller that made Sigourney Weaver a star. Dustin Hoffman and Meryl Streep fought a custody battle in **Kramer versus Kramer**, Woody Allen tried to make some sense of his romantic life in *Manhattan*, and Sylvester Stallone climbed back into the ring in *Rocky II*. There were some agreeable low-budget releases—Walter Hill's *The Warriors* was an evocative fantasy about New York street gangs, while Jonathan Kaplan's *Over the Edge* was a powerful look at disaffected youths in a suburban tract community. Not as good as it could have been, but still pretty damn enjoyable, was **Rock 'n' Roll High School**, in which The Ramones played loud enough to cause deafness in white mice, and helped destroy a suburban high school in the process.

One of the surprise hits of the year, Blake Edwards' **"10,"** made a star out of Bo Derek, who played the object of Dudley Moore's affections. The statuesque Derek, the last of a string of look-alike wives for actor/photographer John Derek, inspired a mercifully brief infatuation among white women for corn-rowed braids.

John Wayne died of cancer on June 11, at the age of seventy-two, but at least "The Duke" could be content in the knowledge that America was still the land of the free and the home of competing roller disco films—both *Roller Boogie* (starring Linda Blair) and *Skatetown, USA* (with Scott Baio

and Flip Wilson) tried to capitalize on the new fad, but with little success.

Palimony Acrimony

The other big news in Hollywood was the "palimony" suit brought against Lee Marvin by former girlfriend Michelle Triola Marvin. Though the couple had broken up in 1970, Ms Marvin claimed half the money Mr Marvin had earned during their six-year relationship. A judge eventually ruled against her, but did award her $104,000 for "purposes of rehabilitation."

TV News

To gauge the utter dearth of ideas in television land, one had only to look at the many new shows taking their cues from successful movies. **Makin' It** starred David Naughton (formerly of the "I'm a Pepper" Dr Pepper commercials) as the Travolta-like star dancer of a New Jersey disco, and was one of the few shows to in history be canceled while its theme song (sung by Naughton) was still in the Top Ten. (Naughton should have tried his luck on *Dance Fever*, a disco game show which gave out cash prizes to the best dancers.) **Delta House**, a sanitized version of

National Lampoon's Animal House, featured a handful of that movie's supporting players, but failed to hang on for more than a few months. Although John Belushi was still committed to *Saturday Night Live*, someone at CBS had the bright idea of cashing in on Belushi's new-found fame by casting his less talented brother Jim in the short-lived sitcom *Working Stiffs*, which also starred a young Michael Keaton.

'79 Bo Derek.

Other shows cashed in on previous or present hits. *Trapper John, MD* starred Pernell Roberts as an older version of Wayne Rogers' *M*A*S*H** character; *Archie Bunker's Place* shifted the scenario from Archie's house to his bar; *Knots Landing* was essentially *Dallas, Jr*; and *The Facts of Life* (later known colloquially as "The Fats of Life," thanks to a cast-wide weight gain) was merely a spin-off for Charlotte Rae's *Diff'rent Strokes* character.

Though absolutely witless, **The Dukes of Hazzard** (*right*) didn't need to exploit a TV or movie connection to score a hit. The white-trash action comedy starred Tom Wopat and John Schneider as Luke and Bo Duke, the short-shorted Catharine Bach as their cousin Daisy, and Sorrell Brooke as their nemesis, "Boss" Hogg, but many viewers tuned in just for the car chases featuring "General Lee," a '69 Dodge Charger.

Tate Succeeds Ali

In boxing, Muhammad Ali retired yet again; in his absence, the heavyweight championship went to John Tate, who defeated Gerrie Coetzee in October.

Street Cred

Nike's Tailwind shoe became the first air-cushioned athletic shoe on the market, and it became increasingly acceptable to wear running shoes with street clothes—although not with the designer jeans that were currently very much the rage. Though made for both sexes, the narrowly fitted, high-priced jeans were much more popular with women; favored brands included Gloria Vanderbilt, Chic, Chemin de Fer, Jordache, Britannia, and Sergio Valente.

'80

Only fifty-four percent of registered voters went to the polls for the 1980 presidential election, **the worst level of turnout since Dewey nearly defeated Truman** in 1948. In retrospect, such apathy was understandable; the pitiful state of the economy and Jimmy Carter's inability to resolve the **Iranian hostage crisis** gave voters **two good reasons not to re-elect** the incumbent.

In addition Ronald Reagan's blatant disregard for facts (on the campaign trail, Reagan asserted that trees caused more pollution than industry, and that new evidence had surfaced giving credence to the biblical view of creation) and the CIA connections of running-mate George Bush gave voters ample reason to be very, very frightened. In the end, Reagan's recurring cry of "**We want to be respected again**" resonated strongly with Americans shamed and frustrated by the hostage crisis; whatever happened, voters reasoned, it had to be better than another four years of Carter.

Detroit In Dire Straits

Still, if it hadn't been for Carter, Detroit would have been in even worse shape than it was by the end of 1980. On January 7, Carter signed a bill authorizing a federal bailout for the floundering Chrysler Corporation to the tune of fifteen hundred million dollars in federal loan guarantees. For Chrysler chairman Lee Iacocca, who was instrumental in swinging the deal, it was a bittersweet year; 1980 saw the introduction of Dodge's Aries and Plymouth's Reliant, the first of several successful permutations of Chrysler's "K-Car" compact, but it also witnessed the closing of Dodge's main plant in Detroit. In general, US auto sales were at their worst in nineteen years, down twenty percent from a dismal 1979; the Ford Motor Company reported a third-quarter loss of five hundred and ninety-five million dollars, the biggest ever for a US corporation.

Hollywood Highs...And Lows

Richard Pryor was also having a particularly lousy 1980. Not only did the talented comedian (who made his name with such raunchy albums as *That Nigger's Crazy* and *Bicentennial Nigger*) star in three terrible films (*Stir Crazy*, *Wholly Moses!*, and *In God We Trust*),

but he also severely burned over half of his body in a **freebasing** accident. The ensuing news coverage marked the first time most Americans had even heard of freebasing cocaine.

Michael Cimino's self-indulgent *Heaven's Gate* was the talk of the industry (it cost a then-record forty-five million dollars), but for the most part Hollywood was doing very well for itself. *The Empire Strikes Back*, the second film in the *Star Wars* trilogy, was a huge hit, as was *Nine to Five*, an office comedy starring Dolly Parton and Jane Fonda. *Urban Cowboy*, starring John Travolta, started a brief western wear fad, although *Cruising* didn't exactly do the same for the

'80 Sony's Walkman, introduced in 1980, for music on the move.

'80 Lily Tomlin, Dolly Parton, and Jane Fonda plot in *Nine to Five*.

leatherman look. The film, which starred Al Pacino as a cop tracking a killer through New York City's gay bars, was the subject of vociferous protests by various homosexual organizations.

Prom Night and *Friday the 13th* were popular additions to the slasher-film genre, although **The Shining** proved that no one could swing an axe quite like Jack Nicholson. Although the saccharine Olivia Newton-John vehicle *Xanadu* came close, none of the above were quite as frightening as *Can't Stop the Music*, a disco musical starring The Village People, Bruce Jenner, and Valerie Perrine.

Black And Blue

Neil Diamond, one of the best pop songwriters of the sixties, sank to self-aggrandizing lows in his update of *The Jazz Singer*, although the scene with him in blackface still must be seen to be believed. Faring much better were Dan Aykroyd and John Belushi, who brought their R&B-loving **Blues Brothers** characters to the screen in John Landis' film of the same name. While Aykroyd and Belushi's own musical contributions were negligible, the film did at least give Ray Charles, James Brown and Aretha Franklin more exposure than they'd had in years.

Fashion Claims Further Victims

Reagan's election ushered in a new age of American conservatism, and the "preppy" collegiate look popular with high school and college students fit right in with it. Sales of Brooks Brothers, LL Bean, and Ralph Lauren's Polo clothes were up, thanks partially to the publication of Lisa Birnbach's **The Preppy Handbook**. Though the book was intended as satire, it was taken at face value by most of its teenaged readers, who regarded it as a fashion bible.

Also making waves was the new, controversial ad campaign for Calvin Klein jeans. "Nothing comes between me and my Calvins," claimed fifteen year-old actress Brooke Shields (star of the risible *Blue Lagoon*), and sales of the designer jeans went through the roof.

'80 "Blues Brothers" Aykroyd and Belushi enlist Ray Charles' help in their mission.

Shotguns and Shoguns

For television viewers, "Who shot JR?" was the most important question of 1980. *Dallas* had ended its spring season with the shooting of Larry Hagman's **JR Ewing** character, and nearly everyone had a theory about who actually pulled the trigger. The November 21 episode, which provided

TOP ALBUMS

PINK FLOYD
The Wall

JOHN LENNON/YOKO ONO
Double Fantasy

THE ROLLING STONES
Emotional Rescue

BILLY JOEL
Glass Houses

BOB SEGER AND THE SILVER BULLET BAND
Against the Wind

the answer to the mystery (JR's wife's sister did it), was watched by more viewers than any other program in TV history.

Also highly rated was *Shogun*, a four-part mini-series based on James Clavell's novel of seventeenth-century Japan. The mini-series, which starred **Richard Chamberlain** as English ship captain John Blackthorne, utilized plenty of Japanese dialogue, thus introducing "Domo Arigato" to the American lexicon.

1980's popular new shows included *Flo*, a spin-off of *Alice*, *Bosom Buddies*, starring a young Tom Hanks, and *Magnum, PI*, which starred Tom Selleck as a detective living in Hawaii. ABC's **Fridays** was criticized for being a *Saturday Night Live* clone, but with the entire original cast of *SNL* gone, *Fridays* was often the funnier show of the two. *Fridays* also had a much hipper musical booking policy than *SNL*, regularly featuring bands like The Clash, The Jam, and The Pretenders.

Walter Cronkite announced his intention to retire in 1981 as anchorman of the *CBS Evening News*, a position he'd held since 1950. Mackenzie Phillips exited *One Day at a Time*, although not of her own volition; once recovered from her addiction to cocaine, she returned to the show in 1981.

Pop, Rap... And Pap

Disco continued to sell well in 1980, with songs like Blondie's "Call Me (Theme From American Gigolo)," Diana Ross' "Upside Down," Irene Cara's "Fame," and Lipps, Inc's "Funkytown" among the year's top smashes, but listeners' tastes were definitely changing. "Average Joe" rockers like Bruce Springsteen, Billy Joel, and Bob Seger were all at the height of their popularity, but mushy, adult-oriented ballads like The Captain and Tennille's "Do That To Me One More Time," Kenny Rogers' "Lady," and Christopher Cross's "Sailing" also spent time at the top of the charts. In January, The Sugarhill Gang's "Rapper's Delight" became the first rap record to make the Top Hundred, peaking at number thirty-six on the Billboard charts.

Digitally recorded LPs were widely marketed for the first time, but more important was the introduction of Sony's **Walkman** portable stereo to the United States. The lightweight tape player virtually changed the listening habits of the entire country, and was probably single-handedly responsible for the tremendous boom in cassette sales during the early half of the decade.

January 2 – The Nuclear Regulatory Commission reports that 38 of the 68 functioning nuclear power plants in the US have failed to meet the January 1 deadline for changes in equipment and procedures. These improvements were mandated in response to the accident at Three Mile Island.

January 4 – President Carter responds to the Soviet invasion of Afghanistan by reneging on a deal to send 17,000,000 metric tons of grain to Russia. On January 20, he also announces a US boycott of the Summer Olympics in Moscow.

April 7 – The US breaks off diplomatic relations with Iran over the continuing hostage crisis.

April 15 – A flood of Cuban refugees leave their homeland, with Fidel Castro's blessing. Over the next two months, over 100,000 enter the US, most of them through Florida. The US initially welcomes them, then—fearing that Castro is using the exodus as a means to empty out his prisons—takes steps to screen the refugees.

April 24 – An airborne attempt to rescue the hostages in Iran ends in disaster, as a helicopter collides with a C-130 troop transport. Eight troops die in the accident, and five are injured.

April 26 – Secretary of State Cyrus Vance resigns in opposition to the military rescue attempt of the hostages. Senator Edmund Muskie takes his place.

April 29 – A "Washington for Jesus" rally brings 200,000 evangelical Christians to the nation's capital.

In Arcade-ia

The videogame industry continued to thrive, with Atari still leading the pack; when the company released a home version of Space Invaders, Atari 2600 sales hit their highest level to date. Atari's first serious challenger was Mattel, who introduced a home videogame system of its own; Intellivision, which included such games as baseball, poker, and blackjack, was more expensive than Atari, but boasted better graphics. 1980 was also the year of **Pac-Man**, the most popular arcade game yet. Originally titled Puck-Man, the name was changed when Namco executives realized that vandals could easily alter the machine's lettering to read, well, something else.

Cubism

Americans who weren't glued to their videogames went nuts over Rubik's Cube, a three-dimensional puzzle invented by Hungarian architectural professor Erno Rubik *(pictured left)*. Manufactured in the states by the Ideal Toy Company, the cube sold millions; its success was quickly followed by spate of books and computer programs that could solve the puzzle for you.

Fame And Shame

In sports, the US Olympic hockey team surprised everyone by defeating the highly favored Finnish and Russian teams at the Winter Olympics in Lake Placid, New York. Muhammad Ali came out of retirement yet again, but went right back after being beaten by Larry Holmes. Rosie Ruiz, named the female winner of the Boston Marathon, was stripped of the medal eight days later when it was revealed that she took the subway for part of the race.

May 17–19 – Race riots in the Liberty City area of Miami, Florida leave fourteen dead, 300 injured, and cause $100 million in damage. The riots erupt after an all-white jury acquits four former Miami policemen in the fatal beating of a black man.

May 18 – Mt St Helens, a Washington State volcano dormant since 1857, erupts. The blast blows the top of the mountain completely off, and sets off a series of fires, mudslides and floods in the 120-square-mile area surrounding the volcano. Fifteen people are killed, and at least 40 are listed as missing.

June 27 – President Carter signs a law requiring draft registration by men nineteen to twenty years of age, although no draft is actually contemplated.

July 14–17 – The Republican National Convention nominates Ronald Reagan for president, and George Bush for vice-president.

August 11–14 – Carter and Mondale are nominated for re-election by the Democratic National Convention.

November 4 – Ronald Reagan wins the presidential election by a margin of 8 million votes. Independent candidate John Anderson receives 7 percent of the popular vote.

So Long, Colonel

December 16 was a sad day for fried-chicken lovers everywhere, as Col Harland Sanders, founder of Kentucky Fried Chicken, left for the great chicken shack in the sky. He was ninety.

TOP SINGLES

KENNY ROGERS
"Lady"

BLONDIE
"Call Me (Theme From *American Gigolo*)"

JOHN LENNON
"(Just Like) Starting Over"

DIANA ROSS
"Upside Down"

PINK FLOYD
"Another Brick In The Wall (Part II)"

"This Is The End..."

Thanks to the use of "The End" in *Apocalypse Now*, a new generation of teenagers was discovering Jim Morrison and The Doors. Morrison became such a popular icon for early eighties teenagers that *Rolling Stone* was moved to do a cover story on him. The headline: "**He's Hot. He's Sexy. He's Dead**." Nobody joked much about John Lennon, however. In the weeks that followed his assassination in New York City by former mental patient Mark David Chapman, each spin of "(Just Like) Starting Over" only seemed to compound the sad irony of his death.

81

When Ronald Reagan entered office in 1981, the American economy was in sad shape. The worldwide recession was taking its toll on an already hurting US; inflation rose by 14 percent, while the unemployment rate hit 7.4 percent. According to the Census Bureau, the average household income before taxes had declined an average of 2.6 percent per household; in a not-unrelated statistic, Americans filed for a record 1,210,000 divorces.

Medical costs also hit an all-time high in 1981. *The New England Journal of Medicine* linked heart disease and coronary death to consumption of large amounts of cholesterol, and also announced that herpes simplex, the country's most rapidly spreading sexually transmitted disease, could be suppressed by acyclovir, an experimental drug. The disease that would eventually become known as **AIDS** also began to surface in 1981, killing mostly gay men in large urban areas. For the time being, it was known in medical circles as GRID, or Gay Related Immune Deficiency.

In Memoriam

In Washington DC the competition to design the Vietnam War Memorial was won by Maya Yand Lin, a twenty-one-year-old Yale architectural student. The design, a low granite V inscribed with the names of the US war dead, received mixed reviews from the public, but most Nam vets were pleased to finally receive a monument of their own. A less permanent monument was erected in Boston, when the Hostess company celebrated

the Twinkie's fiftieth anniversary by making a ten-foot-long version of the spongy snack cake. According to press reports, the über-Twinkie was filled with seventy-five gallons of creme.

Videogame News

Atari's success continued with the release of a home version of Asteroids, while newcomer Sega released an American version of Konami's popular Frogger. Video arcades in the US raked in five billion dollars in 1981, their highest revenues to date. In other microchip news, **IBM** developed its first personal computer.

More Misery For Motown

Hard times continued to plague Detroit's auto makers; between them, they produced only 6.2 million cars in 1981, the lowest level of production in twenty years. General Motors was mired in a massive recall campaign, in which 6.4 million mid-size cars built between 1978 and 1981 had to be returned in order to have two bolts replaced in their rear suspensions. The lone automotive bright spot of 1981 was reserved for lovers of convertibles; after several years in which no American-made convertibles were manufactured, Buick got back into the swing of things with its new Riviera Ragtop.

Fans Favour Football

The popularity of professional football was at an all-time high in 1981, as the NFL set a record attendance average of sixty thousand fans per game. Many fans were beginning to become disillusioned with baseball, especially in light of a mid-season strike by the players' union.

Victory For Video

In a landmark move, the Federal Communications Commission eased restrictions on radio stations regarding time allotted for commercials; as a result, stations could now air as many commercials as they liked, with no obligation to allocate time for news or public affairs programming. While the new ruling was a boon for radio-station coffers, it gave music fans all the more reason to turn off their radios and turn on **MTV**, the new all-music video cable channel that was, for the time being, relatively commercial free. Debuting with a transmission of the Buggles' prophetic "Video Killed The Radio Star," MTV was an immediate sensation, at least among those lucky enough to get it through their local cable service; in a move that echoed the early days of television, many bars drew in extra business by hanging "We have MTV" signs in the window. The network's original "veejays" included Alan Hunter, Martha Quinn, JJ Jackson, Mark Goodman, and Nina Blackwood. As most American recording acts (and record companies) were not in the habit of making videos, the channel was initially dominated by English artists. While this was fine for folks interested in the latest bands (and

'81 Hall and Oates.

fashions) coming out of the UK, many critics noticed a pronounced lack of black artists.

Black Musicians Marginalized

Caught up in the continuing disco backlash (many white record buyers now considered anything black to be "disco"), black recording artists were having a difficult time crossing over onto the pop world. "Punk-funk" king Rick James had a number three album with *Street Songs*, and a Top Twenty hit with "Super Freak," yet couldn't get his video played on MTV. **Prince**, currently racking up critical plaudits for his new *Controversy* LP, was booed off the stage at the LA Coliseum while opening for The Rolling Stones. (Within three years, a Prince show would be the most sought-after ticket in town; right now, Stones fans much preferred the bar-band blues of fellow openers George Thorogood and The Destroyers to Prince's sensual Sly Stone grooves.) Only two records by black artists topped the charts in 1981—Diana Ross

and Lionel Richie's schmaltzy "Endless Love," and "Celebration," Kool and The Gang's available-for-weddings-and-bar-mitzvahs anthem. Blondie experimented with rap in "Rapture," though rap was still too much of an underground phenomenon for the mainstream. For the most part, white America was digging the anemic arena-rock of REO Speedwagon, Styx, and Journey, the pop-country sounds of Eddie Rabbit and Dolly Parton, and the pretty-boy pop of Daryl Hall and John Oates and **Rick Springfield**. Springfield, an Australian actor and musician who'd had a fluke hit in 1972 with "Speak To The Sky," was now one of America's leading heartthrobs, thanks to his regular role as Dr Noah Drake on top-rated daytime soap opera *General Hospital*.

TV News

Two of Springfield's co-stars, Anthony Geary and Genie Francis, were the darlings of daytime TV viewers; when their characters, Luke and Laura, got married in November, the wedding

Dynasty's soap scandals won massive TV audiences.

episode scored the highest ever rating largest for a daytime dramatic series. In the wake of *Dallas*, **nighttime soaps** were poping up everywhere; *Dynasty*, starring Linda Evans and John Forsythe, and *Falcon Crest*, starring Robert Foxworth and Ronald Reagan's former spouse Jane Wyman, were two of the most popular.

Bored with the stale skits of *Saturday Night Live* and *Fridays*, many viewers began to switch their late-night allegiances to **SCTV Network**, an innovative and surreal comedy show from Canada. The talented cast included such future film stars as John Candy, Rick Moranis, and Martin Short. Otherwise, the funniest new show on TV was *The People's Court*, a syndicated show in which real-life small claims cases were tried by retired California Superior Court judge Joseph Wapner.

Smurfs, a phenomenally popular Saturday morning cartoon concerning the adventures of blue, forest-dwelling humanoids, did appeal to certain stoned sensibilities, but the show was primarily the domain of the younger set.

Movie News

The films of 1981 were a diverse lot: Henry Fonda (in his final role) raged against the onslaught of old age in *On Golden Pond*, while Burt Lancaster played an aging gambler in Louis Malle's bleak *Atlantic City*. Superman (Christopher Reeve) married Lois Lane (Margot Kidder) in *Superman 2*, while an inebriated Dudley Moore charmed Liza Minelli in *Arthur*. Already popular for his *Star Wars* appearances, Harrison Ford became a major star on the strength of **Raiders of the Lost Ark**, Steven Spielberg's exciting throwback to the days of Saturday afternoon serials.

Kathleen Turner made a stunning debut in Lawrence Kasdan's *noir*-ish *Body Heat*, while Faye Dunaway's

portrayal of Joan Crawford in *Mommie Dearest* was so over the top ("No more wire hangers, *ever!*") that audiences didn't know whether to laugh or recoil. Burt Reynolds sleepwalked through another series of uninspired films (*The Cannonball Run*, *Paternity*, *Sharky's Machine*), but he could seemingly do no wrong in the eyes of the moviegoing public. Warren Beatty, on the other hand, fell flat with *Reds*, an overlong romance set against the Russian Revolution. The **horror genre** continued to thrive, with films like *Friday the 13th Part Two*, *Halloween Two*, *Happy Birthday to Me*, *My Bloody Valentine*, *An American Werewolf in London*, and *Scanners* all doing well at the box office despite their variable quality. The year's biggest horror, however, was Brooke Shields' listless performance in Franco Zeffirelli's *Endless Love*; it was slowly dawning on the public that, though beautiful, Brooke couldn't act her way out of a bag.

John Waters would have known what to do with Brooke Shields. Notorious for such cult gross-outs as *Pink Flamingos* and *Desperate Living*, Waters had a knack for putting familiar faces in unexpected roles. *Polyester*, Waters' first mainstream film, featured such oddball casting choices as 1950s teen idol Tab Hunter and Dead Boys vocalist Stiv Bators, as well as a scratch-and-sniff "Odorama" gimmick. It also, like most of Waters' best films, starred 300-pound transvestite **Divine**, this time in the role of a suburban housewife.

'81 Harrison Ford in cracking form as Indiana Jones in *Raiders of the Lost Ark,* and Faye Dunaway (*above*) in *Mommie Dearest.*

'82

Whether it was due to "Reaganomics," or just the result of the economy running its natural course, inflation dropped to six percent in 1982. Unemployment, however, continued to climb, hitting 10.8 percent by the end of the year. A record 4.6 million people were on unemployment by October. Over thirty banks failed, and interest rates went through the roof.

TOP TELEVISION SHOWS

Dallas

60 Minutes

Three's Company

*M*A*S*H*

Magnum, PI

Despite the drop in inflation, Detroit was still hit hard by the popularity of imports, which now comprised thirty-five to forty percent of the entire US auto market. Ford tried to improve matters by releasing its 1983 Mustang, which sported a rounded "aero" look that bore little resemblance to its predecessors; though not a failure, the change in styling didn't exactly kickstart sales. Independent auto maker **John De Lorean** got the worst news of all in the fall, when he was busted by federal agents for participation in a twenty-four-million-dollar cocaine deal.

Things were much sunnier over at **EPCOT Center**, the latest addition the Disney World theme park in Orlando, Florida. A geodesic dome featuring educational exhibits with futuristic themes, EPCOT (ie, Experimental Prototype Community of Tomorrow) immediately boosted attendance at the park.

PR Falls In Videogame War

Apple Computer had reason to celebrate in 1982, becoming the first personal-computer firm to reach one billion dollars in annual sales. Atari, on the other hand, was running into trouble. First the company released a home version of Pac-Man, but its cheap graphics and poor playability rendered it extremely unpopular. Then Atari introduced its new 5200 system, an updated version of the Atari 2600; unfortunately, as the 5200 was initially incompatible with 2600 game cartridges, customers had to buy all new games. The company eventually got around to releasing a 2600/5200 adapter, but it came too late to repair the public relations damage.

Other companies were only too happy to capitalize on Atari's mistakes. Coleco released ColecoVision, a programmable home system with the best graphics and sounds to date,

while General Consumer Electronics (GCE) released **Vectrex**, the first home console system to incorporate vector graphics technology. Midway introduced Ms. Pac-Man, which proved even more popular down at the arcade than its predecessor; despite this, arcade revenues were down from the previous year, a trend that would continue during the next fifteen years.

Out Of This World

Hollywood had one of its best years yet, with profits up nine percent from 1981. Much of these profits, of course, came from the success of **ET** The Extra-Terrestrial, Steven Spielberg's heartwarming tale of a lost

alien boy. Other big money-makers included **Tootsie**, a comedy starring Dustin Hoffman as an actor who pretends to be a woman in order to get work, and the melodramatic *An Officer and a Gentleman*, starring Richard Gere and Debra Winger. Tobe Hooper, leaving the low-budget gore of *The Texas Chainsaw Massacre* behind him, made *Poltergeist*, a ghost story as scary as it was successful at the box office.

Arnold Schwarzenegger returned "to hear ze lamentations of ze women" in **Conan the Barbarian**, the popularity of which inspired a whole string of broadswords-and-biceps epics.

Sylvester Stallone also had ample opportunity to flex his pecs, thanks to **Rocky III** (in which he fought the mohawked- and-muttonchopped Mr T and jogged through endless training montages to the

tune of Survivor's "Eye of the Tiger") and *First Blood*, the story of a Nam vet squaring off against smalltown police.

Burt Reynolds was still America's most popular leading man, even if his film choices (*The Best Little Whorehouse in Texas*, which also starred the massively popular Dolly Parton, and *Best Friends*) were dubious at best. In *Fast Times At Ridgemont High*, Sean Penn attracted plenty of attention as a stoned troublemaker named Spicoli, while little-known actors Mickey Rourke, Kevin Bacon, Ellen Barkin, and Paul Reiser all gave impressive performances in Barry Levinson's **Diner**. Meryl Streep gave a typically breathtaking performance as a holocaust survivor in *Sophie's Choice*.

Tron, starring Jeff Bridges as a computer expert trapped in a giant videogame, was notable only for its computer-generated special effects. **Blade Runner**, Ridley Scott's disturbing vision of the not-so-distant future, failed at the box office despite the presence of Harrison Ford, though it has since become a cult favorite. Even more disturbing was the X-rated

'82 Harrison Ford hangs on in *Blade Runner*.

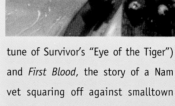

'82 "Thief. Warrior. Gladiator. King." A sword-wielding Arnie plays Conan the Barbarian.

BEST PICTURE

Gandhi

directed by Sir Richard Attenborough

BEST ACTOR

Ben Kingsley

Gandhi

BEST ACTRESS

Meryl Streep

Sophie's Choice

Café Flesh, in which "positives" perform sex acts for the enjoyment of "negatives," who cannot participate. Though often seen as a prescient analogy for the AIDS epidemic to come, the film could easily have been inspired by the wave of genital herpes then sweeping the country—By the end of 1982, twenty million Americans were thought to have the sexually transmitted disease.

Tragedy hit Hollywood twice in 1982. On March 5, hard-partying **John Belushi** died in a bungalow at the Beverly Hills Hotel; an autopsy ruled that his death was caused by a lethal dose of heroin and cocaine. On July 23, Vic Morrow and two child actors were killed in a helicopter accident on the set of *The Twilight Zone*. Director John Landis and four others were indicted on charges of involuntary manslaughter, but later acquitted.

A Blast From The Ghetto

Little noticed in 1982 was an independent film called *Wild Style*. Directed by Charlie Ahearn, the film explored the burgeoning rap music, breakdancing and graffiti art scenes in the black community of New York's South Bronx. Grandmaster Flash and the Furious Five, one of the rap acts to appear in the movie, released a 1982 single called "**The Message**." A departure from the group's usual party-down chants, "The Message" was the first rap hit to comment on the social issues and pressures facing urban blacks; though not a huge pop hit, the single crossed over just enough to let white folks know that something interesting was afoot in the ghettos of America.

For the most part, 1982 was a pretty dull year for American music. Hall and Oates and Lionel Richie continued to dominate the charts; heartland rocker John Cougar found success with watered-down Springsteenisms; and seventies faves like Steve Miller and Chicago came back for another helping of consumer dollars. There were a few highlights, however. Joan Jett (former guitarist for The Runaways, the controversial all-girl band managed by LA entrepreneur extraordinaire Kim Fowley) kicked some real rock 'n' roll back into the charts; The Blasters and The Stray Cats reintroduced American kids to the joys of rockabilly; and The Go-Go's, products of a wide-ranging LA punk scene that included The Blasters, The Circle Jerks, and Black Flag, had melodic guitar-pop to spare. **Frank Zappa** teamed up with his daughter Moon Unit for "Valley Girl," a novelty song which parodied the "val-speaking" residents of LA's San Fernando Valley, and actually gave Zappa the biggest hit of his career.

Liberace's Frame Claim

After a couple of decades' absence, Liberace was back in the headlines when Scott Thorson, his chauffeur and "companion," filed a lawsuit against the flamboyant entertainer. Although Thorson, who had recently broken up with Liberace, really only wanted his belongings back, the press had a field day trumpeting the case as a "palimony" suit. Liberace, for his part, denied being gay, telling journalists that he was the victim of a homosexual conspiracy.

TV News

Introduced in February, *Late Night with David Letterman* was an immediate hit; though Letterman and Johnny Carson were contracted to the same network, many felt that the irreverence of *Late Night* was a much-needed antidote to the increasingly predictable *Tonight Show*. Thanks to recurring appearances by Larry "Bud"

JOAN JETT AND THE BLACKHEARTS

"**I Love Rock N Roll**"

PAUL MCCARTNEY WITH STEVIE WONDER

"**Ebony and Ivory**"

SURVIVOR

"**Eye Of The Tiger**"

J GEILS BAND

"**Centerfold**"

DARYL HALL AND JOHN OATES

"**Maneater**"

Melman and Chris Elliot and regular features like "Stupid Pet Tricks," *Late Night* became *the* show to discuss around the office water cooler.

Cheers was another long-running favorite that debuted in 1982; the

'82 Joan Jett.

sitcom, which followed the lives of a handful of regulars at a Boston bar, starred Ted Danson and Shelley Long. Less enduring was *Joanie Loves Chachi*, a dull *Happy Days* spin-off starring Scott Baio and Erin Moran.

Knight Rider, starring former soap star David Hasselhoff, certainly took the prize for the most unlikely premise: An undercover cop (played by Hasselhoff) is killed, brought back to life by a reclusive millionaire, and given a new identity and a Pontiac Trans Am with a talking computer. Believable? Hell, no. Popular? Hell, yes.

Now that the hysteria over Luke and Laura's wedding had died down, *General Hospital* star Tony Geary capitalized on his newfound name-recognition by appearing in ads for the **"Members Only"** line of men's jackets. Unfortunately, as Geary's TV character was somewhat disreputable,

'82 *Knight Rider* David Hasselhoff.

lavish *Cats*, which opened October 7 at the Winter Garden in New York City. Harvey Fierstein's *Torch Song Trilogy* finally made it to Broadway after a successful off-Broadway run, and *Little Shop of Horrors*, a musical based on the 1960 Roger Corman film of the same name, opened at the New York's WPA Theater to rave reviews.

NFL Strikes Out...

A year after the divisive players' strike, major league baseball was back in top form, setting an attendance record of 44,500,000. This year, it was the NFL's turn to go on strike; the walk-out lasted from September 21 to November 16, cutting the season to nine games apiece per team.

...And Fonda Feels The Burn

Aerobic excercise was becoming increasingly popular, with *Jane Fonda's Workout Book* topping the best-seller list, and as a result, headbands and workout clothes became a regular sight outside of gyms as well as in.

his endorsement only confirmed what many already believed—that "Members Only" jackets were for sleazebags.

Big On Broadway

Big-budget Broadway productions proliferated in 1982, thanks in part to the success of Andrew Lloyd Webber's

Tensions were rising in Lebanon, relations with the Soviet Union were growing ever more strained, and the **invasion of Grenada** gave Ronald Reagan's approval ratings a quick shot in the arm. But for most Americans, 1983 would forever be remembered as the **Year of the Cabbage Patch Doll** *(below)*. No two of the pudgy, stuffed-cloth dolls looked exactly alike; their handmade construction meant that supplies were limited, and kept prices prohibitively high.

TOP TELEVISION SHOWS

60 Minutes

Dallas

Dynasty

Magnum, PI

Simon and Simon

S till, every child had to have one—or so the media claimed. In actuality, it was the parents who were going crazy over the doll; in the possessions-conscious atmosphere of the early eighties, it became a virtual badge of honor to be wealthy enough to shell out the required $125, and tenacious enough to hack your way through the mini-riots occurring inside toy stores which had the dolls in stock.

Conspicious Consumption

But the Cabbage Patch Doll was just the proverbial tip of the iceberg; not since the Eisenhower years had America reveled in such unapologetic materialism. The rise of the "**Yuppie**" class was partially to blame, as young urban professionals ostentatiously stocked their condominium apartments with expensive appliances and the latest in high-end stereo and video gear, and drove to work in shiny new Benzes and Beamers. Additionally, the Reagan

administration's barely concealed contempt for the poor gave tacit approval to those who viewed abundance as their inalienable right. The have-nots weren't going away, however; America's poverty rate was at its highest level in eighteen years, with

over thirty-five million citizens living below the poverty line.

Watt A...!

1983 was also the year that US Secretary of the Interior James Watt talked himself out of a job. Already

despised by conservationists for his scorched-earth attitude towards the environment (like Reagan, he also seemed to believe that trees were the primary cause of the country's pollution problem), Watt became embroiled in further controversy for speaking out against a planned Beach Boys' Independence Day concert at Washington DC's Washington Monument; Watt feared that the band would attract "the wrong element" to the nation's birthday celebration. Watt put his foot in his mouth for the last time in October, when he was forced to resign over publicly describing a newly appointed coal-lease commission as consisting of "a black, a woman, two Jews, and a cripple." National Security Adviser William P Clark was named as his replacement.

Beauty Queen Loses Her Crown

Controversy also swirled around Vanessa Williams *(above)*, a stunning twenty-year-old from New York. Not only was Ms Williams the first black woman to win the Miss America pageant, but she was probably also the first Miss America to have posed nude for lesbian- and bondage-themed photos. Yielding to extreme pressure from pageant officials, Vanessa abdicated her throne after the pictures (which had been taken the previous year) appeared in an issue of *Penthouse*.

Detroit Battles On...

The Chrysler Corporation regained its financial footing in 1983, thanks to the introduction of Dodge's 1984 Caravan and Plymouth"s 1984 Voyager, America's first mini-vans. The vehicles, which could seat up to eight people, became the eighties equivalent of the family station wagon. Lincoln, usually the very definition of excess, did an about-face with the 1984 Continental Mark VII, a semi-fastback coupe with smoother, more rounded styling than any Continental before it. Priced between twenty-two and twenty-five thousand dollars, the Mark VII aimed squarely (and successfully) at the Yuppie demographic, which was currently paying twice as much for high-priced imports like BMW.

...But Atari Ships Out

Atari had a difficult year in 1983; oversaturation of the home videogame market was hurting everyone's sales, but buyers increasingly seemed to favor Mattel's Intellivision or Coleco's ColecoVision. Looking to cut costs, Atari was forced to move its operations overseas, and the company never quite regained its hold on the market.

'83 Vanna White says little but reveals all.

TV News

With cocaine abuse on the rise in the US, First Lady Nancy Reagan took a hands-on approach to the problem by making an appearance on a "very special" episode of *Diff'rent Strokes* (any time a sitcom episode dealt with serious issues such as drugs, sexual abuse, or the evils of punk rock, it was invariably advertised as "very special"). The solution, the First Lady told Little Arnold (Gary Coleman), was simple: "**Just say no.**" Upon hearing these sage words of advice, a nation of freebasers would presumably throw down their bunsen burners, never to get high again.

Really, who needed drugs when you had **Star Search**? A talent contest for aspiring singers, dancers, actors, comics and "model/spokespersons," hosted by by Johnny Carson

sidekick Ed McMahon, *Star Search* was so banal as to be positively hallucinatory. A year after its debut, the show actually made a star out of singer Sam Harris, who briefly pierced the Top Forty with the disturbingly titled "Sugar Don't Bite."

Another "very special" television event was the November 20 broadcast of **The Day After**; the made-for-TV movie, about the effects of nuclear conflagration, was watched by an estimated 100 million viewers. An even larger audience—125 million—tuned in for the final two-and-a-half-hour episode of **M*A*S*H***; after eleven years on television (most of them spent at the top of the ratings), the men and women of the 4077 said farewell to the Korean War. *After MASH*, which debuted

IN THE NEWS

April 11 – A presidential panel recommends the installation of 100 ICBM missles in silos in Wyoming and Nebraska, as well as the development of the single-warhead "Midgetman" missles.

April 18 – The US embassy in Beirut, Lebanon is almost completely destroyed by a car bomb. Pro-Iranian terrorists are blamed in the blast, which kills 63.

May 24 – Congress approves spending $625 million on the research and development of MX missiles.

June – Homosexuals across the country march in protest of what they view as the media's sensationalization of AIDS, which to date has killed over 600 Americans.

September 5 – The US imposes light sanctions against the USSR (including suspension of negotations for a US embassy in Kiev) over the Soviet downing of a South Korean passenger airliner.

in the fall, followed the post-war adventures of several *M*A*S*H** characters, but the show failed to hold the interest of even the most diehard *M*A*S*H** fans.

Beauty And The Beast

Wheel of Fortune, the highest-rated daytime game show in TV history, went into syndication in 1983. The latest incarnation of the show was hosted by Pat Sajak, but letter-turner **Vanna White** became the program's most popular attraction, despite the fact that she rarely (if ever) said

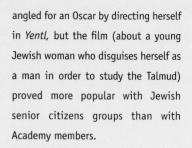

angled for an Oscar by directing herself in *Yentl*, but the film (about a young Jewish woman who disguises herself as a man in order to study the Talmud) proved more popular with Jewish senior citizens groups than with Academy members.

A Star Is Reborn

Shirley MacLaine had better luck, nailing an Academy Award for her role as the mother of dying daughter Debra Winger in *Terms of Endearment*. MacLaine also published *Out on a Limb* in 1983; the book, an account of her involvement with various forms of spirituality, would have been met with ridicule a decade earlier, but now many Americans were acquainting themselves with "New Age" concepts.

Scarface, a cocaine-laden update of the 1932 gangster classic, was criticized for being too violent, while *Staying Alive*, the Sylvester Stallone-directed sequel to *Saturday Night Fever*, was widely assailed for being just plain terrible. Worst of all, according to those who actually

anything. Vanna later posed for *Playboy*, and her fascinating auto-biography, *Vanna Speaks!*, became a best-seller.

Mr T cashed in on his memorable appearance in *Rocky III* with a role on the popular new adventure show, *The A Team*. Born Laurence Tureaud, the gold-bedecked Mr T soon had an entire country imitating his gruff cry of "I pity the fool!" But the year's most unlikely new TV idol had to a dog by the name of **Spuds MacKenzie**; billed as "The original party animal," Spuds did little in his commercials for Bud Light beer except let scantily clad

models fawn over him (or her; a small scandal erupted when it was revealed that Spuds was actually a bitch). Nevertheless, Spuds merchandise (T-shirts, posters, statuettes) quickly became big business, and Spuds was regularly mobbed during personal appearances at bars and taverns.

Movie News

Though 4.1 million VCRs were sold in 1983, and subscribers to cable TV now numbered over twenty-five million, Hollywood barely felt the pinch, thanks to the popularity of *The Return of the Jedi*, *Terms of Endearment*, and *The Big*

Chill. Tom Cruise danced around in his underwear in *Risky Business*, Meryl Streep played a reluctant nuclear activist in *Silkwood*, and Jennifer Beal's **Flashdance** wardrobe inspired a vogue for torn-collared, off-the-shoulder sweatshirts; combined with a headband and brightly colored leg-warmers, the look was quintessentially eighties.

Jerry Lewis, who had made only one film since his 1972 pet project, "The Day the Clown Cried" (about a clown who cheers up children at Nazi prison camps) failed to find release, made a rare return to the silver screen in *The King of Comedy*. Barbra Streisand

ACADEMY AWARDS

BEST PICTURE

Terms of Endearment

directed by James L Brooks

BEST ACTOR

Robert Duvall

Tender Mercies

BEST ACTRESS

Shirley MacLaine

Terms of Endearment

caught it during its brief stay in the theaters, was *The Lonely Lady*, a trashy vehicle for would-be actress **Pia Zadora**. The multi-talented Pia did at least score a minor hit in 1984 with "And When The Rain Begins To Fall," a duet with Jermaine Jackson.

Music News

Jermaine's brother Michael was the

music business's most valuable player in 1983. *Off The Wall*, his 1979 LP, had been a huge success, but it seemed like small potatoes next to *Thriller*. The album boasted no less than six Top Ten hits ("Billie Jean," "Beat It," "Wanna Be Startin' Somethin," "Human Nature," "PYT," and the title track), and Michael's face (with its suspiciously altered-looking nose) seemed to be on MTV twenty-four hours a day. *Thriller* eventually went on to sell forty million copies, breaking nearly every industry record in the process.

Colleges Rock

Metal Health, an album by LA rockers Quiet Riot, presaged the coming popularity of heavy metal (spandex-trousers-and-big-hair version), while Styx's overblown *Kilroy Was Here* signified the last gasp of prog-rock concept albums. Talking Heads, a New York-based art-rock combo, cracked the Top Ten with "Burning Down The House," while **REM** (*right*), an enigmatic quartet from Athens, Georgia, made it into the Top Forty with *Murmur*, despite receiving very

'83 Al Pacino plays a trigger-happy gangster in *Scarface*.

little commercial air-play. College stations, on the other hand, were playing the hell out of *Murmur*; record companies reasoned that there might be more gold in thar hills, and thus REM's success single-handedly paved the way for the rise of "college rock." It also led to the rediscovery of **The Velvet Underground**, a band REM regularly cited as an important influence. By 1985, all of the Velvet Underground's records were back in print, and were selling far better than they had back in the late sixties; no

September 20 – Congress authorizes US marines to remain in Lebanon for another eighteen months.

October 23 – A truck loaded with explosives destroys the US Marine headquarters in Beirut, killing 241 Marine and Navy personnel.

October 25 – In response to a bloody coup by pro-Marxist guerillas, US forces invade the Caribbean island of Grenada. Hostilities end on November 2, with eighteen US soldiers dead and 115 wounded.

November 2 – President Reagan signs a bill designating a federal holiday to honor the late Dr Martin Luther King, Jr.

November 11 – The US sends the first of 160 cruise missles to Great Britain; in response, the USSR withdraws from arms limitation negotiations.

December 3 – Syrian forces near Beirut fire on US reconnaissance planes, prompting an attack from US warplanes the following day.

longer would they be remembered only as "that band Lou Reed was in before *Walk On The Wild Side*."

nineteen

'84

Having won re-election by the largest Republican landslide in history, President Reagan interpreted his massive victory as a "mandate" to run the country in whatever manner he deemed necessary. In actuality, Reagan was re-elected on the strength of the economy, which was at its healthiest since 1951.

Certainly, most Americans would have been hard pressed to rationalize the inherent contradictions in the Reagan administration's foreign policy: At the same time the US was sending military aid to El Salvador, in order to help the established Salvadorian government fend off insurgent forces, it was also supporting the Contra rebels trying to topple Nicaragua's Marxist Sandanista government. (Reagan even showed his solidarity with the Contra "freedom fighters" by posing for photo ops while wearing an "**I'm A Contra, Too**!" baseball cap.)

Rising Population Triggers Boom

In any case, people were buying new homes again; 1.7 million homes were built in 1984, the most since 1979. Of course, the prison construction business was booming as well; over 454,000 Americans were doing time, nearly double the total from a decade ago. The US population swelled to 236,158,000 in 1984, with most of the growth taking place in the South and West. Chicago, traditionally known as

'84 Popular cop Eddie Murphy.

"The Second City," had its role as the country's second largest city usurped by Los Angeles. People were also buying cars. Detroit's "Big Three" auto makers earned nearly ten billion dollars in 1984, an industry record. Riding high on his company's bust-to-boom turnaround, Chrysler chairman **Lee Iacocca**'s *Iacocca: An Autobiography* began a two-year run at the top of the best-seller list.

Big And Beefy

The 1980s ushered in a new age of hostile corporate takeovers, and they didn't come much bigger than Beatrice Foods' purchase of Esmark, Inc. for $2.8 billion. The deal made the Chicago-based Beatrice the second largest food and consumer product company in the world, and the company proudly trumpeted the fact with its appropriately Orwellian "**We're Beatrice**" ad campaign, which covered everything from orange juice to tampons. Wendy's Hamburgers launched its enormously successful "**Where's the Beef?**" TV ads, which provided America with a new buzz-phrase (men's underwear emblazoned with "Here's the Beef!" became big sellers at lingerie shops), and gave elderly character actress Clara Peller her fifteen minutes of fame.

Bell Go Over Big

Good news for the eight percent of American households that owned personal computers: Bell Laboratories announced the development of a megabit memory chip, capable of storing more than one million bits of electronic data. Bad news for the videogame industry: No longer able to bear the glut of games, home systems and other related products, the videogame market crashed hard. Atari 2600 software could be found in the budget bins of supermarkets everywhere; fearing a similar fate, Mattel and Coleco hurriedly got out of the videogame business. Many observers opined that the videogame fad had reached the "**game over**" stage.

Running On Air

Sales of home exercise equipment passed the billion-dollar mark, as the fitness industry continued to boom. Then again, being in good shape wasn't everything, as Jim Fixx found out; at the age of fifty-two, the fitness guru (and author of the best-selling *Running*) dropped dead of a heart attack—while running, of course. 1984 also saw the introduction of Nike's Air Jordans, basketball shoes endorsed by the Chicago Bulls' phenomenal Michael Jordan.

Movie News

Breakdancers were everywhere in 1984—from TV commercials and music videos to the opening ceremonies of LA's Summer Olympics, if it didn't feature someone spinning on their head, it just wasn't happening. Hollywood moved quickly to cash in on the fad, releasing four low-budget "**breaksploitation**" flicks (*Beat Street, Body Rock, Breakin'* and *Breakin' 2: Electric Boogaloo*) before the year was out. Barely three years old, MTV was already exerting a powerful influence on the music and film industries. The quick edits and garish lighting that were an integral part of music videos now found their way into films as varied as *Beverly Hills Cop* (starring Eddie Murphy), *Footloose* (starring Kevin Bacon), Walter Hill's *Streets of Fire,* and *Purple Rain*, Prince's screen debut. Record and movie executives also realized that, by integrating scenes from a current film into a music video, you could sell a movie *and* its accompanying soundtrack, effectively killing two birds with one stone. Still, the combination of music and film didn't necessarily guarantee a hit. *Rhinestone*, in which Dolly Parton tried to turn Sylvester Stallone into a country singer, was too stupid for even the most undemanding viewers, while **This Is Spinal Tap**, Rob Reiner's "mockumentary" of a

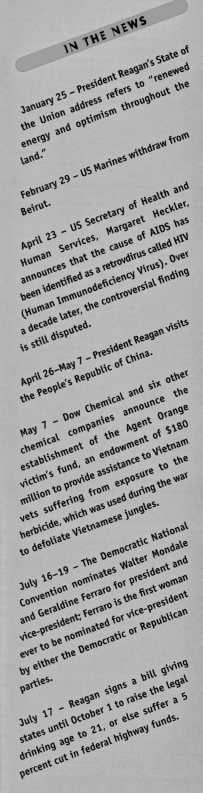

'84 Spoof rock-doc *Spinal Tap*— almost too convincing.

continued to sell by the truckload; in addition, he also found himself roped into singing the hook on Rockwell's "Somebody's Watching Me," and appearing (and doing the bulk of the work) on The Jacksons' *Victory* tour. Michael *had* to work hard, though; unlike the previous year, he had some serious competition this time around. In **Purple Rain**, Prince had both a blockbuster film and a multi-platinum album, while Bruce Springsteen's **Born In The USA** took him almost overnight from basketball arenas to eighty-thousand-seat football stadiums. Tina Turner's comeback was so strong that her Ike and Tina years seemed like a

faded British metal band, may have been too subtle for its own good; members of several preview audiences were heard to ask, "How come they didn't make a movie about a *good* band?" The film became a cult hit among musicians, however, and rare indeed is the guitarist who can't recite Nigel Tufnel's "**This one goes to eleven**" routine in its entirety.

In fact, most of 1984's biggest films had little to do with music. *Indiana Jones and the Temple of Doom* earned forty-two million dollars in the first six days of its release, despite a weak script and a shrill performance by Kate Capshaw as Harrison Ford's love interest. Pat Morita taught Ralph Macchio to stand up for himself in *The Karate Kid*, while Melanie Griffith played a porno star caught up in a murder mystery in Brian De Palma's *Body Double*. The one-two punch of *The Terminator* and *Conan The Destroyer* turned **Arnold Schwarzenegger** into a superstar, and John Hughes' *Sixteen Candles* marked Molly Ringwald as an actress to watch.

What A Nightmare!

Slasher films were so formulaic by 1984 that any semblance of creativity was usually reserved for their ad campaigns: *Silent Night, Deadly Night* featured an axe-wielding Santa and the slogan "He knows when you've been naughty," while print ads for *Pieces* opted for a picture of a chainsaw and the subtle tag-line, "You *know* what it's about!" Into this gory and redundant fray came Wes Craven's *A Nightmare on Elm Street*; while certainly flawed, audiences responded to the film's hallucinatory images and Robert Englund's frightening turn as the blade-fingered Freddy Krueger.

Music News

Like Big Brother himself, Michael Jackson was everywhere in 1984. Stoked by Jackson's million-dollar video for its title track, *Thriller*

TOP ALBUMS

PRINCE AND THE REVOLUTION
PURPLE RAIN
soundtrack

FOOTLOOSE
soundtrack

BRUCE SPRINGSTEEN
Born In The USA

HUEY LEWIS AND THE NEWS
Sports

MADONNA
Like A Virgin

mere warm-up, while newcomers Madonna and Cyndi Lauper quickly became the idols of millions of girls for their independent attitudes and bag-lady fashion sense.

Head Bangers

Heavy metal was back with a vengeance. Eddie Van Halen's blazing guitar solo on "Beat It" had helped Michael Jackson cross over to rock radio, but it also turned a lot of pop fans on to Van Halen, the band; *1984*, the band's final album with extroverted frontman David Lee Roth,

was its most successful yet, spawning the popular singles (and videos) "Jump," "Panama," and "Hot For Teacher." Fellow Sunset Strip denizens Ratt and Motley Crue got heads banging with *Out Of The Cellar* and *Shout At The Devil*, respectively, while Twisted Sister's years of toiling in Long Island bars paid off with the Top Twenty-Five single, "We're Not Gonna Take It." Rocking hardest of all was "Rock Box," an inspired stew of street raps and metallic guitars from New York rap duo Joseph Simmons and Darryl McDaniels, better known as RUN-DMC.

Soul Giant Gunned Down

Plagued for years by drug and tax problems, Marvin Gaye made a major comeback in 1983 with "Sexual Healing." Gaye was working on the follow-up to his successful *Midnight Love* LP when, on April 1, he was shot and killed by his father during an argument. It was a sad and ignominious end to one of soul music's greatest singers.

The Right Prescription

Comedian Bill Cosby already had plenty of hit movies, TV series, and records under his belt by 1984, but nothing on his resume even came close to matching the runaway success of **The Cosby Show** (above). A family-oriented sitcom based around the everyday lives of the Huxtables, an upper-middle-class black doctor's family in Brooklyn, New York, *The Cosby Show* became the most popular series, comedy or otherwise, of the 1980s. Also debuting in 1984 was long-running mystery series *Murder, She Wrote*, starring Angela Lansbury, and *Who's the Boss?*, a popular sitcom featuring former *Taxi* star Tony Danza. The new **Miami Vice** came off like a slick cross between a cleaned-up *Scarface* and a music video, and became an immediate hit; *Dreams*, starring John Stamos, tried to incorporate the MTV vibe into a sitcom format, and barely lasted a month. With *Little House On The Prairie* and *Bonanza* behind him, Michael Landon scored his third popular series in a row with **Highway to Heaven**. The story of an angel who comes down to

earth to help people, *Highway To Heaven* was singled out by President Reagan as one of the year's best shows.

1985 was the year

that Mattel's Barbie, kitted out with business suit and briefcase, joined the ranks of the young urban professionals; her new outfit reflected the fact that, for the first time in history, the majority of professional positions were now held by women. The good news for Barbie and her colleagues was that the **US economy continued to grow**, albeit at a slower rate than in 1984, and that the **unemployment rate of 6.8 percent** was the country's lowest in nearly five years.

TOP TELEVISION SHOWS

The Cosby Show
Family Ties
Dallas
Dynasty
60 Minutes

ACADEMY AWARDS

Out of Africa
directed by Sydney Pollack

BEST ACTOR
William Hurt
Kiss of the Spider Woman

BEST ACTRESS
Geraldine Page
The Trip to Bountiful

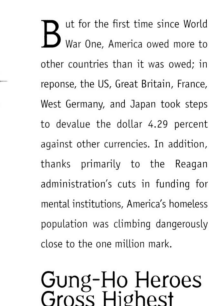

'85 *Left:* **Cher, dressed to kill at the Academy Awards, and (***below***) Stallone shoots to kill in *Rambo*.**

But for the first time since World War One, America owed more to other countries than it was owed; in reponse, the US, Great Britain, France, West Germany, and Japan took steps to devalue the dollar 4.29 percent against other currencies. In addition, thanks primarily to the Reagan administration's cuts in funding for mental institutions, America's homeless population was climbing dangerously close to the one million mark.

Gung-Ho Heroes Gross Highest Profits

Movie profits were down seven percent in 1985, a drop which was widely blamed on the increasing sales of VCRs and the rise of video rental stores. Still, it was hardly like people were avoiding the theaters. *Back to the Future* (a sci-fi comedy starring *Family Ties*' Michael J Fox), *Witness* (with Harrison Ford as a policeman hiding out in Pennsylvania's Amish community), *The Color Purple* (Steven Spielberg's controversial adaptation of Alice Walker's novel about the life of a Southern black woman), and *Out of Africa* (in which Robert Redford and Meryl Streep found romance against the backdrop of early-twentieth-century Kenya) were all enormously successful at the box office, as was the Schwarzenegger shoot-'em-up *Commando*. Sylvester Stallone climbed into the ring yet again in *Rocky IV*, but it was **Rambo: First Blood Part II** that made the biggest impression on American viewers. Released during the tenth anniversary of the Vietnam War, *Rambo* (about a Nam vet who returns to Cambodia to rescue American MIAs) exploited the country's continuing inability to come to terms with losing the conflict; failing to beat the Viet Cong on the battlefield, America could now at least exact revenge (over and over again) on the silver screen. The film was an immediate smash, and Ronald Reagan publicly praised Rambo as "America's Hero." A similar "back to Nam" premise turned the **Chuck Norris** action vehicles *Missing in Action* and *Missing In Action 2—The Beginning* into box-office bonanzas, and Norris also found time to whup him some Commie ass in *Invasion USA*, which (like 1984's *Red Dawn*) was an un-ironic throwback to the Cold War paranoia of the 1950s. *Gymkata* was even more gloriously absurd, starring diminutive Olympic gymnast Kurt Thomas as a US agent

using a singular style of martial arts ("The skill of gymnastics—The kill of karate!") to complete a mission in an Albania-like kingdom.

A popular regular guest on *Late Night With David Letterman*, Pee-wee Herman (aka Paul Reubens) scored a screen hit with *Pee-wee's Big Adventure*, while Madonna played a character resembling her current public image in *Desperately Seeking Susan*. Cher was not nominated for an Academy Award for her part in *Mask* (in which she played the mother of a severely deformed teenaged boy), but she easily won "Most bizarre getup" on Oscar Night with her Bob Mackie-designed outfit (one hesitated to call it a dress) and matching frightwig.

John Hughes, who had tallied previous hits with *Mr Mom*, *National Lampoon's Vacation*, and 1984's

Sixteen Candles, was now one of Hollywood's most successful directors: *National Lampoon's European Vacation*, *Weird Science,* and *The Breakfast Club* were all hits in 1985. The latter film, starring Emilio Estevez, Judd Nelson, Molly Ringwald, Anthony Michael Hall, and Ally Sheedy, marked the rise of "**The Brat Pack**," an aggregation of up-and-coming young actors, many of whom also appeared (along with Rob Lowe,

'85 Brat Packers play teens from Shermer High in *The Breakfast Club*.

Demi Moore, and Andrew McCarthy) in 1985's *St Elmo's Fire*. Although much hyped at the time, none of the Brat Packers (with the possible exception of Demi Moore) would go on to have anything approaching a distinguished career.

RIP Rock

On October 2, Rock Hudson became the first high-profile figure to die of AIDS. His futile search for a cure focused some much-needed attention on the growing epidemic; his former lover, Marc Christian, later successfully sued Hudson's estate, claiming that Hudson had jeopardized Christian's life by refusing to admit to his condition during their relationship.

Cool CD's

In music, 1985 was the year of Live Aid, Farm Aid (a Live Aid-style concert benefitting America's economically embattled farmers), and the founding of the Rock and Roll Hall of Fame, established in the rock 'n' roll hotbed of Cleveland, Ohio. It was also the year of the **compact disc**; despite being substantially higher-priced than turntables and LPs, CD players and CDs were immediately so successful that many predicted vinyl would be rendered completely obsolete by the end of the decade. Sales of vinyl singles were also down substantially, due to the introduction of the "cassingle" format.

Musicians Take Moral Stance

Rock music came under fire in 1985 when the **PMRC**, a self-appointed moral watchdog committee formed by the wives of several prominent politicos, began to pressure record companies to save the youth of America by putting warning stickers on records containing "**offensive**" lyrical content. Despite the popular image of rockers as anti-establishment rebels, Frank Zappa and Twisted Sister's Dee Snider were the only prominent musicians with the courage to appear at the PMRC hearings; both men spoke eloquently of their opposition to the album-labeling plan. Unsurprisingly, the music industry knuckled under with a minimum of fuss, and twenty-two record companies pledged to slap parental warnings on any product containing potentially offensive material. Ironically, the careers of previously obscure bands The Mentors and WASP experienced a sudden boost, after the song lyrics to their respective "Golden Showers" and "Animal (F*ck Like A Beast)" were read aloud at the PMRC hearings.

Don't Give Up The Day Job

Former Credence Clearwater Revival leader John Fogerty returned after an absence of over a decade with the best-selling *Centerfield* LP, acclaimed underground bands The Replacements and Hüsker Dü signed deals with major labels, and a brash youngster named **LL Cool J** established himself as rap's newest superstar with the block-rockin' debut album *Radio*. But for the most part, the airwaves seemed to be filled with faceless pop (Starship's "We Built This City," Mr Mister's "Broken Wings"), syrupy ballads (Whitney Houston's "Saving All My Love For You," Lionel Richie's "Say You, Say Me"), and songs with tie-ins to current films (Madonna's "Crazy For You," John Parr's "St Elmo's Fire," Huey Lewis and The News' "The Power of Love"). **Eddie Murphy**, one of the funniest men in America, made a misguided attempt at a career in music; although the sung-

'85 David Bowie, Alison Moyet, Pete Townsend, Bob Geldof, and Paul McCartney—stars supporting the starving in Live Aid.

with-the-utmost-seriousness "Party All The Time" made it to number two in the charts, the Rick James-produced single proved that, as a vocalist, Eddie was one hell of a comedian.

Razor-Sharp Style?

If Madonna was single-handedly popularizing the crop-top-and-exposed-bra look for young women, Don Johnson's *Miami Vice* wardrobe was similarly influential on the male clothing styles of the day. With *Miami Vice* high in the ratings, it suddenly became the height of fashion to wear pastel-colored, European-cut sports jackets with solid T-shirts and baggy, beltless pants. Special razors that could help you attain Johnson's "permanent stubble" look were also briefly marketed, but never really caught on—even though Bruce Willis, of TV's new *Moonlighting*, also sported a pretty serious five o'clock shadow. A screwball comedy loosely based on the 1940 film *His Girl Friday*,

Moonlighting quickly became a viewer favorite for its knowing wit and the obvious chemistry between Willis and co-star Cybill Shepherd.

Other popular new shows in 1985 included *MacGyver*, an adventure series starring Richard Dean Anderson as a resourceful secret agent; *The Golden Girls*, which starred Bea Arthur, Betty White and Rue McClanahan and was the first successful TV sitcom with an all-female cast; *Growing Pains*, a sitcom starring Alan Thicke (whose late-night talk show, *Thicke of The Night*, had been one of 1983's most critically savaged programs) as a psychiatrist working out of his Long Island home; and *Puttin' on the Hits*, a mind-numbing game show that featured contestants lip-synching to their favorite pop songs.

US Says Yes To NES...

Pronounced dead the year before, home videogames started to make a comeback, thanks to the new Nintendo Entertainment System. Burned by the recent videogame crash, retailers were initially reluctant to stock the NES, but the popularity of Nintendo titles like Donkey Kong, Super Mario Brothers, and The Legend of Zelda soon revitalized the industry.

...But No To New Coke

The biggest marketing gaffe of the decade occurred on April 23, when the Coca-Cola Company, in an attempt to fend off the rapidly expanding Pepsi-Cola, suddenly replaced its venerable Coca-Cola soft drink with the heavily hyped New Coke. From Coke loyalists, the howls of outrage were immediate and deafening; the new, sweeter formula tasted too much like Pepsi, they said. Despite the outpouring of criticism, the company stubbornly stood by its new product, even as

'85
"Cop Chic"—*Miami Vice*.

IN THE NEWS

August – The A H Robins Company, producer of the Dalkon Shield IUD, declares bankruptcy, as thousands of women file lawsuits claiming that they were injured or made infertile by the birth-control device.

September 9 – Reagan announces comparatively mild US sanctions—including bans on the sale of computers and the importing of Kruggerands—against South Africa, in protest of that country's apartheid policies.

October 7 – The US announces that it will no longer automatically comply with World Court decisions, charging that its procedures have been "abused for political ends."

November 20–21 – Reagan and Communist Party Secretary Mikhail Gorbachev hold a summit meeting in Geneva, Switzerland. No major breakthroughs are reached, but the meeting between the two countries is the friendliest in years.

newspapers ran story after story of people making car trips to other cities and states where old Coke was still available, in order to stock up before supplies ran out forever. Finally, the utter failure of the new product forced the company to relent, and the old formula was brought back on July 10, under the name of **Coca-Cola Classic**. Coca-Cola continued to try to push New Coke, but to no avail; like the Ford Edsel before it, New Coke was an improvement that no one had asked for, and it was quietly withdrawn from the shelves before the decade was out.

TOP TELEVISION SHOWS

The Cosby Show

Family Ties

Murder, She Wrote

Cheers

60 Minutes

'86

With only two years remaining in his presidential career, Ronald Reagan decided that the **Strategic Defense Initiative** would be a nice little something for Americans to remember him by. Nicknamed "Star Wars" for maximum soundbite value, the missile defense system could supposedly destroy enemy missiles before they struck American targets, thanks to a complex network of missiles, ground-based lasers, and particle beam sensors that would be **stationed in outer space.**

In July, Senate budget cuts considerably slowed the SDI's development, but Reagan would not let go; in October, a summit meeting between the US and the Soviet Union ended in a stalemate, solely because Reagan refused to even consider limiting or delaying the "Star Wars" program any further.

Contra-Dictory

Unfortunately for the president, there were more pressing issues to worry about. The "**Iran-Contra scandal**," as it came to be known, began in November with rumors that the US had sold arms to Iran, with the understanding that Iran might be able to influence Lebanon to release its

American hostages. Though Reagan had claimed to be virulently against trading arms for hostages, American intelligence sources confirmed that the sales had indeed taken place. Reagan first admitted that he knew of the arms sale, then quickly backpedalled, saying he didn't really understand the full extent of the situation.

Things got even more complicated on November 25, when it was revealed that some of the profits from the Iranian arms sale had been diverted to the Nicaraguan Contras. National Security Council adviser John Poindexter hurriedly resigned, while his assistant, Lieutenant Colonel Oliver North, was fired. On November 26, Reagan appointed a "blue ribbon" panel, headed by former senator John Tower, to investigate the actions of North and the National Security Council.

Movie News

While Oliver North was being investigated, Oliver Stone was being feted. *Salvador* and *Platoon*, both of which were written and directed by Stone, were two of the year's most critically praised films; the latter picture, based on Stone's own experiences as a soldier in Vietnam, was also the director's first major commercial success. The low-budget comedy *She's Gotta Have It* was another critical and commercial hit, with **Spike Lee** winning praise as one of America's most promising young directors. John Hughes continued his string of teen-oriented successes with *Pretty in Pink* and *Ferris Bueller's Day Off*.

'86 Spike Lee—a director to watch.

Tom Cruise was America's hottest star in 1986, playing a pool hustler in *The Color of Money* and a hot-shot jet pilot in **Top Gun**. Bette Midler was filmdom's most popular female, thanks to leads in the hit comedies *Down and Out in Beverly Hills* and *Ruthless People*, while Sigourney Weaver took on an army of slimy extra-terrestrials in *Aliens*. Arnold Schwarzenegger played yet another wise-cracking, ass-kicking tough guy in *Raw Deal*, but the failure of *Cobra* seemed to indicate that audiences were only interested in seeing Sylvester Stallone as Rocky or Rambo. The "Comeback of the Year" award went to **Dennis Hopper** (*below*, with Isabella Rossellini) who played three troubled (but extremely diverse) characters in *Hoosiers*, *River's Edge*, and David Lynch's *Blue Velvet*—the latter of which featured him as the oxygen-swilling Frank Booth, one of the most genuinely frightening psychopaths in film history.

Not Just For Kids

Based on one of Stephen "Just call me the Master of Horror" King's short stories, **Stand by Me** was actually a moving study of childhood friendship; directed by Rob Reiner, the film brought a talented young actor named River Phoenix into the public eye. *Crossroads*, starring Ralph Macchio, could easily have been titled *The Karate Kid Plays the Blues*; with Ry Cooder overdubbing his parts, Macchio challenged the Devil (guitar whiz Steve Vai) to a battle of the blues that surely had Robert Johnson spinning in his grave. In other child actor news, over one hundred X-rated videos starring porn star **Traci Lords** had to be pulled from the shelves, when it was revealed that Lords made them while still under the age of sixteen.

Out Of Their Heads

By June of 1986, 21,915 cases of AIDS had been reported in America, over half of them already fatal. Officials predicted that the number of

'86 Hopping mad in *Blue Velvet*.

DIONNE AND FRIENDS

"That's What Friends Are For"

THE BANGLES

"Walk Like An Egyptian"

PATTI LABELLE AND MICHAEL McDONALD

"On My Own"

WHITNEY HOUSTON

"The Greatest Love of All"

FALCO

"Rock Me Amadeus"

deaths from AIDS would increase more than tenfold over the next five years. Predictably, the network news shows were more interested in the country's escalating drug problems, especially in light of the cocaine-related deaths of college basketball star Len Bias and professional football player Don Rogers. During one week in September, CBS and NBC each tried to out-coke the other, CBS leading with the news special "48 Hours on Crack Street," while NBC followed up with the news special "Cocaine Country." **ALF** was one of the year's most popular new sitcoms. Short for "Alien Life Form," ALF (played alternately by a puppet and by midget Michu Meszaros) was a furry alien who crash-landed on Earth (below), and decided to shack up with a suburban family; hilarity and "wry" commentary on human ways ensued. *Pee Wee's Playhouse*, a highly creative Saturday morning series starring Pee Wee Herman, took the opposite approach, transporting kids (and quite a large number of adult fans) into a surreal world of talking furniture, friendly robots, and disembodied heads. If that wasn't weird enough for you, there were always those California Raisins commercials, in which a soul train of finger-poppin' raisins sang "I Heard It Through The Grapevine."

Videogame News

In the world of videogames, Nintendo still ruled the roost. Sega introduced its new Sega Master System in 1986, while Atari tried to relive past glories with its new 7800 console, but Nintendo's NES still outsold both products by a margin of ten to one.

Music News

With her third album, *True Blue*, Madonna shortened her tresses and generally tried to "class up" her image, a move no doubt motivated by her recent marriage to actor Sean Penn, with whom she made the virtually unwatchable *Shanghai Surprise*. **The Bangles**, an all-female quartet with roots in LA's early-eighties "paisley underground" scene (which included such neo-psychedelic combos as The Three o' Clock, The Dream Syndicate, and Rain Parade), had two massive pop hits in 1986 with "Manic Monday" (written by Prince) and "Walk Like An Egyptian." **Bon Jovi**, who sounded like a cross between Bruce Springsteen and a metal band, scored a pair of chart-toppers with "You Give Love A Bad Name" and "Livin' On A Prayer." **Metallica**'s thrash-metal classic *Master of Puppets* made it into the Top Thirty without the benefit of any commercial radio support, but their momentum was lost when bassist Cliff Burton died in a bus crash during the band's Swedish tour.

Miami Vice's Don Johnson scored a Top Five hit with "Heartbeat," although he seemed much more comfortable in front of a camera than a microphone. Janet Jackson, younger sister of Michael, stepped out on her own with *Control*, while James Brown entered his fourth decade of hits with the success of "Living In America." Paul Simon's use of South African musicians on his new *Graceland* LP inspired a flurry of interest in "world music," while **Run DMC** further fused rock and rap by teaming up with Aerosmith for a revamp of the latter's "Walk This Way." All was not well in the rap world, however; regular reports of violence (gang-related and otherwise) at rap shows caused many big-time concert promoters to steer clear of rap acts.

Missing Links

If 1985 was the summer of Live Aid, 1986 was supposed to be the summer of Hands Across America. The event, which was supposed to raise money for the homeless, involved forming a human chain that would stretch across

WHITNEY HOUSTON

Whitney Houston

BON JOVI

Slippery When Wet

BRUCE SPRINGSTEEN AND THE E STREET BAND

Live 1975–85

MADONNA

True Blue

Top Gun

soundtrack

the country from New York City to Long Beach, California. Unfortunately, the whole thing was completely disorganized; on the day of the event, endless stretches of ribbon had to be substituted for human beings in many parts of the country.

'86 Girl band The Bangles.

The Young Pretender

On November 22, Mike Tyson, aged just twenty, became the youngest heavyweight boxing champion in history, knocking out Trevor Berbick in the second round of the WBC heavyweight title fight.

Power Trips

Sixteen million cars and trucks were bought by Americans in 1986; only 28.2 percent of them were imported, a smaller percentage than in previous years. Chevrolet gave Corvette buffs a reason to celebrate with the release of the first Corvette convertible in a decade; just in case buyers needed any further incentive, Chevrolet raised the car's horse-power to two hundred and forty, up ten from their previous models. General Motors, the largest American company with business interests in South Africa, made headlines in October by withdrawing its operations in protest of the country's apartheid policies. Following GM's lead, IBM, Eastman Kodak, and Citibank would all do the same over the course of the next twelve months.

'86 "Iron" Mike Tyson becomes heavyweight champion.

May 13 – A Justice Department commission on pornography, headed by Attorney General Edwin Meese, rules that such material is potentially harmful and can lead to violent behavior against women and children. The Meese Commission urges stringent action against the pornography industry, and puts pressure on convenience stores to remove magazines like *Playboy*, *Penthouse*, and *Hustler* from their shelves.

June 17 – Chief Justice Warren Burger retires from the US Supreme Court. Reagan names the more conservative William Rehnquist as his successor, and also names Antonin Scalia to the court.

July 27 – The International Court of Justice orders the US to stop training and arming Nicaragua's Contra rebels, and to pay restitution to Nicaragua.

October 22 – Reagan signs a revised federal income tax law, lowering taxes for everyone, especially those in the highest tax brackets, as of January 1, 1987.

November 3 – A Lebanese magazine reports that the US has been secretly selling arms to Iran, in hopes of securing the release of US hostages currently being held in Lebanon.

November 14 – Financier Ivan Boesky agrees to pay the government $100 million as a penalty for illegal insider trading on the security exchange. The Securities and Exchange Commission bars Boesky from participating in the securities business for the rest of his life, although he is allowed to liquidate stocks in order to pay off the $1.4 billion debt still owed by his firm. Boesky is also sentenced to three years in prison.

However sordid it may have seemed at the time, 1987 was certainly one of the most entertaining years in recent memory.

If Gary Hart's extramarital indiscretions, the Iran-Contra hearings and Reagan's endless wranglings over Supreme Court nominees couldn't get you to crack a smile, there was always the **endless saga of televangelist Jim Bakker** to keep you amused.

ACADEMY AWARDS

BEST PICTURE
The Last Emperor
directed by Bernardo Bertolucci

BEST ACTOR
Michael Douglas
Wall Street

BEST ACTRESS
Cher
Moonstruck

TOP TELEVISION SHOWS

The Cosby Show
Cheers
The Golden Girls
Growing Pains
Night Court

A long with his wife, the mascara-caked Tammy Faye, Rev Bakker ran the Soutch Carolina-based PTL ministry, one of the most prominent of the country's many televised pulpits. On March 19, Bakker shocked his flock by resigning, having admitted to an extramarital affair with church secretary Jessica Hahn. Bakker's troubles were only beginning; on June 12, the PTL's new management filed for bankruptcy, and later sued Bakker for helping himself to over fifty-two million dollars from the ministry's coffers. Finally, in October of 1989, Bakker was convicted on twenty-four counts of fraud and conspiracy, and sentenced to forty-five years in prison (the sentence was later reduced to a far more lenient four and a half years). Along with the 1988 sex scandal involving televangelist (and Bakker rival) Jimmy Swaggart, the PTL affair went a long way towards diminishing the power of the religious right in America.

'87 Michael Douglas succumbs to fatally attractive Glenn Close.

North Comes Clean

If Iran-Contra was supposed to be the Watergate of the eighties, someone forgot to tell the congressional committee investigating the affair. The televised congressional hearings, which ran from May 5 to August 6, were marked by the Democrats' unenthusiastic cross-examination of witnesses, while the Republican panelists mostly used the hearings as a forum for pro-Contra rhetoric. Though obviously set up as a **fall guy** by the Reagan administration, Lt Col Oliver North nonetheless

defended the the administration's involvement in the affair. North also admitted to willfully flouting US laws, lying to Congress, destroying evidence, and taking bribes, saying that, if he did wrong, he did so in defense of America. This disingenuous explanation was good enough for American conservatives, who promptly branded North a hero. Fawn Hall, North's attractive secretary (who admitted on the stand to helping North shred classified documents), received numerous offers to pose nude for men's magazines.

On November 17, the bi-partisan panel released a 690-page congressional report on the affair, criticizing Reagan for being oblivious to the illegal behavior of his national security advisors, but otherwise linked the whole mess to a "cabal of zealots" within the White House. The American public, confused by the complexities of the case, had lost interest completely; ten out of of the eleven resulting convictions (including North's) were eventually overturned in court or by presidential pardon, but howls of public protest were almost non-existent.

Black Monday

The worst stock crash in the history of the New York Stock Exchange occured on October 19, when the Dow Jones industrial average fell 508 points in heavy trading. The panic quickly extended to markets around the globe, but the blame could be laid squarely at the doorstep of the US's enormous trade deficit. In *Newsweek*, Economist John Kenneth Galbraith called the crash "the last chapter of Reaganomics," and linked it to "the [government's]

irresponsible tax reduction, the high interest rates that bid up the dollar and subsidized imports, and the trade deficit that put a lot of unstable money in foreign hands." The Dow managed to rebound over the following weeks, but Americans would be spending a lot less on Christmas presents that year.

Hollywood Plays Dirty

Just as Three Mile Island kick-started the box-office success of *The China Syndrome* in 1979, the "Black Monday" crash was the best advance publicity that Oliver Stone's *Wall Street* could have asked for. Stone's gripping morality tale starred Michael Douglas as sleazy trader Gordon Gekko, whose motto, "**Greed is good**," perfectly encapsulated the dominant philosophy of the era; after all, at the time of the film's release, real estate mogul Donald Trump was topping the best-seller lists with his self-aggrandizing *Trump: The Art of the Deal*. Douglas also starred in the popular ***Fatal Attraction***, as a married man whose weekend fling (Glenn Close) turns out to be a raving homicidal looney. Eddie Murphy returned as Axel Foley in *Beverly Hills Cop II*, and also made an uncredited cameo appearance in *Hollywood Shuffle*, Robert Townsend's comedic look at racial stereotyping in the film world. Arnold Schwarzenegger continued his string of successes with *The Running Man* and *Predator*, while *Over the Top*, Sylvester Stallone's idiotic arm-wrestling epic, only extended Sly's post-*Rambo* slump. Cher had her best year yet, garnering raves for three roles—as a public defender in *Suspect*, as one of a trio of gorgeous witches in **The Witches of Eastwick**, and as a young widow torn between two brothers in *Moonstruck*. Barbra Streisand bombed with *Nuts*, but Faye Dunaway made an impressive comeback as a gin-mill moll in *Barfly*, Barbet Schroeder's film based on the writings of Charles Bukowski; Mickey Rourke wasn't bad in the Bukowski role, either. Having played small roles for his entire career, Kevin Costner began to take himself extremely seriously after his turn as Eliot Ness in *The Untouchables* made him a star. Robert De Niro, who played Al Capone in *The Untouchables*, also played the satanic Louis Cyphre in *Angel Heart*, a film which got plenty of publicity mileage out of a nude scene by *The Cosby Show*'s Lisa Bonet. **Patrick Swayze**, best known for films like *Skatetown, USA*, and *Red Dawn*, became a full-blown heartthrob after playing a hunky dance instructor in *Dirty Dancing*.

'87 *Barfly* Mickey Rourke.

Theaters Scrape The Barrel

Cineplexes, huge theater complexes featuring up to eighteen screens, were opening up across the country; as there weren't enough prints of the big hits to go around, theater owners showed whatever they could get their hands on. Thus, certain audiences were treated to such gems as *The Allnighter*, a terrible teen sex comedy (even by teen sex comedy standards) starring Bangles vocalist Susanna Hoffs, and *Disorderlies*, a witless comedy starring influential (but past their sell-by date) rappers The Fat Boys.

Music News

With sales of over 102 million in 1987, the CD market continued to swell. Industry bean-counters had been counting on **Bad**, Michael Jackson's highly anticipated follow-up to *Thriller*, to make a serious contribution to year-end sales figures, and they weren't disappointed. While *Bad* wasn't quite the all-encompassing smash that its predecessor was, it still sold eight million copies and generated five Number One singles, including "Man In The Mirror" and the title track.

"Who's better—Tiffany or Debbie Gibson?" was the question upon the

'87 Number One at sixteen—Tiffany.

lips of young record buyers everywhere (not to mention several pop culture observers with nothing better to do). Sixteen-year-old shopping mall diva Tiffany (last name: Darwinsch) topped the charts with "Could've Been" and a cover of Tommy James' "I Think We're Alone Now," and the seventeen-year-old Gibson placed her own compositions "Only In My Dreams" and "Shake Your Love" in the Top Five.

Some older folks got in on the pop action, as well: The venerable **Grateful Dead** scored their first Top Ten hit with "Touch of Grey," but longtime fans weren't celebrating; Deadheads complained that the single was making the band *too* popular, and that newcomers were ruining the "vibe" of the Dead's concerts. Bruce Willis took advantage of his moonlighting fame by croaking his way through *The Return of Bruno*, a collection of R&B chestnuts. His cover of "Respect Yourself" made it

'87 Debbie Gibson.

to number five on the charts—seven positions higher than the Staple Singers' original hit in 1971. **Metal** was more popular than ever, with new faces like Poison, Dokken, and Slayer replacing Twisted Sister and Quiet Riot in the hearts of headbangers. Slayer's Kerry King shredded some additional guitar on *Licensed To Ill,* the debut LP by New York's white rap trio **The Beastie Boys**. Stoked by the runaway success of "(You Gotta) Fight For Your Right (To Party!)," *Licensed To Ill* sold 5 million copies and became the first rap record to top the pop album charts.

Ten Years After

In August twenty thousand fans from around the world rolled into Memphis to observe the tenth anniversary of Elvis Presley's death. 1987 witnessed the passing of Liberace and Andy Warhol, the former from AIDS and the latter from complications following a gall bladder operation. Though neither could have been classified as a rocker, both these men had an incredible influence on popular music—Liberace with his outrageous sense of onstage style, and Warhol with his concepts of self-reinvention. Indeed, without either of them, it's

'87 "Touch of Grey"—the Dead's Jerry Garcia.

hard to imagine David Bowie, Elton John or Madonna even existing.

Family Dramas

By 1987, 49.5 percent of all American households had cable TV; more and more, viewers were ignoring the three major networks in favor of MTV, VH-1, or various other specialty channels. The brand new Fox network made a run at becoming the Big Three's hold on network television, thanks to the success of *Married...with Children*. Many found the show's characters repugnant in the extreme, but others felt it was a breath of fresh air in a world of generic sitcoms. Fox also offered up *21 Jump Street*, a teen-oriented cop series which turned Johnny Depp into a teen idol. Popular new network series included *A Different World*, a *Cosby Show* spin-off starring Lisa Bonet, and *Thirtysomething*, a baby-boomer-centric dramatic series that followed the interconnected lives of seven adult friends. The series was set in Pennsylvania, home of Pennsylvania State Treasurer R Budd Dwyer, who made some television history of his own in 1987. While holding a televised press conference regarding his up-coming prison sentence for financial improprieties, Dwyer pulled a gun and promptly blew his brains out in front of the TV cameras.

IN THE NEWS

October 23 – The Senate rejects the Supreme Court nomination of Robert Bork. Bork, nominated by Reagan to replace the retiring Lewis Powell, Jr, is considered to be too much of a right-wing extremist for the job.

November 7 – Douglas Ginsburg, another Reagan nominee for the Supreme Court, withdraws himself from consideration over charges of prior conflicts of interest, as well as the admission that he had used marijuana while teaching at Harvard Law School.

December 8 – Reagan and Gorbachev sign the first US-Soviet treaty to reduce nuclear arsenals. According to the agreement, 2,611 US and Soviet medium- and short-range missiles are marked for destruction.

December 22 – Barred by International Court of Justice from sending any further arms or military supplies to the Nicaraguan Contras, Reagan authorizes $14 million in "non-lethal" Contra aid.

'87 The Beastie Boys.

Welcome to the **Land of thirtysomethings.** For the first time in US history, the median age of American citizens was now over thirty-two. **The baby boomers were creating a baby boom of their own, with a record 3.8 million births in 1988,** but parental roles were changing; according to the Census Bureau, over fifty percent of all new mothers were remaining in the work force.

With more and more Americans abandoning their farms (or getting them foreclosed on), the country's farm population was now at its lowest in one hundred and twenty-five years. Another sign of changing times was the closing of the last **Playboy Club**, in Lansing, Michigan. Playboy clubs, which had boasted a membership of over one million men during the early seventies, were considered an embarrassing anachronism by the time the eighties rolled around. In an effort to shore up *Playboy*'s declining fortunes (which included a massive circulation drop in the wake of the Meese Commission's war on pornography) the company decided to phase out the clubs entirely.

Morals Outraged

Playboy (along with every other publication in the country) could at least take heart in the US Supreme Court decision of February 24, which ruled that **free speech** has to be protected even when it is "outrageous," and that the right to criticize public figures is part of free

speech—overturning a $200,000 libel award to Moral Majority leader Rev Jerry Falwell, who had sued *Hustler* magazine over an insulting parody.

On November 18, President Reagan signed an anti-drug bill calling for the death penalty for drug-related murders, and a ten-thousand-dollar fine for possession of even small amounts of controlled substances. A cabinet-level "Drug Czar" position was also established to oversee the "**war on drugs**."

'88 With thawing East-West relations, McDonald's open in Moscow, and the "Bolshoi Mak" is born.

Regan Spills The Beans

In his new book, *For the Record,* ousted White House chief of staff Donald Regan alleged that Nancy Reagan was the real power behind the Oval Office, and that President Reagan made many of his public moves based on the readings of his wife's astrologer. The

news caused a minor uproar but, like most of the criticisms aimed at the "**Teflon president**" during his eight years in office, failed to noticeably damage Reagan's popularity. Nor did it adversely effect the campaign of Vice-President George Bush; despite being dogged by further Iran-Contra allegations, and being saddled with air-headed running mate Dan Quayle, Bush won November's presidential election by a handy plurality. The economy was still in good shape, after all, and many Americans assumed it would continue to stay that way under Bush's administration.

Movie News

Falwell and his colleagues had plenty to get upset about in 1988. Not only was leading televangelist Jimmy Swaggart very publicly defrocked for committing "lewd acts" with a prostitute, but Martin Scorsese's *The Last Temptation of Christ* was

'88 Willem Dafoe stars in *The Last Temptation of Christ.*

committing **blasphemy** by bringing its depiction of a sensual, all-too-human Jesus Christ to movie theaters everywhere. At least, that's what the Christian Right claimed; most of the fundamentalist Protestants and Roman Catholics who picketed the film's screenings hadn't actually seen it. The film, which received mixed reviews from secular critics, further solidified Willem Dafoe's status as one of the decade's top leading men.

With its eye-popping blend of live action and animation, **Who Framed Roger Rabbit** was one of the year's biggest hits, making the curvaceous Jessica Rabbit America's first cartoon sex symbol since Betty Boop. *Hairspray*, a hilarious send-up of early-sixties dance shows, was John Waters' finest commercial work to date; sadly, longtime co-conspirator Divine (who had a starring role) died just as the film was being released. Other hits included *Working Girl* (starring Melanie Griffith as a naive secretary), **Big** (starring Tom Hanks as a twelve-

year-old boy who suddenly turns into a thirty-year-old man), and *Dangerous Liaisons*, an eighteenth-century costumer which showed that bed-hopping wasn't just an invention of the 1960s. Also worth seeing (if you could find it), was Todd Haynes' disturbing *Superstar: The Karen Carpenter Story*, a low-budget film which used Barbie dolls to illustrate both the rise of The Carpenters and Karen's death from anorexia.

Cruisin' For A Bruisin'

Tom Cruise, having played a hot-shot jet pilot in *Top Gun* and a hot-shot pool player in *The Color of Money*, now essayed the part of a hot-shot bartender in *Cocktail*. Such redundant role choices didn't hurt his massive popularity any, although *Rain Man* (in which he played the selfish younger brother of the autistic Dustin Hoffman) proved that he could at least stretch a bit. Arnold Schwarzenegger, who showed a flair for droll one-liners in his previous action roles, successfully ventured into the world of comedy with **Twins**. Sylvester Stallone hoped that *Rambo III* would reverse his declining box-office fortunes, but the

film's plot (Rambo goes to Afghanistan to blow up the Russians) didn't quite resonate with audiences in the same way its predecessor had. Jean-Claude Van Damme, the latest inarticulate man of steel to grace the screen, scored action hits with *Bloodsport* and *Black Eagle*.

TV News

With 52.8 percent of all American households having cable TV, 56 percent owning VCRs, and over twenty-five thousand video stores nationwide, network ratings took a serious hit in 1988. When the fall TV season was delayed by a writer's strike, many viewers tuned out completely. Two of the year's few bright spots, as far as commercial

television was concerned, were *Murphy Brown* and **Roseanne**. The former starred Candice Bergen as a TV news reporter fresh out of rehab, who never seemed to be able to find a decent secretary; the latter starred comedienne Roseanne Barr (who later legally jettisoned her surname) as a working-class mother of three. With their charismatic stars and sharper-than-average writing, both new shows quickly established dedicated followings.

Wrestling Revival

The 1987–1988 theater season was Broadway's most successful in history, thanks to *The Phantom of the Opera*, *Les Miserables*, *Starlight Express*, *Madame Butterfly,* and *Me and My Girl*. But in terms of sheer theatricality, Broadway had nothing on professional wrestling. The sport was at its most popular in three decades, and wrestlers like Hulk Hogan and

'88 King of the ring Hulk Hogan.

"Rowdy" Roddy Piper experienced the sort of name recognition that would have turned "Gorgeous George" Wagner green with envy. On February 5, pro wrestling made prime-time TV for the first time since 1955, as Hogan faced off against the aptly named Andre the Giant in a match billed as "The Main Event."

Videogame News

"Hypermarkets," gigantic "malls without walls," started to spring up around the country. Visit one, and you might come home with fresh produce, an armchair, or a copy of **Tetris**, the video puzzle game that eveyone was playing in 1988. Despite Tetris's popularity, Nintendo stayed at the top of the videogame heap, thanks to the popularity of the company's new Adventures of Link (Zelda 2) and Super Mario 2.

Enter GNR

Heavy metal was bringing in more bucks than ever in 1988, but a Los Angeles band called Guns N' Roses was quickly changing the face and sound of the music. Instead of lipstick, teased hair, and spandex, the band favored leathers, bandanas, and a fresh-from-the-gutter mien; instead of using pointy guitars to crank out catchy bubblegum anthems, Guns N' Roses brandished Les Pauls and sang songs about heroin abuse. Thousands of American rock bands threw down their hair extensions and followed suit. Along with **Public Enemy**'s *It Takes A Nation Of Millions To Hold Us Back* (a groundbreaking rap album that mixed articulate rage with an overwhelming sonic barrage of tape loops, big beats, and samples), GNR's

IN THE NEWS

February 5 – General Manuel Noriega, commander of Panama's armed forces, is indicted by a federal grand jury in Miami, Florida, for letting large-scale drug dealers use Panamanian airstrips under his protection. Panamanian president Eric Delvalle tries to dismiss Noriega, but Noriega's forces drive Delvalle from office.

March 16 – 3,200 US troops arrive in Honduras, in response to reports that Nicaraguan forces are gearing up to attack Contra bases in Honduran territory. No fighting occurs, and the troops return to the US on March 28.

April 18 – In retaliation for Iranian mining of Persian Gulf waters, the US Navy destroys two Iranian oil platforms and six armed Iranian vessels.

May 13 – The Congress and President Reagan approve a $1-billion program for AIDS education, treatment and reasearch. 35,000 Americans have already died from the disease.

May 27 – In the first US-Soviet arms accord since 1972, the Intermediate-Range Nuclear Forces Treaty calls for the elimination of land-based medium-range and short-range missiles installed in Europe by the US and the Soviet Union.

July 3 – In the midst of fighting off an attack from Iranian gunboats, the US cruiser *Vincennes* shoots down an Iranian passenger airliner over the Persian Gulf, killing 290 people. A military report blames the crew error on psychological stress caused by first-time combat.

'88 "Appetite For Destruction"—Guns N' Rose's Axl Rose.

Appetite For Destruction was a welcome relief from the saccharine pap currently cluttering the airwaves. One of the year's bigger hits was Will To Power's "Free Baby," a disco-muzak medley of Peter Frampton's "Baby I Love Your Way" and Lynyrd Skynyrd's "Free Bird," while former pop greats Cheap Trick and The Beach Boys had to play dentist's office music in order to get their first hits in years ("The Flame" and "Kokomo," respectively). Jazz vocalist Bobby McFerrin had a fluke pop hit with **"Don't Worry, Be Happy,"** a song George Bush would later try to appropriate as the theme for his 1992 campaign.

James Jailed, Joe Released

James Brown was arrested in the fall, after leading several Georgia state police cars on a chase while under the influence of PCP. The Godfather of Soul received a six-year jail sentence, which was later reduced to slightly over twenty-five months. In other addictive substance news, "Joe Camel" made his American debut as the mascot for Camel cigarettes. The cartoon character (which some claimed was intentionally drawn to resemble male genitalia) ironically showed up just as a ban on smoking went into effect on all airplane flights two hours or less.

IN THE NEWS

July 5 – Attorney General Edwin Meese, under fire for various alleged criminal misdeeds, announces his resignation.

18–21 – Massachusetts Governor George Dukakis is nominated for president by the Democratic National Convention; Texas Senator Lloyd Bentsen, Jr is nominated as his running mate.

August 15–18 – The Republican National Convention nominates George Bush for president and Indiana Senator Dan Quayle for vice president.

October 13 – Reagan signs a welfare reform bill requiring single parents with children over three years of age to get regular jobs, or enroll in job training or education courses if they can't find work.

October 21 – Ferdinand and Imelda Marcos, former President and First Lady of the Philippines, are indicted by a federal grand jury in New York City. The pair are accused of embezzling more than $100 million of their government's money and using it to buy office buildings in New York, as well as to add to Imelda's ever-expanding shoe collection.

November 8 – George Bush is elected president, winning by a margin of nearly 7 million popular votes.

December 21 – En route to New York City from London, a Pan American Boeing 747 explodes over Lockerbie, Scotland, killing 270 people. After a thorough investigation, British and US officials later indict two Libyan intelligence agents for planting plastic explosives on board the aircraft.

Talk about good timing—just as Ronald Reagan began his first term with the release of the Iranian Embassy hostages, George Bush made it into the White House only a few months before the **collapse of Communism** in Eastern Europe. Whether the Cold War was brought to an end by the Reagan administration's exorbitant weapons spending, or just by an increasing lust behind the Iron Curtain for blue jeans, bad rock 'n' roll (Russian underground rock hero Boris Grebenshikov made his American debut with 1989's "Radio Silence", which sounded suspiciously like Bryan Adams) and other capitalist luxuries, **America was now rid of its foremost foe.**

Of course, this created a bit of a problem for defense contractors; deprived of the Red Menace, the defense industry found it increasingly difficult to justify its own existence. But many Americans hoped that, with Communism out of the way, the US government would pay a little more attention to problems on the home front. Unemployment was down slightly in 1989, but most of the 2.5 million new jobs created during the year were in the service industry, rather than in manufacturing. The population of **federal prisons** had nearly doubled since 1980, and a recent educational survey showed that thirteen-year-old students in South Korea, Great Britain, Ireland, Spain, and four Canadian provinces all ranked higher in math and science than Americans of the same age group.

Exhibitionism

Unfortunately, Congress seemed far more preoccupied with a debate over whether or not the National Endowment for the Arts should fund so-called "offensive" art. One casualty of this controversy was an exhibition of photographs by the late Robert Mapplethorpe, which was slated to open in June at Washington DC's Corocoran Gallery of Art, but was canceled when certain politicos objected to the gay S&M themes of some of the photographs. The Washington Project for the Arts, a private group, wound up taking over the exhibit and opening it in their own facilities.

Thinking Big

Given the eighties' reputation as "the greed decade," it was only fitting that 1989 would witness two of the biggest corporate mergers to date. The merger of Warner Communications and Time, Inc. created Time-Warner, Inc., the world's largest media and entertainment conglomerate, and Kohlberg Kravis and Roberts, which had acquired the Beatrice Companies in 1986, acquired RJR Nabisco for twenty-five billion dollars. The combination of Beatrice and Nabisco properties meant that KKR now accounted for thirteen percent of all US food manufacturing. Luxury hotel owner Leona Helmsley made headlines when she was indicted for tax evasion; according to court

transcripts, Leona's response to the charges was, **"Only little people pay taxes."** Little people everywhere rejoiced when she was sentenced to four years in prison, fined $7.2 million, and ordered to perform seventy-five hours of community service.

Batmania

1989 box-office receipts totalled a record five billion dollars; *Batman*, Tim Burton's incredibly over-hyped adaptation of the DC comic, accounted for roughly half of that. Indeed, with one hundred and sixty varieties of merchandise on the shelves (including T-shirts, coffee mugs, action figures, and separate soundtacks by Prince and Danny Elfman), it was impossible to go anywhere without having the stylized Batman logo stare you in the face.

'89 *Opposite:* **Batman confronts The Joker.**

Though it featured atmospheric sets and Jack Nicholson in fine scenery-chewing form as The Joker, the film suffered from a lousy script and a wooden performance by Michael Keaton in the title role. Still, Batman's runaway success ensured that a sequel would be along shortly.

Other **over-hyped and under-written** hits included *Indiana Jones and the Last Crusade* and *Ghostbusters II*, but 1989 still had more than its share of filmic highlights. Steven

'89 The establishment did wrong by Spike Lee's *Do the Right Thing*.

Soderbergh's sharply scripted *sex, lies, and videotape* was a surprise hit, and Gus Van Sant's **Drugstore Cowboy** (starring Matt Dillon in one of his finest performances) looked at drug abuse with such an non-judgmental eye that it was hard to believe the film was made during the Reagan-Bush era. Michael Moore explored the closing of a General Motors plant in the darkly humorous semi-

'89 Sally (Meg Ryan) meets Harry (Billy Crystal).

documentary *Roger & Me*, **Meg Ryan** faked an orgasm in a delicatessen in *When Harry Met Sally*, and in *The Fabulous Baker Boys*, Michelle Pfeiffer firmly established her place in the Hollywood firmament with an unbelievably sexy rendition of "Makin' Whoopee." Best of all was Spike Lee's angry and poetic **Do the Right Thing**, though it was snubbed by the Academy of Motion Picture Arts and Sciences, which failed to even honor it with a "Best Picture" nomination.

Excellent!

Disney cleaned up with *The Little Mermaid*, a cartoon loosely based on the Hans Christian Andersen story of the same name, and the Rick Moranis vehicle *Honey, I Shrunk the Kids*. Popular teen fare included *Heathers* (starring Winona Ryder and Christian Slater), *Bill and Ted's Excellent Adventure* (with Keanu Reeves), and

Say Anything, which further increased the popularity of John Cusack.

Lying Lowe

In the year's biggest Hollywood scandal, teen idol Rob Lowe was sued by a woman in Atlanta, Georgia, who claimed that Lowe had coerced her underage daughter into performing sex acts in front of a video camera. Lowe tried to keep a low profile for a while, but bootleg copies of the videotape made the rounds for years afterwards.

Rose Blighted, But Shoe Sales Bloom

In sports, Cincinnati Reds player and manager Pete Rose was banned from baseball for life for betting on baseball games, allegedly including ones by his own team. One of the best players of his (or any other) era, Rose was virtually guaranteed a spot in the Baseball Hall of Fame; unfortunately,

the betting scandal all but nullified his chances of getting in. The future looked far more promising for the sports footwear industry; sneaker companies reported sales of more than four hundred million shoes during the year. Converse claimed that children eighteen and under were responsible for fifty-eight percent of their revenues—even though the company's most popular pairs were priced at over a hundred dollars. **Timberland boots** were also selling especially well, thanks to their popularity among hip-hoppers, who regularly wore them with extra-baggy jeans and triple-fat goosedown coats.

Music News

With new releases as disparate as De La Soul's groovy *Three Feet High and Rising* and NWA's incendiary *Straight Outta Compton*, rap music provided 1989 with its most stimulating sounds. Even novelty rap singles like Young MC's

"Bust A Move," 2 Live Crew's "Me So Horny," and Tone Loc's "Funky Cold Medina" were preferable to the **bland pop** of Paula Abdul, Richard Marx, and New Kids on the Block, who dominated the charts for most of the year. Madonna went brunette and made *Like A Prayer*, her strongest album to date, while former New Edition vocalist Bobby Brown left his teeny-bopper past behind him with the tough *Don't Be Cruel*. Harry Connick, Jr, a twenty-two-year-old jazz pianist from New Orleans, became the crooner of the hour, thanks to the success of the *When Harry Met Sally* soundtrack. When Guns N' Roses had an all-acoustic hit with "Patience," a lightbulb went on above MTV's progammers, and **"MTV Unplugged"** debuted in November with a performance by singer-songwriter Jules Shear. An ideal way to resuscitate flagging careers, the show would inspire a spate of "Unplugged" albums throughout the nineties.

'89 Bill and Ted (Alex Winter and Keanu Reeves), ready for adventure.

TV News

With 56.4 percent of American households subscribing to cable TV, and 62 percent now owning VCRs, ABC, CBS, and NBC all lost viewers for the sixth consecutive year. The young Fox network also chipped away at the Big Three, thanks to popular "reality" shows like *Cops*, *Totally Hidden Video*, and *America's Most Wanted*, and viewers were further distracted by such pay-per-view events as **Thunder and Mud**, a women's mud-wrestling special hosted by former Jim Bakker paramour Jessica Hahn. Teenagers, who could normally be counted on to watch almost anything, were busy playing with Nintendo's hand-held **Game Boy**, Atari's portable Lynx, or Sega's Genesis system, which included a version of the popular arcade game Altered Beast.

Talk Isn't Cheap

Two of the year's more popular non-sitcom network offerings were NBC's *LA Law* and ABC's nostalgic *The Wonder Years*, both of which had already been around for a few years; *Rescue 911*, hosted by William Shatner, was CBS's popular response to shows like *Cops*. But for the most part, syndicated talk show hosts Arsenio Hall (who became the first black man to host a successful late-night talk show) and Oprah Winfrey (dubbed "**the richest woman on television**" by *TV Guide*) were among the few who could honestly say that they'd had a good year.

Lucy And Mel Mourned

1989 also witnessed the deaths of two of television's most significant early stars. Lucille Ball passed away on April 25, aged seventy-seven, and Mel Blanc, the voice of Bugs Bunny, Daffy Duck, Porky Pig and the rest of Warner Brothers' cartoon menagerie, died July 10 at age eighty-one. His headstone inscription? "**That's all, folks!**"

TOP SINGLES

PHIL COLLINS
"**Another Day In Paradise**"

JANET JACKSON
"**Miss You Much**"

PAULA ABDUL
"**Straight Up**"

RICHARD MARX
"**Right Here Waiting**"

MADONNA
"**Like A Prayer**"

'89 Oprah—undisputed queen of the talk show.

'90

The recession of 1990, **after the boom of the 1980s,** provided a rather inauspicious beginning to the new decade. By the end of the year, unemployment was up, sales of new homes were down by a whopping 17.5 percent, the Gross National Product improved only 0.9 percent from 1989, and economists were forecasting more of the same for 1991. **The US population hit 249 million in 1990,** an increase of 23 million over the last decade. For the first time ever, over fifty percent of Americans were living in metropolitan areas.

Not that big cities were necessarily any safer to live in; during the year, murder rates hit record highs in Dallas, Memphis, Milwaukee, New York, Phoenix, San Antonio, and Washington DC.

Saturnalia

With sales of new cars down 5.1 percent, the time seemed totally wrong for General Motors to introduce Saturn, its first new brand name in over sixty years. Saturn wasn't just another American car, however; designed specifically to lure younger buyers back from Honda, Toyota and other Japanese brands, Saturn combined the quality construction of its foreign counterparts with a customer-friendly approach. A "no ups, no extras" sales policy meant that customers were guaranteed a fair shake from Saturn dealers; if dissatisfied with the car for any reason, a buyer could return it before thirty days or fifteen hundred miles, no questions asked. Saturn quickly became the industry leader in car sales per dealer, causing other American companies to

reconsider (at least briefly) their lackadaisical attitude towards customer satisfaction.

Dirty Photos?

In Cincinnati, the city's Contemporary Art Center faced an indictment for obscenity, in connection with an exhibit of photographs by that perennial right-wing favorite, Robert Mapplethorpe. The case marked the first time that a museum or its director faced such charges; both were acquitted by a jury in October.

Rock World Rocked

A record store clerk in Florida was arrested for selling a 2 Live Crew abum to a minor; in response, Luke featuring 2 Live Crew's next album was titled **Banned In The USA**. Geffen Records refused to distribute

'90 Mill Vanilli collect a Grammy Award(but don't get to keep it).

The Geto Boys' new record because of the lyrical content of tracks like "Mind of a Lunatic," "Let a Ho Be a Ho," and "Trigga Happy Nigga," and Madonna was excoriated for simulating masturbation onstage during her "Blonde Ambition" tour.

Then there was the question of sampling; while Deee-Lite (whose "Groove Is In The Heart" was one of the year's slinkiest dance hits) and Public Enemy (who released *Fear Of A Black Planet*, their most uncompromising record yet) were among the many artists who sampled other people's records in a creative (and often unrecognizable) fashion, many others opted for a simpler approach, lifting the hooks wholesale from previous hits. Of this latter faction, **MC Hammer**'s "U Can't Touch This" and white rapper **Vanilla Ice**'s "Ice Ice Baby" were the most egregious, utilizing already familiar riffs from Rick James' "Super Freak" and Queen's "Under Pressure," respectively. Not coincidentally, they also became two of the year's biggest rap hits.

But the loudest howls of outrage were reserved for producer Frank Farian's revelation that Europop duo **Milli Vanilli**, who had recently won the Grammy Award for "Best New Artist," did not actually sing on their multi-platinum *Girl You Know It's True* LP. While the cheekbones and dance moves of "frontmen" Rob Pilatus and Fabrice Morvan certainly had as much to do with the album's sales as the bubblegum grooves within (anyone familiar with Boney M, Farian's late-seventies space-disco creations, should have suspected that all was not as it seemed), the National Academy of Recording Arts and Sciences stripped Pilatus and Morvan of their Grammy in November. The duo made another go of it a few years later, this time as Rob & Fab, but only sold a few thousand copies of their record. Pilatus' life became a downward spiral of drug and legal problems; in 1998, he died in a German hotel room from a mixture of pills and booze.

Wood OD's

Another victim of rock 'n' roll excess was Andrew Wood, lead singer of Seattle hard-rock band Mother Love Bone, who died of a heroin overdose shortly before his band's full-length debut was scheduled to be released. With heroin now cheaper, purer and more plentiful then it had been in decades, many observers predicted an marked increase in overdoses (and needle-related HIV cases) over the next few years.

TV News

Saturday Night Live, currently struggling through yet another uninspired season, created quite a hubub when it announced that controversial comedian Andrew Dice Clay would host an upcoming broadcast. As a protest against Dice's lewd and crude stand-up routines, cast member Nora Dunn boycotted the show, joined by scheduled musical guest Sinead O'Connor. A fresh (in several senses of the word) contrast to *SNL* was provided by **In Living Color**, Fox's new comedy-variety series; created by filmmaker Keenen Ivory Wayans, the show featured such memorable characters as "Homey the Clown" and the gay hosts of "Men on Film," as well as a talented young comedian named Jim Carrey. Fox also

IN THE NEWS

March 25 – After being ejected from the Happy Land Social Club in the Bronx, New York, Julio Gonzalez spills gasoline on the entrance and sets it on fire. The ensuing conflagration kills 87 people, and Gonzalez is given 25 years to life in prison.

April 22 – The 20th anniversary of Earth Day is celebrated worldwide, with 200 million people in 140 countries participating in tree planting, recycling, and other earth-friendly events.

June 30 – The National Academy of Science announces that the AIDS epidemic is not leveling off, but rather spreading to new groups, including black and Hispanic women.

July 26 – Bush signs a landmark law forbidding discrimination against disabled persons in employment, public accommodations, and transportation.

90 Jim Carrey *(far right)* with the cast of *In Living Color*.

scored big with **The Simpsons**, the animated brainchild of "Life in Hell" comic artist Matt Groening. Bart Simpson, the show's troublemaking fourth-grader, immediately became an icon for underachievers of all ages, leading to a rapid proliferation of T-shirts bearing Bart's mantra, "Don't Have a Cow, Man." **Twin Peaks**, which also touched a nerve with viewers, was more of an acquired taste. Directed by David Lynch, the unsettling, dream-like serial revolved around the question of "Who killed Laura Palmer?" The plot became impossibly convoluted—and the ratings dropped severely—by the time detective Kyle Maclachlan got around to solving the mystery (answer: her dad, who became a homicidal maniac when possessed by an evil spirit named Bob), but the show further confirmed Lynch's reputation as a man with a darkly original vision, as well as making actress Sherilyn Fenn the sex symbol of the hour. Far more wholesome (though it regularly dealt with issues like drinking, drugs, and

teen sex) was **Beverly Hills 90210**, an Aaron Spelling production that followed the lives of eight Beverly Hills high school students. The show became incredibly popular with teenage viewers, who tuned in religiously to catch the latest crisis, and the success of the series paved the way for such future Spelling favorites as *Melrose Place* and *Models Inc.*

Muppet Man Dies

On February 4, Eddie Murphy, Michael Jackson, Frank Sinatra, and Shirley MacLaine all appeared and performed as part of ABC's "Sammy Davis, Jr's Sixtieth Anniversary Celebration" special. The tribute came none too

soon, as Sammy died a few months later of throat cancer at the age of sixty-four. The country was further saddened by the sudden death (from pneumonia) of Jim Henson, creator of Kermit the Frog, Miss Piggy, and the rest of the Muppet gang. He was fifty-three.

Movie News

1990 saw the revision of the Motion Picture Association of America's rating system, which replaced X ratings with NC-17, meaning that no one under age seventeen would be admitted. *Henry and June*, Philip Kaufman's adaptation of Anais Nin's erotic diaries, was the first film to be classified NC-17 under the new system. The year's biggest hit,

however, was strictly PG—**Home Alone**, in which a young boy outwits a duo of burglars with an intricate series of booby traps, turned child star Macaulay Culkin into one of Hollywood's highest paid actors. *Teenage Mutant Ninja Turtles*, a live-action film based on the popular comic book, was another huge hit with kids, who gobbled up millions of dollars' worth of Ninja Turtle toys and costumes. Expecting a success of *Batman*-like proportions, a line of *Dick Tracy* memorabilia was marketed in well in

'90 Doh! It's *The Simpsons*.

advance of the movie's release. Unfortunately, reviews of the film (which starred Warren Beatty and Madonna) were mixed at best, and the merchandise collected dust on the shelves.

Arnold Schwarzenegger, who continued to alternate action roles and light-hearted comedy with *Total Recall* and *Kindergarten Cop*, was the year's most popular male star, while **Julia Roberts** (*Pretty Woman*, *Sleeping with the Enemy*) was the top female draw.

'90 Teenage Mutant Ninja Turtles.

'90 The ghost of a kiss for Demi Moore from Patrick Swayze.

Patrick Swayze romanced Demi Moore from beyond the grave in *Ghost*; Kevin Costner bonded with Native Americans in *Dances with Wolves*; and mob movie fans were offered the double treat of Martin Scorsese's *GoodFellas* and Francis Ford Coppola's *The Godfather, Part III*. Less enticing was *Ghost Dad*, starring Bill Cosby as a deceased parent continuing to raise his brood, and *Lambada* and *The Forbidden Dance*, both of which tried to exploit the current **Lambada** dance craze (although the former did feature the many talents of Adolpho "Shabba-Doo" Quinones, last seen in *Breakin' 2: Electric Boogaloo*). Worst of all was *Wild Orchid*, in which an orange-colored Mickey Rourke seduced real-life galpal Carre Otis during Carnival in Rio de Janeiro. Ostensibly an "erotic thriller" along the lines of Rourke's earlier *Nine and a Half Weeks*, the film was way too silly to be even remotely sexy.

Millions Netted

Though it had yet to become a household word, more and more Americans were logging onto the Internet. 1990 witnessed the introduction of America Online, which competed with the already established Prodigy and CompuServe networks by specializing in chat folders and offering an easy-to-use interface.

Videogame News

Nintendo rocked the videogame world with the release of Super Mario 3, which quickly became the best-selling game cartridge to date. Meanwhile, the company filed suit against Blockbuster Video, alleging that Blockbuster's rental of video-games severely dented Nintendo sales.

Bud Dries Up

And just when you were wondering if technological wonders would never cease, the Anheuser-Busch Brewing Company introduced Bud Dry, which was specially brewed to have no bite or aftertaste. Unfortunately, the beer had no flavor, either, and poor sales caused it to be pulled off the market in 1994.

As 1991 began, George Bush was riding high. Having spent months demonizing Saddam Hussein (Bush insisted on pronouncing the Iraqi leader's name as "Sodom," apparently for extra righteousness value) before the American public, the president was rewarded with a massive groundswell of popular support for the Gulf War.

Though the war lasted barely a month and a half, Desert Storm Generals Norman Schwarzkopf and Colin Powell became household names, thanks to hourly televised updates of events in the Persian Gulf (Desert Storm trading cards helped the young 'uns keep abreast of the latest weaponry). By the end of February, Iraq was out of Kuwait, Bush was out from under Reagan's shadow (and almost assured of re-election in 1992), and America was "standing tall" again after successive humiliations in Vietnam and Iran.

Recession Deepens

But when the smoke finally cleared and the victory parades were over, things weren't quite so rosy. The recession, which had started the previous year, only seemed to be getting worse; unemployment was up to 7.2 percent, new home sales were down 5.6 percent, and new car sales were down 11.2 percent, giving Detroit its worst year since 1983. General Motors laid off seventy thousand workers, and

'91 Costner as DA Jim Garrison in *JFK*.

IBM axed another twenty thousand. In October, usually their busiest month, Las Vegas casinos reported severe drops in revenue, which in turn caused two of the city's gaming establishments to go bankrupt. In addition, studies revealed that 5.5 million American children were currently going hungry.

Movie News

It wasn't a particularly good year for Hollywood, either; whether it was because of the recession, or just due to the fact that everyone stayed home in January and February to watch the Gulf War on TV, theaters reported their lowest box-office attendance totals in twenty years. Certainly, 1991 didn't lack for blockbusters—the hundred-million-dollar *Terminator 2: Judgment Day* was easily the year's most popular film, as Arnold Schwarzenegger continued to reign as Hollywood's pre-eminent action star. **Kevin Costner**, currently the most popular male box-office attraction, starred in *Robin Hood: Prince of Thieves* and Oliver Stone's controversial *JFK*. (Though many complained that *JFK* played fast and loose with the facts surrounding the Kennedy assassination, the inaccuracies were minor compared to those of Stone's *The Doors*, which was released the same year.)

Madonna's "Blonde Ambition" tour was documented in *Truth or Dare*, and Ice-T and Ice Cube delivered competent performances in *New Jack City* and *Boyz N the Hood*, respectively. But the hands-down winner of the "Worst Performance by a Popular Recording Artist" trophy had to be **Vanilla Ice**, who mumbled his way through the mind-numbingly stupid *Cool As Ice*. The surprise indie hit of the year was *Slacker*, Richard Linklater's plotless trawl through the

January 15 – The UN-authorized, US-led "Operation Desert Storm" begins in Kuwait with an all-out air attack.

January 25 – The AIDS death toll hits 100,000, with over 161,000 cases reported since 1981.

February 27 – After three days of ground offensive, Desert Storm troops rout the Iraqi forces in Kuwait. 146 American troops are killed in the fighting; 467 are wounded.

March 3 – After leading LA police on a car chase of several miles, black motorist Rodney King is arrested and severely beaten by four LAPD officers. The incident is captured on videotape by bystander George Holliday, and shown repeatedly on news programs across the country.

April 4 – The Environmental Protection Agency announces that the ozone layer over the US is being depleted at twice the rate previously thought.

April 16 – Seventy tornadoes touch down in seven states in the Midwest and Southwest, killing 23 people.

June 27 – Thurgood Marshall, the first black US Supreme Court justice, resigns after 24 years on the bench.

July 25 – Jeffrey Dahmer arrested in Milwaukee, Wisconsin for killing, dismembering, and possibly eating at least seventeen people. Dahmer confesses to the sex-related killings, and receives fifteen consecutive life sentences. In 1994, Dahmer is beaten to death in prison by a fellow inmate.

'91 Costner stars again, this time as *Robin Hood: Prince of Thieves*.

lives of idiosyncratic folks living in the college town of Austin, Texas. Alternately hilarious and annoying, the film launched Linklater's career as a director, and gave pop sociologists a handy new name for the post-Boomer generation.

Buddies Team Up On Film

In a year that saw the publication of such new-feminist best-sellers as Susan Faludi's *Backlash: The Undeclared War Against American Women* and Naomi Wolf's *The Beauty Myth*, 1991 fittingly offered numerous films with strong female characters. In **The Silence of the Lambs**, Jodie Foster played a tough FBI trainee tracking a serial killer with help from an imprisoned cannibal (Anthony Hopkins), while Mary Stuart Masterson helped Mary-Louise Parker stand up to an abusive husband in *Fried Green Tomatoes*. *Thelma and Louise*, starring Susan Sarandon and Geena Davis as two road buddies wanted for the murder of an attempted

rapist, inspired a popular T-shirt that sported a picture of the gun-toting pair and the legend, "George Bush— Meet Thelma and Louise!"

Of course, it was also the year that Robert Bly's **Iron John**: *A Book about Men* became the bible of the burgeoning "Men's Movement," and so there were also plenty of male-bonding films to go around. **Keanu Reeves** starred in no less than three "buddy" films, *Bill and Ted's Bogus Journey*, the goofy action-thriller *Point Break* (with Patrick Swayze), and Gus Van Sant's haunting *My Own Private Idaho*. The latter also starred River Phoenix, who received rave reviews for his portrayal of a narcoleptic street hustler.

TV News

Introduced briefly in 1990, *Northern Exposure*, a low-key comedy-drama about a young New York physician (Rob Morrow) assigned to a remote Alaskan village, became a smash in 1991 upon finally finding a permanent time slot. **Seinfeld**, a sitcom revolving around

stand-up comic Jerry Seinfeld and his three neurotic, self-involved friends (Jason Alexander, Julia Louis-Dreyfus, and Michael Richards), also inspired a devoted following, although it wouldn't really break through to the mainstream until 1993, when it was rescheduled to follow the phenomenally successful *Cheers*. The abrasive cartoon **Ren and Stimpy** was a smash with both children and young hipsters, who found the scatalogical humor and John Kricfalusi's eye-popping animation to be very much to their liking.

'91 Seinfield and friends make their TV debut.

Pee Wee Busted

Paul Reubens, aka Pee Wee Herman, made headlines in July when he was arrested for "exposing himself" in a Florida porno theater. In response, CBS quickly removed *Pee Wee's Playhouse* from its Saturday morning schedule, and Pee Wee Herman dolls disappeared overnight from the nation's toy stores, becoming instant collectables in the process. Clearly, Pee Wee should have stayed at home with his VCR, like most porno aficionados. In the triple-X world, "amateur porn" was now the latest fad, with over fifty different video companies buying and repackaging homemade sex tapes for sale or rent.

Videogame News

In other joystick news, Nintendo introduced its new Super NES system, which retailed for $249.95. Nintendo

'91 *Thelma and Louise*, women on the run.

was less than pleased with Galoob Toys, who introduced The Game Genie, a device which allowed players to cheat on Nintendo games and win more easily. Atari, still trying to recover from a disastrous second half of the eighties, announced the development of a new 16-bit system, which the company hoped would effectively compete with Sega and Nintendo; but with Sega's new **Sonic the Hedgehog** game setting sales records, Atari would have its work cut out for itself. Over at the arcade, business was picking up considerably, thanks to Capcom's new, ultra-violent Street Fighter II.

'91 Ren and Stimpy.

Music News

Michael Jackson became the world's highest-paid recording artist in March, when he signed a one-billion-dollar multimedia deal with Sony Software. He also came under fire for the video of his new single, "**Black Or White**," which featured him breaking windows; concerned parents worried that young fans might want to imitate his acts of destructiveness. Though Michael's new *Dangerous* CD sold six million copies, it was hardly the zeitgeist-defining success of *Thriller*; Garth Brooks, Mariah Carey, and Michael Bolton all sold more records than Michael in 1991.

Alternative Source Of Cash

Music lovers who didn't care for any of the above artists could at least take heart in the surprise success of Nirvana; *Bleach*, the Seattle band's previous album, was a college radio favorite, but **Nevermind**, their first record for Geffen Records, shot to the top of the charts, thanks in part to the anarchic video for "Smells Like Teen

Spirit." The success of *Nevermind*, REM's *Out of Time*, and the summer's Lollapalooza festival (which was founded by Jane's Addiction leader Perry Farrell, and featured appearances by The Rollins Band, Ice-T's Body Count, Siouxsie and the Banshees, The Butthole Surfers, and Nine Inch Nails) convinced record executives that "alternative rock" was where it was at. Major labels quickly swooped down on Seattle, signing any band in sight with guitars and flannel shirts; it seemed as if every time Nirvana leader **Kurt Cobain** praised an indie band in an interview, said band were immediately offered a multi-album deal.

As with previous industry feeding frenzies, the mediocre signings far outweighed the good ones, but it was obvious to observers that rock music was turning another corner; almost overnight, hair-metal bands—the music industry's bread-and-butter during the late-eighties—vanished completely from MTV. In their place, an army of "**grunge**" rockers (including Pearl Jam, Soundgarden, and Alice in Chains) expressed a vague dissatisfaction with their lot in life. It was progress, certainly, but it wasn't a whole lot of fun.

The Magic's Gone

In the NBA championships, Michael Jordan led the Chicago Bulls to a four-games-to-one victory over Magic Johnson and the Los Angeles Lakers. In November, Johnson shocked the sports world by suddenly announcing his retirement, due to the fact that he was HIV-positive. Johnson changed his mind and rejoined the team for the 1991–92 season, but retired again in November 1992.

1992 was, as George Bush so eloquently put it, "a weird year."

For Bush, it began with a very public (and embarrassing) display of vomiting during a diplomatic visit to Japan, and ended with a resounding defeat at the hands of a man young enough to be his son. Certainly, Bush's re-election campaign was dogged by unforseen circumstances—the **worsening recession, the LA riots,** Texas billionaire H Ross Perot's third-party candidacy—but the president did little to help his own cause.

TOP TELEVISION SHOWS

60 Minutes
Roseanne
Murphy Brown
Home Improvement
Coach

ACADEMY AWARDS

BEST PICTURE
Unforgiven
directed by Clint Eastwood

BEST ACTOR
Al Pacino
Scent of a Woman

BEST ACTRESS
Emma Thompson
Howards End

Never the warmest of individuals, Bush sounded increasingly shrill and pinched as the campaign wore on and his approval ratings dipped; for all the controversy surrounding Democratic challenger Bill Clinton (he equivocated on several important issues, and was accused of carrying on at least one extramarital affair while presiding as the governor of Arkansas), Clinton at least came across like he cared about people. In the end, incidents like the takeover of the Republican Convention by Pat Robertson's **"Christian Coalition,"** and Bush's confusion during a staged question-and-answer session (he was visibly shaken when the order of questions was accidentally shuffled) only served to illustrate how deeply out of touch Bush was with the mood of the country. Americans showed their displeasure by making sure that Bush would go down in the history books as a one-term-only president.

'92 *Barney & Friends* **became a merchandising bonanza.**

Clinton Plays It Cool

Among the more amusing missteps of the Bush/Quayle re-election campaign was Dan Quayle's blistering attack on Murphy Brown. In a May speech bemoaning America's "poverty of values," Quayle lit into the popular TV show, taking Candice Bergen's character to task for having a baby out of wedlock. The ensuing media hubub helped the show attain its highest ratings to date, while further diminishing the public's ability to take Quayle's seriously. Bill Clinton took a far more media-savvy (and friendly) approach, blowing saxophone (albeit terribly) as part of an appearance on *The Arsenio Hall Show*.

TV News

In retrospect, many parents would have been happier if Quayle had attacked *Barney & Friends*, the inane PBS children's show about a stuffed purple dinosaur who grows and comes to life. *Barney* quickly developed a devoted following among pre-schoolers, who of course petitioned their parents for stuffed purple dinosaurs of their own. By the end of 1993, over three hundred million dollars in Barney merchandise had been sold.

"Babewatch"

Had they been available, stuffed Pamela Anderson dolls would probably have been a big hit with men of all ages; as it was, male viewers had to be content with watching the buxom blonde actress (formerly *Home Improvement*'s "Tool Time Girl") run around in a red lifeguard's swimsuit

on *Baywatch*. The show, which failed to capture a regular audience on its introduction in 1989, was now an international hit, thanks to the charms of such cast members as Anderson, Nicole Eggert, and Erika Eleniak.

Sitcoms And Talk Shows Come And Go

Melrose Place, Aaron Spelling's new dramatic series, also made good use of an attractive cast, including Heather Locklear, Josie Bissett, Courtney Thorne-Smith, Andrew Shue, and Grant Show. Some of the year's more popular

sitcoms included *Love and War* (starring former Partridge Family member Susan Dey, replaced after one season by Annie Potts), *Mad About You* (with Paul Reiser and Helen Hunt), and *Martin* (featuring stand-up comedian Martin Lawrence), while *The Cosby Show*, the most popular sitcom of the last decade, ended its impressive run on April 30.

HBO's popular new *Larry Sanders Show* starred **Garry Shandling** as a neurotic talk-show host; the program's talk-show segments often included real-life guests like Sharon Stone and Elvis Costello, and were filmed in front

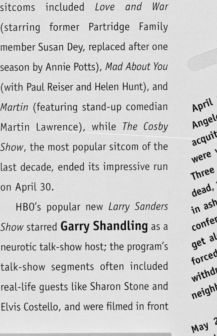

IN THE NEWS

April 29 – Rioting breaks out in Los Angeles, following an all-white jury's acquittal of the four LA policemen who were videotaped beating Rodney King. Three days of violence leave 51 people dead, 1,800 injured, and 3,767 buildings in ashes. On May 2, King holds a press conference, asking, "People, can we all get along?" LAPD Chief Daryl Gates is forced to retire in June, in part for withdrawing his men from LA's poorer neighborhoods at the start of the riots.

May 23 – With the USSR dissolved, President Bush signs an agreement with Russia, Belarus, Kazakhstan, and Ukraine to abide by the nuclear arms reduction treaty signed between the US and USSR in 1991.

June 22 – In the wake of the LA riots, Bush signs a bill providing $1.3 billion for relief to Los Angeles, and which will appropriate funds for a summer employment program in 75 cities.

June 23 – John Gotti, head of the Gambino crime family, is sentenced to life in prison for thirteen charges of murder, conspiracy, tax fraud, and obstruction of justice.

June 24 – The US Supreme Court rules that warning labels on cigarette packages do not protect tobacco companies from damage claims. The court also reaffirms its stance that state-sponsored prayer in public schools is unconstitutional.

June 29 – The US Supreme Court upholds women's constitutional right to abortion by a 5-4 vote, although the court does permit individual states to impose some restrictions.

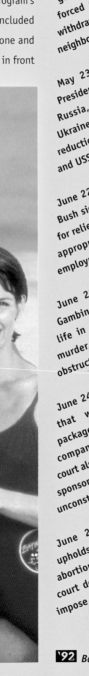

'92 *Baywatch* babes and hunks.

of a live audience. Johnny Carson signed off from *The Tonight Show* in May, and was replaced by stand-up comedian Jay Leno. NBC's decision to hire Leno didn't sit well with David Letterman, who had also coveted the *Tonight Show* job, and industry insiders guessed that Letterman would soon take his sarcastic sense of humor to another network.

Dumb And Dumber

If *The Hat Squad*, a short-lived crime series about three hunky vigilantes who wore fedoras, stood out as the year's dumbest show, it was hard to beat NBC's *Amy Fisher: My Story* for sheer real-life stupidity. The TV movie starred Noelle Parker as the "Long Island Lolita" who attempted to murder the wife of her lover, auto mechanic Joey Buttafuocco. In real life, Buttafuocco did six months for statutory rape, and became something of a minor celebrity (the tabloids gleefully reported that he'd been kicked out of an exclusive Manhattan swinger's club for eating a pastrami sandwich in the communal hot tub), while Fisher was sentenced to five to fifteen years in jail.

Movie News

Movie attendance was still down in 1992, but controversy was way up. Spike Lee got in trouble for recommending that black kids skip school to see his new **Malcolm X**, starring Denzel Washington; gay and feminist activists picketed *Basic Instinct*, protesting Sharon Stone's role as a rapacious bisexual murderess; and Ernest Dickerson's *Juice* (starring Tupac Shakur), Abel Ferrara's *The Bad Lieutenant* (with Harvey Keitel as a *really* bad lieutenant), and **Reservoir Dogs** (Quentin Tarantino's acclaimed directorial debut) all came under fire for their extreme violence.

Party On!

Home Alone 2: Lost in New York and Disney's animated *Aladdin* were huge hits with the kids, as was the eighty-million-dollar *Batman Returns,* which featured Danny DeVito as The Penguin and Michelle Pfeiffer as Catwoman. Younger viewers also flocked to see **Wayne's World**, a film adaptation

of Mike Myers' and Dana Carvey's regular *Saturday Night Live* sketch; the film's soundtrack, which featured such classic rock gems as Queen's "Bohemian Rhapsody" and Gary Wright's "Dream Weaver," topped the charts for several weeks. Other popular soundtracks included *Boomerang* (featuring Boyz II Men, Babyface, and Toni Braxton), *Singles* (with tracks by Seattle bands Mudhoney, Pearl Jam, and Soundgarden), and Whitney Houston's soundtrack to **The Bodyguard**, which sold over fifteen million copies.

Music News

In music, 1992 was the year where juvenile rappers Kriss Kross had kids wearing their clothes backwards, Billy Ray Cyrus started a line-dancing revival with "Achy Breaky Heart," and Prince signed a one-hundred-million-dollar recording contract with Warner Brothers. Madonna released *Erotica*, the aural companion to *Sex*, her controversial photo book, and Body Count, Ice-T's speed-metal band,

caused a stir with a track called "Cop Killer;" under pressure from the White House, Time-Warner stockholders and various right-wing organizations, Sire Records eventually dropped Ice-T from their roster. Lollapalooza had a prosperous second year, thanks to an all-star lineup consisting of the Red Hot Chili Peppers (currently riding high with "Under the Bridge"), Ice Cube, Pearl Jam, Lush, The Jesus and Mary Chain, Soundgarden, and Ministry. The **HORDE** ("Horizons of Rock Developing Everywhere") Tour was a successful "hippie" alternative to Lollapalooza, featuring such jam-happy acts as Blues Traveler, the Spin Doctors, Phish, Widespread Panic, The Aquarium Rescue Unit, Bela Fleck and the Flecktones.

Car Industry Bullish

Though the economy was still hurting, Detroit bounced back impressively, with automobile sales up twenty-one percent from the previous year. Ford's Taurus was the year's top-

selling American car, moving over three hundred and ninety-seven thousand units, and sales would rise even higher during the next two years. While the dependable Taurus appealed to the conservative impulses of American auto buyers, Dodge's new **Viper**, a voluptuously styled sports car that could go 0 to 60 in 4.5 seconds, was all about sex and speed. Though it was priced at fifty thousand dollars, demand for the car far out-stripped the supply.

18–30s Targeted

Observing the runaway success of alternative rock, marketers increasingly geared their advertising campaigns towards eighteen-to-thirty-year-olds, the "Generation X" demographic (usually by featuring young guys with goatees and big shorts in their commercials), and tried hard to give their products an "alternative" spin, whether or not they actually warranted one. **Zima**, the Coors Company's new "clear malt beverage" was a typical example—the alcoholic brew was

marketed as a cool alternative to beer, even though its sweet taste was more appealing to the wine-cooler crowd. **Adidas**, a company that connected easily with the eighteen-to-thirties, responded to a sudden demand for old three-striped styles by reactivating its Gazelle and "shell-toe" lines.

They Fell For It!

In an effort to help the public (and advertisers) more fully understand those mysterious Gen-Xers, *The New York Times* published a glossary of "grunge" terminology in its November 15 issue. Unfortunately for the *Times*, the glossary turned out to be a hoax, perpetrated by Megan Jasper of New York indie label Caroline Records. In retrospect, it's hard to believe that there wasn't anyone at the paper hip enough to know that "swingin' on the flippity-flop" was *not* slacker slang for "hanging out."

Nor was it grunge lingo for **bungee jumping**, which was all the rage at the time. For fifty dollars you could jump from an elevated

platform with an elastic cord tied to your ankles. Though scary, the sport was surprisingly safe; only two bungee-related deaths were reported during the year.

'92 The US boasted over 200 bungee-jump sites in 1992.

IN THE NEWS

July 15–16 – The Democratic National Convention nominates Arkansas Governor Bill Clinton and Tennessee Senator Al Gore for president and vice-president.

August 19–20 – The Republican National Convention nominates President Bush and Vice-President Quayle for re-election.

August 23 – Secretary of State James Baker resigns his post in order to take over Bush's re-election campaign, which is widely seen to be in serious trouble.

August 24 – Hurricane Andrew hits southern Florida; the hurricane's 150 mph winds kill 38, destroy 85,000 homes, and leave 250,000 homeless.

September 24 – Following an inquiry into allegations of sexual harassment at the US Navy's 1991 Tailhook Convention in Las Vegas, two Navy admirals are forced to retire, and a third is reassigned.

November 3 – Bill Clinton is elected president by a margin of 5 million votes. Third-party candidate H Ross Perot logs a surprising 19 percent of the vote.

December 24 – Outgoing President Bush pardons six former federal officials, including former secretary of defense Caspar Weinberger and former national security advisor Robert McFarlane, for their roles in the Iran-Contra scandal.

'93

"Drugs don't work," announced the Partnership for a Drug-Free America's new ad campaign, but the truth of the matter was that, for many, drugs were working just fine—a University of Michigan study showed that pot use among teens was up for the first time in thirteen years. **Marijuana chic** was everywhere, from the cover of Dr Dre's *The Chronic* to the popular **pot-leaf** insignias sported on T-shirts and baseball caps.

A drug-induced heart attack put an end to River Phoenix's promising film career, but his very public death (on Halloween, outside the entrance to LA's Viper Room) did little to diminish the hip cachet of hard drugs in film and music circles. In other addictive substance news, Anheuser-Busch proudly announced that their new **Budweiser Ice Draft** had a smoother taste than regular beer, but it's likely that more people bought it for the increased alcoholic content.

Bad Behavior

In Ohio, a woman claimed that MTV's new *Beavis and Butthead* cartoon caused her five-year-old son to set the fire that torched their trailer park home and killed his two-year-old sister. In LA, rapper Snoop Doggy Dogg was arrested by the Los Angeles Police Department in connection with a drive-by shooting; just across town, the LAPD was investigating allegations that Michael Jackson had molested a twelve-year-old boy. (Beavis and Butthead would have

enjoyed Jackson's televised denial, if only because the "**King of Pop**" actually used the word "penis" in his prepared statement.) Also of note in the City of Angels, "Hollywood Madam" Heidi Fleiss was arrested for running a high-priced call-girl ring (actor Charlie Sheen was known to be one of her many showbiz-related clients), and brothers Erik and Lyle Menendez admitted to the brutal shotgun slaying of their parents, a crime which had gone unsolved for nearly four years. After years of abuse at the hands of her husband, housewife Lorena Bobbitt fought back by chopping off his penis while he slept. Doctors were able to reattach the severed member, thus enabling **John Wayne Bobbitt** to find fame in the best-selling porno videos *John Wayne Bobbitt: Uncut* and the appropriately titled *Frankenpenis*. On the big screen, Woody Allen's *Manhattan Murder Mystery* stalled at the box office, due to the lingering controversy over his relationship with

'93 Wanted: Snoop Doggy Dogg.

Soon-Yi Previn, adopted daughter of Allen's long-time girlfriend Mia Farrow.

Painful Pranks

Mortal Kombat, the year's most popular videogame, included a "finishing moves" feature that allowed you to rip the heart out of your opponent; parental groups were, predictably, less than thrilled. Nor were they particularly happy to see **body-piercing** become a nationwide fad, thanks in part to Alicia Silverstone's navel-piercing scene in Aerosmith's "Cryin'" video. The youth of America was further corrupted (and inspired) by The Jerky Boys, three New Yorkers who sold thousands of copies of a CD consisting solely of obnoxious prank phone calls.

"Girls And Boys Come Out..."

"Lesbian Chic—the Bold, Brave New World of Gay Women," trumpeted *New York* magazine's May issue, which featured singer kd lang on the cover. Public acceptance of "alternative lifestyles" was hardly widespread, however; it was all right for entertainers like lang or Melissa Etheridge to come out of the closet, but—thanks to the military's confusing new **"don't ask, don't tell"** policy—gays were allowed to enlist in the armed forces only so long as they didn't identify themselves as such. And the Mattel Toy company was clearly embarrassed when their Earring Magic Ken doll became the best-selling Ken doll of all time; clad in a purple mesh top and sporting a familiar-looking ring on a necklace, the doll was much more popular with gay men than with little girls.

TV News

The big news in TV land was that, after eleven years on NBC, David Letterman signed a contract with CBS for sixteen million dollars. That amount was strictly small potatoes compared to the sales of Mighty Morphin Power Rangers merchandise; within months of the show's debut, American toy stores had sold over three hundred and fifty million dollars' worth of Power Rangers toys and gear. *The X-Files* made its debut in September to relatively little fanfare, but the adventures of agents Mulder (David Duchovny) and Scully (Gillian Anderson) quickly built a cult following before the year was out. Also debuting was *Star Trek: Deep Space Nine*, a spin-off of *Star Trek: The*

'93 "The truth is out there." *The X-Files'* David Duchovny and Gillian Anderson

IN THE NEWS

January 3 – George Bush and Boris Yeltsin sign the second Strategic Arms Reduction Treaty, calling for the US and Russia to cut their nuclear arsenals by two-thirds over the next decade.

January 8 – Second-hand smoke is deemed a serious health threat by the Environmental Protection Agency.

January 13 – Over 100 US, French, and British warplanes attack Iraqi missile bases and radar stations in response to Iraq's violations of various UN resolutions.

January 20 – Bill Clinton is inaugurated as America's 42nd president, the first president to be born after World War Two.

February 26 – A bomb planted by Islamic terrorists kills six people and injures 1,000 at New York's World Trade Center. Nine people are arrested in connection with the blast.

March 11 – Janet Reno becomes the first woman to be named US Attorney General.

April 19 – David Koresh and over 70 members of the Branch Davidian cult die when, after a 51-day standoff, federal agents attack the cult's compound in Waco, Texas. Many criticize Attorney General Janet Reno for her handling of the whole affair.

April–July – The "Great Flood of 1993" leaves 33 dead and over 70,000 homeless, and causes $12 billion in property damage in the Midwest.

Mariah Carey
"Dreamlover"

Janet Jackson
"That's The Way Love Goes"

UB40
"Can't Help Falling in Love"

SNOW
"Informer"

MEAT LOAF
"I'd Do Anything For Love (But I Won't Do That)"

'93 "I'm listening." Frasier (Kelsey Grammer) on the couch with Eddie

Next Generation. Lois and Clark: The New Adventures of Superman made stars out of previously obscure actors Dean Cain and Teri Hatcher, while *NYPD Blue* made producer **Steven Bochco** a household name, thanks to controversy over the show's steamy content. Among the year's popular new sitcoms were *The Nanny*, starring Fran Drescher (previously best-known for her role as Bobbie Fleckman in *This Is Spinal Tap*); *Grace Under Fire*, starring Brett Butler; *Frasier*, a *Cheers* spin-off starring Kelsey Grammer; and *These Friends of Mine*, which was later renamed *Ellen* after its star, comedienne Ellen Degeneres. 1993 brought more variations on the **Amy Fisher/Joey Buttofuco** saga—ABC offered *The Amy Fisher Story*, starring the recently rehabbed Drew Barrymore, while CBS weighed in with *Casualties of Love: The Long Island Lolita Story*, starring former *Who's the Boss?* nymphette Alyssa Milano. In the top-rated special of the 92–93 season, Oprah Winfrey

interviewed Michael Jackson for ABC; Jackson amused viewers by admitting to having had a "minor" amount of plastic surgery. Talk-radio DJ Howard Stern closed out 1993 with a pay-per-view New Year's special; featuring an army of scantily clad female extras, the program scored the highest all-time rating for a pay-per-view special.

One of Stern's favorite guests, busty Guess jeans model **Anna Nicole Smith**, was the hot babe of the moment, thanks to being crowned *Playboy*'s "Playmate of the Year" and topping the charts with a best-selling video. Though she would star in the following year's *Naked Gun 33⅓: The Final Insult*, Smith's acting career never really got off the ground, although she did make headlines a few years later by marrying ninety-year-old billionaire oil tycoon J Howard Marshall.

The Naked And The Dead

In Hollywood, it was a year of extremes. Steven Spielberg's dinosaur

thriller **Jurassic Park** grossed a record three hundred and fifty million dollars at the box office, while Arnold Schwarzenegger's *Last Action Hero* was an unexpected flop. Films like *Philadelphia*, *Schindler's List*, and *The Piano* were box-office successes despite their serious themes, while *Indecent Proposal* (in which Robert Redford offered Woody Harrelson a million dollars to sleep with Demi

Moore) succeeded in spite of its ludicrous premise. Tim Burton's *The Nightmare Before Christmas* received rave reviews for its special effects, yet they were no match for the stunning visuals of **The Crow**. Already dark in theme and design, the film gained additional weight (and drawing power) from the death of star Brandon Lee (son of Bruce), who was accidentally shot by a prop gun near

'93 Hot playmate Anna Nicole Smith.

'93 Spielberg's *Jurassic Park* was a monster hit at the box office.

the end of the production. **Tom Hanks** starred in the romantic comedy *Sleepless in Seattle*, and won an Oscar for his performance as a dying AIDS patient in *Philadelphia*. Richard Linklater didn't win any Oscars for *Dazed and Confused*, his semi-nostalgic look at high school life in the mid-seventies, but the film did introduce future stars Parker Posey, Ben Affleck and Matthew McConaughey to the movie-going public.

'93 Liam Neeson and Ben Kingsley in *Schindler's List*.

Music News

In April, the American music industry finally did away with the 6- by 12-inch cardboard longbox it had been using for CD packaging. It was not missed. Greatly mourned, however, was the passing of **Frank Zappa**. The idiosyncratic composer died of prostate cancer on December 4th; it is possible he hastened off this mortal coil to escape the new country craze that saw Garth Brooks sell five million copies of *In Pieces* and Brooks and Dunn sell three million of *Hard Workin' Man*.

Gangsta Rap did exceptionally well in 1993, thanks to albums like Dr Dre's *The Chronic*, Cypress Hill's *Black Sunday*, Snoop Doggy Dogg's *Doggy Style*, and Ice Cube's *Lethal Injection*. Janet Jackson dipped back into the sound of old-school soul for her new *Janet* CD, and Rupaul (born Rupaul Andre Charles) became the highest-charting transvestite in history with the club smash, "Supermodel (You Better Work)." Grunge rock, still a year or two away at this point from complete self-parody, carved out out a pretty decent market share of its own. Produced by Steve Albini for maximum sonic discomfort, Nirvana's ***In Utero*** debuted at the top of the charts in October, while Pearl Jam's *Vs* did the same in November, despite the band's marked refusal to do videos. Regular video play helped The Stone Temple Pilots' *Core* sell three million copies, ditto for The Smashing Pumpkins' three-million-selling *Siamese Dream*.

Alternative Airwaves

Indeed, alternative rock was quickly becoming as mainstream as the music it purported to be an alternative to. AAA radio ("Adult Album Alternative") was born in late 1993 on San Francisco's KFOG-FM and Seattle's KMTT-FM. The format, which mixed mildly alternative rock tracks with inoffensive classic rock, was an immediate success among slightly older, slightly less hip individuals. Meanwhile, designer Marc Jacobs integrated "the grunge look" into his Perry Ellis collection, and Anna Sui and Isaac Mizrahi co-opted the "baby doll" fashions popularized by Hole singer Courtney Love and Babes in Toyland leader Kat Bjelland.

Bullseye!

In sports, Cincinnati Reds owner Marge Schott received a year's suspension from baseball for making racist and anti-Semitic remarks about her players. In basketball, the Chicago Bulls won the NBA championship for the third straight year, beating the the Phoenix Suns four games to two. Michael Jordan, who'd led the league in scoring for seven out of his nine seasons, announced his retirement shortly afterwards, but would return to lead the Bulls to the championship in 1996 and 1997.

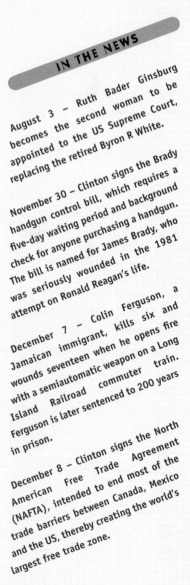

IN THE NEWS

August 3 – Ruth Bader Ginsburg becomes the second woman to be appointed to the US Supreme Court, replacing the retired Byron R White.

November 30 – Clinton signs the Brady handgun control bill, which requires a five-day waiting period and background check for anyone purchasing a handgun. The bill is named for James Brady, who was seriously wounded in the 1981 attempt on Ronald Reagan's life.

December 7 – Colin Ferguson, a Jamaican immigrant, kills six and wounds seventeen when he opens fire with a semiautomatic weapon on a Long Island Railroad commuter train. Ferguson is later sentenced to 200 years in prison.

December 8 – Clinton signs the North American Free Trade Agreement (NAFTA), intended to end most of the trade barriers between Canada, Mexico and the US, thereby creating the world's largest free trade zone.

'94

The American tabloid press, long vilified by adherents of "real" journalism, received a serious credibility boost in 1994, thanks to the scandals surrounding Michael Jackson and OJ Simpson. In both cases, the *National Enquirer*, the *Star*, and the *Globe* all regularly broke stories well ahead of the other, more conventional media outlets.

There was plenty of grist for the tabloid mills, of course; in January, Jackson agreed to settle out of court with the twelve-year-old boy who'd brought a sexual abuse case against him. Though Jackson continued to proclaim his innocence, the settlement was believed to be worth over fifteen million dollars. In August, the boy's stepfather filed a lawsuit against Jackson, alleging that the singer had used his power and influence to try to ruin the boy's family; the suit was thrown out in September, when the boy refused to testify against Jackson in court. Jackson's life took an even more bizarre turn in March, when he married **Lisa Marie Presley**, daughter of Elvis, in a civil ceremony in the Dominican Republic. Rumors about the munion abounded (Was Michael after Lisa Marie's inheritance? Was she trying to convert him to Scientology? Would he help her land a recording

'94 LAPD picture of OJ Simpson, taken following his arrest on suspicion of murdering his ex-wife and her male companion.

contract?), but mostly it seemed like a calculated ploy to help shore up Michael's crumbling reputation.

Did He Do It?

OJ Simpson's reputation was quite another matter. With his smooth manner and good looks, the former football star was extremely popular as an actor, pitchman, and sports commentator; when his ex-wife Nicole and her male acquaintance Ron Goldman were brutally murdered on the night of June 12, it seemed unthinkable that OJ could have been involved. But as evidenced mounted against him, the LA police department decided on June 17 that it had no choice but to make an arrest. By then, unfortunately, OJ had disappeared; when the police finally tracked him down, he was holding a gun to his own head in the back of a white Ford Bronco, driven by former teammate Al "AC" Cowlings. As television viewers across the country looked on, Cowlings led police on a bizarre slow-speed car chase back to Simpson's abode, where Simpson was arrested. Police found his

Vice On Ice

In another strange-but-true incident, figure skater Tonya Harding and three others (including Harding's husband) pleaded guilty of conspiracy to assault Nancy Kerrigan, Harding's rival in the Lillehammer Olympic games. Kerrigan had been attacked by a "mystery assailant" on January 6, five weeks before the games were to begin; though her leg had been injured in the attack, she still skated away with the silver medal. Harding came in eighth, but achieved immortality of a different sort when the X-rated home video of her wedding night became an oft-bootlegged VCR favorite.

Americans Approve Rough Justice

In May, American teenager Michael Fay found his fifteen minutes of fame after being arrested in Singapore for spray-painting parked cars. Though the Clinton administration tried to intervene, Fay received the country's standard punishment for the crime— four strokes on the backside with a wet rattan cane. Rather than protest the caning, most Americans seemed to be in favor of it; with a recent study showing a 154-percent increase since the mid-eighties in violent crimes committed by young men between ages fifteen and nineteen, many suggested that the US would benefit from meting out similar punishments to youthful offenders.

passport and ten thousand dollars in cash in the vehicle.

TV News

Many television viewers only had eyes for the neverending jury selection process of the OJ trial, which was televised live from the courtroom by day and subjected to continual analysis on evening news programs. Despite this, many new shows were able to thrive. Hospital dramas *ER* (*above*), which turned George Clooney into a popular heartthrob, and *Chicago Hope* found a devoted audience, as did the syndicated sci-fi show *Babylon 5* and the gritty crime series *New York Undercover*. **Friends**, which revolved around six young and attractive New Yorkers, was the year's most popular sitcom; as the US Bureau of Labor estimated that twenty percent of American graduates now held jobs that didn't require a college degree, the show's over-educated, under-achieving characters struck a chord with twentysomething viewers. The "**Rachel**," named for Jennifer Aniston's character on the show, became the most popular women's hairstyle of the mid-decade. Less popular, though highly acclaimed, were *South Central* (a comedy-drama about a single-parent black family living in Los Angeles), *My So-Called Life* (starring Claire Danes as a smart-but-confused teen), and *Party of Five*, a dramatic series about five children (including Matthew Fox and Neve Campbell) trying to carry on in the

'94 Close *Friends*.

wake of their parents' deaths. Of the three, only *Party of Five* managed to last more than a season on the air. *Beverly Hills 90210* remained as popular as ever, but it went into the fall season without **Shannon Doherty**; the volatile actress, whose tantrums and drinking binges were the stuff of legend, left the show for greener pastures in the spring.

Music News

Shannon Doherty and Lisa "Left Eye" Lopes probably would have made one hell of a team; Lopes, of the popular rap trio TLC, made headlines in June by burning down the mansion of her boyfriend, Atlanta Falcons wide receiver Andre Rison, in a drunken rage. Rison was forgiving, as were courts, which only sentenced Lopes to five years' probation.

Without question, the saddest news of the year was that of **Kurt Cobain**'s suicide. Always uncomfortable with his degree of celebrity (to say nothing of the media's attempts to brand him as a "spokesman for his generation"), the Nirvana leader had been plagued throughout his short career by depression and a heroin problem, and the mounting pressures of the music business simply became too great for him. After disappearing from an LA rehab clinic where he was supposed to be detoxing, Cobain went back to his home in Seattle and blew his head off with a shotgun. **Hole**, featuring Courtney Love, Cobain's widow, released the ironically titled *Live Through This* shortly thereafter.

Red-Hot Lineups At Festivals

With the disparate likes of A Tribe Called Quest, The Beastie Boys, The Smashing Pumpkins, The Breeders, Nick Cave, George Clinton and The P-Funk Allstars, Green Day, The Verve, and The Boredoms on hand (as well as Stereolab, Guided By Voices, The Pharcyde, and Luscious Jackson playing the second stage), Lollapalooza featured its strongest lineup to date. Green Day, whose multi-platinum *Dookie* CD showed that there was indeed room for punk rock in the mainstream, also put on an impressive, mud-caked performance at **Woodstock '94**, the twenty-fifth anniversary concert event that featured sets by Nine Inch Nails, Soundgarden, Porno for Pyros, and the Red Hot Chili Peppers, as well as old-timers like Santana and Crosby, Stills and Nash. This time around, the love beads and moccasins were replaced by **Doc Martins** (*below*) and navel, nipple, nose, and eyelid piercings, ecstasy was substituted for LSD, and the organizers weren't letting anyone in for free; tickets were available at a hundred and thirty-five dollars apiece for a block of four, or two hundred dollars apiece for individual admission.

Easier Listening

Henry Mancini, composer of the themes for *Peter Gunn*, *The Pink Panther*, *Charade,* and countless other film and TV projects, died June 14 at the age of seventy. Sadly, he passed away just as his music was starting to be appreciated by a new generation of listeners. Lounge and easy-listening sounds of the fifties and sixties were back in style, thanks to the release of *I, Swinger*, the debut record by cocktail revivalists Combustible Edison, and **Space Age Bachelor Pad Music**, Bar/None Records' new compilation of hard-to-find Esquivel tracks. Many listeners found these whimsical records to be a refreshing antidote to the dull grind of grunge; soon, venerable labels like RCA and Capitol were raiding their own vaults for long-lost classics of the Rat Pack era.

Movie News

You couldn't go anywhere in 1994 without hearing the songs from Disney's new animated musical, *The Lion King*, just as it was simply impossible to get away from people riffing on the "Life is like a box of chocolates" line from *Forrest Gump*. Thankfully, there was also Quentin Tarantino's **Pulp Fiction**, which featured dialogue so amusing ("You know what they call a Quarter Pounder in Amsterdam? A Royale with Cheese!") and a soundtrack so cool (featuring such 1960s surf classics as Dick Dale's "Misirlou" and The Centurions' "Bullwinkle, Pt 2") that you didn't mind hearing them replayed. John Travolta, mired for years in *Look Who's Talking* purgatory, proved that he could still do great work, but

it was Samuel L Jackson—as the Bible-quoting hitman—who really stole the show. Oliver Stone also added to the year's violence quotient with the bloody *Natural Born Killers*.

Jim Carrey, who came on like a mutant version of Jerry Lewis, scored big box-office hits with *Ace Ventura, Pet Detective, Dumb and Dumber*, and *The Mask*. Tim Allen also made the transition from small screen to large with the popular holiday entry, *The Santa Clause*, but the year's funniest film was probably Kevin Smith's **Clerks**, a comedy about a couple of foul-mouthed guys working at a convenience store and video shop. Shot in black-and-white on a budget of twenty-seven thousand dollars, *Clerks* proved (once again) that you didn't need special effects or big-name stars to get a hit. Of course, it didn't hurt, either; *True Lies* (Arnold Schwarzenegger's latest) and *Speed* (with Keanu Reeves and Sandra Bullock) both lured in millions with a combination of big-budget explosions

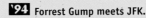

and high-profile stars. **_Interview with the Vampire: The Vampire Chronicles_** may not have had any explosions, but it did have Brad Pitt and Tom Cruise—though Anne Rice fans were appalled at the very thought of having Cruise portray their beloved Lestat. Even more appalling was the fact that **_Hoop Dreams_**, an excellent film charting four years in the lives of two young inner-city basketball players and

their families, was completely passed over for a "Best Documentary" Oscar nomination. The ensuing outcry caused the Academy to re-examine

its judging procedures, but the changes came too late to help *Hoop Dreams*.

Not Excused

In a class-action lawsuit against silicone breast implant manufacturers, sixty companies were ordered to pay a total of 4.25 billion dollars to 90,500 women who claimed to have been injured by their implants. Luckily, Sara Lee's uplifting Wonderbra debuted in 1994, thus diminishing the need for implants, at least for women outside of the sex industry. In related news, **supermodels** Elle McPherson, Naomi Campbell and Claudia Schiffer opened the Fashion Café in New York City. Though she'd recently made fifty thousand dollars modeling a pair of black jeans for No Excuses

jeans ad, Paula Jones—the former Arkansas government worker currently suing President Clinton for sexual harassment—was not invited to the opening.

IN THE NEWS

November 8 – In congressional elections, the Republican party wins control of the Senate and the House of Representatives for the first time in 40 years. The election results are thought to be indicative of voter dissatisfaction with the Clinton Administration. In California, 59 percent of the voters cast their ballots in favor of Proposition 187, which makes illegal immigrants residing in the state ineligible for medical care and public education.

TOP ALBUMS

The Lion King
soundtrack

BOYZ II MEN
II

PINK FLOYD
The Division Bell

STONE TEMPLE PILOTS
Purple

KENNY G
Miracles: The Holiday Album

On January 25, opening statements began in the case of *The People of the State of California v Orenthal James Simpson*, better known as "the trial of the century." With television crews allowed into the courtroom by LA Superior Court Judge Lance Ito, the trial quickly became a circus; everyone, from Simpson lawyer Johnnie Cochran to Judge Ito himself, seemed to be playing to the cameras.

Prosecutors Marcia Clark and Christopher Darden painted a picture of Simpson as a control freak who had previously stalked and beaten Nicole, while Simpson's "dream team" of Cochran, Robert Shapiro, and F Lee Bailey argued that their client was the innocent victim of either the sheer incompetence of the LA police department, or a massive conspiracy masterminded by racist LAPD officer Mark Fuhrman.

Polls showed that American opinions about the case were split along racial lines, with the majority of blacks believing OJ to be innocent, and most whites judging him guilty; in Los Angeles, where the police department and the criminal justice system had long given minorities the shaft, this disparity was even more pronounced. Despite compelling evidence pointing to Simpson's guilt, few were truly surprised when, on October 3, he was **acquitted** by the jury of nine blacks, two whites, and one latino after only four hours of deliberation.

During the trial and its aftermath, fame smiled briefly on many of those

'95 Trial by television—OJ Simpson in court.

involved with the case. Over thirty books about the trial were published in 1995, including the autobiography of Brian "**Kato**" Kaelin, OJ's hunky houseguest. Kato parlayed his newfound celebrity into unsuccessful gigs as a stand-up comic and talk-radio host, while Al "AC" Cowlings began appearing at autograph conventions in the company of the white Bronco. Paula Barbieri, who

had broken off a relationship with OJ on the night of the murders, took the place of soft-porn star Shannon Tweed in the straight-to-video *Night Eyes* series. Prism Pictures, who produced the series, further played up the OJ connection by putting a figure with a black ski mask and long knife (both of which Simpson was alleged to have used in the murders) on the video box.

That's THEIRstory...

With Michael Jackson's two-CD set of old and new material, the modestly titled *HIStory: Past, Present And Future—Book 1*, due for a July release, Jackson and wife Lisa Marie appeared on *ABC's Primetime Live* in June to do some advance promotion. Viewers hoping to see Jackson answer some pointed questions about the recent sexual molestation allegations were sorely disappointed, as an obviously awestruck Diane Sawyer only lobbed the softest possible queries in Michael's direction. Though the couple did their best to act affectionately towards each other, it was hardly a convincing performance; Michael tried to flash a studly grin when Lisa Marie offered an unprompted, "**Do we have sex?** Yes, yes, yes!", but no one seemed especially surprised when the pair divorced seven months later.

Music News

What was especially surprising in 1995 was the runaway success of Hootie and The Blowfish's *Cracked Rear View*,

which was still selling like hot cakes a year after its initial release. Though the music itself was basically just drab bar-band rock, something about the singles "Hold My Hand," "Let Her Cry," and "Only Wanna Be With You" struck a chord with the American public, who scarfed up over fourteen million copies of the album. Also striking an unexpected nerve was Canadian singer-songwriter **Alanis Morissette**, who moved over eleven million copies of her American debut, *Jagged Little Pill*. Although there was nothing new about Morissette's off-pitch singing style or her liberal use of four-letter expletives (Chicago singer-songwriter Liz Phair had recently racked up critical raves for the same shtick), her angry-young-woman attitude immediately won her a dedicated legion of followers.

After years without an actual home, the **Rock and Roll Hall of Fame** finally opened in Cleveland, housed in a new, ninety-two-million-dollar structure designed by award-winning architect IM Pei. The Hall's opening ceremonies featured concert performances by Chuck Berry, Little Richard, The Kinks, Bruce Springsteen, and **Sheryl Crow**, who was currently high in the charts with *Tuesday Night Music Club*. This year's Lollapalooza festival featured Hole, Sonic Youth, Pavement, Beck, Jesus Lizard, the Mighty Mighty Bosstones, Sinead O' Connor (who had to split early due to pregnancy), and Cypress Hill, although it was obvious that most of the attendees were just there to display their tattoos and piercings or surf the mosh pit, regardless of who happened to be onstage at the time.

'95 Alanis Morissette.

More Musicians Leave The Stage

Latina singer Selena (full name: Selena Quintanilla) was on the verge of crossover success when she was shot to death, on March 31, by the founder of her fan club. Months later, her commercial breakthrough came in the form of *Dreaming Of You*, her first English-language recording. **Tupac Shakur**, having recently survived a murder attempt, received a jail sentence in February in connection with a 1993 sexual assault. Released while the rapper was in prison (he was out on parole by the year's end), the aptly titled *Me Against The World* became Tupac's best-selling record to date. Former NWA rapper **Eazy-E** (Eric Wright) died on March 26th of AIDS, now the leading killer of Americans aged twenty-four to forty-four; his last album, *Str8 Off Tha Streetz Of Muthaphukkin Compton*, would top the charts the following year, leaving such sentimental musings as "Hit The Hooker" and "Nutz On Ya Chin" to remember him by. Other passings in the music world included the overdose death of Shannon Hoon, lead singer of Blind Melon, and Dean Martin, who went to the great lounge in the sky at the age of seventy-eight. **Jerry Garcia**, who had been plagued by drug problems for the last two decades, died in a rehab clinic at the age of fifty-three, effectively bringing the long, strange trip of the Grateful Dead to an end.

Movie News

In 1995, Hollywood offered a little something for everyone. At any given multiplex, you could find moving dramas (*Leaving Las Vegas*, *Dead Man Walking*, *Apollo 13*) nestled cheek-by-jowl with witty comedies (*Get Shorty*, *To Die For*), nostalgic rehashes (*The Little Rascals*, *The Brady Bunch Movie*), dumb farces with *Saturday Night Live* alums, trashy Tarantino knock-offs (*Things to Do In Denver When You're Dead*; *From Dusk Till Dawn*, which actually featured Tarantino in a supporting role), and just plain trash (*Showgirls*).

Kevin Costner's post-apocalyptic *Waterworld* was a $235-million flop, while ***Batman Forever*** (starring Val Kilmer as the caped crusader, and Jim Carrey as The Riddler) raked in $184 million at the box office, making it the year's biggest film. Kids of all ages went to see *Toy Story*, *Pocahontas*, and *Babe*, but no one under the age of eighteen could get in to see *Kids*, Larry Clark's controversial look at a bunch of amoral high schoolers; Alicia Silverstone's ***Clueless*** character, on the other hand, preferred to get her kicks from shopping instead of unsafe sex and illicit drug use.

Demi Moore took off her clothes again in *The Scarlet Letter*; Whitney Houston, currently married to troubled singer Bobby Brown, sounded all too convincing complaining about the lack of decent men in her life in *Waiting to Exhale*; and Sharon Stone's ludicrously drawn-out death scene almost sank Martin Scorsese's otherwise excellent *Casino*.

Surfing for Thrills

With Americans logging onto the Internet in record numbers, it wasn't at all surprising to see a handful of "**techno-thrillers**" pop up in theaters in 1995. Unfortunately for Hollywood, most folks preferred to stay home and surf the Net than go see stinkers like *Hackers*, *Johnny Mnemonic* (with Keanu Reeves), and *The Net* (starring Sandra Bullock).

Bad Connections

Attempting a hard-hitting exposé about pornography on the Internet, *Time* magazine's panic-stricken "**Cyber Porn**" cover story only succeeded in increasing the amount of one-handed net-surfing going on

'95 *Toy Story* characters.

across the country. When Nebraska Senator Jim Exon proposed the so-called Communications Decency Act as a way to ban porn from the net, online companies responded by offering Adult Check and other filtering products to keep minors from viewing X-rated websites. Sales were slow for videogames in 1995, perhaps because of the increased interest (prurient or otherwise) in the Internet. The most popular game system by far was Sony's new **PlayStation**, which offered a hefty amount of quality titles, and retailed for around $299.

TV News

TV Talk Shows—Have They Gone Too Far? That was the topic on the table in March, when the "Secret Admirers" segment of the **Jenny Jones** show ended in tragedy. After learning on the show that his secret admirer was a man, enraged guest Jonathan Schmitz allegedly drove to the house of his secret admirer and killed him. It sounded like a future case for **Murder One**, Steven Bocho's acclaimed new crime series, which took the novel approach of following the

progression of a single murder case over the entire season. Other popular shows included *The Drew Carey Show*, *The Single Guy*, and *Caroline In the City* (sitcoms which took their cues from *Seinfeld* and *Friends*), *Star Trek: Voyager* (the first regular series aired on the new UPN network), and *Cybill*, Cybill Shepherd's new sitcom. The surprise hits of the year were *Hercules—The Legendary Journeys* and *Xena: Warrior Princess*, both of which mixed **swords-'n'-sorcery**

scenarios with knowing humor and attractive leads; in no time, *Hercules'* Kevin Sorbo and *Xena's* Lucy Lawless were two of America's more popular pin-ups.

Café Society

As Starbucks continued to spread the gospel of gourmet coffee, coffee bars were now the most popular places for young professionals to hang out. Cybercafés, where you could order a cup of joe while surfing the Net and arguing the merits of Microsoft's new Windows 95, were also increasing in number. As a result of the recent cigar boom—sales of premium cigars were up twenty-nine percent over the past three years—cigar bars started to pop up in urban areas. Usually, though, cigar aficionados had to go to special "cigar nights" at restaurants or bars in order to socialize and smoke with other stogie fanciers. The fad wasn't limited to men, either; studies showed that women now made up five percent of the cigar-chomping populace.

'95 Middle-aged fun in *Cybill*.

IN THE NEWS

December 31 – The federal government shuts down in a dispute between President Clinton and the Republican-controlled Congress over balancing the budget. Over 260,000 federal employees are furloughed for two weeks, and many public services are halted. House speaker Newt Gingrich and his fellow Republicans engineered the shutdown in an attempt to embarrass Clinton, but the plan backfires when the public blames Congress for the impasse.

'95 Star Trek's *Voyager*.

'95 Pin-up princess Lucy Lawless

'96

1996 saw Bill Clinton become the first Democratic president since Franklin Roosevelt to be elected to two full terms. For the most part, his victory was something of a foregone conclusion; the economy remained in good shape, and his opponent, long-serving Republican senator Bob Dole, couldn't seem to come up with a platform more compelling than that it was *his* turn to be president.

TOP TELEVISION SHOWS

ER
Seinfeld
Friends
Suddenly Susan
Home Improvement

ACADEMY AWARDS

BEST PICTURE
The English Patient
directed by Anthony Minghella

BEST ACTOR
Geoffrey Rush
Shine

BEST ACTRESS
Frances McDormand
Fargo

Dole's major gaffes on the campaign trail—which included lambasting death-metal bands who hadn't existed for at least a decade, falling off a podium in Chico, California, and claiming on national television that tobacco was not, in fact, addictive—were compounded by his austere mein and the fact that he was over two decades older than Clinton.

After some hemming and hawing, H Ross Perot ran again as a third-party candidate, but his showing was less impressive this time around; although Perot did manage to wangle 7.8 million votes (three hundred thousand more than Clinton's margin of victory over Dole), it was less than half the total he received in 1992.

Primary Colors, a scabrous, anonymously written "novel" about Clinton's presidential campaign, was one of the year's best-selling books. After months of speculation, the author's identity was revealed to be that of Joe Klein, a conservative *Newsweek* columnist who'd previously denied authorship.

'96 "Don't cry for me, Argentina..." Madonna as Evita.

Gore-geous!

Clinton's secret re-election weapon, of course, was that he had a vice-president who could do the macarena at any time or place. The dance—sort of an advanced hokey-pokey—was currently sweeping the country, erupting seemingly whenever a large group of people were gathered, and VP Al Gore's repeated willingness to throw some macarena shapes couldn't help but reflect positively on the Clinton/Gore campaign.

Music News

Ska and swing were two other musical crazes beginning to infiltrate the mass consciousness. While the former remained primarily a club phenomenon and had yet to penetrate the charts, LA's ska-poppers **No Doubt** managed to sell several million copies of their *Tragic Kingdom* CD; though the band's sound was hardly authentic bluebeat (and though "Don't Speak," their smash power ballad, sounded like a slowed-down version of Irene Cara's "Fame"),

their success inspired a frenzied major label trawl for other ska acts. Gwen Stefani, No Doubt's Madonna-esque frontperson, was romantically linked with Gavin Rossdale of Bush, a British grunge band whose *Sixteen Stone* album proved far more popular in the states than in their homeland. **Snoop Doggy Dogg** (real name: Calvin Broadus) had two reasons to celebrate in 1996; not only was he back in the charts with *The Doggfather*, his second album, but he was also finally acquitted of murder charges stemming from a 1993 shooting. Tupac Shakur wasn't so lucky; his two records, *All Eyez On Me* and *Don Killuminati: The 7 Day Theory* (released under the name Makaveli) charted well, but he died from wounds received in a September 13 shooting in Las Vegas. To date, the crime hasn't been solved. The year's other popular rap records included Bone Thugs-N-Harmony's *E1999 Eternal* and Lil' Kim's *Hard Core*. **Beck** (full name: Beck Hansen), who had first attracted

'96 Mega-bucks sci-fi movie *Independence Day.*

attention with 1994's "Loser," proved that his previous hit was no fluke; *Odelay*, an innovative mixture of breakbeats, samples, and general weirdness, was voted "Album of the Year" in countless critics' polls.

Radio Rivals

The US government's Telecommunications Act of 1996 lifted limits on the number of radio stations big businesses could purchase; as a result, commercial radio became increasingly generic. Alanis Morissette continued to dominate the "commercial alternative" stations, but she had some serious competition in the form of **Fiona Apple** and **Jewel**. The former's *Tidal* was an angry, brooding record featuring songs like "Shadowboxer" and "Criminal," while the latter's *Pieces Of Me* was filled with sweet pop-folk numbers like "You Were Meant For Me." Most likely, neither were in attendance when the original members of **Kiss** slapped on the old

makeup and reunited to pillage the nation's enormo-domes. The group was in fine, filthy form, and the reunion tour grossed over forty-four million dollars.

Movie News

Widely touted as "the year of the independent film," 1996 did indeed have more than its fair share of low-budget successes. Jon Favreau's *Swingers* took an amusing look at young hipsters in LA, and made a star out of Vince Vaughn; Billy Bob Thornton's *Sling Blade* won an Oscar for "Best Screenplay Adaptation," Todd Solondz's *Welcome to the Dollhouse* won praise for its unflinching portrayal of the horrors of adolescence, and Joel and Ethan Coen had the biggest hit of their careers with **Fargo**, a droll crime story starring Frances McDormand as a pregnant Minnesota police chief. But when all was said and done, it was still the big-budget flicks that brought home the bacon. *Independence Day* (essentially a nineties update of the cheesy flying-saucer films of the fifties) and *Twister*, two of the year's highest-grossing films, were short on substance but boasted eye-popping special effects. *Space Jam*, in which Michael Jordan helped Bugs Bunny and Porky Pig defeat an alien basketball team, fared extremely well at the box office, as did *Evita*, starring Madonna. Woody Harrelson and Courtney Love gave impressive performances as the *Hustler* publisher and his junkie wife in Milos Forman's *The People Versus Larry Flynt*. Eddie Murphy regained some commercial momentum with his remake of *The Nutty Professor*, Honk Kong action star Jackie Chan finally had his first American hit with *Rumble in the Bronx*, and Wes Craven had his biggest hit since *Nightmare on Elm Street* with *Scream*, featuring Neve Campbell as a teenager menaced by a killer obsessed with horror films. *Jerry Maguire* starred Tom Cruise as a struggling sports agent, but it was fellow actor Cuba Gooding's Oscar-winning supporting performance that had all of America shouting, "**Show me the money!**"

March 13 – The Liggett Group, the smallest of the nation's five major tobacco companies, shocks the tobacco industry by settling a class action lawsuit over the detrimental health effects of smoking.

April 3 – US Secretary of Commerce Ronald H Brown perishes, along with 34 others, when his military plane crashes into a mountain in Dubrovnik, Croatia. The same day, Theodore J Kaczynski, a 53-year-old loner, is arrested and charged with being the so-called Unabomber.

June 13 – After an 81-day standoff, sixteen members of the Freemen, a right-wing extremist group, surrender to federal officials in Montana. Fourteen members are charged with threatening federal officers and defrauding banks and businesses of more than $1.8 million.

June 25 – A truck bomb kills nineteen American soldiers and wounds 300 people in Dhahran, Saudi Arabia. No suspects are apprehended.

Un-bare-able

Some of the year's major losers included *Barb Wire*, Pamela Anderson Lee's disastrous screen debut; *Kazaam*, starring basketball star Shaquille O'Neal as a friendly genie "owned" by an obnoxious little white boy; *Grace of My Heart*, Alison Anders' botched look at pop music in the Brill Building era; and **Striptease**, Demi Moore's unbelievably awful comedy-drama about a young mother who has to strip to raise funds for an upcoming child-custody hearing. The latter triggered some unintentional political hilarity when Bob Dole, desperately digging for a relevant issue on the campaign trail, condemned Moore for baring all in the film. Bruce Willis, Moore's husband (and a prominent supporter of the Republican party), suggested that the candidate mind his own damn business, and an embarrassed Dole quickly apologized.

TV News

In February, responding to widespread viewer criticism about the violent content of prime-time TV programs, the four major networks announced an agreement to establish a rating system for television shows. By the end of the year, they proposed a plan to rate programs "TV-Y" (suitable for all children) to "TV-M" (mature audiences only), but many critics complained that the system was not specific enough.

Some of the year's most popular new shows included **Third Rock From the Sun**, starring John Lithgow and Jane Curtin as space aliens trying to blend into the American suburbs, and

Just Shoot Me, starring David Spade as Laura San Giacomo's blisteringly sarcastic secretary. The biggest small-screen surprise had to be *Suddenly Susan*, which proved, after years of awful film appearances, that Brooke Shields actually had something of a flair for comedy.

Centenarian Dies

George Burns, one of early TV's most popular comedians (and one of the first TV stars to "break the fourth wall" by speaking directly to the camera) died on March 9th after a long and distinguished career. He was a hundred.

Fat Chance

1996 brought good news for weight-conscious snackers, when the Food and Drug Administration approved the use of Olestra, a fat substitute, for snack foods such as potato chips; the fact that many people reported experiencing stomach cramps and "anal leakage" after ingesting Olestra products didn't seem to bother anyone at the FDA. McDonald's introduced the **Arch Deluxe**, a sandwich aimed at the adult demographic, but it flopped; adults, it seemed, preferred the less "sophisticated" pleasures of a Big Mac. The home fitness business continued to boom, perhaps spurred by studies showing that Americans were more obese than ever. Marketed in slightly variant versions by several different infomercials, the AbRoller was the year's most popular piece of home-exercise equipment.

'96 Tickle Me Elmo, the "must-have" toy of '96.

Centenary Edition Hits The Road

1996 witnessed the passing of the American auto industry's one-hundredth anniversary, which Plymouth celebrated in fine style by producing the limited-edition Prowler roadster. With its small cockpit and retro styling, the aluminum-skeletoned two-seater agreeably harkened back to the custom hot rods of the forties and fifties.

Playing With Danger

If Tyco's giggling Tickle Me Elmo doll was the year's hottest Christmas toy, Cabbage Patch Snacktime Kids were the most controversial. In nearly one hundred separate incidents, the dolls—which had a mechanism enabling it to "eat" plastic carrots and french fries—actually chewed the hair and fingers of children feeding it. Eidos Interactive's **Tomb Raider**, a 3-D adventure game starring buxom cyber-heroine Lara Croft (*Newsweek* called her "the perfect fantasy girl for the digital generation"), became one of the year's most popular computer games.

TOP ALBUMS

ALANIS MORISSETTE

Jagged Little Pill

MARIAH CAREY

Daydream

CELINE DION

Falling Into You

Waiting to Exhale

soundtrack

FUGEES

The Score

July 17 – A TWA Boeing 747 jet explodes over the Atlantic Ocean shortly after takeoff from New York's Kennedy International Airport, killing all 230 people aboard. Theories about the blast blame mechanical failure, terrorist action, or accidental downing by a missile from a nearby military base, but findings remain inconclusive.

July 27 – A bomb explodes in a park in Atlanta, Georgia, during Summer Olympics festivities, killing one and injuring 100. Security guard Richard Jewell is briefly held as a suspect, then released; he later files defamation suits against the FBI and various media outlets.

September 26 – Astronaut Shannon Lucid sets an American record for time in space after spending 188 days aboard Russia's MIR space station.

November 5 – Clinton is re-elected president.

December 5 – Clinton appoints Madeline Albright, US representative to the UN, to be his new Secretary of State. She becomes the first woman ever to hold the post.

December 18 – The Oakland CA school board passes a resolution to treat black English, or "ebonics," as a second language. Controversy predictably ensues.

December 26 – The body of six-year-old beauty pageant contestant JonBenet Ramsey is found dead in the basement of her Boulder, Colorado, home. Her death is originally thought to be the result of a bungled kidnapping, but when her wealthy parents John and Patsy refuse to cooperate with the investigation, speculation increases that they were somehow involved, and that local police have bungled crucial evidence in the case.

As 1997 began, people across the country began to make plans to celebrate an important milestone in American pop culture—the fiftieth anniversary of the crash of an alleged flying saucer in Roswell, New Mexico. Though few people were aware of the incident fifty years ago, word of it had since spread to such an extent that "Roswell" was now virtually synonymous (at least among UFO buffs) with "government cover-up."

In the spring, the US military attempted to quell the storm of conjecture by releasing a 231-page report on the matter; according to the report, the "flying saucer" that witnesses reported was actually a disc-shaped NASA test craft, and that the dead and mutilated "aliens" spotted at the scene were actually several parachute test dummies and an injured air force crewman. As the military had already changed its story several times regarding the incident, Ufologists scoffed at the explanation, noting that the military did not even use parachute test dummies back in 1947. The truth, as *X-Files* fans were fond of saying, was still out there.

Star Comes Out

1997 also marked the fiftieth anniversary of the birth of commercial television; and oddly enough, it was the liveliest TV year in recent memory. *Ellen*'s **Ellen DeGeneres** caused a stir with her decision to come out of the closet, but that was nothing compared to the decision to have her character come out as well. Thirty-six million viewers tuned in on April 30 to watch Ellen kiss guest star Laura Dern; fearing a boycott by conservative Christians, Wendy's, Chrysler, and JC Penney all pulled their ads. DeGeneres' very public relationship with actress Anne Heche was also a source of criticism from both straights and gays; the two were photographed hanging all over each other at a White House function, which many folks felt was in poor taste.

'97 The one where Ellen comes out...

Others called Heche's sincerity into question—she and Ellen had made their relationship public just days before Heche's new *Volcano* hit the multiplexes—and felt her admission that she'd "been straight before I met Ellen" only reinforced the image of homosexuals as predatory creatures.

Albert Crosses The Line

Not that heterosexuals were any less predatory, of course. In September, NBC sportscaster Marv Albert lost his job after pleading guilty to charges of sodomy and assault and battery, stemming from an incident that involved him savagely biting a female acquaintance in a hotel room. Albert had originally denied all charges, but when further revelations came to light

regarding Albert's alleged bisexuality and penchant for wearing garter belts and ladies lingerie, the toupeed announcer finally had no choice but to throw in the towel.

Dry Humor

New hits were few and far between in 1997. *Veronica's Closet*, featuring Kirstie Alley as a former fashion model, and *Dharma and Greg*, starring newcomer Jenna Elfman as a hippie who impulsively marries a yuppie, were the year's biggest new sitcoms; **Jenny**, a comedy variety show starring obnoxious former *Playboy* playmate/*MTV Singled Out* hostess Jenny McCarthy, was one of the year's biggest flops, despite reviews hyping McCarthy as "the next Lucille Ball."

Public opinion was sharply divided on **Ally McBeal**, a comedy-drama starring Calista Flockhart (*right*) as a

yuppie lawyer with a hyperactive imagination; the show inspired a fanatic following, but many of the unconverted thought the title character was pathetic and in desperate need of a life. Not so with **Buffy the Vampire Slayer**, played by Sarah Michelle Gellar; the poor girl was so occupied with staving off the undead, she barely had time to worry about her social life.

Over-Exposed

In an attempt to boost its TV ratings, which had sagged considerably over the past few years, contestants in the seventy-seventh Annual Miss America Pageant were allowed to wear two-piece swimsuits, and sport navel rings and tattoos. You could see most of the above—and a whole lot

more—in the Pamela Anderson and Tommy Lee video currently being sold on the Internet. Allegedly stolen from a locked safe in their home, the video depicted the happy couple swimming nude, having sex, rolling joints, and uttering endless inanities.

Blue Brew

It did not, however, show either of them drinking Motley Brue, a beverage manufactured by the Skeleteens soda company in honor of the reunited Motley Crue's new *Generation Swine* CD. In addition to a tangy ginseng-and-jalapeno flavor, the soda boasted the added attraction of turning your feces blue.

Music News

According to the music industry, 1997 was supposed to be the year that electronica became "the next big thing." **Electronic music** was enthusiastically supported by the country's music press, and MTV (which these days rarely played videos for more than an hour at a time) actually devoted a weekly program to ambient

TOP SINGLES

ELTON JOHN
"Candle In The Wind 1997"

JEWEL
"You Were Meant For Me"

PUFF DADDY AND FAITH EVANS
"I'll Be Missing You"

TONI BRAXTON
"Unbreak My Heart"

PUFF DADDY
"Can't Nobody Hold Me Down"

and electronica videos, but—with the exception of England's Prodigy—electronica failed to succeed outside of the rave/dance-club circuit. Part of the problem was radio, which was offering less and less support to music outside the parameters of "commercial alternative." The airwaves were jammed with one-hit wonders like OMC ("How Bizarre"), Sugar Ray ("Fly"), Smash Mouth ("Walking On The Sun"), Meredith Brooks ("Bitch"), Squirrel Nut Zippers ("Hell"), and teeny "MMMBop"-ers Hanson. Rap radio was dominated by Sean "**Puff Daddy**" Coombs (*above*), crowned "The New King of Hip-Hop" by *Rolling Stone* after the March 9 death by shooting of his friend and colleague Christopher Wallace, aka Notorious BIG.

Religious Unrest

Thanks to the success of *Antichrist Superstar*, Marilyn Manson (real name: Brian Warner) could lay uncontested claim to the title of "the Alice Cooper of the nineties." And, as with Alice before him, the rumors about the goings-on at his shows were far more bizarre than anything he actually got up to. According to the right-wing Christians who picketed his shows, Marilyn regularly slaughtered animals onstage, passed out drugs to the audience, and engaged in public sex with nine-year-old boys.

The religious right were no more tolerant of their own kind—after **Pat Boone** appeared at the American Music Awards dressed in leather and

wearing studded wristbands and fake tattoos (a publicity stunt to promote his new album of heavy metal covers), the Trinity Broadcast Network promptly Boone's *Gospel America* TV show.

Girls Make It On Their Own

Lilith Fair, a traveling festival made up entirely of female acts, was the surprise hit of the summer. Organized by Canadian singer-songwriter Sarah McLachlan, the tour featured sets by Jewel, Paula Cole, Tracy Chapman, Suzanne Vega, the Indigo Girls, and others, and proved to the previously skeptical music industry that an all-girl bill could be successful.

Titanic Sinks Also-Rans

Five months late and way over budget, James Cameron's *Titanic* confounded the cynical expectations of industry odds makers by becoming the top-grossing film of all time. Not even *The Lost World* (Steven Spielberg's follow-up to *Jurassic Park*) or *The Men in Black* (an enormously popular sci-fi comedy starring Will Smith) were any match for the commercial onslaught of Cameron's film, nor for the outpouring of love and worship heaped by fans upon *Titanic* star **Leonardo DiCaprio**.

1997 was, in many ways, a year of comebacks. Jim Carrey bounced back from the relative failure of 1996's *The Cable Guy* with *Liar, Liar*, and 1970s blaxploitation goddess Pam Grier scored her most high-profile role in years as the star of Quentin Tarantino's *Jackie Brown*. Sylvester Stallone and Kim Basinger racked up raves for their respective performances in *Cop Land* and *LA Confidential*, with

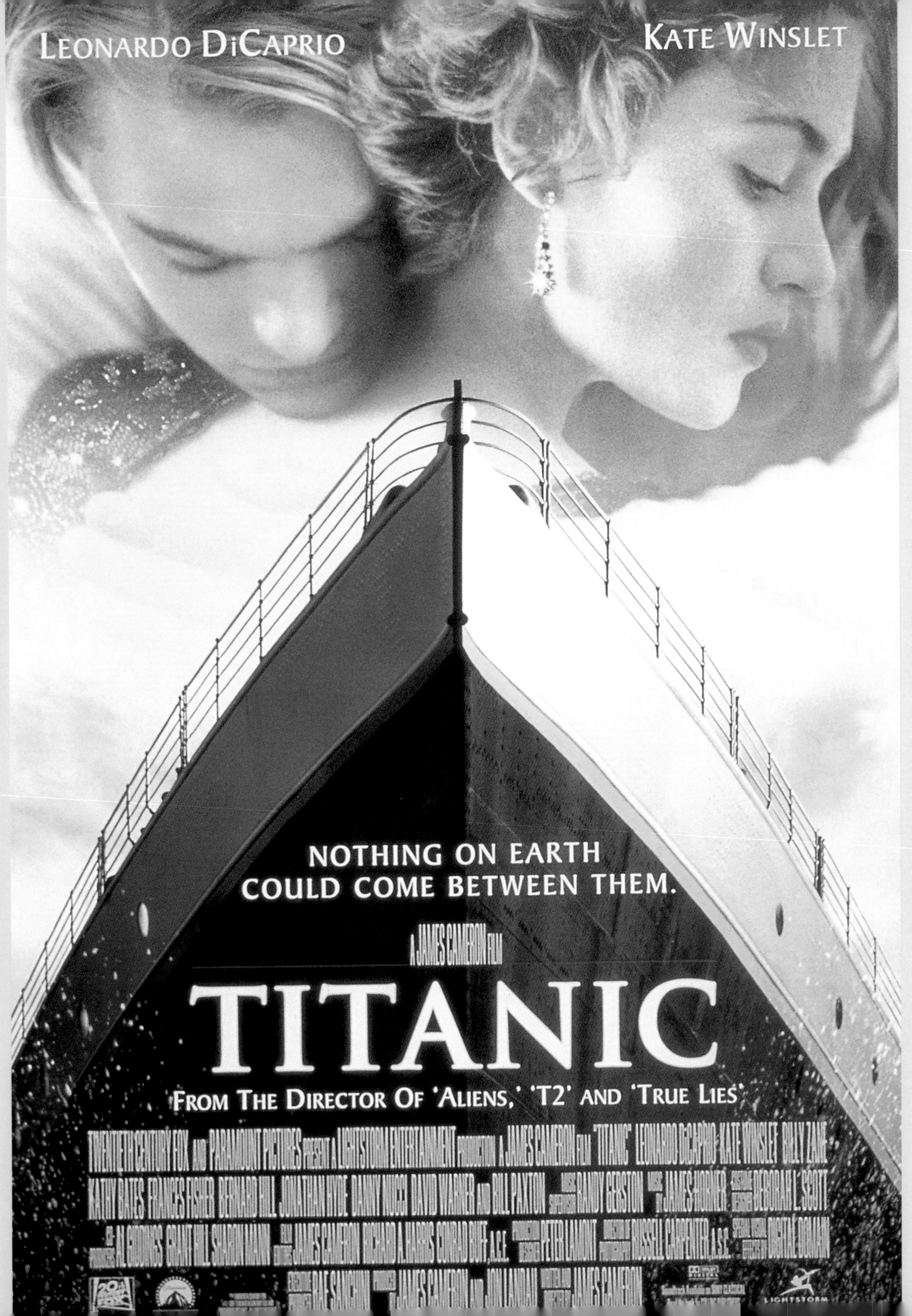

LEONARDO DiCAPRIO
KATE WINSLET
NOTHING ON EARTH
COULD COME BETWEEN THEM.
A JAMES CAMERON FILM
TITANIC
FROM THE DIRECTOR OF 'ALIENS,' 'T2' AND 'TRUE LIES'
TWENTIETH CENTURY FOX AND PARAMOUNT PICTURES PRESENT A LIGHTSTORM ENTERTAINMENT PRODUCTION A JAMES CAMERON FILM "TITANIC" LEONARDO DiCAPRIO KATE WINSLET BILLY ZANE
KATHY BATES FRANCES FISHER BERNARD HILL JONATHAN HYDE DANNY NUCCI DAVID WARNER AND BILL PAXTON MUSIC SUPERVISOR RANDY GERSTON MUSIC BY JAMES HORNER COSTUME DESIGNER DEBORAH L. SCOTT
CO-PRODUCERS AL GIDDINGS GRANT HILL SHARON MANN EDITED BY JAMES CAMERON RICHARD A. HARRIS CONRAD BUFF, A.C.E. PRODUCTION DESIGNER PETER LAMONT DIRECTOR OF PHOTOGRAPHY RUSSELL CARPENTER, A.S.C. SPECIAL VISUAL EFFECTS BY DIGITAL DOMAIN
EXECUTIVE PRODUCER RAE SANCHINI PRODUCED BY JAMES CAMERON AND JON LANDAU WRITTEN AND DIRECTED BY JAMES CAMERON
LIGHTSTORM

Basinger even winning a "Best Supporting Actress" Oscar for her role in the neo-*noir* thriller. But the biggest comeback of all belonged to **Burt Reynolds**. Hoping for a break the previous year, he'd taken the role of the perverted congressman in *Striptease* for a cut-rate fee. When that movie stiffed, things looked especially bleak—until Burt's performance in *Boogie Nights* (as the porn director who gave Mark "Marky-Mark" Wahlberg his big break) won him a "Best Supporting Actor" Oscar nomination.

There were other highlights, as well: Mike Myers spoofed James Bond films of the sixties with *Austin Powers*, a crusty Jack Nicholson romanced waitress Helen Hunt in *As Good As It Gets*, Jennifer Lopez sizzled as *Selena*, Howard Stern played himself in *Private Parts*, and Ben Affleck and Matt Damon made hearts flutter in *Good Will Hunting*.

Farley Follows His Hero

The dire action-comedy *Beverly Hills Ninja*, briefly a hit in the theaters, was sadly notable only for the fact that it was the last Chris Farley vehicle released while he was still alive. An obese, eager-to-please comic with a flair for physical comedy, Farley adhered too closely to the hard-living aesthetic of his hero, John Belushi, and so it came as no surprise when he died of a drug-related heart attack in December. Like Belushi, he was thirty-three at the time of his death.

Kids Demand Care-ful Designs

Already hugely popular in Japan, Bandai's Tamagotchis, or "virtual pets," were all the rage in the US in 1997. Retailing for between $9.99 and $12.99, the little electronic buggers (which required you to take care of their needs by pushing specific buttons, lest they "die" from neglect) were moving out of New York's FAO Schwarz at a rate of around eighty thousand a week. Smelling a good thing, the Tiger Electronics and Playmates companies released respective knock-off versions known as Giga Pets and Nanos. Educators, parents and sociologists were all wondering the same thing: Are Tamagotchis teaching kids responsibility, or are they just stressing them out?

Mattel brought Barbie into the computer age with Talk with Me Barbie, who came with a little computer and a CD-Rom that enabled the doll to talk to you. The company also introduced **Becky**, Barbie's disabled pal (who came with a pink and purple wheelchair), and teamed up with MasterCard to launch Cool Shoppin' Barbie, who came complete with a tiny MasterCard and a credit card scanner.

'97 Pam Grier as Jackie Brown.

nineteen

Hate crimes against gays and lesbians were up across the country, according to statistics, and the "El Niño" weather system caused the wettest US winter on record—but this was nothing compared to the storm clouds that hung over the White House during 1998. Saddam Hussein threatened several times over the course of the year to halt all UN inspections of Iraqi weapons facilities, demanding an end to the US's damaging economic sanctions against his country.

'98

TOP TELEVISION SHOWS

ER

Seinfeld

Friends

Touched By An Angel

Veronica's Closet

ACADEMY AWARDS

BEST PICTURE

Shakespeare in Love

directed by John Madden

BEST ACTOR

Roberto Benigni

Life Is Beautiful

BEST ACTRESS

Gwyneth Paltrow

Shakespeare in Love

'98 Clinton puts his credibility on the line.

With Americans split over whether to use force against Saddam (and how *much*), the US failed to form a coherent strategy for dealing with the situation, opting for the occasional bombing run (or threat thereof) each time Saddam Hussein ejected weapons inspectors.

But the biggest bomb dropped on the home front: Having spent some forty million dollars on the convoluted Whitewater real estate scandal, independent counsel Kenneth Starr expanded his inquiry to include the allegations that President Clinton had had an affair with White House intern **Monica Lewinsky**, and that the President had coerced her into lying about it to investigators. Clinton stated several times that he "never had sex with that woman," but finally admitted to having a relationship with

Lewinsky after evidence to that effect proved insurmountable. He did, however, continue to insist that his statements had been "legally accurate," drawing a hair-splitting distinction between oral sex and actual fornication.

An Upstanding Man

As far as the media seemed to be concerned, everything else going on in the world paled in importance next to "Zippergate" or "Monicagate," as the scandal was variously known. It became virtually impossible to turn on the TV or open a newspaper without seeing a picture of Lewinsky, hearing some titillating new detail about the case, or being subjected to someone's opinion about the seriousness of the charges against the President. Some commentators called for his immediate resignation—or, failing that, his impeachment; others condemned Starr for conducting a "**sexual witch-hunt**" with taxpayers' money, likening him to Joe McCarthy. (For his part, Starr preferred to think of himself as Joe Friday from *Dragnet*.) About the only thing anyone seemed to agree upon was that Linda Tripp (the government employee and "friend" of Lewinsky's, who had surreptitiously taped their discussions of the intern's affair with Clinton) was a vindictive and generally repulsive person. Meanwhile, parents across the country wrung their hands over how exactly to answer their children's persistent questions about oral sex, while stand-up comics alternated Lewinsky jokes with cracks about **Viagra**, the popular new anti-impotence drug currently being endorsed by Bob Dole.

In September, Starr's exhaustive

report on the matter was released to the media, and million of people from around the world logged on to read it from various websites. And yet, for all of Starr's findings and allegations, Clinton's approval polls remained remarkably high. The robust health of the country's economy didn't hurt, to be sure, nor did his role in brokering the Wye River peace accord between the PLO and Israel.

Though poll after poll showed that the majority of Americans wished to "move on," the US House of Representatives voted in October to open **impeachment** hearings. Voters responded to the Republican Party's increasingly shrill and self-righteous anti-Clinton tirades by handing Republican candidates a series of surprise defeats in the November elections; hours later, House speaker Newt Gingrich resigned from his post. (In another election-day surprise, former pro wrestler Jesse "The Body" Ventura won the race for governor of Minnesota.)

The Republicans continued to press on, however; a week before Christmas, the House of Representatives voted on four articles of impeachment against Clinton. Two passed—one alleging that the President committed perjury, one that he obstructed justice. To no one's surprise, the vote fell mostly along party lines. The matter would move to the Senate during the first weeks of 1999.

Net Profit

The only real respite from the continuing Clinton scandal came during the baseball season, as Mark McGwire and Sammy Sosa chased Roger Maris' seasonal home run record. Their record-setting seasons (McGwire finished with seventy; Sosa with sixty-six) inspired a renewed interest in the game, even though McGwire came under criticism for using androstenedione, a dietary steroid supplement.

In other sports news, the Chicago Bulls won their third straight NBA

championship in the spring, but a players' strike pre-empted the entire basketball schedule for the fall. Dennis Rodman kept himself by marrying TV babe Carmen Electra in a civil ceremony in Las Vegas. Rodman's publicist immediately sent out a press release stating that Electra had coerced a drunken Rodman into marriage, a charge Rodman denied.

Rat Pack Rendezvous Closes

On the subject of Vegas weddings, the Aladdin Hotel—site of Elvis and Priscilla's 1968 wedding—was demolished in April to make way for a new resort, due to open in the year 2000. While the Aladdin was never one of the jewels of the Vegas "strip," it was one of the few casinos remaining from the Rat Pack era. Ironically, just as Americans were becoming more interested in that period of Vegas history, the city razed all but the last

TOP ALBUMS

Titanic
soundtrack

CELINE DION
Let's Talk About Love

BACKSTREET BOYS
Backstreet Boys

City of Angels
soundtrack

SHANIA TWAIN
Come On Over

remnants of its golden era. But with the gambling mecca almost exclusively given over to theme hotels (Hard Rock, Excalibur, Treasure Island, New York New York), it seemed like it would be be just a matter of time before somebody opened a Rat Pack-styled joint.

Cartoons Are In As Comics Bow Out

Just months after it debuted on Comedy Central, *South Park*, the crudely animated cartoon that revolved around four foul-mouthed elementary schoolers, made it onto the covers of *Newsweek, Spin,* and *Rolling Stone*. Along with Mike "Beavis and Butthead" Judge's new series, *King of the Hill, South Park* was the most popular cartoon on nighttime TV; by the end of the year, even toupee-wearing newscasters were fishing for laughs by blurting out, "Ohmigod, they killed Kenny!"

Another show which crossed demographic lines was **Dawson's Creek**, a teen soap which dealt frankly with sexual issues and

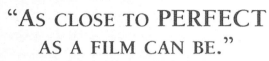
elevated young Katie Holmes to stardom. **The Jerry Springer Show** was now the most popular syndicated talk show in the country, thanks to a booking policy that seemed to encourage both the sleaziest topics and the most violent confrontations.

Coming under fire for his show's violent content, Springer promised he'd tone it down, but never seemed to get around to doing it.

After eight years on the air, **Jerry Seinfeld** decided to call it quits, much to the chagrin of millions of fans

around the country. The script for the show's final broadcast was subject of much hype, conjecture, and secrecy, with various fake scripts floating around on the Internet; but in the end, the May 14 finale was largely judged to be a letdown. The spring season also marked the end of the road for *Ellen*; low ratings, as well as a continuing battle between the show's producers and ABC over Ellen's "gay content," apparently contributed to the network's decision to pull the plug. Also getting the hook was *The Magic Hour*, a talk show hosted by former basketball great Magic Johnson, which was yanked after only eight weeks on the air.

Hollywood Fare Lukewarm To Hot

Wag the Dog, released in late '97, received a new lease on life thanks to the Monica Lewinsky scandal and the concurrent situation in Iraq. In the film, Dustin Hoffman played a director hired to film a phony war in order to distract the American public from a presidential scandal. Would President Clinton bomb Iraq in order to achieve a similar purpose? Americans could only wait and see.

Lost In Space was the first film of the year to best *Titanic* in the weekly box-office tallies, despite predominantly lukewarm reviews; many wondered if there were any old TV shows left for Hollywood to recycle. Of course, for a full-on nostalgic experience, you couldn't beat the twentieth-anniversary re-release of *Grease*; in packed multiplexes across the country, Americans were doing the hand jive and singing along. *Primary Colors*, starring John Travolta as a

Clintonesque president, had the misfortune to open the same week as *Grease*; even with the Lewinsky scandal adding extra marquee value to *Primary Colors*, moviegoers preferred to pay money to see the younger, buffer Travolta of twenty years earlier.

1998 featured not one but two meteor-hits-the-earth films—*Armageddon* and *Deep Impact*; it also made way for *Godzilla*, the first Godzilla film to not use a man dressed in a latex lizard suit. Sporting a budget of a hundred and twenty million dollars, the film was trashed by critics but did quite well at the box office. Other big hits included Steven Spielberg's World War Two film *Saving Private Ryan*; *City of Angels*, a blatant *Wings of Desire* rip-off; two Adam Sandler vehicles, *The Waterboy* and 1980s nostalgia comedy *The Wedding Singer*; *Lethal Weapon 4*; *Dr Dolittle*, starring Eddie Murphy in the title role; gross-out comedy *There's Something about Mary*; and **The Truman Show**, which starred Jim Carrey as a man whose every waking move was surreptitiously followed by TV cameras.

Teensploitation films continued to rake in the cash, with *I Know What You Did Last Summer*, *The Faculty,* and *Wild Things* (the latter featuring a much remarked-upon three-way sex scene with Matt Dillon, Neve Campbell, and Denise Richards) heading the list. But while Gwyneth Paltrow may have racked up a mantelful of awards for her performance in *Shakespeare in Love*, **Christina Ricci**, who played vastly different characters in *Buffalo 66*, *The Opposite of Sex*, and *Pecker*, was generally considered to be the indie-film babe of the year.

Music News

In a year where singles were almost phased out entirely by the music industry, film soundtracks did an unprecedented amount of business. The *Titanic* CD continued to fend off all comers, but the soundtracks to *City of Angels* and *Armageddon* also charted well. **Ray Of Light**, Madonna's much-ballyhooed foray into electronica, sold well too, although it turned out to be her blandest record yet. Indeed, it seemed that her influence was beginning to wane: hardly anyone was copying her fake English accent or new "pre-Raphaelite" hairstyle. Cher made an unexpected comeback with *Believe*, while **Bob Dylan**, then touting his new *Time Out Of Mind* album, received something of a shock while playing at the Grammy Awards; Michael Portnoy, a twenty-six-year-old performance artist/stand-up comic, crashed the stage with "Soy Bomb" written on his bare stomach, and proceeded to dance spastically until removed by security.

'98 *Left:* '98 movie releases *Godzilla* and the highly acclaimed *Life Is Beautiful*, and *(below)* back on track, Pearl Jam.

Rock Falls

Pearl Jam's new *Yield* was widely hailed as a return to form, as was *Hello Nasty*, the first Beastie Boys release in several years. *Van Halen III*, the new album by the latest incarnation of Van Halen (with former Extreme singer Gary Cherone replacing Sammy Hagar), sold impressively in its first week of release, but quickly dropped off the charts. People had been saying "**Rock 'n' roll is dead**" for years, but now many in the industry were starting to believe it. Much-hyped new records by Marilyn Manson, Hole, and The Smashing Pumpkins all fell short of sales expectations by several million; meanwhile, rap records by Lauryn Hill, Jay-Z, Master P, Jermaine Dupri, and rap-metal hybrids Korn never seemed to stop selling. After simmering in the background for several years, the **swing revival** came to the boil, thanks to records by Brian Setzer, Cherry Poppin' Daddies, The Squirrel Nut Zippers, and Big Bad Voodoo Daddy.

"Chairman Of The Board" Dies

All fedoras were doffed in sorrow on the evening of May 14, when news spread that Frank Sinatra had died of a heart attack. He was eighty-two.

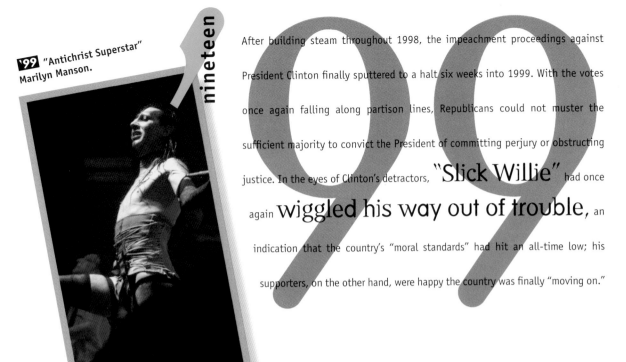

'99 "Antichrist Superstar" Marilyn Manson.

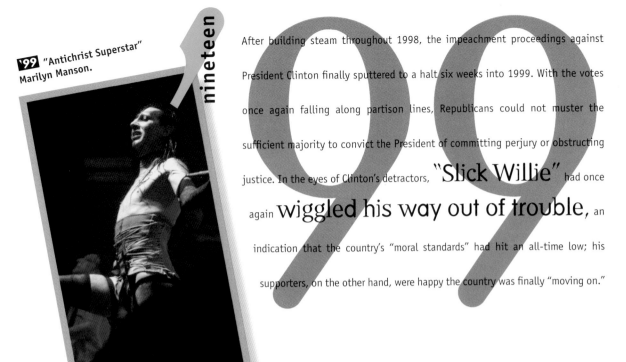

nineteen

99

After building steam throughout 1998, the impeachment proceedings against President Clinton finally sputtered to a halt six weeks into 1999. With the votes once again falling along partisan lines, Republicans could not muster the sufficient majority to convict the President of committing perjury or obstructing justice. In the eyes of Clinton's detractors, "Slick Willie" had once again wiggled his way out of trouble, an indication that the country's "moral standards" had hit an all-time low; his supporters, on the other hand, were happy the country was finally "moving on."

Opposing Forces

Other conversations in the nation's capitol concerned the possibility of Hillary Clinton running for Senator of New York in 2000, as well as the upcoming presidential elections. Several Republicans, including Bob Dole's wife Liddy, were said to have their hats in the ring, while Vice-President Gore and Senator Bill Bradley looked set to duke it out in the Democratic primaries. More pressing, however, was the worsening situation in **the Balkans**; as March drew to a close, NATO forces began air strikes against Kosovo, but government officials and American voters were still divided over whether or not the US should send ground troops.

Movie News

None of the above debates were quite as heated as those surrounding *Episode 1: The Phantom Menace*, however. Previews of the *Star Wars* prequel had been shown in selected theaters before screenings of the otherwise unremarkable *Meet Joe*

For his part, the President—whose current public approval rating of sixty-six percent was the second highest during his tenure—made a solemn vow to spend the rest of his time in office attending to "the people's business."

The scandal didn't suddenly dry up and blow away, however. *Monica's Story*, Lewinsky's perspective on the

scandal, became an immediate best-seller; her giggly appearance on Barbara Walters' March special pulled in so many female viewers that some media watchers dubbed it "the Super Bowl for women."

Flynt Digs Up Dirt

After vowing for many months to "reveal the hypocrisy" of politicians

who publicly denounced Clinton's affair with Lewinsky, *Hustler* publisher Larry Flynt put out his "Flynt Report," which featured plenty of dirt on Bob Barr, Henry Hyde, Newt Gingrich, Mary Bono (who was elected to the House of Representatives after her husband, singer/politician Sonny Bono, was killed in a 1998 skiing accident), and several others.

'99 Clinton gets back to the people.

Black and Wing Commander, and it seemed as if everyone had an opinion about them. Some said that the star, nine-year-old Jake Lloyd, couldn't act; others opined that the computer-generated special effects looked cheesy. In any case, the film—and accompanying merchandise—seemed set to do record-breaking business.

Teensploitation films kept up their reign of terror at the box office, with *Jawbreaker*, *Cruel Intentions*, *10 Things I Hate About You*, *Never Been Kissed*, *Varsity Blues*, *She's All That*, and *Go* (the only one of the bunch to receive positive reviews) all raking in truckloads of cash. Less successful were **200 Cigarettes**, MTV Films' inept attempt to drum up some nostalgia for the "New Wave" era, and **The Mod Squad**, a TV rehash so dead on arrival that even a Levi's merchandising tie-in couldn't save it.

Some of the year's early winners (at least in terms of ticket sales) included *Forces of Nature*, a romantic comedy with Ben Affleck and Sandra Bullock; *The Matrix*, a cyber-thriller with Keanu Reeves and Laurence Fishburne; *EDtv*, a Ron Howard-directed comedy suspiciously similar to *The Truman Show*; and *Life*, a "bittersweet" comedy with Eddie Murphy and Martin Lawrence. But at last check, all the groovy guys and gals were still saving their money for the forthcoming *Austin Powers: The Spy Who Shagged Me*.

Abnormal TV Success

There was little in the way of remarkable new programming in 1999, save for HBO's *The Sopranos*, which starred James Gandolfini as a New Jersey mob capo on Prozac. An immediate cult hit, the show was far more intelligent and humorous than anything else on TV. Comedian **Norm MacDonald**, recently fired from *Saturday Night Live*, returned with his own sitcom, *The Norm Show*, while former child star Alyssa Milano and former über-bitch Shannen Doherty rebounded as well-meaning witches with expensive wardrobes on *Charmed*. But "Most Surprising Comeback" award had to go to **Pamela Anderson Lee**, whose *VIP*—a campy *Charlie's Angels* knock-off with a bigger explosives budget—completely trounced *Baywatch* in the ratings.

Cartoon Cornucopia

There also seemed to be an abundance of prime-time animated shows on the tube in '99; joining *The Simpsons*, *King of the Hill*, and the rapidly-deteriorating *South Park* were *Family Guy*, *Dilbert*, *The PJs*, and *Futurama*, the new futuristic comedy by *Simpsons* creator Matt Groening. The Cartoon Network's *Powerpuff Girls* were a big daytime hit with the kids, while Britain's *Teletubbies* got on the wrong side of right-wing Christian leader Jerry Falwell, who accused "Tinky-Winky" of being a homosexual. (The purse was apparently the tip-off.)

Making Moral Judgments

In other daytime TV news, *Judge Judy* proved so popular that several other networks rushed out their own courtroom shows; Ed Koch, formerly the mayor of the largest city in the US, could now be seen banging a gavel on a revival of *The People's Court*. And in protest at *Jerry Springer*'s high ratings—and of "trash TV" in general—Oprah Winfrey announced that she would be leaving talk TV when her current contract expired.

Music News

With the exception of records by rap artists like DMX, TLC, Eminem, The Roots, Redman, and C-Murder—and the almost weekly arrests of Wu-Tang Clan member Ol' Durty Bastard—there wasn't much interesting happening in American music, either. **Bubblegum** was back in a big way, with teen wet-dream Britney Spears outselling the already popular 'N Sync and Backstreet Boys. Hungry for another piece of the action, former New Kids on the Block Jordan Knight and Joey McIntyre released new albums; if they didn't sell as well as their old stuff, at least they could be content in the knowledge that they'd outsold *Hard To Swallow*, Vanilla Ice's aptly-named 1998 comeback attempt. The much-ballyhooed **Marilyn Manson**/Hole tour collapsed after less than two weeks, the victim of poor ticket sales, monetary disputes, and a fall that injured Manson's leg; at least Manson's engagement to actress Rose MacGowan, supposedly already pregnant with his child, seemed like something the "Antichrist Superstar" could be happy about. The "Hard Knock Life Tour," with Jay-Z, Redman, and Method Man, was the first successful hardcore rap tour in years; as spring progressed, however, the organizers of Woodstock '99 still hadn't nailed down any rap acts to join the already-confirmed likes of Jewel, Alanis Morissette, Rage Against the Machine, Korn, Aerosmith, and John Fogerty for the summer event.

Mostly, talk around the music industry concerned the availability of MP3 music files on **the Internet**, with many pundits predicting the end of the industry as we know it. Many online music stores now also included a feature where you could make your own CD mix from a database of one hundred thousand songs. With CD burners priced ever cheaper, and a

growing number of cyber-savvy musicians looking to circumvent the hassles of record labels, it seemed that retail record chains could soon be a thing of the past.

US Bugged By Millennium Threat

In other cyber-news, new studies showed that a distressing number of government agencies were still unprepared for the Y2K bug, which was expected to muck up computers not already programmed to make the transition to the new millennium. In addition to debating whether 2000 or 2001 would mark the "real" beginning of the millennium, many Americans pondered the effect the Y2K bug would have upon daily life. Would airplanes fall out of the sky? Would there be food shortages and rioting in the streets? Or would life continue pretty much as we now knew it, with only a few minor complications to mark the changing of the decade? We could only wait and see.

Picture Credits

The publishers would like to thank the following sources for their kind permission to reproduce the pictures in this book:

The Advertising Archives

AKG, London

Corbis/Tom Bean, Bettmann, J M Chenet, Jerry Cooke, Henry Diltz, Everett Collection, Eye Ubiquitous, Mitch Gerber, Hulton-Deutsch Collection, Dewitt Jones, Lake County Museum, The National Archives, Photo Reporters, Neal Preston, Roger Ressmeyer, D Rudgers, Flip Schulke, Harry Takeda, David Turnley, UPI, Larry White, Ronnie Wright; *Jaws*/ Universal/.Zanuck-Brown, Rocky/ UA/Chartoff-Winkler, *Carrie*/ Paramount, *Mommie Dearest*/ Paramount/Frank Yablans, *Conan The Barbarian*/Dino de Laurentiis/Edward R. Pressman, *Top Gun*/Paramount/ Don Simpson, Jerry Bruckheimer, *Blue Velvet*/De Laurentiis, *She's Gotta Have It*/40 Acres And A Mule Filmworks, *Roseanne*/Viacom, Batman/Warner, *Forrest Gump*/ Panavision, Toy Story/Buena Vista/ Walt Disney/Pixar, *Independence Day*/TCF/Centropolis, *Jackie Brown*/ Buena Vista/Miramax/A Band Apart, *Godzilla*/Columbia Tristar/ Centropolis/Fried/Independent.

Ronald Grant Archive/*Taxi Driver*/ Columbia/Italo-Judeo, *Star Wars*/ TCF/Lucasfilm, *Up In Smoke*/ Paramount, Scarface/Howard Hughes, *This Is Spinal Tap*/Mainline/Embassy, *Purple Rain*/Columbia-EMI-Warner, *Barfly*/Cannon/Barbet Schroeder/ Fred Roos, Tom Luddy, *The Last Temptation of Christ*/ Universal/ Cineplex Odeon.

Hulton Getty

The Image Bank/Archive Photos, Frank Driggs Collection.
London Features International Ltd./ Agencja Piekna, Angie, J Bangay, Neil Leifer/Camera 5, Lawny, J

Gordon Levitt, Phil Loftus, V Malafronte/ Celebrity Photo Agency, K Mazur, L. McAfee, K Regan/Camera 5, A Vereecke; *Saturday Night Fever*/ Paramount/Robert Stigwood, *Annie Hall*/UA/Jack Rollins-Charles H. Joffe, *Close Encounters of the Third Kind*/Columbia/EMI, *National Lampoon's Animal House*/Universal, *The Blues Brother*/Universal, *Raiders Of The Lost Ark*/MPTV/Paramount/ Lucasfilm, *ET*/Universal/Steven Spielberg, Kathleen Kennedy, *Beverly Hills Cop*/Paramount/Don Simpson/ Jerry Bruckheimer, *Bill & Ted's Excellent Adventure*/P Caruso, *Schindler's List*/Universal/Amblin, *Natural Born Killers*/Warner/Regency/ Alcor/JD/Ixtlan/New Regency.

©1999 MTV Networks Europe. All Rights Reserved. MTV: MUSIC TELEVISION® MTV: MUSIC TELEVISION and all related titles, logos and characters are trademarks owned and licensed for use by MTV Networks, a division of Viacom International Inc.

Courtesy Nintendo

The Robert Opie Collection
Pictorial Press Limited/Cover/ Showtime/Sunstills; *One Flew Over The Cuckoos Nest*/UA/ Fantasy Films, *Grease*/Paramount/ Robert Stigwood/ Allan Carr, *Superman*/Warner/ Alexander Salkind, *9 to 5*/TCF/IPC, *The Terminator*/ Orion/Hemdale/ Pacific Western, *Rambo*/Anabasis Investments NV/ Buzz Feitshans, *The Breakfast Club*/ A&M/Universal, *Fatal Attraction*/ Paramount/Jaffe-Lansing, *Dirty Dancing*/Vestron, *Reservoir Dogs*/Rank/Live America/Dog Eat Dog.

Courtesy Sony Computer Entertainment

Every effort has been made to acknowledge correctly and contact the source and/copyright holder of each picture, and Carlton Books Limited apologises for any unintentional errors or omissions which will be corrected in future editions of this book